THE INTIMACIES OF CONFLICT

D1521252

The Intimacies of Conflict

Cultural Memory and the Korean War

Daniel Y. Kim

NEW YORK UNIVERSITY PRESS
New York

NEW YORK UNIVERSITY PRESS
New York
www.nyupress.org

© 2020 by New York University
All rights reserved

References to Internet websites (URLs) were accurate at the time of writing. Neither the author nor New York University Press is responsible for URLs that may have expired or changed since the manuscript was prepared.

Library of Congress Cataloging-in-Publication Data

Names: Kim, Daniel Y., author.
Title: The intimacies of conflict : cultural memory and the Korean War / Daniel Y. Kim.
Other titles: Cultural memory and the Korean War
Description: New York : New York University Press, [2020] | Includes bibliographical references and index.
Identifiers: LCCN 2020016523 (print) | LCCN 2020016524 (ebook) | ISBN 9781479800797 (cloth) | ISBN 9781479805365 (paperback) | ISBN 9781479800018 (ebook) | ISBN 9781479800032 (ebook)
Subjects: LCSH: Korean War, 1950–1953—Social aspects—United States. | Korean War, 1950–1953—Literature and the war. | Korean War, 1950–1953—Motion pictures and the war. | Orientalism—United States—History—20th century. | Race awareness—United States—History and criticism. | Race in literature. | United States—Armed Forces—Minorities—History—20th century. | Minorities in motion pictures. | Collective memory—United States.
Classification: LCC DS921.5.S63 K557 2020 (print) | LCC DS921.5.S63 (ebook) | DDC 951.904/21—dc23
LC record available at https://lccn.loc.gov/2020016523
LC ebook record available at https://lccn.loc.gov/2020016524

A portion of the introduction has been adapted from "The Korean War," in *Asian American Society: An Encyclopedia*, ed. Mary Yu Danico, Anthony Christian Ocampo, and Association for Asian American Studies (Los Angeles: SAGE, 2014), 607–10.

An earlier version of a portion of chapter 4 appeared in "'The Case of the Mysterious Koreans': The Meaning of Life, American Orientalism and the Korean War in the Age of the World Target," *Trans-Humanities* 8, no. 3 (October 2015): 7–32.

An earlier version of some of the material in chapter 6 was published as "'Bled in Letter by Letter': Translation, Postmemory, and the Subject of Korean War History in Susan Choi's *The Foreign Student*," *American Literary History* 21, no. 3 (Fall 2009): 550–83.

An earlier version of material from chapter 7 was published as "The Borderlands of the Korean War and the Fiction of Rolando Hinojosa," *positions: asia critique* 23, no. 4 (2015): 665–94.

A more expansive account of the discussion of the War Memorial of Korea in the conclusion can be found in "Nationalist Technologies of Cultural Memory and the Korean War: Militarism and Neo-Liberalism in *The Price of Freedom* and the War Memorial of Korea," *Cross-Currents* 4, no. 1 (2015): 40–70.

New York University Press books are printed on acid-free paper, and their binding materials are chosen for strength and durability. We strive to use environmentally responsible suppliers and materials to the greatest extent possible in publishing our books.

Manufactured in the United States of America

10 9 8 7 6 5 4 3 2 1

Also available as an ebook

For my halmoni

CONTENTS

Introduction

The Korean War in Color

Described as "one of the enduring images of the Korean War," this photograph accompanied the *Washington Post* obituary of Al Chang, a well-respected combat photographer who had passed away on September 30, 2007, at the age of eighty-five.[1] Taken on August 28, 1950, it "shows a distraught soldier who has learned that his replacement as a radio operator had been killed. In vivid contrast, it also shows a corpsman in the background sifting through casualty information with apparent detachment."[2] If this is one of the most famous American photographs of the Korean War (1950–53), what makes it so exemplary is the fact that there is practically nothing about it that identifies it as

Figure I.1. A forgotten image of a forgotten war. Adam Bernstein, "Al Chang, 85; Trained Lens on 3 Wars," *Washington Post*, October 5, 2007, www.washingtonpost.com.

such. Indeed, what makes it such a disturbing yet moving image is that it seems to speak to something *universal* about the modern experience of war—the juxtaposition of the open and anguished intimacy of the two men in the foreground and the "apparent detachment" of the man in the background. While most readers will likely not be familiar with this image, they will probably be able to call to mind ones from World War II or the Vietnam War: perhaps the raising of the flag on Iwo Jima, the mushroom cloud over Hiroshima, or a naked girl running in terror from her napalmed village in Vietnam. The ubiquity of these latter images suggests how central to American historical memory these other military conflicts have become. The relative obscurity of the former image, by contrast, highlights the fact that what we have left of the Korean War are mainly a handful of phrases untethered from any easily visualizable referent: the thirty-eighth parallel, the demilitarized zone (DMZ), the "forgotten war."

The relative invisibility of this conflict may be explained in part by its chronological bracketing by these other, more dramatic American wars in Asia. The popularity of the television series *M*A*S*H* makes it abundantly clear how the Vietnam War—and its immediate and traumatic significance—has shaped and even displaced any historical sense of the Korean War that Americans might possess. And the fact that the Korean War took place a mere five years after the end of the Second World War also suggests how it has been overshadowed from a different historical direction.

If the Korean War seems to lack the world-shattering significance of either World War II or the Vietnam War—if it fails to register a weighty enough sense of its own discrete eventfulness—this is not a consequence of its insignificance. Indeed, as this study will make clear, this conflict was a watershed event in numerous ways—and not simply because it was the first "hot war" that took place during the Cold War. For one thing, it was the first of many unpopular and undeclared wars that the United States has waged against Third World enemies since its ascendance as a global superpower—a history that obviously stretches into the present. Like many of these conflicts, moreover, much of the military violence unleashed by the United States was directed not only at conventional forces but also at insurgents, and much of the devastation was inflicted from the air—a combination of factors that has always led to a significant number of civilian casualties.

Moreover, the Korean War marked a turning point in the US history of race. Indeed, one year before he filed the brief that would bring the issue of segregation before the Supreme Court, Thurgood Marshall was dispatched to Korea by the National Association for the Advancement of Colored People (NAACP) to investigate the disproportionate number of black soldiers facing courts-martial. While they had been serving in segregated all-black units, the exigencies of the Korean War necessitated the rapid implementation of President Harry Truman's Executive Order 9981, which had been issued in 1948, mandating the integration of the armed forces.[3] As such this conflict was the first in which black soldiers fought side by side with white soldiers. Japanese American soldiers were also integrated into formerly all-white combat units for the first time, many of whom had spent much of the prior war in internment camps, their loyalty suspect because of their racial background.

The Korean War inaugurated a wholesale transformation in the *transnational* conception of race as well. Five years after a conflict that ended with the deaths of 150,000 Japanese civilians in Hiroshima and Nagasaki and during which 120,000 Americans of Japanese descent were placed in internment camps came one in which Japan was trumpeted as the most important Asian ally of the United States and the heroism of Japanese American soldiers was celebrated. China, an important ally in the earlier war, became the most imposing enemy that US forces would face in the current one. And Koreans? Few Americans knew much about them—mainly that some apparently yearned for freedom, while others had fallen under the sway of Communism.

To Koreans themselves, however, this conflict was at root the most dramatic episode in a civil conflict that had erupted with the liberation of the peninsula from Japanese occupation in 1945 and that continues in a suspended form to this day. Korea was one of the many nonwhite countries that sought to emerge from the shadow of empire in the wake of World War II, though in this case, the colonial power that had collapsed was Japan. For Koreans, then, the conflict was at its core a civil war waged by two nascent postcolonial nation-states, each seeking to enact its own vision of a unified Korea, greatly aided and guided by the global powers who intervened. Although it officially lasted just over three years, the war resulted in an extraordinary number of noncombatant casualties. The *Encyclopedia Britannica* estimates that there were roughly 4 million casualties, half of which were civilians,[4] which, as historian Bruce Cumings notes, reflects "a higher percentage than in World War II or Vietnam."[5] The number of dead is estimated at 2.5 million.[6] This is an especially chilling number given that the prewar population of the country was, according to Cumings, 10 million. Moreover, "two-fifths of Korea's industrial facilities were destroyed and one-third of its homes devastated."[7]

To the extent that most Americans remain unaware of not only the carnage that took place but the historical context surrounding it, we bear some resemblance to the soldier in Chang's photograph who looks away in "apparent detachment"—most of us simply have not registered that an event of significance and sorrow has, as it were, taken place before us. Part of my aim in *The Intimacies of Conflict* is simply to shift our gaze. In the first half of this study, I return to the time in which that photograph was taken to gain a sense of what this event meant to Americans as it was taking place—to develop a picture of what the Korean War looked like before it was forgotten. In so doing, I will reveal not a paucity of cultural artifacts—neither a ghostly absence nor an emptiness. After all, the war was hardly conducted in secret. It was entered into with the full knowledge and initial support of the American public if not exactly its formal consent.[8] The propaganda machinery developed during World War II still functioned as a potent force in 1950. During the fighting, a significant body of material on the conflict was generated by Hollywood and the mainstream press, very little of which questioned the war's justness in any significant way despite its increasing unpopularity.

In returning to American culture during the time of the Korean War, moreover, I intend to draw attention to something that is not quite visible in Chang's photograph but that becomes apparent when we consider the ramifications of the photographer's ethnic and racial identity: he was Korean American. There is another invisible thread of intimacy that we can trace from this image. Although the anguish and the comfort that are the subject of this photograph remain unseen and unacknowledged by the soldier in the background, they are certainly registered by the man who stands unseen in the foreground, Chang himself. To the extent that he participates in the drama of shared loss he visually records, the photographer adds an interracial dimension to the male intimacy he depicts. What we might discern beyond the edges of its frame is an Asian American subject who is joined to the white American subjects whose drama of loss he both shares and records.

Looking at this image in the way I suggest is made easier when we look at how Chang was memorialized in a very different kind of American newspaper. The obituary that ran in the *Honolulu Star-Bulletin*, "Photographer Brought War Home," also refers to the photograph included with the *Post* article.[9] However, it includes a different image (see figure I.2), which is captioned "This Korean War photo by Al Chang shows Sgts. 1st Class Robert Muramoto, Castro Corpuz and David Kauanui relaxing with canned poi, dried squid and a ukulele." Included with this obituary are the reflections of Retired Brigadier General Irwin Cockett, who recalls how Chang "really made the 5th Regimental Combat Team, which was made up of a lot of guys from Hawaii, famous with his pictures of the fighting in Korea." This photograph also captures the intimacy of US soldiers, but what is different is both the mood and the fact that the men pictured are clearly of Asian descent.

In bringing these images together, I offer a sense of how I will be looking at the materials I address in this study, for I will not simply be addressing what is there to be looked at, the forms of intimacy that

Figure I.2. Asian American soldiers from Hawaii during the Korean War. Gregg K. Kakesako, "Al Chang, 1922–2007: Photographer Brought War Home," October 2, 2007, http://archives.starbulletin.com.

occupy center stage in the works I examine; I will also be addressing what lies outside the frame, which will entail, among other things, offering an Asian American perspective on the war's significance. *The Intimacies of Conflict* is mainly a work of cultural and literary criticism built through detailed analyses of cinematic and journalistic texts as well as novels, all of which center on the affective connections that were engendered by the Korean War, the myriad intimacies that were born of this conflict.

The constant through all the cultural works I examine here is the issue of intimacy. The popular depictions of the Korean War from the 1950s that I examine in the four chapters that compose part 1 frame the interracial intimacies they celebrate within what I term a *humanitarian and military Orientalism*. As such, they traffic in the sentimentalism that is, as Christina Klein has argued, the dominant "cultural mode" in which Asian subjects appeared in US representations of the Cold War.[10] In contrast, the novelistic depictions of interracial and transnational intimacy from the past two decades I examine in part 2, which also comprises four chapters, are far more vexed. These works draw attention to the darker aspects of the interracial and transnational intimacies that the conflict engendered, evoking a wider web of suffering and complicity and speaking eloquently and expansively to the troubling implications of not only the US role in the Korean War but also the part played by black, Latinx, Asian American, and Korean combatants in the violence. In their rendering of the affective intimacies—the "tense and tender ties," to use Ann Laura Stoler's phrase—that emerge through the brutality of war and out of its lingering aftermath, these novels reimagine community in ways that exceed conventional notions of national, racial, or ethnic identity.[11] Additionally, as I will later elaborate, the title of this study is also indicative of its concerns with issues of history and memory. What I have assembled here is an archive of cultural memory that suggests the intimacy of the various histories, both national and transnational, refracted in the Korean War—histories that have to do with the structure of race in the United States and the formations of empire that emerged during the Cold War.

The Militarized Dimensions of Cold War Orientalism

Part 1 of this study takes up cultural artifacts that are, like Chang's photographs, contemporaneous with the conflict or produced in the decade after. These works have been selected because they highlight the pivotal role the Korean War played in US histories of race: Hollywood films that foreground military integration and the coverage of the war in the mainstream press as well as in black and Japanese American newspapers. As we shall see, the theater of war was particularly suited for the staging of a number of compelling domestic dramas: tales extolling the bonds formed among white, black, and Japanese American servicemen and marriages between US soldiers and Japanese war brides and transforming Korean war orphans into objects of humanitarian care. The midcentury cultural works I examine in part 1 compose a middlebrow archive of US imperial aspirations as they took shape during the early years of the Cold War.

An influential body of scholarship that has emerged in the past two decades has altered our view of this period to better recognize how the conflict between the capitalist East and the Communist West took shape alongside and interacted with decolonization and the emergence of what came to be known as the Third World. Leerom Medovoi, for example, has argued for "thinking of the Cold War era not simply as a squaring off between two superpowers, but instead as a triangulated 'Age of Three Worlds,'" which would entail recognizing their imperial dimensions.[12] However, as Medovoi notes, "while the United States and the Soviet Union, without question, aimed to claim new territories for their social systems around the world, it was no longer permissible to do so in the old modality of empire," and "whatever rich techniques of neo-colonial domination did in fact emerge in the Cold War era, they could not be made explicit in the face of the new geopolitical norm of anti-colonialism."[13] Medovoi emphasizes that in the propaganda war this entailed—the war for the hearts and minds of Third World subjects—both the United States and the Soviet Union characterized their military incursions as acts of liberation and couched their justifications in "[a] language of fraternal good will and international consensus regarding the right to popular sovereignty and freedom."[14]

In addition to Medovoi, a number of scholars, including Mary L. Dudziak, Jodi Kim, Christina Klein, Jodi Melamed, Nikhil Singh, and Penny Von Eschen, have illuminated how vital the idea of the nation as multiracial became to US Cold War liberalism.[15] Much of the labor of constructing this ideology was carried out by middlebrow cultural producers who, as Klein puts it, propounded "the idea of America as a harmonious nation made up of people from diverse ethnic, racial, national, and religious backgrounds," thereby "mobiliz[ing] this idea of a racially and ethnically diverse America in the service of U.S. global expansion."[16] Christina Klein's work is particularly germane here, for many of the popular depictions taken up in this study are not only set in Korea and sometimes Japan; they also focus on the connections that white Americans forged with Japanese Americans and with Koreans and Japanese. As such, they are clearly part of the archive that Klein examines in *Cold War Orientalism: Asia in the Middlebrow Imagination, 1945–1961.* The extensive and sweeping imperial endeavors undertaken by the United States during this period engendered, as she notes, a massive transnational movement of Americans: "Hundreds of thousands of Americans flowed into Asia during the 1940s and 1950s as soldiers, diplomats, foreign aid workers, missionaries, technicians, professors, students, businesspeople, and tourists. Never before had American influence reached so far and so wide into Asia and the Pacific."[17] This same period witnessed a proliferation of US popular representations of Asians and Asian Americans that depicted them in largely positive terms rather than as figures of yellow peril, works that "imagined and facilitated the forging of a new set of affiliations—nationally, among diverse social and political groups with the United States, and transnationally, between the United States and the noncommunist parts of Asia."[18] These "envisioned U.S. global expansion taking place within a system of reciprocity" and were therefore "full of exchanges between Americans and Asians: intellectual exchanges of conversation, economic exchanges of shopping, emotional exchanges of love, physical exchanges of tourism and immigration."[19]

Klein's study has been exceptionally generative in terms of reframing Cold War studies to be more attentive to the pivotal position that Asians and Asian Americans occupied within the global order that the United States sought to establish through the expansion of its empire, one premised on capitalism and liberalism. However, the emphasis on the networks of affiliation linking East and West that emerged tends to reaffirm a central fallacy embedded in the dominant conception of the historical period she addresses, for the Cold War was only cold insofar as no direct military conflict emerged between the United States and the Soviet Union, one that could easily have led to nuclear Armageddon. The absurdity of that designation becomes clear, though, when we consider the perspectives of those who were enmeshed in the brutal conflicts that erupted in places like Korea and Vietnam. Moreover, the "hundreds of thousands of Americans [who] flowed into Asia during the 1940s and 1950s" did so for different reasons.[20] It was the experiences of those who came to Korea during the war in relation to military and humanitarian endeavors that were highlighted in US representations of the Korean War. And if the Cold War Orientalism Klein exhaustively anatomizes is redolent with the promise of a peaceable coexistence, the cultural works I examine in part 1 of this study reveal how it is underwritten by the violence of war. Indeed, these texts call attention to the emergence of what I term a humanitarian Orientalism that is explicitly militarized.

The two Hollywood films I examine in the fourth chapter, *One Minute to Zero* (1952) and *Battle Hymn* (1957), along with the coverage of the conflict in *Life* magazine, justify the American intervention in Korea on humanitarian grounds, highlighting the role that US servicemen played as protectors and saviors of Korean war orphans.[21] As they do so, however, they openly acknowledge that the tactics used by US military forces on the ground and in the air resulted in the deaths of many Korean civilians. These texts foreground the vulnerability of Korean civilians to the violence of war by centering on refugees and orphans. The innocence of these noncombatants and the precarity of their lives is emphasized, suggesting their potential to become loyal subjects. They are placed in a sentimental framework that, as Klein asserts, testifies to their humanity. Their construction as worthy objects of a humanitarian Orientalism is premised, however, on their capacity to be distinguished from the enemy they resemble, a distinction that is not only difficult to make but also tenuous and unstable.

Korean noncombatants who remain uncontaminated by an allegiance to Communism are examples of what Josephine Park has termed "the friendly," a figure that features prominently in US representations of the Korean War and the Vietnam War. In her book *Cold War Friendships*, she writes, "An adjective first turned into a noun to describe unthreatening natives, 'friendlies' became military terminology most often used to distinguish between raced others," to identify those who were inclined to support US Cold War efforts and with whom one could form "provisional and weak alliances."[22] Such figures, as Park demonstrates, played a central role in justifying US military interventions in "wars that remained dangerously murky" to most Americans, as they signified who was being saved.[23]

Nonetheless, as the films I examine in part 1 make clear, the task of distinguishing those Koreans who are due objects of humanitarian care emerges as a difficult one. To a significant degree, this stems from the insurgent tactics deployed by North Korean forces. A scenario that emerges in many US representations of the Korean War is a column of refugees that has been infiltrated by North Korean soldiers disguised as civilians. This epistemological uncertainty is compounded by the homogenizing effect of Orientalism writ large, which renders all Asians indistinguishable to the Western eye. Sergeant Zack, the protagonist of the Sam Fuller film *The Steel Helmet* (1951), which I will examine in chapter 1, offers this sardonic opinion on how US soldiers might be able to tell the difference between hostile and friendly Koreans: "He's a South Korean when he's running with you, and he's a North Korean when he's running after you."[24] This comment frames the essential difference between the two as a matter of bodily orientation—as a matter of whether the Korean body in question is moving in alignment with one's own or in the opposite direction. The orientation of bodies is always, as Sara Ahmed powerfully suggests in much of her work, a matter of affect: how bodies orient themselves and extend into the world is coextensive with the emotions they inhabit.[25] And hence the premium that US cultural representations of the Korean War place on a capacity to discern the emotions that might lie behind the performative movement of Korean bodies.

The bodily gestures that testify best to a Korean subject's alignment with the US cause, her friendly political orientation, are ones that express a sense of gratitude: the hand of the orphan outstretched for a gift of candy, the hands of a Christian clasped in prayer, the embrace of refugees who have been taken out of harm's way. In such renderings of the Korean civilian, we can see a forerunner of the Vietnam War refugee as she has been figured in US liberalism. As Yen Le Espiritu has argued, "The production of the assimilated and grateful refugee—the 'good refugee'—enables a potent narrative of America(ns) rescuing and caring for Vietnam's 'runaways,' which powerfully remakes the case for the rightness of the U.S. war in Vietnam."[26] Refugee subjects, as Mimi Nguyen asserts, are construed as grateful for the "gift of freedom" they have received in being rescued by the United States—a gift that entails "the right to have rights, the choice of life direction, the improvement of body and mind, the opportunity to prosper" and thereby incurs a never-ending sense of debt. They can strive to repay it in part by reiterating "a benign, rational story about the United States as the uncontested superpower on the world stage today."[27]

The three films I've mentioned—*The Steel Helmet*, *One Minute to Zero*, and *Battle Hymn*—foreground how this humanitarian Orientalism, which identifies certain Korean civilians as objects of care, is embedded within a mode of warfare that designates the very populations of which refugees are a part as legitimately killable. While these films grant a measure of humanity to Koreans and openly grieve the civilian deaths that are the result of *US* military violence, they nonetheless disclose that the right to live of certain humans can be abrogated in the context of war. A character in *One Minute to Zero*, a physician working with the United Nations, offers this clinical analogy for such deaths in reference to an incident when a number of refugees were killed in an artillery barrage unleashed by US military forces: "War is the most malignant disease of the human race. It is an infection. It is contagious. When we doctors amputate, we sometimes cut good tissue along with bad because we can't take the chances."

Such Korean War representations of the refugee reveal that humanitarian Orientalism is part of a biopolitical project, to invoke the conceptualization of governmentality that Michel Foucault undertook in his later writings, which centers on the management of life while maintaining the sovereign right to kill: they are part of a population whose relationship to life comes under humanitarian management even as some are allowed to die. Or, to evoke the work of Giorgio Agamben, these Korean civilians inevitably might seem to constitute a species of bare life. Additionally, they might constitute an example of the "living dead," to draw on Achille Mbembe's allegorical rendering of those who are consigned to the death worlds that are constitutive of a global ordering structured around necropolitics and necropower. Finally, they might be counted among what Judith Butler has described as the ungrievable, those who are simply not recognized as fully human within the normative frames of war.[28]

While *The Intimacies of Conflict* is not intended primarily as a systematic intervention into the rich discussions that have emerged around the constellation of theoretical works cited earlier, it draws broadly from them in its analyses of the humanitarian Orientalism that arises in US representations of the Korean War, for the form of intimacy that humanitarian Orientalism extends to civilians acknowledges their humanity while simultaneously designating their deaths as a tragic but necessary consequence of war-making.

These figures occupy what I will term a *racial DMZ*, or a zone of indiscrimination, and are subjected to technologies of knowledge production that purport to distinguish between those who constitute the proper objects of humanitarian care and those who are legitimate objects of military violence. These representations reveal, however, that despite the allegedly surgical precision with which such distinctions are made, the violence required for segments of the population identified as malignant is somewhat indiscriminate: that "we sometimes cut good tissue along with bad because we can't take the chances." If this cutting away reveals how all Koreans are in fact constituted as bare life or the living dead within the frames of war, the performative gestures of mourning that follow enact a mystification: by clothing them within the fabric of the sacred, their deaths are sanctified as sacrifices.

I have coined the term *military Orientalism* to name another strain of Cold War Orientalism that remains largely unaddressed in Klein's scholarship, one that stresses the humanity of Asian American combatants even as it also suggests that they, like Korean civilians, may necessarily be sacrificed to the cause of war.[29] Two of the US films I examine in part 1—*The Steel Helmet* (1951) and *Pork Chop Hill* (1959)—call attention to how Japanese American soldiers, whose racial identity had rendered their loyalty suspect in World War II, fought valiantly alongside white soldiers during the Korean War.[30] In the Nisei characters who appear in these films,[31] we witness the reconstruction and rehabilitation of Japanese Americans as citizen-subjects par excellence whose prior experiences with racial discrimination only enhance their value to the American cause, asserting that their loyalty has only been strengthened by having been so sorely tested. Military Orientalism, which is the focus of the third chapter, constitutes a distinct component of what Melanie McAllister has termed "military multiculturalism," the notion that "the diversity of its armed forces made the United States a world citizen, with all the races and nations of the globe represented in its population."[32]

I address the more prominent manifestation of this ideology in chapter 2, which examines the depictions of African American soldiers in a rapidly integrating military that are found on the pages of black newspapers and also in Hollywood films, including *All the Young Men* (1960), starring Sidney Poitier.[33]

A pertinent biopolitical perspective on the precise role that soldiers perform in the apparatus of war-making can be found in Jin-kyung Lee's *Service Economies: Militarism, Sex Work, and Migrant Labor in South Korea*. She notes that the soldier "occup[ie]s an inherently paradoxical and contradictory position" in that he serves simultaneously as

> the agent of the state's necropolitical power and as its very potential victim. On the one hand, military labor carries out the will of the state in conquering and subjugating the enemy, that is, those "deemed worthy of being exterminated," while soldiers—especially or exclusively those who fill the lower ranks—carry the risk of themselves being exterminated by their enemy. In the state's ability to mobilize a sector of population as military workers who are potentially expendable, I argue that the state already constructs them as subject to its own necropolitical authority.[34]

The military Orientalist narratives I examine in chapter 3 celebrate Japanese American soldiers for embracing "the risk of themselves being exterminated by their enemy," presenting their potential sacrifice as constituting their best wager for proving their loyalty to the United States. This ethos of sacrifice is explicitly thematized in *Go for Broke!* (1951), a film set in World War II that nonetheless inflects the Korean War context of its release.[35] That the production of this film received extensive coverage on the pages of the Japanese American newspaper the *Pacific*

Citizen alongside tributes to Nisei soldiers who had been killed in Korea and those who had been decorated suggests how these two conflicts became integral to the dominant narrative that emerged in the 1950s constructing Japanese Americans as a model minority. Samuel Fuller's *The Crimson Kimono* (1959) features a Nisei Korean War veteran as one of its protagonists, and through him, this film dramatizes the culmination of this narrative: an assertion that their wager of sacrifice had been successful and that the winnings Japanese Americans had thereby secured were the rewards and comforts of bourgeois domesticity.[36]

Taken together, humanitarian and military Orientalism comprise the militarized edge of the Cold War Orientalism that took shape during the Korean War, one that was deployed to distinguish Asian and Asian American populations loyal to the United States from those that threatened its existence. The deaths of innocent Asian noncombatants and loyal Japanese American combatants underwrite their full integration into the human family, enabling them to achieve an aim that may have been withheld from them in life.

Reframing the 1950s

The archive of cultural works from the 1950s that I examine in part 1 of this study is in no way intended to be exhaustive. The films selected either highlight the racially integrated nature of the US military forces that took part in the conflict or draw particular attention to the plight of Korean refugees and sometimes both.[37] Similarly, *The Intimacies of Conflict* does not offer a comprehensive account of how journalists covered the war; instead, it highlights the perspectives of African American and Japanese American reporters and columnists.[38] Finally, this is not a study that attempts to uncover a hitherto hidden archive of Korean War cultural works that explicitly question the liberal consensus that took shape in the United States at midcentury. By and large, the texts from the 1950s taken up in part 1 of this study are decidedly middle of the road both politically and aesthetically.

What I hope to accomplish in subjecting these cinematic and journalistic works to detailed close readings is a kind of reframing very much akin to the mode of analysis that Judith Butler deploys in her book *The*

Frames of War: When Is Life Grievable? which centers on twenty-first-century representations of US war-making. Most of the archive Butler takes up consists of works that reveal the dominant framing of the wars waged since September 11 that has been offered by the US government and supporters of its efforts. Journalistic and photographic depictions are embedded in and contribute to this framing by confining themselves to the rather restricted visual field in which conflict is made knowable. Butler's analyses stress how the necessary iterability of visual representations (her case study being the infamous photographs of the war crimes committed at Abu Ghraib) can actualize their potential as critique. As she asserts of such images, "this very reproducibility entails a constant breaking from context, a constant delimitation of new context, which means that the 'frame' does not quite contain what it conveys" but is actually characterized by a "vulnerability to reversal, to subversion, even to critical instrumentalization."[39] In looking at the images of the Korean War brought before the American public by Hollywood, I will be, as Butler suggests, looking closely at how they frame the war in ways that reiterate and confirm the US government's justifications of it. However, in making this ideological framing part of the picture, as it were, we can engage in "disobedient act[s] of seeing" that "consider what forms of social and state power are 'embedded' in the frame, including state and military regulatory regimes," and employ "a social critique of regulatory and censorious power."[40]

Facilitating this reframing of popular representations of the Korean War from the 1950s is the fact that the conflict they depict will likely seem strangely familiar to readers today. It is a war waged against an enemy who subscribes to an ideology regarded as posing an existential threat to the West, one capable of astonishing acts of brutality. This enemy can easily blend into the civilian population, whose loyalties are difficult to discern. Because of this, and even as due care is taken in identifying legitimate military targets, the countermeasures required to kill the enemy will necessarily result in the deaths of civilians—in "collateral damage." Finally, defeating this enemy will require that the overwhelmingly superior technology of US military forces be brought to bear, especially in terms of airpower. In these respects, the Korean War that emerges from these representations will have an uncanny resemblance to the conflicts the US military has been engaged in since it entered Afghanistan on October 7, 2001, as well as to the Vietnam War, which it officially entered on August 7, 1964.

In her discussion of reframing, Butler cites the work of Walter Benjamin, who famously asserts in his much-cited essay "Theses on the Philosophy of History" that "to articulate the past historically does not mean to recognize it 'the way it really was'" but rather "to seize hold of a memory as it flashes up at a moment of danger."[41] The task of the historian, as Benjamin captures it in perhaps his most oft-cited phrase, is "to brush history against the grain."[42] While *The Intimacies of Conflict* is not a conventional historical study, it is driven by an impulse kindred to the spirit of the "historical materialism" that Benjamin advocates.

Reframing 1950–53

Given that most readers will likely not be very familiar with the Korean War, it is worth taking a moment to outline how that conflict has been conventionally understood, as a proxy conflict, and how that historical framing was dismantled by the path-breaking scholarship of Bruce Cumings. The traditional historical understanding of the conflict that largely continues to reign in the United States has situated it wholly within the bipolar framework of the Cold War and within the temporal markers of 1950–53, the years during which, officially speaking, the war took place.[43] When placed strictly in those confines, one can think of the Korean War as taking place in four phases. It began in the early hours of June 25, 1950, when Korean People's Army (KPA) forces engaged Republic of Korea Army (ROKA) units on the Ongjin peninsula, northwest of Seoul, the South Korean capital. KPA forces quickly pushed their way to Seoul, meeting little significant resistance. The Truman administration's decision to intervene was sanctioned by the United Nations—the first time the charter of the newly formed United Nations (UN) had been used to justify military intervention. The KPA came quite close—and quickly—to achieving a decisive military victory. By the end of July, US, ROKA, and UN troops had been driven into the southeastern corner of the peninsula, hemmed in at what came to be known as the "Pusan Perimeter."

The second phase of the war began on September 15, when General Douglas MacArthur led a surprise amphibious assault on the port city of Inchon, just west of Seoul. As a result, US-led forces were able to push the KPA northward, and they eventually crossed the thirty-eighth parallel on October 1. By Thanksgiving, the KPA was cornered in the far north of Korea, on the verge of the border with China. In the final days of November, a massive deployment of soldiers from the People's Republic of China entered the fight, and the tide of the war turned once again. In the subsequent four months, Seoul changed hands two more times. With both sides taking and losing such wide swaths of territory with such rapidity during this first year of the war, multitudes of civilians streamed back and forth, seeking refuge from the violence. By the end of April 1951, the front line stabilized at a point quite close to the thirty-eighth parallel. In the fourth and final stage of the war, which composed the last two years of fighting, little ground was gained or lost, but the violence and destruction continued. Massive numbers of soldiers lost their lives taking and retaking hill after hill. Guerrilla warfare and counterinsurgency efforts continued in the South. The North was subjected to a massive air campaign that involved carpet-bombing, napalm, and the eradication of cities, dams, and factories and resulted in a staggering number of civilian deaths.

Negotiations took place throughout the final two years of the conflict. A major sticking point concerned the repatriation of prisoners of war. While China and North Korea maintained that they should be returned to their country of origin as stipulated by the Geneva Conventions, the United States and South Korea insisted that they should be allowed to choose the country to which they would be released. The issue was settled in July 1953 through a compromise: the release would be managed by a "neutral nation," India. As negotiations continued over the exact location of the final line of demarcation, fierce fighting continued as both sides sought to maximize the territory under their control. Though Syngman Rhee, president of South Korea, eventually agreed to the terms of the agreement, he sent no representative to the signing ceremony, which is why the two Koreas technically remain in a state of war. On July 27, 1953, the armistice agreement was signed by General Mark W. Clark for the United Nations Command, Peng Dehuai for China, and Kim Il Sung for North Korea.

A more nuanced and capacious global perspective has emerged since the 1980s that views the conflict through the lens of decolonization—a revisionist perspective inaugurated by Cumings's scholarship. The first part of his two-volume study *The Origins of the Korean War* was published in 1981 and the second in 1990.[44] From this standpoint, the Korean War was, at bottom, a civil war—one that came out of a longer complex struggle for national liberation that began in resistance to Japanese colonialism and was subsequently shaped by the imperial aspirations of the two competing global powers that emerged at the end of World War II. In his 2008 appraisal of five decades of historical scholarship on the war, military historian Allan R. Millet, while questioning Cumings's "position that the Communists had the edge in legitimacy and popularity," characterizes the conflict in similar terms when he asserts that "the best approach to understanding the interaction of external and internal factors in shaping the Korean War is to forget that it began on 25 June 1950" and to "see it as a three-phase Maoist war of national liberation in which *two* competitive parallel political movements, neither strong enough to stand alone, started their struggle to prevail in 1945–48."[45]

Cumings's scholarship points us even earlier in the century, to the colonial era, when Korea was enfolded into the rising Japanese empire, a process that began in earnest in 1905 at the close of the Russo-Japanese War. The peace treaty brokered by Theodore Roosevelt essentially ceded Korea to Japan, and it marked the beginning of a much-hated occupation that ended in 1945. The Japanese inflicted much cruelty on the Koreans and sought to eradicate their language and culture. The form of economic modernization they imposed diverted the most valuable resources to Japan and depended on fortifying the power of traditional local elites. Syngman Rhee, who would become the first president of the Republic of Korea, spent much of that time in exile in the United States, devoting his efforts to the cause of Korean independence. Kim Il Sung, who would become the first premier of the Democratic People's Republic of Korea, gained fame as part of a contingent of Koreans who had joined the Chinese People's Army in the 1930s in its fight against the Japanese in Manchuria.

The colonial period came to an abrupt end in 1945, when the Japanese surrendered and the Soviets capitulated to the hastily devised partitioning of the peninsula at the thirty-eighth parallel proposed by the United States. While the two administrative units thereby created were to be temporary, this division catalyzed the development of two opposed nation-states, each seeking to create its own version of a liberated and unified Korea. The Republic of Korea (ROK)—which proclaimed itself a sovereign state on August 15, 1948—was largely built upon a colonial apparatus that had been imposed by the Japanese and essentially repurposed by occupying US forces. Local movements for land reform and the redistribution of other resources had flourished throughout the peninsula after 1945, and these tended to be dominated by peasants, who had borne the brunt of the Japanese occupation. Many of these "people's committees" were socialist in their leanings. In the South, leftist Koreans (as well as suspected sympathizers) were subjected to the repressive violence of the South Korean military, the National Police, and various anti-Communist paramilitary organizations. At the same time, a parallel campaign of violence was launched in the Democratic People's Republic of Korea (DPRK), which targeted Christians and nonleftist opposition parties, while the energies of the people's committee were funneled into shoring up the newly established state, which also proclaimed its independence in 1948. Atrocities took place in both Koreas, though the scale of the violence committed by anti-Communist forces in the South was significantly greater. More broadly, during the five years before the conventional war began, factions that harbored opposing visions of the nation had already been in violent conflict in many parts of Korea, underscoring the inadequacy of the temporal markers of 1950–53 in characterizing its civil war.

The Intimacies of Cultural Memory

If Cumings's initial studies of the Korean War situated the conflict in a significantly wider temporal framework stretching back to the turn of the nineteenth and twentieth centuries, his most recent book on the conflict extends that framework in the opposite direction. His *Korean War: A History* (2010) devotes a good deal of attention to the competing regimes of remembrance that have taken shape north and south of the demilitarized zone as well as the culture of forgetting that emerged in the United States. Symptomatic of the latter is the fact that no significant literary works concerning the conflict have been produced by American authors: "If this war exists in American literature, it is usually wallpaper for people who may or may not have fought there, but came of age in the 1950s. From this war came nothing like Norman Mailer's *The Naked and the Dead*, Joseph Heller's *Catch-22*, or Michael Herr's *Dispatches*."[46] Cumings's appraisal is partially accurate, for it is certainly true that no white male authors comparable in reputation to the ones he cites have devoted much attention to the Korean War. Whatever references crop up do tend to treat it as "wallpaper," as he puts it, serving primarily as an empty temporal marker that helps identify the 1950s as a work's historical setting.

It is one of the primary contentions of *The Intimacies of Conflict*, however, that a rich and vibrant tradition of novels about the conflict has in fact emerged in the United States over the past two decades—one composed primarily of works by authors of color. Part 2 comprises four chapters that address a body of novels that take the Korean War as a central object of concern: well-regarded works by a number of US minority writers (Toni Morrison, Chang-rae Lee, Susan Choi, Rolando Hinojosa, and Ha Jin), a white Southern author (Jayne Anne Phillips), and a South Korean writer (Hwang Sok-yong); I also briefly address a memoir by an African American veteran of the Korean War, Clarence Adams.[47] These constitute, I contend, an exemplary literary archive of transnational cultural memory, one that illuminates the interlocking imperial and racial histories that converged in this conflict and the domestic and transnational transformations it helped engender. None of these works takes the form of conventional historical fiction, a genre that might promise a totalizing and comprehensive account of the Korean War. Instead, in their formal experimentation, these novels all intimate that any given work of cultural memory is necessarily partial and must be seen as part of a larger constellation of remembrance.

As this study's aperture widens to encompass the novels examined in part 2, it situates the Korean War in a complex nexus of formations that highlights the conflict's significance for US minorities—particularly for Asian Americans, Mexican Americans, and African Americans—while maintaining the postcolonial trajectory of Cumings's historical work to engage with the intertwined imperial formations that converged in the origins of the conflict and that have been restructured over the course of its long afterlife. This study therefore draws on and brings together scholarship from fields that are not often in dialogue: African American,

Asian American, and Latinx studies, as well as East Asian studies. In so doing, *The Intimacies of Conflict* adopts an approach somewhat analogous to the one elaborated by Alexander G. Weheliye in *Habeas Viscus: Racializing Assemblages, Biopolitics, and Black Feminist Theories of the Human*. In that work, Weheliye positions black studies in relation to "other forms of racialized minority discourse," including Asian American, Latinx, and postcolonial studies.[48] While he locates his "argument principally within black studies as a (non)disciplinary formation that brings to the fore blackness," his focus is on what he calls "racializing assemblages," which entail other racialized groups.[49]

While the approach adopted by *The Intimacies of Conflict* might be termed "comparative," I find in Weheliye's conceptualization of "relationality" a more compelling account of my own aims. Particularly salient is his concern with a particular form of comparison that can arise as lesser-known histories of marginalization become objects of study: "While thinking through the political and institutional dimensions of how certain forms of violence and suffering are monumentalized and others are relegated to the margins of history remains significant, their direct comparison tends to lead to hierarchization and foreclose further discussion."[50] Weheliye finds an alternative to this "grammar of comparison" in the notion of relationality, which he draws from the work of Edouard Glissant. "Relationality," he writes, "provides a productive model for critical inquiry and political action within the context of black and critical ethnic studies, because it reveals the global and systemic dimensions of racialized, sexualized, and gendered subjugation, while not losing sight of the many ways political violence has given rise to ongoing practices of freedom within various traditions of the oppressed."[51] *The Intimacies of Conflict* strives for a version of the relationality that Weheliye models in *Habeas Corpus*, departing from approaches that tend to be constructed around a single racial, ethnic, or national category. The novels I examine in part 2 constitute an exemplary archive of cultural memory in which the traumatic meanings of the Korean War are conjured to consolidate not nationalist, ethnonationalist, or racially distinctive forms of identity but a form that is more open-ended and dynamic.

The multiracial and transnational approach to cultural memory that shapes this project is also akin to what Michael Rothberg has termed "multidirectional memory." In *Multidirectional Memory: Remembering the Holocaust in the Age of Decolonization,* he offers a critique of what he dubs "competitive memory," which is a "framework that understands collective memory . . . as a zero-sum struggle over scarce resources" and is resonant with Weheliye's critique of "the grammar of comparison."[52] Multidirectional memory, in contrast, involves "opening up the separate containers of memory and identity that buttress competitive thinking and becoming aware of the mutual constitution and ongoing transformation of the objects of comparison."[53] It acknowledges that "the borders of memory and identity are jagged; what looks at first like my own property often turns out to be a borrowing or adaptation from a history that initially might seem foreign or distant. Memory's anachronistic quality—its bringing together of now and then, here and there—is actually the source of its powerful creativity, its ability to build new worlds out of the materials of older ones."[54] Because cultural memory is always "multilayered," perpetually reconstructed through the "restless rearticulations" of various subjects, it can be approached in ways that "construct solidarity out of the specificities, overlaps, and echoes of different historical experiences."[55] The focus of Rothberg's study is on how "the emergence of collective memory of the Nazi genocide in the 1950s and 1960s takes place in a punctual dialogue with ongoing processes of decolonization and civil rights struggle and their modes of coming to terms with colonialism, slavery, and racism."[56]

In stitching together approaches from Holocaust and postcolonial studies, Rothberg stresses "the rhetorical and cultural *intimacy* of seemingly opposed traditions of remembrance," a formulation that obviously speaks to the memorial and historiographical ambitions of my book as well.[57] Like Rothberg's study, *The Intimacies of Conflict* seeks to expose the "jagged" edges of memory, the tense and tender forms of "borrowing or adaptation," that are required to conjure memories of the Korean War that speak not only to the experiences of those who are linked to their authors by race, ethnicity, or nation but also to those who are "foreign or distant." To borrow from Weheliye's formulations, this study also conjures an assemblage of cultural memories that do not cohere into an organic whole. It is, rather, shot through with tensions and gaps; it is thus presented as necessarily partial and incomplete, tending toward a totality at which it will never arrive.

Thus while my analyses of the novels in part 2 address how the cultural memory of the Korean War is animated by authors in ways that speak to their own racial and national backgrounds, its aim is not to confine them to discrete containers of remembrance. When I take up the writings of Clarence Adams, Toni Morrison, and Rolando Hinojosa, for example, I explore the resonances between what the Korean War might have meant to African Americans and Mexican Americans, respectively; however, I also examine how their writings expose the intimacies, both loving and violent, that emerged between black and brown servicemen on the one hand and Asian combatants and civilians on the other. The protagonist of Morrison's *Home* (2012) is a veteran of the Korean War who struggles with post-traumatic stress disorder and returns to a still white supremacist country, highlighting the ghost in the machinery of 1950s military multiculturalism. He is haunted most, however, by the atrocities that he and other US soldiers inflicted on Korean civilians.

The protagonists of Hinojosa's trilogy of Korean War novels—*Korean Love Songs* (1978), *Rites and Witnesses* (1989), and *The Useless Servants* (1993)—are also soldiers. Their experiences cast light on a racial history that was nowhere apparent in contemporaneous popular depictions—another forgotten aspect of the forgotten war. While the US military had classified Mexican Americans as white, the racism his protagonists negotiate both in Korea and back home in South Texas suggests affinities between their experiences and those of African Americans. Like Morrison's, Hinojosa's novels are also notable for their depictions of their encounters with Asians. The portrayals in his trilogy of Japanese and Korean civilians as well as of Chinese soldiers suggest at times a sense of interracial and transnational solidarity, while at others they grapple with the fact that colored soldiers during this war directed their violence at a colored enemy and with the US Army's dark history in regards to Mexican Americans. Hinojosa's trilogy also encourages readers to reflect on parallels between that conflict and the US-Mexico War, which ended in 1848 with the partitioning of a long-standing community that resided on both banks of the Rio Grande River. The transnational dimensions of the war are also explored in Ha Jin's *War Trash* (2005). That novel offers a critical account of the Chinese perspective on the conflict, which renders it as a great victory against a great imperial power, the United States. It does so, however, from the viewpoint of Chinese prisoners of war who, along with the hardships of incarceration, faced excruciating choices and were treated as "war trash" by their own government upon their return.

While the archive of works I take up in this study is obviously multiracial and while I draw from a wide range of disciplinary and interdisciplinary traditions, Asian American studies—a field that has embraced transnational approaches—constitutes its primary point of departure. As such, novels by Korean American and Korean authors— Susan Choi, Chang-rae Lee, and Hwang Sok-yong—assume a prominent place in it. One aim *The Intimacies of Conflict* shares with their works is to draw attention to the devastating effects this war had on the Koreans who survived it, including those who emigrated to the United States as well as their descendants. What has largely been forgotten by Americans along with the war is the trauma experienced by the people in whose country the fighting took place. In this respect, a kindred scholarly work to this one is Grace M. Cho's *Haunting the Korean Diaspora: Shame, Secrecy, and the Forgotten War*. Cho's study, like mine, emanates from the positionality of having been raised by immigrant parents who have largely been silent about their wartime experiences. My study forwards a diasporic perspective insofar as it assumes that, as Cho puts it, "the Korean diaspora in the United States has been haunted by the traumatic effects of what we are not allowed to know—the terror and devastation inflicted by the Korean War, the failure to resolve it, and the multiple silences surrounding this violent history."[58] In the readings I offer of Lee's *The Surrendered* (2010) and Choi's *The Foreign Student* (1998) in chapter 6, however, I underline how these novels signal to readers that they should be taken not as "authentic" or authoritative accounts of what those who lived through the war actually experienced but rather, as I will elaborate, as second-generation translations—literary renderings of what Marianne Hirsch terms "postmemory."[59]

In addition to these Korean American perspectives, in chapter 8 I also take up Hwang Sok-yong's *The Guest*. This novel, which was released to great acclaim in South Korea in 2001, dramatizes how some of the most egregious violence committed during the conflict was of the most intimate kind—how the perpetrators of atrocities were often neighbors and friends of the victims and even family in some cases. My conclusion delves a bit more fully into South Korean perspectives, primarily through an analysis of the War Memorial of Korea, a monumental site that opened in 1994 in which several somewhat contradictory nationalist narratives about the conflict are housed. It also examines *Taegukgi: The Brotherhood of War*, a South Korean film released in 2004. In my account of these cultural objects, I will elaborate on how military Orientalism names more than a mode of representation aimed at eliciting the loyalties of Asian and Asian American subjects.[60] These narratives, in pointing toward the collaboration of South Korean soldiers with US military forces, open the way to an understanding of how they came to function, in Jin-kyung Lee's formulation, as "a subimperial force," an outsourced supply of military labor that the United States drew on as it established and maintained its neocolonial presence in East and Southeast Asia.[61] Military Orientalism ultimately took shape as a transnational military labor force in which Asian as well as Asian American subjects were conscripted, though sometimes voluntarily, as essential cogs in the machinery of US war-making.[62]

This study does depart from most scholarship in Asian American studies, however, in its multiracial scope and particularly from diasporic approaches that tend to take shape around a particular ethnic group. In reference to this second point, it is worth underlining that while this project takes up South Korean perspectives, it has been motivated by an ambivalence and skepticism toward the nationalisms, ethnic and otherwise, that circulate around the Pacific along with an intimate awareness of their allure. It thus shares the critical stance that Jin-kyung Lee adopts toward what she terms *Pan-Koreanism*, the South Korean notion that both citizens and those in the diaspora share a singular ethnic identity that persists in a coherent form. As she writes, this is "an ideology [that is] becoming gradually pronounced in the mass media, and as a more explicit policy and concerted practice in the South Korean government and corporations."[63] The advent of this notion of identity, she writes, "is, in part, related to the newfound usefulness of overseas diasporic ethnic Korean populations as human resources in multiple locations in the age of globalization. This newly emergent deterritorialized Korean identity is also related to the continuing emigration and fast-growing cosmopolitanism of middle-class and elite South Koreans to various locations, including North America and Australia."[64] While Lee issues this critique of Pan-Koreanism from the vantage point of critical Korean and East Asian studies, somewhat comparable critiques of essentialist notions of identity can be found in the work of two Asian Americanist scholars who happen to be Korean American: Kandice Chuh and Laura Kang.[65] I might speculate that like myself, one reason why Chuh and Kang are especially sensitive to the dangers of certain forms of ethnic and diasporic identity politics might be because of the way they have been practiced by Korean American communities in particular. Particularly germane here is Chuh's exceptionally generative elaboration of a "subjectless" approach to Asian American studies. In *Imagine Otherwise: On Asian Americanist Critique*, she argues for a turning away from approaches that explicitly or implicitly aim at the construction of a coherent subject and toward one that would orient itself around "a strategic *anti*-essentialism" as "the common ethos underwriting the coherence of the field."[66]

The approach I take in this book also has affinities with the one adopted by Lisa Lowe in her study *The Intimacies of Four Continents*, which "investigates the often obscured connections between the emergence of European liberalism, settler colonialism in the Americas, the transatlantic African slave trade, and the East Indies and China trades in the late eighteenth and early nineteenth centuries."[67] While Lowe's work takes up earlier formations of liberalism, race, and empire, the description she offers of its methodology has clear resonances with my own project. She notes that her "approach does not foreground comprehensiveness and teleology, in either a historical or geographical sense, but rather emphasizes the relationality and differentiation of peoples, cultures, and societies, as well as the convergence and divergence of ideas, concepts, and themes. In pursuing particular intimacies and contemporaneities that traverse distinct and separately studied 'areas,' the practice of reading across archives unsettles the discretely bounded objects, methods, and temporal frameworks canonized by a national history invested in isolated origins and independent progressive development."[68] In historiographical terms, *The Intimacies of Conflict* similarly seeks to illuminate the complex intimacies that connect domestic histories of race to the multiple colonial trajectories that converged in the Korean War. Rather than confining that event within discrete temporal and geographical boundaries (the Korean peninsula, 1950–53), this study situates the war in a longer and wider set of histories that involve not only the United States and the two Koreas but also China, Japan, Vietnam, and even Mexico.

Thus the historiographical trajectory that part 2 travels runs parallel to the genealogical itinerary traced by Lowe's *The Intimacies of Four Contents*, which "questions the apparent closure of our understanding of historical progress and attempts to contribute to what Michel Foucault has discussed as a historical ontology of ourselves, or a history of the present."[69] My analyses are driven by an analogous desire to explore how a deeper understanding of a war that took place in the middle of the last century and its contemporary resonances might contribute to "a history of the present." To better understand this present entails recognizing, as Christine Hong powerfully insists, how "the Korean War has fostered a formidable, crisis-generating, self-perpetuating, institutional architecture—the national security state, the military industrial complex, and the perpetual war economy."[70]

Finally, by showing how the works examined make multiple pasts—involving African American, Mexican American, Chinese American, and Korean and Korean American subjects—intimate with our present, I likewise hope to contribute to what Lowe terms "a historical ontology of ourselves." In this respect, my analyses of the novels in part 2 of this study strive to destabilize the "given categories and concepts" that ground our notions of collective identity—that invite us to reconsider who "we" are when we come to them and ponder who they ask us to become. For at the emotional core of these works are protagonists who are drawn together into circles of intimacy that do not always conform to the usual logics of race, nation, or even gender and sexuality—it is not always easy to identify in them the shapes that love and affection customarily take, shot through as they are with aggression, violence, and betrayal. In their mappings of the affective bonds that can emerge from the brutality of war and out of its lingering aftermath, however, these works move "us" toward an exemplary and capacious ethical framework for coming to terms with the legacy of war's violence.

PART I

The "Forgotten War" Before It Was Forgotten

1

"He's a South Korean When He's Running with You, and He's a North Korean When He's Running after You"

Military Orientalism and Military Humanitarianism

I will begin this study by examining Samuel Fuller's *The Steel Helmet*, the first Hollywood movie set during the Korean War. It was released in February 1951, as US-led United Nations (UN) forces were attempting to retake Seoul for the second time, two months before the front line would stabilize, more or less, near the thirty-eighth parallel. While it provoked some criticism from conservatives, *The Steel Helmet* did very well at the box office. In his autobiography, *A Third Face*, Fuller—who wrote, directed, and produced the film—recounts that his aim in making it was "to show audiences that war was more complex than the front-page newspaper articles."[1] He wanted to depict "the confusion and brutality of war, not phony heroism," and recalls that he wrote the screenplay "quickly, like a reporter on a scoop, the story 'torn from the headlines,' as they used to say."[2]

This "torn from the headlines" quality makes *The Steel Helmet* an exceptionally useful point of departure for this study. Indeed, the film encapsulates many of the tropes that appear in subsequent productions and in the coverage of the war. Its inclusion of a Japanese American soldier in the diverse unit of US soldiers it centers on illustrates how what I have termed *military Orientalism* is an aspect of the nascent form of military multiculturalism that took shape during the conflict. The film also prominently features an orphan as its sentimental fulcrum, and in him we can see the military humanitarianism that emerged as a central feature of cultural representations of the Korean War.

An exceptional feature of this first Korean War film is its personification of the enemy in the character of a North Korean major who is captured by men in the unit; in most movies, as we shall see, opposing

soldiers are simply depicted as members of a faceless horde. In this figure, we can see the remnants of a conception of Asian racial difference
that had been formed in the prior war and the advent of one that oper-
ated quite differently—one premised on the ability to distinguish between friendly and hostile Asians. As I will show, nearly all the nonwhite
characters in this film make their initial appearance in a racial demilitarized zone (DMZ) before they are properly identified as either benign
or threatening, revealing the dynamic structure of racial difference that
took shape during the Korean War.

The Remaking of a Genre: The Korean War Combat Film

The main protagonist of *The Steel Helmet* is Sergeant Zack (Gene Evans),
who is a "retread," which is what World War II veterans who fought in
the Korean War were called. The film in which he appears is also somewhat of a "retread" in that it recycles many of the generic conventions
that had been codified in the 1940s. As Jeanine Basinger notes in her
study *The World War II Combat Film*, "When the Korean conflict broke
out, and the need for combat stories arose, the model of the World War II
film was readily available for usage," and "with a minimum of temper-
ing and tampering, the Korean combat film—about an entirely different
kind of war—became only a variation of the World War II combat film."[3]
Of the film's plot, Fuller has this to say in his memoir: "I concocted a
squad of GIs in Korea cut off behind enemy lines. They're of different
races and backgrounds. Together, they must assault a Buddhist temple,
now an enemy observation post, as part of a big offensive operation."[4]
While in actuality the men's takeover of the temple happens quite easily
and the climactic battle is defensive in nature, the elements of his film, as
Fuller describes them, conform to well-established conventions. These
include, according to Basinger's itemization, a group of soldiers comprising "a democratic ethnic mix" that serves as a collective protagonist, the
journey of a patrol lost behind enemy lines, and a heroic final stand.[5]

One of the notable wrinkles Fuller adds to the genre in *The Steel Helmet* is an expansion of the diversity represented by its unit of US soldiers. In films depicting the prior war, this diversity would have been
limited to white ethnicities, but this film includes a Japanese American

and an African American soldier—Sergeant Tanaka (Richard Loo) and Corporal Thompson (James Edwards), respectively.

Another innovation of this film, according to Basinger, is that the character personifying the Asian enemy, the North Korean major, is quite different from the analogous figures depicted in World War II combat films. In her estimation, he is depicted as "a human being, educated, and with a clear political ideology" and thus "appears more like the suave Nazi of World War II films than the leering and grinning Oriental we have come to expect."[6] While this is true, the racial ideologies of the earlier conflict are still at play in *The Steel Helmet*, though in a somewhat jumbled form. Indeed, Fuller's film is illuminating precisely because of how it attempts to identify the Asian enemy in terms that do not simply recapitulate the racist cinematic shorthand of a prior war and how it improvises cinematic devices used to assert the loyalty of Asian, Asian American, and African American allies. What we see in *The Steel Helmet* is not just the emergence of the anti-Communism that provided the primary rationale for US entry into the Korean War but also a collision between residual and emergent vocabularies of race. Crucial to this shift, as we shall see, is the film's heavy reliance on a legalistic understanding of the war in relation to both its means and its ends. Out of this clash of ideologies, the film produces a justification for the vast killing of Koreans that the war will require—a justification that ultimately comes across as somewhat less than unwavering.

One sequence that illustrates this shift in racial ideologies is the tracking shot that introduces the North Korean. The camera pans up the roof of the Buddhist temple and zooms in to reveal the enemy, who is looking straight at the viewer, though his face is hidden behind a gargantuan pair of binoculars (figure 1.1). This image immediately conjures the image of the myopic and bucktoothed Jap soldier from countless World War II movies and Warner Brothers cartoons, which suggests that the racist caricatures of the prior war were simply repurposed for a new Asian enemy. The persistence of the figure of the evil Jap would seem to be hardwired into the genre. As Basinger points out, the vast majority of early World War II films were set in the Pacific theater because "the dramatic shock of Pearl Harbor, and the sense of outrage Americans felt made that story the more important one."[7]

Figure 1.1. The North Korean major: A new kind of enemy? *The Steel Helmet*, directed by Samuel Fuller, Eclipse Series 5: The First Films of Samuel Fuller (New York: Criterion, 2007), DVD.

However, when the major lowers his binoculars, the viewer is invited to pause for a moment to ponder his human face. This gesture prefigures a kind of unveiling that will take place much later in the film, when this character exceeds the framework imposed by what had become an immediately legible racist script.

An additional significant modification is that the only character of Japanese ethnicity Fuller places on screen, Sergeant Tanaka, is a Nisei who is presented as a seasoned and loyal fighter. In World War II combat films, as Basinger notes, the diverse unit of soldiers at their center could "have a German in its midst, but during the war itself, never a Japanese."[8] This is due to the fact that "we viewed the war with the Japanese as a race war, and the war with the Germans as an ideological war. When we disliked Germans, it was the Nazis we meant. When we disliked the Japanese it was all of them."[9] "All of them" also included, we might add, the many thousands of Japanese Americans who were herded into internment camps.

In a remarkable scene that I will discuss momentarily, *The Steel Helmet* underscores Tanaka's loyalty by revealing how it had been so severely tested by the injustice of the internment. Fuller is proud of this aspect of this film, as he wanted to dramatize that "it wasn't just blacks who suffered injustices. I wanted to show that other minorities were abused, too, long before the Nisei internment of Japanese Americans was general knowledge, [so] I had my characters in *The Steel Helmet* talking about it."[10]

In its heroic depiction of both Tanaka and black medic Corporal Thompson, the film clearly affirms that because of the military service of their real-life counterparts, African Americans and Japanese Americans have earned the right to be treated as fully American. The most compelling evidence of their loyalty is their willingness to kill or be killed in defense of their country. Moreover, *The Steel Helmet* highlights the particular role that subjects like Thompson and Tanaka can play in the fighting. Thompson frequently lays his hands on other characters, patching up their wounds, giving them medicine, or administering blood transfusions. Tanaka is cool in the face of danger, efficiently helping Zack take out two enemy snipers or calmly defusing a grenade. He, too, seems to be in possession of healing hands: a comic bit repeated several times in the movie involves Tanaka massaging dirt into the scalp—seemingly a Japanese folk remedy for baldness—of an inexperienced private aptly named Baldy. Thompson and Tanaka clearly stand in allegorically for Japanese and African Americans at home, their participation testifying to both the moral and military use value of racial integration.

We have become accustomed to thinking about the 1950s as a period in American history in which certain images of black and white male fraternity became popularized. Leslie Fiedler's provocative but influential thesis in "C'mon Back to the Raft Ag'in Huck Honey" is that the classic canon of American literature had at its heart interracial male romances that celebrated the love of a white man and a colored man.[11] This was the period in which the "canonical architecture" of American culture, to use Robyn Wiegman's phrase, was set in place, and it was apparent in the literary works whose "classic" status was being insistently proclaimed at midcentury by critics like Fiedler: works like Mark Twain's *The Adventures of Huckleberry Finn*.[12] As this study will demonstrate, such narratives of interracial fraternity significantly shaped how Americans viewed the Korean War. Also evident in many of the cultural texts I examine is a nascent version of what cultural historian Melanie McAllister has termed "military multiculturalism."

As will become especially evident in chapter 3, however, the military multiculturalism that emerged during the Korean War also featured images of Asian American and white fraternity, inaugurating the appearance during the Korean War of military Orientalism. This is evident in *The Steel Helmet*, especially in a scene that showcases the efficient and deadly teamwork of the two "retreads," Sergeants Zack and Tanaka, who wordlessly pinpoint the position of the enemy snipers who are firing on the unit and efficiently dispose of them. As they unleash the barrage of gunfire that will kill the attacking North Koreans, the two men are touching, back to back.

The final innovation to the genre I want to note here is the character of Short Round (William Chun), a Korean orphan who forms the crux of a sentimental narrative that runs through this film and plays a key role in the events that take place. Without specifically citing *The Steel Helmet*, Basinger identifies Korean War films as the first to include "an Oriental child who attaches himself to the hero," a motif that would appear in later combat films.[13] Short Round, the first iteration of this cliché, regards the gruff Sergeant Zack as a surrogate father figure and happily totes his guns and ammunition. He offers prayers to Buddha for the men's safety and sings for them a version of the South Korean national anthem. While Basinger does not quite make this link, it would seem that such figures are a humanizing of a prior convention: the mascot, a small dog or other cute animal, who is adopted by one or more men in the unit.[14]

Of Short Round, Josephine Park writes, "In this figure of a Korean boy who assists an American sergeant, *The Steel Helmet* creates the paradigmatic friendly of the Korean War: the orphan."[15] Arguably, such depictions of war orphans are the most enduring legacy of the conflict in American culture.[16] Although the practice did not originate with this war, representations of innocent and victimized Korean children in dire need of American assistance played a crucial role in framing how Americans understood the reasons for fighting, and I will discuss other representations of humanitarian Orientalism in chapter 4. Short Round and the North Korean major are the two Korean characters that appear in *The Steel Helmet*. Short Round's age, innocence, and guileless affection for the curmudgeonly Sergeant Zack clearly distinguish him from the latter, who is clearly his opposite. How Americans might learn to tell the difference between these two different kinds of Asian subjects forms this film's dramatic focus, which goes hand in hand with the task of distinguishing those who should be killed and those who should be saved. As I will argue, Fuller's film primarily deploys a legalistic framework to make this distinction, suggesting that the difference between friendly and hostile raced subjects can be determined by their lawfulness.

Racial Performances of Legality

This legalistic emphasis is not surprising given that the Korean War was, as Sar Conway-Lanz puts it, "the first armed conflict in which the United States attempted to live up to the human rights and humanitarian standards newly institutionalized in the late 1940s," after four new Geneva Conventions were codified in 1949.[17] Because the United States sought and received a UN sanction for its intervention, "American armed forces faced new expectations to meet humanitarian standards as well as new requirements for working with international organizations and allies. The treatment of refugees was a central aspect of these emergent obligations."[18] This new legal framework concerning war is refracted by the obsession with legality that is evident in *The Steel Helmet*, as is a concern with refugees.

Within the body of laws that ostensibly govern the conduct of war, a cornerstone distinction is made between those subjects who can legally be killed during the course of the fighting and those who cannot, which is directly tied to the question of who can be considered a legal combatant, and it is worth taking up this distinction before we examine how it structures *The Steel Helmet*. The state of war constitutes, by its very nature, a state of legal exception in which the laws rendering the intentional killing of other human beings an egregious criminal act are, within certain putatively clear and stable limits, suspended. As Nathaniel Berman has noted, one of "the key doctrines" of the body of laws that govern the conduct of war—*jus in bello* or, as it is now more commonly referred to, "international humanitarian law"—concerns what is termed "the 'combatants' privilege'—the provision of legal immunity for certain kinds of large-scale violence."[19] More recently, in the wake of 9/11 and the controversy over the treatment of "illegal combatants" incarcerated in Guantánamo, the term *legal combatant* has circulated in US culture, but this, according to Berman, merely names those who enjoy, within the "hoary and formerly esoteric doctrine of jus in bello," "the combatant's privilege," which is "an international law immunity that places some violent actions and actors substantially outside the purview of 'normal' criminal law and human rights law. Those who benefit from the combatants' privilege cannot be prosecuted for mere participation in armed conflict and are entitled to prisoner of war ('POW') status."[20] Subjects who qualify as legal combatants are then also—from the standpoint of the enemy, obviously—subjects who can be legally killed. Within the laws governing war, the issue of distinguishing between those who are legally recognized as possessing the right to kill and are therefore also legally killable and those who are not is connected to the principle of *discrimination* or *distinction*. For the rules of war to be observed, it is necessary to discriminate between those who are in legitimate possession of "the combatant's privilege" and those who are not.

In theory, at least, there is one clear way of making this distinction. In the following passage, Michael Walzer describes the criteria involved as well as the kind of warrior that makes such criteria increasingly difficult to apply: "The legal rules are simple and clear-cut, though not without their own problems. To be eligible for the war rights of soldiers, guerrilla fighters must wear 'a fixed distinctive sign visible at a distance' and must 'carry their arms openly.'"[21] The first criterion refers to the definition of military insignia codified in the Hague and Geneva Conventions: a military uniform is, precisely, "a fixed distinctive sign visible at a distance." *The Steel Helmet*, as we will soon see, highlights the issue of military insignia and uniforms in ways that bring into focus the radical rewriting of racial scripts that the film is engaged in, a revision of race ideologies written in the language of legality.

We can better understand the changes in the meaning of race that surface in Fuller's movie in this context if we turn to a well-known observation made by American sociologist Robert E. Park in 1917 concerning the seeming inability of Japanese Americans to assimilate: "The fact that the Japanese bears in his features a distinctive racial hallmark, that he wears, so to speak, *a racial uniform*, classifies him. He cannot become a mere individual, indistinguishable in the cosmopolitan mass of the population. . . . [He] is condemned to remain among us an abstraction, a symbol—and a symbol not merely of his own race but of the Orient and of that vague, ill-defined menace we sometimes refer to as the 'yellow peril.'"[22] If we view the racial ideologies that underwrote the Second World War in relation to Park's assertion, it would seem that the "racial uniform" that all Japanese and Japanese Americans were perceived as wearing functioned as the symbolic and legal equivalent of a military uniform, since the "distinctive racial hallmark" that "the Japanese bears in his features" can so readily serve as "a fixed distinctive sign visible at a distance." As John W. Dower demonstrates in *War without Mercy*, Americans seemed to believe that it was not only Japanese fighting men who were worthy of extermination but civilians as well.[23] That Americans were not particularly interested in distinguishing between Japanese combatants and noncombatants may explain why the hundreds of thousands of civilian deaths that were the consequence of the atomic bombings of Hiroshima and Nagasaki were acceptable to military planners and, to a significant extent, the public.

In 1950, however, no particular Asian racial uniform could serve as a "fixed distinctive sign" designating the legally killable enemy because it was no longer possible to distinguish between friendly and malevolent Asians on the basis of nationality. By the time hostilities had erupted on the Korean peninsula, Japan was in the process of being redefined as the most important American ally in Asia, and the defeat of Chiang Kai-shek's Nationalist forces made it clear that not only were there both friendly and hostile Chinese, but there were far more of the latter. And until the United States decided to intervene in Korea, few Americans knew anything about that country or its people.

The film explicitly addresses the uncertainty this poses, which is heightened by the insurgent tactics used by the enemy. That the US soldiers perceived Koreans generally as inhabiting a kind of racial DMZ is dramatized in a scene where the men come across a group of Korean refugees and force them to submit to a search of their clothing and belongings. Zack explains to Lieutenant Driscoll, the inexperienced commander of the platoon, why this is necessary: "Well, these guys are smart. They hide behind them white pajamas and wear them women's clothes." The grizzled veteran cannot help but admire these tactics, though they violate the laws of war proscribing the deliberate obscuring of military uniforms and weapons that would distinguish combatant from civilian. That the collapse of this distinction is catalyzed by the "racial uniforms" that all Koreans are seen as wearing is confirmed when one of the soldiers observes, "They all look alike to me," a comment that Zack sardonically affirms: "He's a South Korean when he's running with you, and he's a North Korean when he's running after you."

While the ending of the film offers the final word on this issue, much of the film seems devoted to making clear that a certain relationship to legality can reveal the difference between those Koreans who are with us and those who are against us—illuminating the zone of indiscrimination in which all of them are shrouded and distinguishing between those who possess "the combatant's privilege" and can be legally killed and those who do not. Indeed, the link between North Koreans and lawlessness is thematized in the film's opening scene, where we discover that Zack is the sole survivor of his own unit—all the other men have been shot and killed by North Koreans after having been taken prisoner. What we learn about North Koreans from *The Steel Helmet* before we even see one is that they flagrantly violate the rules of war concerning the humane treatment of enemy soldiers who surrender. The second thing we learn in the scene immediately following is that they violate the rules of war mandating that legal combatants must identify themselves through the clear display of their military uniforms: Zack and Short Round are shot at by two North Korean soldiers who are dressed in civilian clothes, or "white pajamas." What is worse is that they are pretending to worship at a Buddhist shrine and one of them is disguised as a woman.

Notably, the film's first scene also dramatizes how Short Round becomes legible as a "friendly" only after he is sited within a racial DMZ. His body is first glimpsed in parts. As ominous music plays, a tracking shot captures him from the knees down, and the tip of the rifle he carries is visible in the frame as he walks barefoot toward Zack, who has his hands tied behind his back and is playing dead. We then get a close-up of only the boy's eyes, highlighting the fact that he is Asian. Next, we see one of his hands pick up a knife lying on the ground nearby. As the music swells and suddenly drops to silence, we see him cutting Zack free. The soundtrack is replaced by Short Round proclaiming "South Korean" as he points to himself. Everything we need to know about Short Round is conveyed by the gestures he makes, literal and figural, here and throughout the rest of the film. As Park notes, he is depicted as "a walking emblem of faith," a devout Buddhist who makes prayers for Zack and the other men and thus answers, as it were, to a divine law.

The issue of whether one is a law-abiding subject also suffuses the depiction of Tanaka and Thompson. By stressing the men's relationship to legality, the film directly answers the question of whether African Americans and Japanese Americans can be counted on to be loyal to the American cause. When Thompson, the African American member of the unit, makes his first appearance in the film, he too emerges from a kind of racial DMZ. Sergeant Zack first sees the corporal as a figure walking toward him in a fog-shrouded forest (figure 1.2). Thompson's racial identity is difficult to determine at first because of the darkness and mist. What is immediately visible, however, is the insignia on his helmet that identifies him as a medic. It is no coincidence that the particulars of Thompson's military uniform are made discernible before those of his racial uniform. His honorable adherence to the obligations that accrue to him because of the insignia that adorns his helmet is what comes to define Thompson most as a character, and it bespeaks what kind of soldier and what kind of American he is.

Figure 1.2. Corporal Thompson's first appearance. *The Steel Helmet*, directed by Samuel Fuller, Eclipse Series 5: The First Films of Samuel Fuller (New York: Criterion, 2007), DVD.

Zack initially voices skepticism about Thompson's worth as a soldier. As he dresses the sergeant's wounds, the medic recounts how all the other men in his unit were murdered after being taken prisoner. When Zack asks why Thompson wasn't killed as well, Thompson replies that the North Koreans only kept him alive so that he could attend to their wounded. In the following exchange, Zack references how Communist propaganda had directly targeted African Americans, asking them to reconsider their loyalty to the American cause in light of the racism they continued to face:

> ZACK: I guess you had plenty of chances to see how those Reds treat
>   you guys.
> THOMPSON: They hate our guts.
> ZACK: That's not what Joe Stalin says.
> THOMPSON: Got fifteen out there to prove it.

The question that this brief conversation implicitly raises, which is whether African Americans might be susceptible to Communist propaganda, is explicitly broached and forms the very pivot of a remarkable scene that comes later in the movie. Thompson is once again tending to an injured soldier, but in this instance, the wounds belong to the North Korean major, whom they have taken prisoner. In this scene (figure 1.3), the two men have a rather extraordinary conversation. The major expresses his incredulity that a black man would fight for a country that sanctions segregation: "I just don't understand you. You can't eat with them unless there's a war. Even then it's difficult. Isn't that so?" Thompson acknowledges the racism he and other blacks have been subjected to but counters with the following: "A hundred years ago I couldn't even ride a bus. At least now I can sit in the back. Maybe in fifty years, sit in the middle. Someday even up front. There's some things you just can't rush, buster." The scene ends with each man telling the other he is stupid.

The physical placement of the actors in this scene visually conveys a sense that the relationship between African American and Asian is inherently antagonistic rather than, as the major suggests, conducive to a kind of interracial solidarity. As the camera revolves around them, Thompson and the major debate American racism face-to-face, which emphasizes both the oppositional nature of their statements and

Figure 1.3. "I just don't understand you." *The Steel Helmet*, directed by Samuel Fuller, Eclipse Series 5: The First Films of Samuel Fuller (New York: Criterion, 2007), DVD.

the difference in the "racial uniforms" the two men wear. Moreover, it calls attention to a key difference in their military uniforms as well. The cross on Thomson's helmet is contrasted with the star on the North Korean's cap. Though both insignias are "red," the difference between them highlights the different relationships to legality that African Americans and North Koreans embody. Thompson's words suggest that he is willing to honor the laws maintaining racial segregation even if he knows they are wrong, that he is willing to wait another fifty years or even longer for them to be changed. Thompson's interactions with the major affirm, moreover, that as a medic he will honor the Geneva Convention's guidelines concerning the treatment of prisoners of war even when he is being provoked into violating them: even as their conversation becomes more heated, Thompson continues to tend to the North Korean's injuries, though less gently as their argument intensifies.

The next scene, in which the North Korean speaks with Tanaka, is also shaped by a collision between racial and legalistic modes of differentiation. It begins with the major noting to Tanaka, "You got the same kind of eyes I have." Instead of talking to Tanaka face-to-face as he had to Thompson, he stands behind the Nisei soldier. The frontal shot that captures their conversation frames their faces side by side, as if confirming the physical resemblance the North Korean asserts (figure 1.4). The major then tells Tanaka, "They hate us because of our eyes." This shot highlights this physical similarity, reflecting back to mainstream viewers their own racism—their tendency to see all Orientals as identical. Further proof of US racism is provided by the major's reference to the internment: "They threw Japanese Americans in prison camps in the last war didn't they? Perhaps even your parents? Perhaps even you?" The camera records Tanaka's reaction in a close-up, sharing in the reflective pause that precedes his affirmation of the major's words: "You rang the bell that time. They did." Anticipating the voice of protest that would be raised six years later in John Okada's novel *No-No Boy* (1957), Tanaka's understated words register the injustice of the internment.[24] As such, the scene suggests that given this recent history, it would make sense for someone like Tanaka to be tempted by the Communist's words.

This moment passes abruptly, however. What provokes the Nisei to assert his absolute difference from the major is the latter's mockery of those Japanese Americans who fought with the 442nd Regimental Combat Team in the prior war: "Were you one of those idiots who fought in

Figure 1.4. "You got the same kind of eyes I have." *The Steel Helmet*, directed by Samuel Fuller, Eclipse Series 5: The First Films of Samuel Fuller (New York: Criterion, 2007), DVD.

Europe? For your country?" After noting that "over three thousand of us idiots got the Purple Heart," Tanaka underscores the difference between them by reimposing the World War II image of the bucktoothed Jap onto the North Korean: "I've got some hot infantry news for you. I'm not a dirty Jap rat. I'm an American. And if we get pushed around back home, well, that's our business. But we don't like it when we get pushed around by—aw, knock off before I forget the Articles of War and slap those rabbit teeth of yours out one at a time."

Because the visuals in the second scene suggest the difficulty of discerning a physical difference between loyal Nisei and commie Korean, the work of distinguishing between the two is performed by the dialogue. The most salient difference between Tanaka and the major is conveyed by the commitment to lawfulness that the former shows. While Tanaka expresses a desire to do violence to the North Korean, he restrains himself: "If I wasn't in the army and you weren't a PW, I'd—ah, in our country we have rules, even about war."[25]

In the end, it is a willing adherence to laws (even to those that one knows to be unjust) that defines and unites Thompson and Tanaka and distinguishes them from the North Korean. If current laws—which have been given constitutional sanction by the Supreme Court's *Plessey v. Ferguson* decision—force Thompson to sit in the back of the bus, he is willing, nonetheless, to abide by them. If a past law—an executive order issued by President Franklin D. Roosevelt, the constitutionality of which was affirmed by the Supreme Court—forced Tanaka and his family into an internment camp, it was a law he was willing to follow. And in the current context, both men prove themselves to be soldiers who will abide by the international laws that govern the conduct of war and the treatment of prisoners.

That the very first Korean War film placed such an overwhelming emphasis on the law is no coincidence, for indeed there was, from a legalistic point of view, something unprecedented about this conflict. It was the first of several undeclared wars that the United States waged during the latter half of the twentieth century.[26] The US entered into hostilities with North Korea not through a congressionally sanctioned declaration of war but on the basis of the Truman administration's assertion that the United States was compelled to take part in a UN-sanctioned military intervention, one that was justified within a novel international legal framework. The newly instituted Security Council of the United Nations was authorized by Article 39 of the UN Charter to "determine the existence of any threat to the peace, breach of the peace, or act of aggression." At the urging of the US, the Security Council voted on June 25, 1950, to define the North Korean attack as a violation of Article 39 and thus as an illegal breach of the peace. Article 42 also authorized the Security Council to take "action by air, sea, or land forces as may be necessary to maintain or restore international peace and security." On June 27, it passed a second resolution on the basis of Article 42 that, in the words of legal scholars Thomas M. Franck and Faiza Patel, "recommend[ed] that members furnish assistance to the South Korean Government necessary to repel the armed attack and to restore international peace and security in the area."[27] On June 26, Truman referred to the North Korean invasion of the South as a "lawless action" and pledged that the United States would "continue to uphold the rule of law," and this legalistic framing of the intervention was found convincing to a majority of the US Congress.[28] It was three days later during a press conference that the term "police action"—long attributed to the president—first emerged, though it was actually introduced by a reporter. Following up on Truman's explicit assertion that "we are not at war," one journalist asked, "Mr. President, would it be correct . . . to call this a police action under the United Nations?," to which Truman replied, "Yes. That is exactly what it amounts to."[29]

As mentioned earlier, the opening scene of *The Steel Helmet* had already affirmed this link between the North Koreans and lawlessness. The opening credits are projected over a full-frontal shot of an eponymous steel helmet—what initially appears to be a still photograph. But gradually the helmet rises, and we see the eyes, then the face, and eventually the body of Zack, the film's protagonist, emerge into the frame. He crawls toward the camera as it tracks slowly backward, and we soon discover that his hands are bound. We then see the bodies of two other American soldiers who, like Zack, have had their hands tied behind their backs. The meaning of this shot would have been self-evident to US moviegoers, as the press had widely reported the discovery of the corpses of many American soldiers found in this state: bound and executed. The North Koreans are thus depicted not only as having committed a crime against the peace, of violating the law *of* war (*jus ad bellum*); they are also presented as flagrantly violating the law *in* war (*jus in bello*), of committing war crimes. They kill their prisoners; they compel captured medics to minister to the wounds of their soldiers; and finally, they disguise themselves in civilian clothes, thereby disregarding the requirement that soldiers be distinguished by the wearing of military insignia.

A Racial DMZ

What ultimately makes *The Steel Helmet* such an exemplary text about the Korean War, however, is not just the tidy ideological schema I have just sketched out but also how the neat distinctions it establishes basically crumble by the end. In concluding my analysis of this film, I want to trace how *The Steel Helmet* asserts that the principle of discrimination it has so carefully elaborated is completely inadequate to the realities of war.

Like any war film, *The Steel Helmet* is inherently engaged in a metacommentary on its own status as a piece of visual technology. Paul Virilio has observed that the very first motion picture cameras were inspired by the Gatling gun and that military aviation originally emerged out of a desire to better see the enemy's forces. "For men at war," he writes, "the function of the weapon is the function of the eye."[30] One of the things the film is trying to demonstrate to its viewers is how *they* might be able to detect the difference between the two different kinds of Koreans, those who are the legitimate targets of military violence and those who are not. The notion that it is possible to *tell* the difference presupposes, however, that there actually *is* a difference. And while the film insistently tells us that both of these things are true—that there is a difference and that it is discernible—it ultimately shows us something else.

The antithetical terms in which the film depicts Short Round and the major, the representative South and North Korean characters, are not quite sustained by the film's ending. When Short Round is killed by a sniper shortly before North Korean forces are about to storm the temple, this would seem the ultimate affirmation of the difference: we are to link the Communists' willingness to kill a child with the Communists' willingness to kill their prisoners. Both convey the North Koreans' treacherous criminality. But the circumstances of Short Round's death make it seem less like a murder, a war crime, than a legally sanctioned act of warfare. The film makes clear that when Short Round is shot, he is wearing the military insignia of the US Armed Forces. When the North Korean sniper first spots him (figure 1.5), Short Round is walking out of the temple wearing a helmet and boots that have been taken from the corpse of an American soldier, and he is carrying an extra rifle for Sergeant Zack. As is evident from the long shot that shows the viewer what the sniper is seeing, in that moment, the South Korean boy looks less like the civilian he is and more like the American soldiers he is helping: that he is wearing a military insignia, visible from a distance, and that he is bearing arms would seem to distinguish him as a legal combatant. The film provides no reason to think that the soldier who shoots Short Round would have known otherwise.

The actions that follow shortly after Short Round's death further erode the distinctions the film has so carefully made. Zack is angered when the North Korean major reads and mocks a prayer that Short Round had written out on a piece of paper that he had pinned to his back, a prayer imploring Buddha to make Sergeant Zack like him. In response to the Communist's derisive comments, Zack shoots him in the stomach. The consequences of this act are spelled out by Lieutenant Driscoll,

Figure 1.5. Short Round's "uniform." *The Steel Helmet*, directed by Samuel Fuller, Eclipse Series 5: The First Films of Samuel Fuller (New York: Criterion, 2007), DVD.

who angrily asserts, "Just because those little rats kill our prisoners doesn't mean we have to do the same thing. . . . If it takes me twenty years, I'll see that you're shot for killing a prisoner of war, understand?" Having placed so much emphasis on the rules of war forbidding the killing of POWs, the film has its protagonist commit the very crime that seemed the essence of North Korean villainy.

And while it is the North Korean's callousness to the boy's death that leads to his own, something of his humanity is revealed in his own death scene. Thompson and Zack cradle the North Korean as he lies dying. They are positioned in front of the large statue of Buddha that dominates the temple in an arrangement that conjures a kind of pietà (figure 1.6). The North Korean's final words are a request to Thompson to offer a prayer to Buddha on his behalf. The sense of religiosity with which this scene is imbued reveals that the seemingly godless Communist, like his conational, Short Round, ultimately answers more to a divine law than to the laws of man. These two kinds of Koreans, whose essential difference the movie has gone to great lengths to underline, come to bear in death a kind of family resemblance.

Figure 1.6. The dying North Korean major asking for a prayer to Buddha. *The Steel Helmet*, directed by Samuel Fuller, Eclipse Series 5: The First Films of Samuel Fuller (New York: Criterion, 2007), DVD.

Overall, the Koreans who appear in this film are thus situated within a kind of chiasmic reversal. Their racial and national identities as framed by the context of war initially locates them in a kind of no-man's-land, a racial DMZ. The fact that the film's US protagonists are facing an enemy who literally clothes himself in the "white pajamas" of civilians makes the discriminations so necessary to war nearly impossible to make. Sergeant Zack's ironic assertion that "he's a South Korean when he's running with you, and he's a North Korean when he's running after you," suggests, however, that bodily orientations—the extension into space of Korean corporeal gestures—might enable such distinctions to be made. This suggestion seems affirmed by the numerous acts of friendship and gratitude performed by Short Round, ones that make him legible as a "friendly" in part by underscoring his Buddhist piety and as the antithesis of the North Korean major. In revealing the latter's own religiosity at the moment of his death, however, *The Steel Helmet* collapses the differences between them, returning both to that zone of racial indiscrimination where *all* Koreans, in the end, reside.

The piety that defines Short Round and, ultimately, the North Korean major as well works to humanize them. Within the schema that Judith Butler outlines in *The Frames of War* that distinguishes between those who are recognized as conforming to the norms of the human and those who are not and, concomitantly, harboring lives whose passing can be grieved or not, these characters do belong to the former category. Moreover, because of the aura of the sacred that surrounds their deaths, they emerge as sacrificial victims. Even as their deaths are thus mourned, however, they are nonetheless depicted as part of the necessary if tragic consequence of war, which constitutes, after all, the state of exception *par excellence*, the ultimate expression of a biopolitical project of governmentality predicated on the simultaneous management of certain populations' access to life and the consignment of others to death.

In chapter 4, I will take up two other films that further illuminate the racial DMZ, the zone of indiscrimination, in which US representations of the Korean War situate the figure of the Korean refugee: *One Minute to Zero* and *Battle Hymn*. In the humanitarian Orientalism they express, we will see a similar identification of the management of Korean civilian populations as the vital strategic and ideological problem posed by the conflict, the difficulty in discriminating between friendly and hostile Koreans. In those films, we will again come across an oscillation between a sacrificial representative mode that depicts the deaths of Korean civilians as a tragic but necessary consequence of war, which will always take the lives of innocent humans whose deaths must be mourned, and a more nakedly biopolitical calculus that reduces them to "good tissue" that must be cut away along with the bad.

It is not only Korean civilians who are reduced by war to the status of bare life, however, in the film's rendering. Notably, while *The Steel Helmet* ends with its US protagonists successfully repelling a North Korean attack despite suffering heavy losses and the revelation that the four survivors will likely be decorated for their performance, its coda is decidedly absent of triumphalism. Zack has succumbed to shellshock, afflicted by flashbacks to World War II, and its final shot is a rather somber one picturing an exhausted Tanaka, Thompson, and Baldy (figure 1.7). Their dialogue suggests that these Japanese American, African American, and white soldiers have been reduced to bodies capable of experiencing only the most primitive of survival instincts:

Figure 1.7. Tanaka, Thompson, and Baldy: A new kind of US Army. *The Steel Helmet*, directed by Samuel Fuller, Eclipse Series 5: The First Films of Samuel Fuller (New York: Criterion, 2007), DVD.

TANAKA: I'm hungry.
THOMPSON: Me too.
BALDY: Me too.
TANAKA: First we'll eat. Then we'll bury 'em.

It is rather fitting that this first Korean War film concludes with such a chastened image of interracial fraternity. Like virtually all war films, *The Steel Helmet* affirms above all the sentiment of brotherhood that connects men on the field of combat, an intimacy that emerges out of being subjected to, witnessing, and also committing acts of horrendous violence. But even as it asserts the value of these male bonds, it evinces an uncertainty over the ultimate value of the larger cause for which the war itself is being fought. Basinger's observation of significant changes to the genre of the combat film as it engaged with the complexities of the conflict is evident from not only this film but the others I take up in this study: "With the Korean War, we begin to see an increasing cynicism about fighting wars, a questioning of whether or not we should let ourselves be talked into it."[31] In the next two chapters, I will examine US popular representations of the Korean War that revolve around the interracial intimacy that emerged in integrated military units like the one that comprises the collective protagonist of *The Steel Helmet*.

In chapter 3, I will explore more fully the military Orientalism that is evident in the crucial part that Tanaka plays in this film. I will look at depictions of the Japanese American soldiers who were integrated into combat units during the Korean War—the most visible of whom had, like Tanaka, also served in the Second World War as members of the segregated 442nd Regiment—by examining films and the *Pacific Citizen*, the official newspaper of the Japanese American Citizens League.

In the next chapter, I turn first to the African American dimensions of the military multiculturalism that began to take shape during the Korean War. I examine cultural works that highlight the role played by African American soldiers in the conflict as they served initially in segregated units and then increasingly in integrated ones. Although these representations, like those in Fuller's film, generally celebrate the interracial brotherhood that develops on the battlefield, they also contain, to a certain degree, more critical perspectives that highlight the racial intimacies that link African Americans with Asians.

2

"Tan Yanks" and Black Korea

Military Multiculturalism and Race War in Movies and the Press

The actor who played Corporal Thompson in *The Steel Helmet*—James Edwards—went on to appear in a number of Korean War films. Viewers today might recognize him as Corporal Melvin in *The Manchurian Candidate* (1962).[1] In the decade between the release of the two films, Edwards would appear in two other Korean War films that I will examine in this study and seems to have made a career out of playing versions of the same character—the courageous, steadfast, and loyal African American GI.

A real-life counterpart to the cinematic soldiers portrayed by Edwards appears on the pages of the August 21, 1950, issue of *Life* magazine (figure 2.1). Pictured here is Corporal Ollie Lin, and the *Atlanta Daily World* applauded his appearance as paying tribute to the "courage, bravery, sacrifice, loyalty, patriotism and conduct of the Mississippi Negro Soldier in the Korean war." Coverage of the Korean War in African American newspapers like the *Atlanta Daily World* was replete with similar images of black military heroism.[2] Generally, black journalists, while not quite enthusiastic about the war, voiced no coherent opposition to it. The most explicit criticisms concerned, as historian Daniel Widener observes, the racial policies of "an army whose commitment to desegregation was uneven at best."[3] Penny Von Eschen similarly notes that the relatively "sparse coverage" of the war in the black press was mainly restricted to "the involvement of black American troops and the issue of segregation in the military."[4]

This marked a stark turnaround from the prior war, when black journalists, intellectuals, and political leaders composed a powerful anti-colonial formation that "elaborated a concept of democracy that put the struggles of black people at the center of world politics but encompassed *all* democratic struggle" and that "understood racism and shared bonds

Figure 2.1. Corporal Ollie Linn, a quintessential "Tan Yank." "In Sweat-Soaked Uniform, Corporal Ollie Linn of Farm Haven, Miss. (Photograph)," *Life*, August 21, 1950.

in the context of the history of slavery, colonialism, and imperialism."[5] In her influential study *Race against Empire: Black Americans and Anticolonialism, 1937–1957*, Von Eschen conveys how these activists "forcefully argued that their struggles against Jim Crow were inextricably bound to the struggles of African and Asian peoples for independence" and were therefore ambivalent about the war effort, since the Allies comprised the leading colonial powers.[6] The contradictory pronouncements issued by the United States concerning the postwar fates of European colonies—and of India in particular—made it difficult for many black cultural and political activists to commit themselves fully to the US war effort.

The Korean War years saw the collapse of this black anticolonial formation, according to Von Eschen, which resulted from "the systematic repression of those anticolonial activists who opposed American foreign policy" as well as "the embrace of Cold War American foreign policy by many African American liberals."[7] Additionally, Widener argues, this conflict "pav[ed] the way for the emergence of the belief that the U.S. military—the primary purveyors of organized violence on the planet today—somehow represents the most meritocratic, socially equal, and ultimately progressive institution in American society."[8] Widener's assertion that the Korean War enabled the construction of the ideology that Melanie McAllister terms *military multiculturalism* is borne out by the depictions of black soldiers I examine in this chapter, which include those in the reports of the black press and two films: *Pork Chop Hill* (1959) and *All the Young Men* (1960).[9]

Opposing currents are also discernible in some of these depictions, remnants of the more radical cultural formation that came into being during the Second World War and adumbrations of the one that would develop more fully during the Vietnam War. Widener asserts that "the unease, anxiety, and opposition generated between 1950 and 1953 produced lasting impressions among a critical swath of black Americans, including several who would play critical roles in the radical era that accompanied the Vietnam War."[10] Toni Morrison, in a similar vein, has asserted that part of her motivation in writing *Home* (a novel taken up in chapter 7) was to explore the effects the Korean War and other events of the 1950s had on African Americans and how these became "the seeds that produced the '60s and '70s."[11]

A little-known and rather singular example of the link between these wars is a statement directed at African American soldiers that aired on Radio Hanoi on August 14, 1965. As reported the next day in the *New York Times*, it was delivered by Clarence Adams, described as "a 36-year old Korean war defector," "a native of Memphis, and dubbed 'the Vietnam version of Tokyo Rose.'"[12] Adams, who was black, had become somewhat infamous during the Korean War as one of twenty-one US prisoners of war (POWs) who had refused repatriation and emigrated to the People's Republic of China in 1953. He begins his statement with the greeting, "Hi, fellows. Let's have a heart-to-heart talk," and recalls that during the Korean War, he and other soldiers "had been told that Asians were barbarians, that it was better to go down fighting than to surrender," but that this was false. "I am the living truth that the American bosses have lied about the Asians in the same way that they have lied about Africans and Latin Americans," he continues, and warns US soldiers in Vietnam that they "are fighting people in Vietnam like the ones I fought in Korea—people who are defending their homes with homemade weapons. . . . The people of Vietnam know what they are fighting for. . . . They know that their enemy is the American big shot. They know that the burning of their homes, schools, towns, and villages is America's doing. Americans will have to get out of Vietnam and the Vietnamese will see that they do." He asks, "Fellows, are you on the right side of this? The Vietnamese are not bombing your churches and killing your children." And he concludes by asserting, "You are in the wrong battle here. . . . You are fighting the wrong war. Brothers, go home. The Negro people need you back there."

Adams's words resonate with the much more well-known statements made by Muhammad Ali a couple years later to explain his refusal to register for the draft. When asked by a journalist in 1967 about his reasons, Ali reportedly said, "Why should they ask me to put on a uniform and go 10,000 miles from home and drop bombs and bullets on Brown people in Vietnam while so-called Negro people in Louisville are treated like dogs and denied simple human rights? No I'm not going 10,000 miles from home to help murder and burn another poor nation simply to continue the domination of white slave masters of the darker people the world over."[13] While both Ali and Adams voice their objection to the wars African American men have been made to fight in Asia, they do not denounce war in general. Their pacifism has a specific object, and it depends on the ability to distinguish between just and unjust wars.

Ali and Adams describe the unjust war that the US is waging in Vietnam (which Adams describes as a repetition of the one that took place in Korea) in racial and colonial terms. Ali characterizes the Vietnam War as part of a much longer conflict, one in which "white slave masters" have been engaged in a race war against "the darker people the world over." Adams similarly asserts that Vietnam is the "wrong war" for black GIs because "the American bosses have lied about the Asians in the same way that they have lied about Africans and Latin Americans." Linking them, in Adams's view, is their shared status as "barbarians" in the eyes of an imperialist racism that lumps them all together. The war that black GIs should be fighting, Adams tells them, is already raging back home, against those who have been "bombing your churches and killing your children."

Structuring both Adams's and Ali's statements is a metaphor of race war—a militarized view of the domestic conflict between black and white Americans that links it to a global conflict between the white and nonwhite races. For them, *race war* functions as a historiographical analytic somewhat in the way it does in Michel Foucault's *Society Must Be Defended*, as a "counter-discourse" that reveals currents of power and domination obscured by Enlightenment discourses of sovereignty.[14] As David Macey describes it, "The central thesis of '*Society Must Be Defended*' is the claim, put forward from at least the 17th century, that 'war is the uninterrupted frame of history' and that: 'The war that is going on beneath order and peace, the war that undermines our society and divides it in a binary mode is, basically, a race war.'"[15] Both Ali and Adams situate twentieth-century US military interventions in Asia in a much deeper history, suggesting that they are simply the most recent flare-ups in a centuries-long race war in which "white slave masters" have sought to dominate "the darker people the world over."

A somewhat similar conception of race war lies at the heart of the political and cultural formation that Bill Mullen has labeled Afro-Orientalism, a formation of which Ali and Adams are clearly a part. Exemplified and inaugurated by W. E. B. Du Bois's writings on the world-historical role that Africa and Asia could play in bringing racism, colonialism, and capitalism to an end, Afro-Orientalism, in Mullen's words, comprises "a counter-discourse that at times shares with its dominant namesake certain features but primarily constitutes an independent critical trajectory of thought. . . . Afro-Orientalism . . . is a signifying discourse on race, nation and global politics constituting a subtradition in indigenous writing on imperialism, colonialism, and the making of capitalist empire."[16] To recognize the central role that race war plays in this formation, one need only consider that the watershed historical event that prompted Du Bois's Afro-Orientalist musings was the victory of the Japanese Empire in the Russo-Japanese War—a war he perceived as the first military defeat of a white colonial power by a colored one (and that also, by the way, opened the door to the annexation of Korea by Japan)—and that his romance, *Dark Princess* (1928), ends by suggesting the possible emergence of a cataclysmic global conflict between the white and colored races.[17]

As we shall see, the more critical perspectives on the Korean War that emerged in some representations of the role that African Americans played in this conflict drew on a similar notion of race war. As Widener notes, a debate did emerge in black newspapers over the issue of "whether the war was a legitimate struggle against aggression or a colonial strike against the self-determination of another 'colored' people."[18] Given that the conflict became increasingly unpopular to all Americans, largely because its aims seemed to lack the moral clarity of the ones that underwrote US participation in the Second World War, the question of why African Americans should support it was a thorny one, which all the texts I will be examining here grapple with. I will first take up the coverage of the war in the black press.[19] Then I will examine two Hollywood films—*Pork Chop Hill* and *All the Young Men*—that explicitly justify the sacrifice and struggle of African American soldiers as crucial in helping the United States live up to its stated ideals of racial equality and inclusion.[20]

From a "Gigantic War of Color" to the Emergence of Military Multiculturalism

The phrase "war of color," as Daniel Widener notes, is used more or less interchangeably with "race war" in the war coverage of black newspapers, indicating the anticolonial framework that some commentators used to frame the US military intervention in Korea and elsewhere. He argues that "the notion of a 'war of color' opened a space for viewing the Korean conflict, the Chinese Revolution, and the insurgencies in Indonesia, Indochina, and the Philippines as part of a worldwide struggle against what the African American radical Malcolm X termed 'world white supremacy.'"[21] He adds, "The perception that the United States was preventing unification caused many to view events in Korea as part of a global struggle for self-determination."[22]

During the Korean conflict, African American journalists actually used the rhetoric of a war of color in two overlapping ways: on the one hand, it was invoked to forward a historiographical perspective on Western imperialism as a centuries-long race war; on the other, it was used to refer to the kind of war Americans were in danger of being *seen* as waging—as a problem of *perception*. This rhetoric was, for the most part, confined to some of the earliest dispatches that characterized Koreans as a colored and colonized people and North Korean military aggression as the local manifestation of a widespread hostility of darker-skinned races toward racism and colonialism.

Several early editorials implicated the United States in Korea's colonial history by pointing to US collusion with other Western imperial powers in sanctioning the Japanese annexation of the peninsula several decades earlier. The July 8, 1950, edition of Lucius C. Harper's column "Dustin' Off the News" in the *Chicago Defender* was titled "All Big Power Nations Have at One Time Betrayed the Koreans." In it he provides an overview of what he calls Korea's "strange and sordid history" of being used as "a sort of political football for all the great powers. England, France, Russia, Japan and the United States have all betrayed it at one time or another."[23] In recounting how the Japanese turned Korea into their colony with the "connivance" of European powers and treated Koreans as "virtual slaves," Harper essentially aligns the former with whites and the latter with blacks. The following week, Harper specifies in his column how Americans were implicated in this "sordid" history of "betrayal," pointing out how President Theodore Roosevelt, by ceding Korea to the Japanese at the end of the Russo-Japanese War, "aided Japan in enslaving the Koreans, changing the whole course of their whole national history, their culture and everything dear to them. That was in 1905—remember! If you don't, the Koreans and Russians do. Does a nation, invaded by its neighbors—aided and abetted by foreign powers—forget and forgive as easily as an individual?"[24] Walter White echoes this account of Korea's colonial history a month later in his column in the *Chicago Defender* and identifies the book that he and Harper both seem to have relied on: *America's Role in Asia* by Harry Paxton Howard, a journalist who during the Second World War had written critically about the internment policy on the pages of the NAACP journal the *Crisis*.[25] Drawing on Howard, White describes the Korean People's Army's invasion of the South as a delayed response to Roosevelt's betrayal in 1905: "It took forty-five years for the Koreans to take revenge. Today they strike with all the pent-up fury of nearly half a century of brooding resentment."[26] He further warns that "bloody chickens are coming home to roost on the stars and stripes," since the military aggression of North Korea reflects "the flaming resentment of non-white peoples all over the world against racial bigotry here in the United States and in places like Asia and Africa."[27]

On January 6, 1951, Harper warns, "Whether he realizes it or not, the Caucasian—a minority group in this world's make-up—is facing a gigantic color war; probably in which will be determined how the affairs of coming generations will be managed from thence on."[28] The Russian enemy, formerly a "white nation," is now one "boasting of some 150 different racial patterns—mostly of mixed breeds."[29] Moreover, it "has cast its lot with the darker Asiatics and is utilizing this great brown-skin horde to obliterate white supremacy and bring about a new world order, minus the caste system." Harper here evokes a staple image of yellow peril—the Asiatic horde—in order to warn of the dire consequences of white racism. "The day is rapidly drawing to a close," Harper intones, "when the Caucasian—a minority world group—can thrust his insults world-wide over the dark majorities and fear no retaliation or attack."

While such commentary invokes the notion of "a gigantic color war" as a historiographical paradigm, it slides into an engagement with the problem of perception and the propaganda war in which the United States is engaged. This is evident in White's column from September 9, 1950, in which he reports that Moscow Radio "has pounded incessantly into the ears of not only Koreans but of people throughout Asia, Africa and Latin America that 'at the command of a southern President,

American G. I.'s are bombing and strafing COLORED PEOPLE in Korea.' Soviet Russia is doing everything within her power to make the war in Korea *appear to be one between white and colored peoples.*"[30] To battle such perceptions, White argues, it is in the vital interests of the United States to support racial quality and integration at home and enlist the support of colored allies abroad. He asserts how "fortunate" it was that India and Pakistan supported the US decision to intervene and "thereby, among many other things, minimize the racial angle in the present imbroglio."[31]

Commentators went on to assert that the best way to combat Communist propaganda that depicted the Korean War—and the Cold War overall—as "a gigantic color war" was to hasten racial integration both on the front lines and back home. While President Truman had issued Executive Order 9981 on July 26, 1948, decreeing that "there shall be equality of treatment and opportunity for all persons in the armed services without regard to race, color, religion or national origin," this policy was only implemented in 1951, when military planners realized that it was more efficient to train new soldiers to serve in integrated units.

Ironically, however, the early coverage of the war that sought to affirm the vital role that African American soldiers could play in challenging Communist perceptions of the conflict in Korea as a race war had to trumpet the accomplishments of "Tan Yanks" (as the *Chicago Defender* called them) who were serving in a still-segregated military. There was one particular unit that drew the lion's share of attention early on: the Twenty-Fourth Infantry Regiment. The ideological value of its performance was underlined in an editorial that ran on August 5, 1950:

> These colored GI's are proving they can take it and dish it out. Moreover, *they're putting color into what otherwise would be a war of whites against colored*, which wouldn't sit too well on the stomachs of the South Koreans themselves. There's no doubt that colored Asia and Africa have their eyes on the United States in these decisive days, and the total battle against the spread of Communism will stand or fall on whether the United States is willing to move forthrightly to accord those fundamental rights to Negro Americans which are everyday guarantees for all other Americans.[32]

Numerous tributes extolling the storied nature of this regiment of "buf-falo soldiers" appeared in all the major black newspapers.

Another irony that emerges in these tributes is that they trumpet a legacy of black military violence that had largely been directed at nonwhite enemies of the United States. The *Atlanta Daily World*, for example, explained on July 1 that the Twenty-Fourth Regiment had "at-tained distinction in World War II as the first all-Negro combat unit to face the Japanese" in 1942.[33] A follow-up piece from July 9 extolling the unit's illustrious past points out that it had "maintain[ed] order among the early settlers and the Indians in the western part of the United States, which was then in the first stage of civilization"; had "helped to save Colonel Teddy Roosevelt's 'Rough Riders' at San Juan Hill in Santiago, Cuba"; was sent to the Philippines three times to quell insurrections after the Spanish-American War; had assisted in pursuing Pancho Villa in Mexico in 1916; and had served as the first colored regiment to fight the Japanese in the Pacific during World War II.[34] Articles like these highlight that the colored soldiers of the Twenty-Fourth had been de-ployed in numerous wars against various colored enemies of the United States: Native American, Cuban, Filipino, Mexican, and Japanese.

The performance of the Twenty-Fourth Regiment was praised in mainstream newspapers as well. A July 22, 1950, report by the Associ-ated Press recounted that "American Negro troops, counter-attacking on South Korea's central front, took the rail and highway city of Yechon Friday in a 16-hour battle with Red forces," describing the action as the "first aggressive victory for the United States Eighth Army in the 4-week-old Korean fighting."[35] Facsimiles of the headlines reporting this victory that appeared in a number of mainstream newspapers were displayed on the front page of the July 29 issue of the *Chicago Defender*. The caption informed readers that "editors North and South gave full credit to the 24th for its signal accomplishment that has been an inspira-tion to a nation unused to the depressing news of withdrawals, retreats and defeats it has been receiving since the Communist invasion began June 25."[36]

As it turned out, however, the late summer of 1950 marked the mo-ment when the reputation of the Twenty-Fourth Regiment would reach its apex, for soon thereafter, reports began to emerge that a notably high number of men from this unit were being court-martialed. In 1951, two widely circulated reports—one in the NAACP's organ, the *Crisis*, and the other in the *Saturday Evening Post*—offered two divergent ways of interpreting this development. The first, which was published in the May 1951 issue of the *Crisis*, was written by Thurgood Marshall, whom the NAACP had sent to Korea in January 1951 in order to investigate possible racial bias in how the men of the Twenty-Fourth Regiment were treated by the military justice system.

Marshall begins his essay, "Summary Justice—the Negro GI in Korea," by expressing his incredulity at the fact that the same regiment that became famous for the victory it helped secure at Yechon "could change from heroes to cowards, all within a few days, even under the violent pressures of warfare."[37] This sudden turnaround could only be explained, Marshall asserts, by racial bias, which was evident from the disproportionate number of black soldiers who were charged: fifty-four of eighty-two US soldiers who were court-martialed in the first months of the war were black. It was also apparent from the "efficient haste" with which courts-martial were carried out, "almost as on an assembly line. As many as four cases in a singled day were tried, running on through the night, with all concerned anxious to get them over with."[38]

From his numerous interviews with men of the unit, Marshall concludes that the high rate of courts-martial reflected not the actual performance of the soldiers but the racism of the white commanding officers, many of whom were Southerners. This racism had a devastating effect on the men's morale, greatly diminishing the effectiveness of the regiment as a fighting unit. "Time and time again," Marshall recounts, "these officers told the men who they were going to order into battle, 'I despise nigger troops. I don't want to command you or any other niggers. This Division is no good, and you are lousy. You don't know how to fight.'"[39]

In his conclusion, Marshall calls for the rapid integration of the armed forces as the only way to prevent such injustices from recurring. If segregation were to remain the norm, he adds, this would further the perception that the United States would "face the potential enmity of hundreds of millions of men whose skins are not white, who look with extreme care to see how white men feel about colored peoples."[40]

Harold H. Martin's profile of the Twenty-Fourth Regiment—"How Do Our Negro Troops Measure Up?"—which appeared in the June 16,

1951, issue of the *Saturday Evening Post*, presented a view of the regiment that was, in significant ways, diametrically opposed to the one Marshall had put forward. For one thing, Martin suggests that the high number of court-martials of men in that unit were justified because it had actually performed poorly in combat. Martin asserts that GIs in the Twenty-Fourth had a marked tendency to "bug out," which, he explains, "is a phrase born of this war, and it means a pell-mell retreat, a stampede from a place of danger."[41] He itemizes "the troubles that beset the colored regiment—the deep fear that came with the darkness when each man felt himself alone, the tendency to exaggerate the enemy's strength and the effectiveness of his fire, the habit of falling wearily to sleep when falling asleep meant almost certain death"; however, he also notes that these "affected white regiments too."[42] The disproportionate degree to which black soldiers were affected by these "troubles," he asserts, could only be explained by their awareness of the racism of the country they were being asked to fight for. He offers this account of what some "Negro officers, in shame and sore humiliation," would say to their "White colleagues" in order to explain the poor performance of black enlisted men: "The trouble is . . . you take a man who in his own country has always been treated as a second-class citizen, and you call upon him to fight as a first-class soldier. You talk to him about democracy, and liberty, and how these things are worth fighting for. But the words don't mean the same to him as they mean to a white soldier who has always been free."[43] After reviewing the dismal performance of the Twenty-Fourth, Martin concludes that it is in the strategic interest of the United States to hasten the integration of the army. After polling several officers, black and white, who had served with the Twenty-Fourth, he reports that "all were agreed that the only way to make efficient use of the Negro infantryman is to integrate him into the line companies without regard to his race" and that if this were to happen, "he will fight as well as any man."[44]

Whatever damage Martin's profile might have done to the reputation of the Twenty-Fourth, his aim was the same as Marshall's: to criticize the racism of US officers and to promote the rapid integration of the army. Indeed, his concluding sentence could have appeared in either report: "To segregate the Negro into units where his resentment of the separation and the strange workings of mass psychology cause him to do less than his best is a waste of fighting talent the nation cannot afford."[45]

Walter White noted as much *in the Chicago Defender*, insisting that Martin's piece should be read "by Generals Douglas MacArthur, Dwight D. Eisenhower and Omar Bradley. And all others who have dragged their feet in obeying President Truman's directive to do away with racial segregation in the armed services."[46]

At any rate, by 1951, celebrating the exploits of a still-segregated military unit had become an anachronistic maneuver. When the disbanding of the unit was announced that summer, the tributes that appeared in the black press suggested that the Twenty-Fourth had outlived its usefulness as a symbol of black aspirations. In the July 29 issue of the *Atlanta Daily World*, it was reported that "Negro soldiers were happy when they heard the news from Washington that the Army was disbanding the 24th Infantry Regiment and integrating its Negro soldiers into regular Army units."[47] The October 4, 1951, issue of the *World* announced the official deactivation of the regiment by celebrating its various accomplishments and alluding to Martin's arguments: "Although there was mixed reaction in the United States both to Martin's article and the decision to deactivate the historic outfit, the men of the 24th welcomed the integration which, at last, placed them on equal footing with white soldiers."[48]

Over the remainder of the war, black newspapers increasingly and then rather incessantly highlighted the successful instances of military integration that the Korean War occasioned. The spirit of such reporting was conveyed in an article on February 3, 1951, by L. Alex Wilson, declaring that "the bloody Korean War has done more to wipe out Jim Crow in the Army than any other campaign—civilian or military—during the past 30 years."[49] A front-page article in the *Atlanta Daily World* from January 23, 1951, similarly announced that "the color line has disappeared in the foxholes of the American division on the central front of Korea. White and colored soldiers are fighting shoulder to shoulder."[50]

While the black press did highlight instances where segregation persisted in the military, its primary emphasis tended to be on the ways in which the war had dramatically hastened the spread of racial integration. On August 15, 1953, two weeks after the armistice was signed, an editorial in the *Chicago Defender* highlighted the fact that "training centers, many of them in the heart of Dixie, now operate on an integrated basis from the squad level up. Negro and white GIs train, play, eat and sleep side by side day in and day out. And what's more, there has never been a report of a major incident of violence as a result of the integration policy."[51] The integration of basic training, the editorial continues, "has resulted in many interracial friendships that otherwise would not have been possible."[52] In order to provide a concrete image of what this new military brotherhood looks like, the *Defender* conjures this scenario: "Negro and white GIs 'on the town' together have broken the segregation laws with impunity. In many a small southern Army post town, Negro GIs can be seen drinking with their white comrades in bars where no Negro except the janitor had ever set foot before."[53]

The Korean War in Black and White: *Pork Chop Hill* and *All the Young Men*

The cinematic resonances of the image that the *Defender* offers of "Negro and white GIs 'on the town' together" are not exhausted by the seeming reference it makes to the 1949 musical *On the Town*, which features Frank Sinatra and Gene Kelly as sailors on shore leave. As Robyn Wiegman has argued, during the late 1950s and early 1960s, narratives centering on the bonds that formed between black and white men became codified into cultural mythology.[54] She points to two Hollywood films in particular, both starring Sidney Poitier—*The Defiant Ones* (1958) and *In the Heat of the Night* (1967)—in which this formula took shape and the overcoming of racial tensions between white and black male protagonists compose the central drama.[55] The two major Hollywood films I will turn to next—*Pork Chop Hill* (1959) and *All the Young Men* (1960)—make clear that the Korean War provided a crucial site for the construction of this canonical architecture. However, they also contain elements that, as Jeanine Basinger notes, foreshadow the darker, more nihilistic cinematic visions that would emerge in the aftermath of the Vietnam War. Like several others released during the Korean War era, these films tell "stories which frequently question military leadership and which often present weak, frightened, or unreliable people in command of troops."[56]

Pork Chop Hill is based on a historical study of the same name written by Brigadier General S. L. A. Marshall that described one of the final battles to take place during the conflict and also one of its bloodiest. The film stars Gregory Peck as the newly promoted Lieutenant Joe Clemons, whose unit has been ordered to take back the eponymous Pork Chop Hill from the Chinese even as peace talks are taking place at Panmunjom. The film focuses on the harrowing battle that ensues as Clemons's men successfully take and defend the hill, a battle that only a few survive. It openly describes their objective as tactically meaningless but somberly insists that this victory had vital strategic value nonetheless.

Notably, the sense of racial mistrust evinced by white soldiers in *The Steel Helmet* is absent for the most part in *Pork Chop Hill*. Clemons's closest friend and confidante is Lieutenant Tsugi Ohashi, who is played by George Shibata, a nonprofessional actor who was the first Japanese American to graduate from West Point, where he had met the real-life Clemons.[57] The easy camaraderie that exists between Ohashi and Clemons is evident at one point when the former agrees to lead a risky bayonet charge and jokingly remarks, "You know my ancestors were pretty good at this banzai business."

Black soldiers are also visible in many shots, suggesting their seamless integration as well. Two of them play a small but pivotal role in *Pork Chop Hill*: Corporal Jurgens, played by the stalwart James Edwards, and Private Franklin, played by Woody Strode. Strode's character initially strikes a dissonant note in the film's ode to military multiculturalism, but it is eventually resolved. Jurgens is introduced at roughly the midpoint, when he is ordered by Clemons to watch Franklin, who has been trying to desert his unit. After forcibly prodding Franklin into a nearby trench and directing him toward the fighting, the two have the following intense exchange:

> FRANKLIN: What are you staring at?
> JURGENS: I'm staring at you. Who you think I'm staring at?
> FRANKLIN: What for? (Grabs Jurgens's wrist.)
> JURGENS: (Looks at Franklin's hand gripping him, apparently noticing its color.) 'Cause I got a special interest in everything you do.

In their juxtaposition, Edwards and Strode embody two competing images of black military manhood and two political possibilities for black America that emerged out of the Korean War. Edwards embodies the heroic "Tan Yank," another iteration of the stock role he played in several Korean War films. Strode, by contrast, seems to recall the men of the Twenty-Fourth Regiment as they were portrayed by Robert Martin in his profile in the *Saturday Evening Post*, prone to "bugging out" in the face of battle.

The intimate link that *Pork Chop Hill* establishes between these characters is conveyed by the intensity with which Franklin clenches Jurgens's wrist and by Franklin's assertion that he has a "special interest" in Jurgens. Jurgens realizes that both of their performances will reflect on the race as a whole. That Franklin is indeed someone who needs to be watched over is dramatically conveyed in a tense scene that takes place roughly two-thirds of the way through the film. At that point, while Clemons's men have successfully taken the hill, they are vastly outnumbered because of the heavy losses they have incurred. As Clemons is assembling the survivors to make their final stand, he discovers Franklin hiding in a bunker. Franklin raises his rifle, points it at his commanding officer, and threatens to kill him (figure 2.2). Clemons calmly asks the private to join the remaining members of the unit, adding that his current actions could result in "ten years" in a military prison. Franklin angrily replies, "Ten years for what? 'Cause I don't want to die for Korea? What I care about this stinkin' hill? You ought to see where I live back home. I sure ain't sure I'd die for that. It's a cinch I ain't gonna die for Korea, serve ten years for it neither." After a brief pause, Clemons replies that all of them are likely to die one way or another, given the impending

Figure 2.2. Franklin (Woody Strode) threatens Clemons (Gregory Peck). *Pork Chop Hill*, directed by Lewis Milestone (1959; Santa Monica, CA: MGM Home Entertainment, 2005), DVD.

Chinese counterattack. He continues, "At least we've got the chance to do it in pretty good company. A lot of men came up here last night. They don't care any more about Korea than you do. A lot of them had it just as rough at home as you did. They came up and fought. About twenty-five of them left. That's a pretty exclusive club. But you can still join up, if you want to. I'm going to move, Franklin. Make up your mind." Franklin, after some hesitation, takes up Clemons's invitation, lowers his rifle, and joins the other men. He becomes, along with Jurgens and Ohashi, part of that "exclusive club" of US soldiers who are willing to die for one another. By the end of the film, the gulf closes between these two black soldiers who were initially so opposed.

Despite its ultimately tidy containment, the degree to which the film gives voice to Franklin's mutinous perspective is notable. Due in part to Strode's bristling performance, Franklin's resentment comes across as understandable, however dismayed and uncomfortable white viewers at the time might have been to confront the image of a mutinous black soldier pointing a rifle at his white commanding officer and threatening to shoot him. To audiences today, this scene might seem to anticipate the more militant forms of black activism that would emerge later in the decade, notably the iconic image of Huey P. Newton brandishing a shotgun in an expression of the Black Panther Party's advocacy of armed self-defense. In *Pork Chop Hill*, however, this image of black militancy and treason is cast as a *past* threat that was, to a significant degree, contained by the integration of the armed forces. The film seeks to reassure its viewers that by joining the exclusive club that was the US military during the Korean War, black men who started out like Woody Strode's Private Franklin came to resemble Edwards's Corporal Jurgens.

I turn now to *All the Young Men* (1960), a Korean War film that features Sidney Poitier playing Sergeant Eddie Towler, a more prominent version of the role Edwards had made his specialty during the previous decade. It was released seven years before the two films that would cement Poitier's reputation as Hollywood's preeminent black actor—*Guess Who's Coming to Dinner* (1967) and *In the Heat of the Night* (1967)—and that would also make his name virtually synonymous with liberal Hollywood films that sought to address head-on the difficult conflicts that emerged as the nation struggled to move toward an integrated future.[58] While the characters Edwards portrayed were consigned to secondary roles, Poitier's Sergeant Towler is the central protagonist of *All the Young Men*, and the actor received equal billing with the film's other lead, Alan Ladd, who starred as Sergeant Kincaid. As we shall see, the kind of part Edwards had played goes to a Native American character portrayed by Mario Alcade.

The plot of *All the Young Men* is a familiar one, echoing that of *The Steel Helmet*. It focuses on a diverse unit of soldiers (a platoon of Marines this time) who battle their way to a key location (a farmhouse overlooking a mountain pass) and find themselves surrounded and outnumbered by hordes of Communist soldiers; it ends with the men making a heroic last stand. While this film, like *Pork Chop Hill*, is littered with moments when, during breaks in the fighting, the men of the unit discuss matters small and large, its dramatic focus is on the tension and then the sense of brotherhood that emerges between its two leads. The shifting dynamic between Poitier's and Ladd's characters—a tense interracial rivalry that is ultimately transformed into intimacy—is also a familiar one, a version of the narratives anatomized by Leslie Fiedler and Robyn Wiegman.

The film takes place in a snowy mountain pass in October 1950, after the Chinese have entered the war. In the first few minutes, the men come under sniper attack: several are killed and their leader, Lieutenant Toland, is fatally injured. His final order is to turn his command over to Towler. This scene introduces the essential dramatic questions around which the narrative will pivot: whether Towler will be up to the responsibility that has been given to him and whether the men will accept his command despite the fact that they see Kincaid as their natural leader. The challenges Towler faces are made apparent by both Kincaid's visible bitter disappointment as he hears the lieutenant's final order and the outrage voiced by Bracken, a white Southerner who makes similar outbursts throughout the film. When Bracken is ordered to bury their lieutenant, he throws down his shovel, calls Towler "black boy," and angrily asserts, "Where I come from, the black man does the digging." Towler replies, "We are not where you come from," and raises his rifle, pointing it directly at the Southerner, who, after a pause, sullenly does as he is told.

We witness here a restaging of the trope of race war, but in this 1959 film, the image of a black soldier raising his rifle at a white soldier is rendered not as a threat to unity but rather as a gesture necessary to maintain it. This black soldier has military regulations and a presidential executive order on his side, and it is the racist Southerner whose insubordination must be checked and who represents the greatest threat to the group's unity. In this scene, Poitier comes to resemble not only Private Franklin but also President Dwight D. Eisenhower, who had, just three years prior to the release of the film, sent the US Army to guard nine African American students who were integrating Little Rock Central High School.

As in *The Steel Helmet* and *Pork Chop Hill*, the cast of *All the Young Men* comprises a multiethnic mix that embodies the diverse and integrated image the United States presented during the Cold War. The vision of integration promoted by the film is literally staged in an early scene that shows the men in a moment of relaxation, entertaining each other in the pause before the expected enemy attack. The opening shot of this interlude shows Bracken drinking from a jug of wine and smoking. As the camera pulls back, we see a group of men sitting around a low Korean table, and we soon realize that the music in the scene is actually part of the diegesis. It is a folk song sung by Torgil, who is, we discover, a Swedish immigrant to the US who hopes to become a citizen. His singing is accompanied by the guitar playing of another member of the platoon, Cotton. As the men begin to banter, they remind the radioman, Corporal Crane, to try to reestablish contact with Battalion Command. Crane, the comedian of the group, launches into a monologue about the ineptitude of military intelligence. The loose and strikingly informal nature of the dialogue gives the impression that it has been improvised, an impression deepened by the chuckles of the other actors, which also sound spontaneous and unrehearsed. In this scene, it almost seems as if a later style of filmmaking—one we might associate with, say, Robert Altman—has suddenly though momentarily intruded into what is otherwise a rather conventional combat film.

It is not, however, a sense of verisimilitude that this scene ultimately conveys. Instead, viewers will likely experience a heightened awareness of its artifice. They may well be jarred by the collision among the acting styles of the various performers, many of whom are celebrities who became famous in fields other than acting. The most straightforward and naturalistic line readings are given by Paul Richards, who had been a regular on a number of television series and plays the racist Bracken. By contrast, it is quite clear from his delivery that the man playing Torgil is not a professional actor. In fact, Torgil is played by Ingemar Johansson, the Swedish boxer who had become famous for defeating Floyd Patterson in the 1959 world heavyweight championship. Johanssen's amateur status as a performer is evident in his singing as well, but the part of his accompanist, Cotton, is played by a professional musician of sorts, the teen idol James Darren. The star of this scene, however, is comedian Mort Sahl, who as Crane simply seems to be delivering the kind of monologue he became famous for: observational, conversational, and mildly subversive. It is, in part, the audience's awareness that they are watching performances by famous nonactors who sometimes seem as if they are acting in slightly different films that gives this scene its somewhat surreal quality. But if this interlude seems dissonant with the film's overall naturalism, the impressive multiethnic cross section of American celebrity it brings before its viewers is in line with its overall message: the integration its characters are fighting for in 1950 is embodied by the mix of stars who appear onscreen in 1960. What the film renders visible in this motley gathering of men—through their easygoing back-and-forth, their casual laughter—is a vision of an American culture in which an affable Swede, a funny Jew, and a drunken Southerner can peaceably cohabit.

At least in the realm of celebrity culture, then, the film presents integration as something that has already been achieved, for it is a site that is roomy enough to accommodate a Mort Sahl, a James Darren, and an Ingemar Johansson. The hierarchy that matters here, moreover, is one structured not by ethnicity, nationality, or race but by the species of merit that defines the Hollywood star system. The actors who receive top billing here are, after all, Ladd and Poitier. What this 1960 film records in its retrospective glance is the struggle it took to get here from there, and it memorializes the Korean War as a key waypoint in that journey.

What it took to get here, on the one hand, was the kind of military struggle against Communism in which the film's integrated platoon is engaged and, on the other, the more intimate struggles of individual men with their own social training and with each other—the intra- and interpersonal dramas that are the film's central concern. The narrative tension that defines *All the Young Men* as a war film—whether the platoon will be able to hold the farmhouse against enemy attack—is deeply entwined with the dramatic tension that structures the relationship between its two protagonists: Ladd's Kincaid and Poitier's Towler.

An early scene elaborates further on the tensions that threaten to fracture the platoon's unity. The men are debating whether they should stay and defend the farmhouse as they have been ordered to do, which will place them in great peril, or whether they should hide in the surrounding woods. Towler insists they must follow orders and remain where they are, and he is backed by Torgil and Crane. Kincaid and Bracken forcefully voice their dissent, and while the latter does so in more crudely racist terms, the former takes a slightly subtler tack. Kincaid accuses Towler of being motivated by both personal ambitions and a political agenda: "Nine marines and one black man with an ax to grind. We'll pull out and you'll be a hero. You might even get the Navy Cross. And when all your people hear what you've done, they'll build a statue for you in the cotton fields." As he had in his earlier exchange with Bracken, Towler resorts to the threat of violence to assert his authority. When Kincaid tells the men to "saddle up," Towler pulls out a grenade. He tells Kincaid, "Go ahead, you move, OK? And I'll pull this pin and push it down your throat. I didn't ask for this command, but that's the way it is. And any man who tries to move out of here without orders I'll shoot in the back." He turns to the men and appeals to their pride: "You're Marines, and you're gonna act like it as long as you're alive."

By the end of the film, however, the relationship between Kincaid and Towler will undergo a dramatic transformation, from near mutiny to an intimate intermingling of blood. The interracial intimacy that ultimately emerges between these two men is brokered through the mediation of a third man, a Navajo character referred to by the others as "Chief." He is the first member of the platoon to convey a belief that Towler may actually be up to the job, telling him, "I think we stand a good chance with you." Chief's appraisal prefigures the respect with which Kincaid will eventually view the sergeant. And the intense connection the black sergeant and the Native American enlisted man quickly form foreshadows the bond that will eventually emerge between Towler and Kincaid.

The connection between Towler and Chief deepens during a tense and attentive moment of waiting they share as they watch for enemy soldiers, one of several similar scenes that punctuate the film. Chief talks about the pleasures of duck hunting with his family back home in Arizona and asks Towler if he himself has ever hunted. Towler replies, "I've been hunting. Never in the country. I've been hunting, city-style. You know what I mean? Right in the middle of a million people. And you hunt plenty more things than jobs and apartments. Answers. People. One person even. One person. . . . I'm still looking. Still hunting. For everything." This exchange offers the sole glimpse into Towler's background, portraying him as a solitary urban figure whose peacetime existence was defined by a search for not only economic security and companionship but apparently also a larger sense of meaning for which he still hungers. In contrast, Chief's words suggest a rural past shaped by close family ties and a connection to his tribal community. He recalls how he and his father would just "lie there in the dark" and "talk about everything," which also offers a metacommentary on the intimacy taking shape between the two men as they stand guard.

A scene that takes place soon thereafter, in which the men repel an enemy attack in a fierce firefight, once again demonstrates Chief's capacity for interracial intimacy, but this time in relation to Kincaid. After Chief shoots and kills an enemy soldier who had been taking aim at Kincaid, the latter says, "Thanks, Chief. You handle that thing like Buffalo Bill." Chief replies, "I wish I could tell you I got it from my old man. But in my tribe, nobody could shoot straight. The cavalry died of old age." In this allusion to the savage battles that opened the American frontier, the film references the race war that helped give the nation its contemporary borders. But the potential ideological unruliness of this reference to what was a genocidal imperial project is contained by situating it within a kind of folksy—Will Rogers–ish, even—family narrative about inept Native American forefathers who never really posed a threat. Their exchange takes on an added irony given that Ladd had starred in several Westerns in which his characters protected white settlers from Native American attacks.

While *All the Young Men* is clearly steeped in the tradition of interracial male romance codified by Fiedler, it offers an interesting innovation. The Native American in this narrative does serve as a loyal sidekick, but much more prominently in relation to Poitier's character, not Ladd's. The bond between them is cemented when Chief insists that he, and not Towler, should scout the surrounding woods for enemy soldiers. He explains, "This is Indian country and you're a city boy. I stand a better chance." Chief specifies the password he will use when he returns: "Yah-tah-hay. That's the way a Navajo says hello to a good friend when he hasn't seen him for a long time. Yah-tah-hay." Enemy soldiers soon capture Chief, however, and attempt to use him to infiltrate the defensive perimeter the men have formed around the farmhouse. They tie a rope around his neck and march him in front of them as they push their way to the security post. Chief refuses to say the password when Towler asks for it and ends up being shot. The enemy soldiers disperse, leaving the mortally wounded Chief to die in Towler's arms.

This death scene clearly recapitulates the hoary trope of the vanishing Native American. But in making the ultimate sacrifice, Chief fulfills his function as a mediating figure who triangulates and transmutes the intense libidinal bond between the film's black and white male protagonists from hate to love. Mirroring the scene in which a dying Lieutenant Toland compelled Towler to take charge of the unit, this exchange also suggests the passing of a legacy. As a Navajo, Chief is clearly aware of the brutal treatment that men of his race have been subjected to by men like Kincaid and Bracken. This history of mistreatment, however, does not diminish his loyalty to the United States. Reminiscent of the characters of Tanaka and Thompson in *The Steel Helmet*, Chief is yet another cinematic example of the colored soldier who maintains his allegiance to America despite his intimate awareness of its legacy of racism.

The idyllic anecdote Chief had recounted about hunting mallards with his father also foreshadows the act that will convert Kincaid's antipathy toward Towler into respect and trust. What transforms these two men into comrades is also a hunting expedition of sorts, though their quarry is a North Korean tank bearing down on the farmhouse the men are defending. When the men hear it rumbling toward their outpost, Towler proposes a plan of attack. By using torches and kerosene to engulf the exterior of the tank in flames, he explains, they will be able to smoke out the crew inside and save the few grenades they have left. The two men execute Towler's plan to perfection, but Kincaid is badly injured when the tank rolls over his leg.

Wade, the medic, informs Towler that the only way to save Kincaid is to amputate his leg. Kincaid will require a significant amount of blood, however, and as it turns out, the only member of the platoon whose blood type matches Kincaid's is Towler. To say that the film's staging of the ensuing blood transfusion homophobically emphasizes its homo-erotic dimensions would be a gross understatement. The scene operati-cally conveys that in losing his leg, Kincaid is being subjected to a kind of castration, but what seems particularly unmanning is that the opera-tion also requires the entry into his body of a precious fluid that flows from the veins of a black man. As Wade prepares the needles and tubing through which Towler's blood will travel, he says to the sergeant, "I want you to listen to me very carefully. It's very important. When I'm ready, I want you to squeeze your hand in a slow, pulse-like rhythm. Don't stop no matter what happens." The racist Bracken has been made to assist in the operation. Successive close-ups show Bracken's hands releasing the clamp to start the flow of blood and Towler's hand slowly and repeatedly clenching into a fist. As Kincaid's leg is lifted up, he lurches his head back and screams. A few more pumps from Towler's hand engender a spasm of pain in Kincaid, who screams loudly and then falls completely uncon-scious. After the successful operation, the camera pulls back to linger on a shot of an empty right boot.

Bracken is not only an intimate witness to this event but a participant as well. In releasing the clamp, he is directly responsible for bringing about the mixing of black and white blood that is a white supremacist's worst nightmare—a miscegenation that, even worse, results from the coming together of *male* bodies. To help save Kincaid, he must overcome a repugnance that results from an aboveboard racism and a down-low homophobia. And while his face registers disgust and horror through-out the scene, it ultimately expresses a sense of resignation. Afterward, the chastened Bracken finally begins to treat Towler with the respect he is due.

In the final moments of the film, Towler steps fully into his role and the men wholly accept his command. As the requisite horde of enemy troops descends upon the farmhouse, he confidently barks orders that are duly followed. He tells his men to seek safety in the surrounding woods and to take with them the Korean civilians who live in the house. Towler carries the injured Kincaid, as he had earlier carried the dying Toland, into a foxhole, and they prepare to make their heroic stand. As the sergeant mans a machine gun, the greatly weakened Kincaid tells him to escape. Towler responds, "I'm not leaving you here, Tiger. I've got an investment in you. Some of my best blood is running through your veins. I don't want nothing to happen to it." As if to prove his point, when a shell lands nearby, Towler covers Kincaid's body with his own.

In what is literally the film's final minute, a formation of US jets appears and bombs the approaching enemy troops. Towler turns to Kincaid to say, "Merry Christmas, Tiger," knowing that the rest of their battalion will soon be arriving to save the day. Kincaid responds, "Same to you . . . sergeant." The film concludes with a shot of Towler happily firing away over the strains of "When the Saints Come Marching In" blaring on the soundtrack. In its concluding image of a black soldier laying waste to hordes of attacking Communist soldiers while protecting his injured white comrade in arms, *All the Young Men* overwrites the vestigial renderings of race war that had appeared in the two scenes in which Towler had threatened to fire on his own men. The film suggests the potency of the fully integrated combat units that served in Korea in not just military but also ideological terms. Poitier's star turn as Towler would also seem to put to rest the image of the sullen Franklin in *Pork Chop Hill*, who had pointedly asserted, "You ought to see where I live back home. I sure ain't sure I'd die for that. It's a cinch I ain't gonna die for Korea."

Madame Butterfly in Black and Yellow: Military Romance and the Korean War

Before I leave *All the Young Men* behind entirely, I want to briefly spotlight a subplot concerning the three Korean characters who appear in it: the residents of the farmhouse that the platoon commandeers as an observation post. When the men first come upon it and realize people are inside, one of them throws a grenade. As they clamber over the wall, they find that they have injured an elderly woman (though not seriously, it turns out) who lives there with her beautiful adult daughter, Maya, and grandson. Maya, the only speaking character of the three, is played in yellowface by Argentinian actress Ana María Lynch (who adopted Ana St. Claire as her stage name after coming to Hollywood). Although she glares at Towler the first time she meets him, angry that his men have injured her mother, an enigmatic bond emerges between them over the course of the film, though they are only alone together in one short scene.

In this scene, she comes upon Towler as he stands over the grave in which he has just buried Chief. She holds a candle, which he quickly puts out, since it would pinpoint their location to any enemy troops in the surrounding darkness. She apologizes and explains to him that she had lit the candle in order "to thank the Lord Buddha" for "sending you to help me," which makes no sense given that his men have occupied her house and wounded her mother. Confused by her gratitude, Towler asks her not to judge him and his men, explaining that they have acted out of fear and because they "have seen too much death." She seems to understand and adds that since the death of her father, she has learned that "time helps all of us," which is a lesson she somehow knows that Towler needs. She intuits his struggle and reassures him, "The day will come when your color makes no difference to any of them."

That there is something mystical about Maya is suggested not only by the fact that her dialogue has the quality of fortune-cookie aphorisms but also because she seems to thank Towler *in advance* for an act he will perform shortly thereafter, when he saves her from being raped by the drunken Bracken. This suggests that she somehow knew what Towler would do on her behalf before he did it.

Although Maya is an adult and the intensity with which she and Towler look at each other intimates a physical attraction, she does recall Short Round in certain ways. Not only is she a Buddhist, but she also comes across as an isolated figure who has been metaphorically if not literally orphaned: her father has died and her mother is injured, and there is no explanation given for why her son's father, presumably her husband, is not present. Additionally, she lends a hand during Kincaid's amputation, mopping the sweat from his fevered brow with a washcloth as his leg is cut away.

While the humanitarian Orientalism of *The Steel Helmet* is somewhat discernible in the figure of Maya, a more conventional and long-standing form is rather more apparent in its underscoring of her exotic allure and empathy, not to mention her apparently supernatural abilities. Although she is Korean, she is not unlike the eponymous figure immortalized in the Puccini opera *Madame Butterfly*, who ultimately commits suicide after being abandoned by her lover, a white American naval officer. This story codifies a fantasy about Asian women that exemplifies the tendency of Orientalism to insist on, in Edward Said's famous formulation, "the separateness of the orient, its eccentricity, its backwardness, its silent indifference, its feminine penetrability, its supine malleability."[59] As Gina Marchetti observes, the postwar era—and especially the US occupation of Japan, which occasioned a significant degree of fraternization between American servicemen and local women—provided fertile ground for the regeneration of the *Butterfly* narrative.[60] The Cold War variant of this narrative, as Marchetti elaborates, is epitomized by *Sayonara*, a Marlon Brando vehicle released in 1957.[61] Brando plays Major Lloyd Gruver, a fighter pilot who, at the beginning of the film, has become emotionally worn down by the missions he has flown in Korea. He finds healing in the arms of a Japanese woman, Hana Ogi (Miiko Tara), and in so doing, Gruver rebels against the racism of his white commanding officers and his own racist social training as a white Southerner.

As a segue to my account in the next chapter of how Japanese Americans came to be constructed during the Korean War era, I want to turn briefly to an African American variant of this more traditional form of Orientalism that was discernible on the pages of black newspapers and is resonant with the odd intimacy between Towler and Maya in *All the Young Men*. While a relatively progressive and anticolonial Afro-Orientalism, to use Bill Mullens's formulation, was evident in some of the early editorials in the *Chicago Defender*, as I demonstrated earlier in this chapter, another more sensationalistic Orientalism emerged in black newspapers at the same time that had much in common with its more hegemonic counterpart and centered on the romantic relationships formed between African American soldiers stationed in Japan and Japanese women.

On November 4, 1950, the *New York Amsterdam News* and the *Chicago Defender* both ran front-page stories reporting that roughly four hundred members of the Twenty-Fourth Infantry Regiment had applied to the army for permission to marry Japanese women. In the *Defender*, L. Alex Wilson reported that "the big problem facing lovesick Tan Yanks, now engaged in mopping up activity in North Korea, is their return to their former base in Gifu in order to complete arrangements for marital unions with their Oriental sweethearts."[62] Both papers treated the plight of these soldiers and their fiancées sympathetically but also noted opposition to these unions.

The allure of these women was the focus of a follow-up article by Wilson that appeared one week later in the *Defender* (figure 2.3). This November 11 story delves deeper into the amorous relationships members of the Twenty-Fourth Regiment had formed with Japanese women, or "musumes." Wilson admits that while he was initially "under the impression the love affairs between the GIs and musumes were of the passing fancy variety," he was soon "amazed to find many as deep-rooted or more so than engagements of a strictly racial kind in the United States."[63] A certain tension exists between the rationale the article itself offers for the appeal of Japanese women and the three largest photographs accompanying it. These pictures are presented as an idealized typology of female beauty, as none of the women's actual names are given. The accompanying captions identify one as "the face of . . . Oriental glamour" and another as "the girlish type." The third pictures a woman holding

Figure 2.3. The allure of Japanese women for "Tan Yanks." L. Alex Wilson, "Why Tan Yanks Go for Japanese Girls," *Chicago Defender*, November 11, 1950.

her baby, which the caption reveals is a biracial daughter fathered by a "Tan Yank." None of these women are pictured in clothes or makeup that would signify Japanese exoticism—in kimonos, for instance. Rather, they resemble a pantheon of *white* American femininity: the sexy glamour girl, the girl next door, and the mother (as well as the adorable infant daughter). The answer these photographs suggest to the question broached by the headline "Why Tan Yanks Go for Japanese Girls" is that the latter look like white girls.

The article itself, however, offers a different account. Ethel Payne, the director of the service club catering to US servicemen, describes the women's appeal this way: "By tradition, the Japanese woman is submissive. To the man of her choice or the one who wins her attention she presents a convincing superficial respectfulness and affection." This sentiment is echoed by another American woman who adds, "It is not unusual . . . for the Japanese girl to shut up when ordered to do so and to voluntarily look after every whim of her mate while he is with her."[64]

This familiar Orientalist conceit is echoed by a soldier who asserts that with a Japanese woman, "always YOU come first in her life." In elaborating further on the submissive femininity of the Japanese woman, he uses terms that connote a more contemporary ideal of domesticity: she "is loyal, devoted, thrifty and a good home-maker." This last term is key, for the allure of the musumes is intimately tied to the kind of homes that the Tan Yanks are able to make with them in Japan. "Before leaving Japan for Korea," Wilson writes, "a number of doughboys bought neat bungalows and furnished them in the latest style from Sear's Roebuck [*sic*] and Montgomery Ward. Other GIs rented Japanese homes and modernized, western style, the interiors." These details suggest that the Japanese woman is prized because she is an angel of domesticity, midcentury style—a necessary accouterment of the middle-class lives that black GIs had come to enjoy in Japan. One soldier tells Wilson that there, they "live like human beings, without suffering from prejudice and segregation."[65] Indeed, what black soldiers seemed to find in Japan was something like the suburban ideal so dear to the heart of Cold War America, but one largely denied to black men under Jim Crow. The Japanese woman functions, then, as a symbol of the life that black men will presumably lay claim to in a postsegregated future—she is valued not only for her sexual desirability but for being the very emblem of a peaceable domesticity.

Given that these women thus symbolize a middle-class prosperity, the seeming whiteness conveyed by the accompanying photographs makes sense, since it is largely available only to white men back home. Payne's commentary on their physical appearance, however, complicates this understanding of the musumes' racial complexion: "There is the color factor. The hue of the girls range from very fair to a nut brown. Hence it can easily be understood why our boys fall for them." Payne seems to suggest that the coloring of Japanese girls actually approximates that of black women, who might similarly range from "very fair" to "nut brown." Still another possibility is that what incites black male desire is not a single shade per se but a range of hues that suggests a racial amorphousness and morphability.

The sense that the musumes are so enticing because of a certain malleability is further conveyed by Wilson's conclusion to his article, which describes how American soldiers have "help[ed] to emancipate the Japanese girl," which is evident from the fact that "most of them no longer trot along on getas (wooden shoes) and in traditional colorful kimonos." Instead, he writes, "through the love of the men, the girls have learned to walk gracefully in high heel shoes and to dress with the taste and finesse of American women. Here too Sears Roebuck did a thumping business."[66] Overall, then, Wilson's article suggests that Japanese women are desired by black men, in other words, both for their exemplification of timeless Oriental values and for their modern capacity for change and assimilation. It is seemingly the combination of their not-quite-white but also not-quite-black bodies, their ability to fashion themselves and their bodies in accordance with American standards of beauty, and their traditionally submissive attitude toward men that composes their allure. The Japan that emerges from this report is not so much a fantasy of a timeless, ancient culture but more of a projection of a future America in which black men will become full beneficiaries of the Cold War dispensation of middle-class prosperity. Their lives there, it is suggested, enable black servicemen to live basically as organization men who are rewarded for their travails with attractive, loyal, and obedient wives and comfortable suburban homes.

This reporting does speak to the construction of the Asian woman as a "sexual model minority," to use Susan Koshy's formulation.[67] To address the economic framework that subtends it, however, it is also useful to consider Colleen Lye's account of what she sees as the particular quality of US Orientalism that distinguishes it from its European counterpart. The "exceptionalism of America's Asia," she writes, associates the peoples of that region with "a putatively unusual capacity for economic modernity," which then frames how Asian immigrants come to be racialized in the United States.[68] While stereotypes of Asian Americans have been "hostile ('yellow peril') as well as admiring ('model minority')," Lye argues that these seemingly antithetical constructions "are best understood as two aspects of the same, long-running racial form, a form whose most salient feature, whether it has been made the basis for exclusion or assimilation, is the trope of economic efficiency."[69]

Lye's thesis enables a speculative reading of Wilson's article—an economic Orientalist analysis, if you will—that enables us to glimpse a certain agency in the musume that extends beyond the support she provides to African American men in seeking a form of upward mobility, for her capacity to effortlessly embody a range of gendered racial and national styles enables *her* to achieve a measure of security. Her morphability appears from this angle not only as a survival skill in a country suffering from a resounding military defeat and occupation by foreign soldiers but also as a form of entrepreneurial prowess. The musume's agency stems from her ability to both engender the affection and desire of African American men and present herself as the ideal helpmeet for achieving the American Dream—from her capacity to offer herself, in other words, as a model collaborator.

While I will traverse a significant gap as I turn in the next chapter to popular representations of Japanese American soldiers during the Korean War, the constant is tied to the economic subtext that is, as Lye insists, the exceptional component of US Orientalism, for the version of agency promoted in the works I examine next constructs the Nisei citizen-soldier as a worthy object of white male affection and loyalty—a model collaborator in a number of ways—by depicting him as a certain kind of economic subject who understands the necessity of a certain calculus of sacrifice.

3

Military Orientalism and the Intimacies of Collaboration

Sacrifice and the Construction of the Nisei Citizen-Soldier as a Model Minority

I want to begin my analysis of the depictions of Nisei soldiering that emerged during the Korean War by returning to the notion of the "pretty exclusive club" Lieutenant Clemons evokes in *Pork Chop Hill* to entice Private Franklin into joining the other surviving members of their unit as they prepare to make their final stand. While this black private must be convinced to become a member of that club, the Nisei soldier who is Clemons's loyal second in command, Tsugi Ohashi, needs no such urging. In this respect, he has something in common with the man who played him, George Shibata, who was, as a 1958 UPI profile of him notes, "a much-decorated Air Force veteran" who had served in the Korean War.[1] The report also points out that he was the first Japanese American to graduate from West Point, where he had been a classmate of the real Joe Clemons, who recommended him for the part of Ohashi even though Shibata had no training as an actor. A profile that had appeared three years earlier in the Utah newspaper the *Ogden Standard-Examiner* fleshes out his biography.[2] Shibata, who was from Utah, joined the army during World War II and qualified as a paratrooper but was too late to see any action. After graduating from West Point, he became a fighter pilot and flew "over 30 ground support missions" during the Korean War. Having completed his service, Shibata was planning to enter law school. While he did become a lawyer, Shibata went on to play small roles in a handful of movies and television shows in the 1960s after performing the role of Ohashi in *Pork Chop Hill*.[3]

Writ small in the outlines of Shibata's life, shaped as it was by both the Korean War and his participation in a film that memorialized the conflict, is a certain narrative about how Japanese American men were remade in this era as model minority subjects, a narrative that many of them collaborated in writing. The sacrifice of military service, how-ever selfless it may be, also appears as a kind of prudent investment, one that will eventually pay dividends in a widening of economic op-portunities: for Shibata not only received a bachelor's degree by attend-ing West Point; he also gained a law degree after his service in Korea, presumably with the help of the GI Bill. Moreover, the connections he formed through his military service opened the door to a modest acting career. This aspect of his life story speaks to "the trope of economic efficiency" that composes the exceptional feature, as Colleen Lye has observed, of US Orientalism.[4] Indeed, economic matters will lie at the heart of the narratives of Nisei soldiering taken up in this chapter. More-over, as we shall see, the story of how Japanese Americans became model minorities during the Korean War era also involves their experiences during the Second World War, when 120,000 of them were incarcerated in internment camps and "over 3,000 of us idiots got the Purple Heart," as Sergeant Tanaka proudly asserts in *The Steel Helmet*, referring to the many Nisei who had fought heroically for the US Army in Europe.

The archive of cultural works explored in this chapter, which elab-orate how this narrative came to be built, does not contain an exact counterpart to a film like *All the Young Men*, one that would make the racism that Japanese American soldiers confronted and overcame dur-ing the Korean War its dramatic pivot. The movie that actually performs this ideological labor and that is the primary focus of this chapter—*Go for Broke!*—will come at this topic from a somewhat oblique angle. Re-leased on May 4, 1951, one month before US-led United Nations (UN) forces would retake the South Korean capital of Seoul and commence its war of rollback by crossing the thirty-eighth parallel on April 1, this work is actually a World War II combat film celebrating the exploits of the 442nd Regiment, a segregated unit consisting wholly of Nisei sol-diers. Nonetheless, as I will demonstrate, the context of its release during the Korean War inflected both its popular reception and its production history. Moreover, the Second World War setting of this film provides valuable insights into how a cross-referencing of both conflicts played a pivotal role in constructing Japanese Americans as a model minority during the early Cold War era. As such, it is a foundational text of the military Orientalism that emerged during the Korean War.

The mainstream press profiled several Japanese American soldiers who had fought valiantly in Korea. Most prominent among them was Hiroshi Miyamura, who received the Medal of Honor, the highest military decoration that can be awarded to a US serviceman. Miyamura was among the men singled out in an October 9, 1966, article that appeared in the *Los Angeles Times* that paid tribute to medal winners, and its title—"One in 10,000 Fighting Men Make This Exclusive Club"—makes clear that it is built around the trope deployed by Clemons in *Pork Chop Hill*. Written by Jerry Cohen, the article was occasioned by an upcoming reunion of medal recipients that would soon take place in Los Angeles. Its particular focus is on the nonwhite soldiers who received this honor, including Miyamura, who is described as "a bespectacled Nisei out of Gallup, N.M."[5] Echoing a central theme of *Pork Chop Hill*, Cohen highlights that a soldier's "creed, color or place of birth" has no bearing on membership in this exclusive club and that the only criterion for entry is the commission of "a deed of personal bravery or self-sacrifice, above and beyond the call of duty."[6]

Miyamura achieved a measure of acclaim in the waning days of the Korean War. He had been among a group of prisoners of war (POWs) who had been released from captivity and were on ships headed home in August 1953 when it was announced that he would be awarded the medal for his actions in an April 25, 1951, battle. Columnist Bill Henry offered this breathless account in the *Los Angeles Times* of Miyamura's heroic actions: "He was a machine-gun leader and, when his position was overrun by the Reds, he grabbed a bayonet, killed at least 10 of the enemy in hand-to-hand combat, went back to care for the wounded men in his group, then stayed to cover their evacuation, manning machineguns and other weapons and killing from 50 to three times that number of the enemy before running out of ammunition and being captured."[7] Miyamura, whom Henry describes as a "slender American boy with Oriental features," and Shibata were real-life counterparts to the cinematic Nisei characters we have already encountered. While not accorded the same level of prominence as African American soldiers, such figures, fictional and actual, make clear that the exclusive club evoked by the military multiculturalism that took shape during the Korean War included Japanese American members. Although neither Tanaka nor

Ohashi assumes a central role in the films in which they appear (the way Sergeant Towler does in *All the Young Men*), their presence onscreen is nonetheless striking, especially from our current vantage point, in which the relative absence of Asian American representation in movies and television has become a matter of discussion and debate. Even more notable in that respect is the fact that nearly all of the parts in *Go for Broke!* were played by Japanese Americans.

The link to World War II in references to Nisei soldiers in the Korean War speaks in part to the commonplace understanding that the US servicemen who fought best in Korea, especially early on, were "retreads" who had served during the earlier conflict. This was true of Murayama (as well as of Shibata), and profiles of him invariably mentioned that he had served "with the famous 442nd Infantry outfit which made military history as the all-Nisei 'Go for Broke' unit which fought in Italy."[8] Similarly, *The Steel Helmet* underscores that the fictional Tanaka, like Sergeant Zack, is a veteran of the 442nd. As we shall see, *Go for Broke!* codifies the terms in which such Nisei citizen-soldiers came to be lionized during the Korean War, ascribing to them a certain ethos of sacrifice that defines their community. This ethos includes a willingness to sacrifice not only one's own life but the lives of those to whom one is closest to the cause of defending the nation. This racialized spirit of sacrifice, moreover, is cast within a set of monetary metaphors that recall Lye's assertion that US conceptions of Asians and Asian Americans are always situated within an economic framework.[9]

To be sure, the use of economic metaphors to render the sacrifice of military service is common in American culture, as is evident in the name of the special exhibit on US wars that is housed in the Smithsonian's National Museum of American History: *The Price of Freedom*. This analogy also finds expression in the final scene of *Pork Chop Hill*, which ends with an extended tracking shot following the survivors of the final battle as they make their way down the hill accompanied by Gregory Peck's voice-over: "Pork Chop Hill was held, bought, and paid for at the same price we commemorate in monuments at Bunker Hill and Gettysburg. Yet you will find no monuments on Pork Chop. Victory is a fragile thing, and history does not linger long in our century. But those who fought there know what they did and the meaning of it. Millions live in freedom today because of what they did." The men who fought in this battle, this patriotic but melancholy conclusion affirms, were willing to pay the ultimate price for freedom: they were willing to sacrifice their lives, and many did. The film thus renders dying or being injured on the field of battle as a kind of blood currency, the price exacted for securing the freedom of millions. The inclusion in this final shot of Ohashi being carried away on a stretcher reminds viewers that he had been from the outset a committed member of the "exclusive" club that the more recalcitrant Franklin had to be cajoled into joining and that other Japanese American soldiers had also been willing to pay the price of freedom.

The Romance of Military Orientalism and the Racial Economy of Sacrifice in *Go for Broke!*

The Korean War erupted at the midpoint of the decade after the end of the Second World War, a period Japanese Americans primarily experienced as an "era of good feelings," according to historian Lon Kurashige.[10] While World War II marked the nadir of their experience, when nearly 120,000 Japanese Americans were incarcerated in internment camps, their loyalty suspect because of their racial identity, "it took less than a decade," Kurashige points out, "for all major anti-Japanese laws and court decisions to be rescinded." By 1946, most of the Nisei who had renounced their US citizenship to protest the internment had it restored; internees who had been imprisoned for resisting the draft were pardoned by President Truman in 1947; in 1948, the Supreme Court ruled that California's Alien Land Law, which had made it illegal for Japanese immigrants to own land, was unconstitutional; and in 1952, the Walter-McCarran Act was passed, bringing an end to racial quotas that had greatly restricted immigration from Japan and granting those who came to the US the right to become naturalized citizens. Kurashige notes that the spotlight on Nisei veterans who had fought during World War II in segregated units like the 442nd played a key role in transforming the status of Japanese Americans during the early Cold War years.[11]

Nisei were still associated with Japan, but that country was being redefined in that period, to use Naoko Shibusawa's phrase, as "America's geisha ally," as the economic linchpin in the free trade zone the United States sought to establish throughout the Pacific Rim as a bulwark against Communist expansion.[12] This international context cast

Japanese Americans in a new light: they became increasingly seen, as scholars like Robert Lee and T. Fujitani have argued, as a "model minority."[13] Given that the plight of US minorities had come front and center in the ideological war that the United States was waging with the Soviet Union over the "hearts and minds" of subjects in the decolonizing world, the internment policy became an embarrassing symbol of America's racial legacy. To counter Soviet propaganda that painted the United States as a racist imperial power, it thus became vital to insist that the legacy of the internment had been transcended. To that end, Japanese American soldiers who had served in the prior war along with those fighting in Korea played a crucial role.

An organization that led the way in advocating for Japanese Americans during this period was the Japanese American Citizens League (JACL), a civil rights organization founded in 1929 that was generally moderate in its political orientation through much of its existence and has been seen as mainly reflecting the interests of the Nisei middle class. During World War II, the JACL had explicitly advocated military service as a crucial means through which Japanese Americans could refute the suspicions of disloyalty that had led to their incarceration—a position that met significant opposition in the camps. The JACL's overall vision was insistently nationalist, focusing primarily on the racism faced by racial minorities within the United States and not particularly concerned with issues of colonialism and empire. Its lobbying efforts in Congress were led by Mike Masaoka, who had served in the 442nd Regiment during World War II and was a technical consultant on *Go for Broke!*

As is evident on the pages of the *Pacific Citizen*, its official newspaper, the leadership of the JACL were well aware that "the Nisei Story," as columnist Larry Tajiri termed it, could prove to be "an effective weapon of democracy's arsenal in the unceasing war of ideas" that the United States was waging with the Soviet Union and the People's Republic of China.[14] In this November 10, 1951, installment of his column in the *Citizen*, "Nisei USA," Tajiri celebrated the fact that Radio Free Asia was now broadcasting in China, whose troops had entered the fighting in Korea a year earlier, and that it was recounting stories of Japanese Americans. He notes that while the internment "provided considerable propaganda for the Japanese militarists" during World War II, recent broadcasts by Radio Free Asia "brought the record up to date by describing the reacceptance of the Japanese Americans on the Pacific Coast, their successful relocation in other areas and the program of the government to pay for evacuation losses." Telling "the Nisei Story" in full, Tajiri asserts, would involve a "heartwarming recital of a minority's victory over discrimination . . . which stresses the ability of a democracy to rectify mistakes," a story "the people of Asia should know."[15]

Crucial to "the Nisei Story" told on the pages of the *Citizen* during the Korean War were highlights of the heroic participation of Japanese American soldiers in the Korean War as well as the prior one. The continuity of these wars in regards to the narrative promoted by this newspaper is evident from the front page of the November 11, 1950, issue, which offered three very short pieces cataloging current Nisei acts of military heroism and sacrifice ("Colorado Nisei Soldier Dies in Korean War," "Report Oakland Nisei Killed in Korea Battle," and "Wounded GI Goes Back on Duty") and a longer article with the title "Movies More Complicated Than Battle, Say 442nd Veterans." This latter article was one of many that would appear in the *Citizen* devoted to *Go for Broke!*, and it focused on how "intrigued and amused" many of the Japanese American actors were as they re-created a battle in which they had actually participated.[16] Another typical front page of the newspaper, this one from December 2, 1950, also featured a trio of short articles itemizing the sacrifices made by Nisei soldiers in Korea: "California Nisei Reported Killed in Korean War," "Sgt. Okanishi Reported Hurt in Korean War," and "Wounded Sergeant Now Recuperating in U.S. Hospital." Page four of that issue featured a full-length article by Tajiri profiling the diverse group of 442nd veterans reenacting their World War II exploits in *Go for Broke!* Tajiri's piece concludes by asserting that the film "has great possibilities in American democratic propaganda, particularly in Japan and in Asia, where the U.S. Army is sometimes regarded as the instrument of white imperialism."[17]

Much of the *Citizen*'s coverage of the film appeared in Tajiri's "Nisei USA" column, which regularly focused on cultural topics. The first mention of the film comes on July 8, 1950, when Tajiri notes that "the Far Eastern crisis," by which he presumably means the Korean War, "may mean that things will open up again for film actors of Japanese ancestry in Hollywood," prompting studios to take a greater interest in "scripts with Oriental backgrounds," and he identifies *Go for Broke!* as "MGM's entry."[18] The *Citizen* provided readers with nearly weekly updates on the film's production in breathless anticipation of its release. Tajiri's actual review of *Go for Broke!*, which appeared on March 31, 1951, almost seems redundant given the avid attention the film had been given for over eight months. This glowing review announces that the film "is vivid and exciting. It has humor as well as pathos. It rings true and it is good entertainment."[19] Tajiri credits both producer Dore Schary and writer-director Robert Pirosh for having "given the picture the quality of documentary realism without loss of warmth of humanity." Pirosh's writing is praised for offering "a well-rounded portrait of a group of Nisei citizen soldiers." Tajiri credits Mike Masaoka for contributing to the film's "technical accuracy" in his role as "special consultant on its script and production." The review also praises the acting of the mainly nonprofessional actors, noting that with one exception, "all of the Nisei principles are veterans of the regiment as are most of the nearly 300 Nisei who were used as extras in the picture." Tajiri insists that the film will have "a special emotional impact" on Japanese American viewers: "It will make them laugh and cry and will make them proud. For the nearly 10,000 Nisei who served in the 442nd, as original volunteers and as replacements, the picture is a tribute; for the 600 men of the 442nd who died in combat, it is a memorial."[20]

Go for Broke! was generally well received by the mainstream press as well. Bosley Crowther's glowing review of the film in the *New York Times* commends it as "a respectful and rousing tribute to the men of the 442d Regimental Combat Team," which is "contained in a simple straightforward M-G-M war film."[21] As Crowther implies, its plot can be easily summarized. *Go for Broke!* features a collective protagonist—the soldiers in a single platoon of the all-Nisei 442nd Regimental Combat Team—but it stars Van Johnson, who plays the unit's commanding officer, Lieutenant Grayson. In following the men from boot camp, through a series of battles in Italy, and then finally to a victory celebration in Washington, DC, where they are honored with a presidential commendation for "outstanding accomplishment in combat," the film records how a group of raw recruits became seasoned and skilled fighters and ultimately war heroes. The collective arc of development of the multiple Nisei characters is mirrored in the transformation of their commander: Grayson, a Texan, is initially upset when he is commissioned to lead a unit of "Japs," but over the course of the film, he develops a deep sense of loyalty and respect for these Nisei soldiers.

As we shall see, *Go for Broke!*'s depiction of the heroism of its Japanese American protagonists highlights the ethos of sacrifice they embody and the interracial intimacy that emerges between them and Grayson. The film also leverages a number of economic metaphors to capture the forms of interracial intimacy it celebrates. This is actually foreshadowed by the film's title: the promotional materials explain that "go for broke" was the regiment's motto and the Hawaiian pidgin phrase for "shoot the works," which is uttered by a craps player when he is wagering everything on the next roll of the dice.

While *Go for Broke!* will likely come across as a fairly flat piece of Hollywood propaganda to viewers today, conveying a rather awkward and woolly liberal antiracism and sentimental multiculturalism, it does openly acknowledge that Nisei soldiers had fought for a government that had incarcerated many of them and their families and plainly acknowledges the racial dimensions of that policy. While it stops short of criticizing the executive order that established the internment as racist, it explicitly condemns the racism of white soldiers who did not want to fight alongside "Japs" and the extralegal acts of racist violence to which Japanese Americans were subjected. It therefore makes clear how this history could have easily produced a bitterness in Japanese Americans and fervently celebrates those who went to war nonetheless. *Go for Broke!* insists, moreover, that such service provides the best way of combatting racism—that the hearts and minds of racist whites can be transformed by Nisei loyalty, patience, courage, and sacrifice.

Perhaps the most remarkable aspect of *Go for Broke!* is its casting: Pirosh insisted that the men of the 442nd should be played by Japanese Americans and not by whites in yellowface or Asian Americans of other ethnicities, as had been the custom in Hollywood. Given the dearth of professional Japanese American actors, Pirosh cast amateurs in the principal Nisei roles: nearly all of them were veterans of the 442nd and were thus playing fictionalized versions of themselves. This unorthodox casting choice results in a film with an uncanny relationship to the sense of verisimilitude it is clearly intended to convey.

In his astute analysis of the film, T. Fujitani argues that *Go for Broke!* "circulated images of the Nisei soldier-citizen that had not been

previously possible," displaying a remarkable "tolerance for both individual and cultural difference."[22] The film particularly highlights the
distinct culture of Nisei from Hawaii, which is exemplified by their
music, dancing, and the pidgin in which they speak. One of them, Kaz,
is openly depicted as Buddhist, and his faith is treated with respect. For
all these reasons, Fujitani asserts, the film exemplifies "a new pattern
of representations and discourses in which values considered to be traditional in Asian societies were celebrated as conducive to Americanism" and marks "the remarkable transformation of Japanese Americans
in general, and especially Japanese American citizen-soldiers, from the
obvious symbol of racial discrimination into a living representation
of America's denunciation of racism."[23] Indeed, "cultural difference is
represented as an asset" in this film—even a *military* asset.[24] This point
is made most dramatically during the climactic battle, when one Nisei
soldier speaks in Japanese on the radio to those in the field in order to
thwart the attempts of English-speaking German soldiers to intercept
their communications, a tactic he chalks up to "that good old Yankee
know-how." Fujitani ultimately underscores the limits of the film's progressive racial politics, which are most evident in how the story of its
Japanese American characters is subordinated to that of its white protagonist, whose narrative "dominates the film and subsumes the 442nd's
heroism."[25]

My own reading of *Go for Broke!* echoes Fujitani's persuasive account
but explores three aspects of the film that his analysis does not delve into
fully: (1) the economic frame of reference in which the film operates,
evident in the trope of gambling that recurs throughout the narrative;
(2) the precise ethos of sacrifice the film celebrates Japanese Americans
for exemplifying, which involves a willingness to sacrifice those to whom
one is closest; and (3) what I term the film's "uncanny verisimilitude,"
which invites viewers to look beyond the edges of its diegetic world and
see its continuities with the world in which they live—an element that
stems partly from its repeated highlighting of *performative* utterances
and Pirosh's decision to cast actual veterans of the 442nd in most of the
principal roles.

The film opens in 1943 at Camp Shelby, Mississippi, where the men
of the platoon have arrived to begin basic training. Grayson, the newly
minted lieutenant who has just been commissioned to lead them, is a

Texan who had hoped to rejoin his former unit, the Thirty-Sixth Division, an "old Texas National Guard outfit." When he expresses his disappointment that he has been assigned to train "Japs," he is immediately chastised by his superiors. Captain Solari offers a brief account of the internment that avoids any judgment about its justness: "The army was facing an emergency at the start of the war, a possible invasion by Japanese troops. So all Japanese Americans were evacuated from the West Coast. There was no loyalty check. No screening. Nothing. If there were any spies among them, I can assure you there are not in the 442. Every man in this outfit has been investigated and reinvestigated and re-reinvestigated." Colonel Pence then specifies the term that should be used to refer to these men: "They're not Japs. They're Japanese Americans, Nisei, or as they call themselves, Buddhaheads. All kinds of Buddhaheads. From Hawaii, Alaska, California, New York, Colorado, and yes, even some from Texas. They're all American citizens, and they're all volunteers. Remember that." The regional diversity Pence refers to is exemplified by the men in the platoon, who are individuated in ways that are in keeping with the conventions of the genre—as representative types. Their diversity is suggested as a synecdoche for that of the larger population, though it is *Japanese* America that the men represent. One distinction the film teaches its viewers to make is between "kotonks," the Hawaiian pidgin term for those from the mainland, and "Buddhaheads," referring to those from the islands.

The first Nisei character to be introduced is the diminutive Tommy (Henry Nakamura), who speaks in pidgin, a sign that he is a "Buddhahead." We soon learn that he is an orphan whose parents were killed during the surprise attack on Pearl Harbor and that he had enlisted in hopes of avenging his parents' deaths. While he is largely a comic character whose small size is often the source of humor, his tragic past gives him a sense of depth. Tommy instantly becomes best friends with Sam (Lane Nakano), a "kotonk" from the mainland. We learn that Sam's family and his fiancée, Terry, are in an internment camp in Arizona. The conditions there and his reasons for volunteering are recounted in an early conversation between them in the barracks. Sam describes the lack of privacy and the crowding in the internment camp, the terrible food, and the scarcity of basic supplies like soap, which is why he is sending them a care package. Tommy asks, "Treat you like that? Hard to figure why a guy volunteer for the army." Sam replies, "We have to do something so we don't ever get a deal like that again," and Tommy agrees: "We show 'em. We show 'em us Buddhaheads good soldiers. Good Americans."

This early conversation introduces the economic subtext that circulates through the rest of the film. The privations of the internment camp are figured as a scarcity of goods that Sam, because of his military service, is in a position to help ameliorate. Additionally, his decision to enlist is framed by a gambling metaphor that likens the internment to a "bad deal" that the Japanese were given; Nisei military service is likewise presented as a wager or bet, the winning of which will entail Japanese Americans being embraced by their countrymen. Their service is thus also rendered, moreover, as a *performance* of sorts aimed at a white audience—an attempt to "*show* 'em" that the Japanese are not only "good soldiers" but also "good Americans."

This notion of military service as a kind of performative gamble is embedded in the film's title, the meaning of which would have been unclear to most Americans in the 1950s; Captain Solari explains its meaning to Grayson early on. "Go for broke!" is thus a performative utterance that both announces and enacts the fact that the shooter is wagering everything on one roll of the dice, risking everything if he loses. That the actual men of the 442nd took this as their regimental motto suggests that they saw their service as a similar performative gamble—that they were risking it all to prove their loyalty to the United States and prevent anything like the internment from happening again.

The first Nisei character to utter the titular phrase is Chick (George Miki), who yells it in an early scene, though he is the least enthusiastic of the recruits. When their craps game is interrupted by news of Grayson's arrival, Chick grumbles that white officers are always put in charge of Nisei soldiers in order to make them more miserable. Through much of the film, Chick's is the voice of Nisei resentment. That he is the first character to shout the regiment's motto, however, foreshadows his transformation in the film's final moments. Notably, he couches his discontent in economic terms. He is from Iowa and therefore had not been interned like those from the West Coast, and he had been making a good living as a chick-sexer. He regrets having listened to an army recruiter and enlisting, mainly because it resulted in the loss of his livelihood. Chick explains that chick-sexing is a "science" that had been developed by the

Japanese: being able to determine the sex of day-old chicks enables white farmers to reserve their feed for just the females, who will mature into productive hens. It "was one of the few ways a Buddhahead could get a break." He bitterly proclaims that he had been earning far more than he is being paid now. He mocks Frank (Akira Fukunaga), who has a degree in architecture from the University of Southern California but had been working as a fruit peddler. When the bespectacled Frank insists that he couldn't find work in his chosen field because his "eyes just couldn't handle all that close work," Chick retorts, "Yeah, eye trouble. That's what it was. All you need is corrective glasses to take the slant out of those eyes." Chick highlights the economic dimension of racism, which the film confirms has impeded Frank's vocational dreams.

While the first part of *Go for Broke!* depicts their training, the middle third takes place in Italy, where the men are first deployed. In the film's first battle sequence, three Nisei soldiers—Tommy, Sam, and Masami (another infantryman from Hawaii)—are shot at by German soldiers from an observation post established atop a hill. The three fight their way uphill and kill the enemy soldiers. In the process, they happen to find a piglet, whom Tommy adopts and names Paisan. The bond he forges with Paisan forms the crux of a comic, sentimental, and ultimately tragic subplot that runs through the remainder of the film. Subsequent scenes show Grayson and his men functioning as a formidable fighting unit. A montage (which mixes in documentary footage) portrays the platoon's progress across Italy and culminates in a firefight in which the men skillfully take out a group of German soldiers in an Italian farmhouse.

During one of the lulls in the fighting, we learn of the growing reputation of the 442nd back home. In one of several scenes in which Sam reads his letters from Terry, his fiancée, aloud to Tommy, the two find out that the regiment's heroic actions have been widely reported in the press. As Sam reads the letter, he and Tommy beam with pride about the transformative effect this recognition has had on those in the camps: "Honestly, Sam, you'd hardly recognize the old homestead. Maybe it looks the same. The barracks. The barbed wire. The MPs. But it isn't the same anymore. Nothing's the same. Because everybody knows what the 442 is doing. And what means [the] most to me is the change in the kids in my class. . . . They were just sad little people. Never laughed. Never made a sound. Today I'm happy to say I have as noisy a classroom as you'll find in America." The changes that have taken place are not merely subjective, however, for there are more material signs of a shift: we see a change of direction in which goods move between the soldiers and the camp, as Sam is now the recipient of a care package containing homemade cookies, and we learn that Sam's younger brother has been granted permission to work on a beet farm. These developments seem to affirm that the wager that men like Sam had made by enlisting is paying off.

Shortly thereafter, however, two scenes in the final third of the film, set in France, suggest the threat to the loyalty of soldiers like Sam and Tommy posed by the continuing racism of white Americans. By this point, Grayson has overcome his antipathy toward "Japs" and come to respect the men in his platoon and is even disappointed when he learns he has been given a new assignment. He is replaced by the newly promoted Lieutenant Ohara, which obviates one of Chick's early complaints about the absence of Nisei commanding officers. The 442nd has been assigned to the Thirty-Sixth Division, Grayson's old unit, and their former commander has assumed the position of liaison officer. Upon hearing of these developments, the men of the 442nd speak to each other in horrible Southern accents, joking that they have become honorary Texans.

The first scene highlighting the persistence of white racism occurs in a French tavern and pivots once again around a bet. As Grayson is driving by in a jeep, he hears the men from the 442nd singing and playing music, and he enters the bar to socialize with them. As he is about to join his former platoon, he spots Culley (Don Haggerty), his old sergeant from the Thirty-Sixth, at the bar and tells the men he wants to say hello to him first. The drunk Culley had been loudly complaining about the "Japs" recently attached to his division, and as Grayson makes his way over to him, Chick complains, "That guy would be a buddy of Grayson's" and wagers "five to one he don't come back for that drink." Chick ends up winning the bet, as Grayson does leave the bar with Culley. However, we soon realize (though the men do not) that he has pulled his former sergeant outside to reprimand him for his racist remarks. Reiterating Colonel Pence's earlier remarks, Grayson tells Culley, "They're not Japs. They're Japanese Americans. Nisei. Or if you prefer, Buddhaheads. But not Japs. They don't like it, and neither do I." Culley accuses Grayson of being a "Jap lover," goading him into a fistfight, and the former knocks Culley unconscious.

A second scene shortly thereafter shows the threat posed by racism at home. Sam receives another letter from Terry, but this one bears the disturbing news that his younger brother and some of his friends are no longer working at the beet farm in Idaho because "a gang beat 'em up to a pulp and said they'd lynch 'em if they ever came back." When Tommy asks why such a thing would have occurred, Sam bitterly replies, "They did it because they've got slant eyes. That's a crime in some places. Didn't you know that? How do you like that? We're good enough to carry rifles, but we're not good enough to pick sugar beets." This story seems to confirm the cynicism Chick has been voicing all along, so he chimes in, "Ain't I been telling you? Suckers. That's what we are."

The concluding battle sequence in the final fifteen minutes of *Go for Broke!* reenacts the engagement that brought fame to the real 442nd Regiment: the October 1944 rescue of the "Lost Battalion," in which the men saved 211 members of the Texas 141st Regiment who had been surrounded by enemy troops. Two hundred soldiers from the 442nd died during this battle, and six hundred were wounded. As the platoon begins to move up the hill into the teeth of the enemy defenses, Chick complains to Tommy and Sam, knowing that Culley is one of the men they have been ordered to rescue, as is Grayson: "This don't make sense. Sticking our necks out for guys like that buddy of Grayson's. That sergeant. That's the kind ganged up on your brother." However, Tommy tells Sam to ignore Chick: "We get to the Lost Battalion, that sergeant gonna change his mind about us Buddhaheads. . . . It's plenty rough. But we know what's it all about. You bet. Mo better we go for broke. Yes, Sam?" Sam replies, "Yes, Tommy. Mo better we go for broke." And so they do. The men of the 442nd engage in a brutal, uphill fight and succeed in rescuing the remnants of the Lost Battalion. Sam, Tommy, and Chick go all in, as it were, staking their very lives on the proposition that their actions will change the minds of even those like Culley.

When they come across Culley and Grayson, who are on a desperate scouting patrol, the former yells out, "Man, I never thought I'd be so happy to see a bunch of Japs! Pardon me, Japanese! I mean Nisei!" Culley also reveals to Tommy, Sam, and Chick that Grayson had "slugged" him for using the word *Jap*, making them aware of their former platoon leader's change of heart. A similar change is also apparent in the grateful Culley, which, in turn, effects a transformation in Chick. When the men reach the rest of the exhausted survivors of the Thirty-Sixth Division, it's Chick who first speaks to them: "Any of you guys want a cigarette?" By the end of the film, Chick is as enthusiastic a member of the 442nd as Sam and Tommy.

Within the terms of the genre, it is unremarkable that neither Grayson nor the three Nisei principals die during the film's climactic battle. The individuated Nisei characters who do perish in the finale are Frank and the newly promoted Lieutenant Ohara. The version of Nisei heroism that the film ends up celebrating most, however, is not linked as much with the relatively minor characters who die as it is with the more prominent characters who survive: Sam, Tommy, and Chick. Their heroism involves not just an ethos of self-sacrifice—a readiness to give up one's own life to a larger cause—but also a willingness to offer up others, even those to whom they are closest, to that same end.

In fact, *Go for Broke!* celebrates this particular form of sacrifice as the signature feature of Nisei heroism: a readiness to offer up the lives of ones' intimates in the name of a greater good. This ethos is epitomized by Tommy in the subplot that focuses on his bond with Paisan, his adopted piglet. Both are orphans, and the two quickly form a surrogate interspecies family. Their relationship is often played for laughs, as in a scene in which Tommy smuggles the pig onto a transport ship by hiding him in his duffel bag. Tommy always manages to find a local family to take care of his pig, paying them in supplies. In one crucial scene, however, he sacrifices his beloved pig to a starving French family. The scene in which a teary-eyed Tommy walks away from the hut in which he's left Paisan, who will be butchered to feed the family, is saturated with sentiment, the sound of the distraught, squealing pig serving as its only soundtrack.

Such sacrifices have an implicit connection to the gambling conceit evoked by the film's title. The film suggests that in "going for broke," these soldiers wager not only their lives but the lives of those closest to them: it is a wager made not just by soldiers themselves but also by the families they left behind in the camps. The film therefore idealizes a very specific vision of Nisei community values in which each member recognizes not only the potential necessity of his or her personal sacrifice but also the possible need to sacrifice others for the good of the community as a whole. To the extent that Nisei military service is thus rendered as a wager, the chips one is willing to sacrifice represent not just one's own well-being but also that of others. It entails a kind of cost-benefit analysis in which the reward of winning over the hearts and minds of the very racists who have incarcerated them and their families is worth the risk of losing not only their own lives but also those of the people they care about most.

What the men of the 442nd have gained through their collective wager is depicted in the film's coda, which includes documentary footage of the actual men of the 442nd receiving a commendation from President Truman and participating in a huge victory parade in Washington, DC. Prominently featured is Truman's attaching of battle honors to the 442nd's regimental flag and a voice-over that explains this gesture's significance: "Battle Honors by order of the secretary of war and the name of the president of the United States. As public evidence of deserved honor and distinction, the 442nd Regimental Combat Team is cited for outstanding accomplishment in combat. The gallantry and esprit de corps displayed by their officers and men in bitter action against a formidable enemy exemplify the finest traditions of the Armed Forces of the United States." These honors, the film concludes, are the hard-won currency gained by going for broke. In highlighting the bond to the nation that was cemented by this commendation, *Go for Broke!* underlines that it, too, is an interracial love story of sorts, one that celebrates the intimacy that formed between Nisei soldiers and the white men who led them.

Given that many of the actors in *Go for Broke!* were actual veterans of the 442nd, the coda's intercutting between documentary footage and cinematic re-creations highlights what I alluded to earlier as the film's uncanny sense of verisimilitude. Pirosh's casting decisions meant that many of his actors and extras may well have been present at the filmed ceremony and were again playing the same roles in the film. In the combat sequences, viewers are aware that the bodies that appear onscreen had actually been engaged in the military actions they are simulating. The contiguity of the ersatz 442nd that appears on the screen and the real regiment that fought in Europe thus invites viewers to consider how the latter had aspects of the former—for the actual 442nd was also engaged in a kind of performance, though one enacted in the theater of war. Both versions of the regiment are intended to "show" white Americans that "us Buddhaheads good soldiers. Good Americans."

Another consequence of Pirosh's choice to use actual veterans of the 442nd is that he, as director and writer, comes to seem like a ghostly double of the commanding white figures—fictional and actual—that appear in his film. This spectral mirroring is suggested in the first diegetic sequence, which is a shot of Nisei infantrymen walking past the camera. Superimposed over them are the presidential words that helped make the 442nd a reality: "The proposal of the War Department to organize a combat team consisting of loyal American citizens of Japanese descent has my full approval. The principle on which this country was founded and by which it has always been governed is that Americanism is a matter of the mind and heart; Americanism is not, and never was, a matter of race or ancestry." Roosevelt's statement, an excerpt from a letter he wrote to Secretary of War Henry Stimson that authorized the formation of an all-Nisei unit, is, like the film's title, another performative utterance: a speech act that brings something into being instead of simply describing it. *Go for Broke!* thus mimics the presidential order, as it too brought the 442nd into being—or at least a reproduction of it that bears significant traces of the real thing. And since it was Pirosh who chose to recruit Nisei veterans to play versions of themselves onscreen, his executive decision seems a virtual repetition of Roosevelt's.

To the extent that the film suggests a kind of doubling between its director and various white commanding figures, it also invites a consideration of the relationship among the corporate entities these men represent: the US Army, the US government, and MGM. The intimacy of these entities is suggested by the entirely conventional opening and closing sequences. Like all films, *Go for Broke!* begins with the studio logo. As the lion's roar recedes and the MGM logo fades to black, it is replaced by the 442nd's regimental flag, which prominently features its motto, making it evident that "Go for Broke" is both a regimental motto and a trademarked film title. The intimate relationship of the corporate entities that made this film possible is also underscored in the closing images. It ends with a single long shot—documentary footage—of troops in a victory parade, with the Capitol building prominently in the background. Above this image, the customary "The End," is superimposed and, below that, "Made in Hollywood, U.S.A. by Metro-Goldwyn-Mayer." These final visual elements thus spotlight the fact that the story of the 442nd had been crafted in two sites: the nation's capital and the capital of the US movie industry.

These entirely conventional elements call attention to its uncanny verisimilitude—a quality that invites us to move beyond thinking of it as a closed box, as it were, and to consider the story behind the story as well—the complex collaborative effort that went into its making. As such, it invites a consideration of not only the Korean War context of its production and release but also the prodigious collaborative labor involved in making it. It is this context that the numerous articles, columns, and editorials that appeared on the pages of the *Pacific Citizen*—which at times make the paper seem like an extension of MGM's publicity department—sought to flesh out.

The Politics of "Constructive Collaboration": The Japanese American Citizens League and the *Pacific Citizen*

As I turn now to the exhaustive reporting on *Go for Broke!* in the *Pacific Citizen*, I want to begin by looking briefly at several short articles that came out in the years after its release that resonate with the film's uncanny verisimilitude and are indicative of how the film is sited in a kind of inflection point between the Korean War and the Second World War. These are profiles of the only Nisei principal in the film who was not an actual veteran of the 442nd: Henry Nakamura, the actor who played Tommy and was too young during the Second World War to have served. These pieces provided readers with updates on his life as it took shape after his star turn, giving special attention to the fact that he followed up his simulated service in World War II with actual service in the Korean War.

"Tommy of 442nd Film Gets Real-Life Training" appeared in the November 24, 1951, issue of the *Citizen*, accompanied by two photographs of Nakamura undergoing military training at an army camp in Hawaii. The caption wryly notes that he "is now reenacting in real life the training experiences he depicted as an actor in *Go for Broke!*" Despite having been in the movies, Nakamura is described by his fellow trainees as hardworking, down to earth, and well liked. Indeed, he apparently received the distinction of being "Trainee of the Week" for his "outstanding progress in training, attention to duty and eagerness to learn."[26] Nakamura appeared again a few months later in a front-page article in the February 23, 1952, issue that announced, "'This Time It's for Real'; Tommy of 'Go for Broke!' Goes Off to War in Korea." This piece reports that having finished both basic training in Hawaii and a further stint at the US Army's Eta Jima Specialist School in Japan, Nakamura was "en route to a Korean assignment."[27] It ascribes to Nakamura the rather Tommy-like phrase quoted in its title—"This time it's for real"—to characterize his deployment. The August 28, 1953, issue included a very brief dispatch that brought his life up to date. It recounts that "he served two years as an interpreter in Korea and was discharged in last June," and he has now enrolled as a student at the University of California, Berkeley to pursue a graduate degree in psychology.[28] In an apt coincidence, this last article on Nakamura appeared on a front page primarily devoted to announcing that Hiroshi Miyamura had been awarded the Medal of Honor.

The sketch of Nakamura's life as it was shaped by his service in Korea—prefaced by the key role he played in reenacting the military performances of the 442nd Regiment in the earlier conflict—is an odd mirror of the brief biography of George Shibata, the Korean War veteran who played Ohashi in *Pork Chop Hill*. For both men, fighting in the Korean War and acting in war films opened up professional opportunities not only in the fields of psychology (in Nakamura's case) and law (in Shibata's) but also in the movies. Like Shibata, Nakamura would enjoy a short-lived acting career, landing small parts in a handful of films in the 1950s.

In Nakamura's case, it would seem that his having played the part of a Nisei serviceman provided a kind of training for the life he would go on to lead—as if the fictional Tommy provided the real Nakamura with a useful template for citizenship. By the same token, the glimpse into Nakamura's postmilitary future these articles provide—a college education that presumably culminates in a career in psychology—indicates the rewards that the fictional Tommy will reap as a result of his service, providing a kind of real-life coda to *Go for Broke!* The echo of Tommy's life in Nakamura's sounded by these articles thus effects a kind of slippage between the Second World War and the Korean War, suggesting how the rehabilitation of Nisei masculinity that began with military service in segregated units in the earlier conflict has only been fulfilled by military service in integrated units in the current one. Nakamura's participation in the Korean War and the presumably comfortable middle-class life he will move on to enjoy after his return to civilian life in 1953 mark the culmination of a process that began nearly a decade earlier when Tommy's real-life counterparts sacrificed themselves and those closest to them in order to "show 'em us Buddhaheads good soldiers."

These profiles of Nakamura and the listing of Nisei casualties and commendations that continued to appear in the *Citizen* highlight the Korean War context in which *Go for Broke!* was produced and released. That being said, it is important to acknowledge that the newspaper did not engage in any substantive reporting on the conflict. In fact, from 1950 to 1953, the political issues featured in the *Citizen* were the legislative efforts to pass the Walter-McCarran Act (which would strike down the racial quotas restricting immigration from Asian countries) and the War Brides Act (which would enable foreign women who had married US servicemen, many of whom were Japanese, to come to America with their husbands), as well as instances of housing discrimination and efforts to secure statehood for Hawaii.

The production and reception of *Go for Broke!* received as much attention on the pages of the *Citizen* during these years as any of the political issues just mentioned, and its release was treated as a watershed event in Japanese American history. Now I want to delve a bit further into this coverage, which offers a virtual primer on the technical and economic aspects of film production and some hints about the US government's possible role in shaping the story it told. The backstory of the film provided by the *Citizen*, much of which appeared in Tajiri's "Nisei USA" column, mirrors the story the film itself tells—it features heroic American men of different races working together on behalf of their country and ultimately reaping the personal rewards that await those who are daring enough to risk it all.

Virtually no aspect of the production process for the film was too trivial for the *Citizen* to cover: the ukulele lessons some actors took and the search to find pigs and piglets to play Paisan are two examples. The detailing of such minutiae highlighted how complex and elaborate an undertaking it was to make a Hollywood movie and render visible the army of cast and crew that were involved. In so doing, the *Citizen* emphasized all the more the prodigious efforts of the three men who emerge as the principal figures: producer Dore Schary, writer and director Robert Pirosh, and consultant Mike Masaoka.

It is not surprising that the *Citizen* would spotlight Masaoka's role in the making of the film. He had been the JACL's first executive secretary and was, at the time, "probably the most well-known Japanese American lobbyist in Washington," as he worked to bring the organization's concerns to members of Congress.[29] Moreover, he was himself a decorated veteran of the 442nd, the first from the mainland to volunteer for it. He was one of five brothers who served in the regiment: all of them were wounded, several left disabled, and one killed. Drawing attention to Masaoka's role is in keeping with the overall aim of *Go for Broke!*, which was to present Nisei veterans as exemplars of Japanese American identity.

In the *Citizen's* story about how the film was made, however, the leading roles go to white men: Schary and Pirosh, and the former gets top billing, as it were. Schary is presented as a daring and visionary figure, commended for his track record of producing films with a liberal message on race. As reported in the October 28, 1950, issue, Schary was given the following citation from the JACL: "Japanese American Citizens League, National Recognitions Committee, honoring Dore Schary for distinguished leadership in the motion picture industry. His courage in exposing the twin evils of discrimination and prejudice without fear, through the medium of the motion picture, has lent stature and dignity to the industry."[30] The newspaper lauded the producer's impeccable business sense as well. Tajiri's column from February 16, 1952, is occasioned by the fact that *Variety* "had placed the picture 20th among 150 Hollywood films" in terms of ticket sales and predicted it would eventually gross $2.5 million, "a figure which should return a handsome profit to the studio." The article praises the "considerable daring" Schary showed in making the film and reflects that his "investment in good citizenship . . . is paying dividends at the box office."[31]

According to Tajiri's April 28, 1951, column, the genesis of the story that would become *Go for Broke!* was Schary's outrage in the late 1940s over the racism Japanese Americans had experienced. While he considered various ideas for a film that would treat that topic, after becoming a producer at MGM, he called upon Pirosh, who

> developed a story idea about a Nisei college student in Los Angeles who volunteers for the army on the day after Pearl Harbor and is turned down. His bitter reaction to prejudice is intensified by the mass evacuation and by detention in a relocation camp. He volunteers for sugar beet work and is in the fields when the formation of the 442nd Combat Team is announced. In his bitterness against discrimination he does not want to volunteer but is induced to do so by his girl who comes to see him from the WRA [Wartime Relocation Authority] center. He joins the 442nd and goes overseas. He is captured by the Nazis and placed in a POW camp where he managed to correspond via the International Red Cross with his girl who is in an internment camp in the United States, a situation which underscores dramatically the contradictions in the government's wartime treatment of Nisei. Later he escapes from the Germans in time to participate in the rescue of the Lost Battalion in the Vosges.[32]

This is certainly a much darker story than the one told by the film version of *Go for Broke!* Particularly notable is its inclusion of scenes depicting the "mass evacuation" and "detention in a relocation camp" of its Japanese American protagonists. And here Tajiri broaches the possibility that this first script was abandoned because of the US government's discomfort: "It may be that the Army Department demurred in its cooperation with a production which would tell the world about an event, the wartime mass evacuation of Japanese Americans, of which it is not proud although it maintains that the mass removal was carried out as a security measure and not as the result of political or economic pressures or because of race prejudice."[33] Tajiri elaborates further on the government's possible reservations: "Whatever the reason, it may have been felt that in this time of the cold war a picture about the mass incarceration of an American group on the basis of ancestry might be exploited by anti-American elements."[34]

While what Tajiri intimates could certainly be construed as a form of censorship, he concludes that the army's influence "has probably made for a more effective picture," since it "places the emphasis on the Nisei

GIs themselves, rather than on the still-controversial mass evacuation."[35] At least two other installments of Tajiri's column tell versions of this story.[36] All three articles explore the possibility of government interference only to highlight its positive effect. Ultimately, Tajiri praises the filmmakers for their ability to negotiate the constraints imposed by the army, for engaging in a kind of productive collaboration with it.

Tajiri's characterization of Schary's response is understandable if we consider the general orientation to the US government that the JACL adopted during the internment. As Jere Takahashi details in *Nisei/Sansei: Shifting Japanese American Identities and Politics*, after Masaoka assumed a leading role in the organization in 1941, he helped devise the organization's response to President Roosevelt's Executive Order 9066, which set the internment in motion. Rather than resisting the government or seeking some sort of compromise, the JACL endorsed a policy that Takahashi terms "constructive cooperation": the JACL would cooperate with and assist the War Relocation Authority (WRA) in "evacuating" Japanese Americans from the West Coast. Doing so, it believed, "would help the war effort and prove to others that the Nisei were in fact loyal Americans, as well as create a moral obligation on the government to reciprocate similarly."[37] Given this history, it only makes sense that the JACL's newspaper would cast Schary's seeming capitulation to governmental pressures in a positive light. After all, Masaoka, the ideological architect of constructive cooperation, served as the film's "special consultant."

Two photographs that picture Schary and Masaoka together epitomize how the *Citizen* depicted the men as figureheads for two of the organizations that collaborated in making *Go for Broke!*, MGM and the JACL. The image first appeared on the front page of the October 28, 1950, issue, accompanying an announcement that the JACL had officially commended Schary for "Distinguished Leadership in the Motion Picture Industry."[38] The photograph captures Masaoka presenting a framed copy of this citation to Schary, who also holds a gold medallion. The two men look at each other, smiling as they stand before the 442nd's regimental flag. The March 31, 1951, photograph looks similar but depicts Schary presenting a check to Masaoka, the two men standing side-by-side and looking directly at the photographer. The caption explains that Schary had made, on MGM's behalf, a $3,500 donation "in appreciation for the JACL's assistance on the film."[39] Suggested here is the studio's willingness to share some of its real dividends with its Nisei "special consultant" and the organization he represents. In these photographs, we see the economic subtext of *Go for Broke!* traveling into the real world, materialized in the gold medallion and the check that cements the bond between Schary and Masaoka and between MGM and the JACL—a celebration of an interracial partnership and a joint investment in good citizenship that have proven profitable for both parties.

The Rewards of Paying the Price of Freedom: *The Crimson Kimono*

In closing this chapter, I want to turn to a film released in 1959, the same year as *Pork Chop Hill*, that offers another oblique angle on the performance of Nisei soldiers in the Korean War: Samuel Fuller's *The Crimson Kimono*. This film fleshes out a fictional endpoint to the narrative that foregrounds the crucial role the Korean War played in constructing Japanese Americans as model minorities. While it is not a war film but rather a convoluted murder mystery set in Los Angeles revolving around the murder of a white stripper, the Korean War is integral to the plot. Its two lead characters, Joe Kojaku (James Shigeta) and Charlie Corbett (Glenn Corbett), became extremely close friends while serving together in Korea and now work together as detectives in the Los Angeles Police Department. In Joe, we get a glimpse of the peacetime lives that other cinematic Nisei characters like Tanaka and Ohashi might have gone on to lead after their service in the Korean War, dramatizing how Nisei veterans who fought in that conflict might have found ample compensation for their sacrifice in the comfortable middle-class lives they went on to enjoy. Moreover, in its depiction of the deep friendship of its lead characters, *The Crimson Kimono* extends and complicates the concern with interracial male bonding so prominent in the Korean War films previously examined.

When the film opens, Joe seems to have already attained a version of the Cold War ideal of middle-class domesticity. He lives in a nicely decorated apartment that he shares with Charlie, and several scenes in the film convey the cozy domestic routine of their lives together, for the two men are not just partners at work; they seem to function much like a modern-day two-career couple at home. An extremely hard worker, Joe is happy with the profession he has entered into since leaving the military. He is keen to rise in the ranks of the police department and has been studying hard for the sergeant's exam. Charlie also enjoys his work, but he is more easygoing, prone to telling his partner to "relax." While the film underscores their heterosexuality, it nonetheless imbues their relationship with a certain queerness. Both men are reluctant to settle down and marry: Charlie relishes the bachelor life, as it enables him to have his pick of women, while Joe is too picky to become serious with any of the women he dates. The name of their apartment building also seems like a wink at what their living arrangement resembles: the Gaylord Hotel. The film largely depicts their relationship as a queer and interracial version of the midcentury suburban ideal, dramatizing the comforts of middle-class domesticity that awaited Korean War veterans.

Ultimately, however, the film presents the homosocial utopia the two men share—which seems to echo Huck and Jim's raft—as simply a prelude to Joe's achieving a more mature heterosexual manhood, for *The Crimson Kimono* is also structured as a coming-of-age narrative and a heterosexual love story with Joe as its central protagonist. The film only offers scant details about the men's wartime experiences: as Charlie recalls, "We met in a foxhole. I was the CO; he was a rifleman. Got the Silver Star. . . . He deserted a hospital bed to rejoin my outfit when we went back into action." That there might be something excessive about their bond and its Korean War origins is conveyed by Mac, a woman who serves as an informant to the two detectives but has also formed a friendship with them: "What those two had together in the war no one could touch. It was Joe's blood that kept Charlie alive in Korea, and now it's Charlie's friendship that's keeping Joe alive. It's like . . . well, it's like mixing two dabs of paint together. You can never separate them." Mac is an artist, which accounts for the painterly metaphor she uses to evoke the miscegenated quality of their intimacy. We also learn that Joe had saved Charlie's life through a blood transfusion. In sketching out how their relationship took shape during the Korean War, one that culminated in an intimate mingling of blood (a trope already encountered in *All the Young Men*), *The Crimson Kimono* memorializes that event primarily as one that engendered intense forms of male intimacy that crossed the borders of race.

In one scene, we get a glimpse of what their partnership might have looked like in combat when they track down a witness named Mr. Shuto, a physically imposing Korean man who is also a martial artist. He becomes violent when Joe and Charlie approach him in a pool hall, but the two men reveal the formidable fighting team they make. They expertly coordinate their punches, karate chops, and kicks and bring down the much larger and more powerful Shuto. In this scene, they subject their Korean foe to a less lethal dose of the violence they would have meted out as soldiers during the war.

Their relationship is thrown into crisis when Joe and Charlie both fall in love with Chris, another female artist who turns out to be a key witness, and the intensity of their friendship is transmuted into a sexual rivalry. Although both men come to feel a jealous rage toward each other, Joe is overwhelmed by his emotions, nearly killing his partner when they compete in a kendo match. Their mutual desire for Chris seems to have brought to the surface in Joe a lifetime of internalized racism and anger at the white men to whom he has been made inferior—an anger he directs at his partner. Even after Chris reveals that she has fallen in love with him rather than Charlie, Joe continues to struggle with his self-hatred, unable to believe that a white woman would ever pick a Japanese American man over a white one.

The film ends, however, with the true identity of the killer revealed and Joe overcoming his racial self-loathing. As Joe passionately kisses Chris in the final shot, we know that this may well spell the end of his friendship with Charlie. For Joe to embrace fully the white woman he loves and to walk into the glorious Japanese American future that awaits him, he must walk away from the most meaningful relationship he had formed to that point, with the white man he had "met in a foxhole" in Korea. With Chris, he will presumably be able to enjoy a more conventional version of the interracial domesticity he had shared with Charlie. Much like the reporting of black newspapers on the lives "Tan Yanks" and "musumes" built together in Japan, *The Crimson Kimono* conjures the midcentury ideal of middle-class domesticity as a symbol of the integrated future that awaits military men of color as a reward for their service.

The sacrifice Joe made in Korea is symbolized by the unspecified injury he received during the fighting, which no longer bothers him.

Fuller's film pauses in one striking scene, however, to underscore that some Japanese American soldiers made an even greater sacrifice. Early on, Joe learns that George Yoshinaga, an elderly Japanese American he is friendly with, may have crucial information about a potential suspect. He meets with Yoshinaga at a cemetery, where he is paying respects at the grave of his son. The camera lingers for a moment on the epitaph that appears on the gravestone, which reveals that his son, Jun Yoshinaga, had been killed in action in Korea and that he had received the Medal of Honor. In pausing on these words, *The Crimson Kimono* asks its viewers to ponder the fact that some Nisei soldiers made the ultimate sacrifice during the Korean War. While Jun Yoshinaga is Fuller's invention, as mentioned earlier, a Japanese American soldier was among the 135 who were given this honor during the Korean War, though Hiroshi Miyamura was very much alive when he received the medal.

Coda: Forgetting and Forgotten

While my analysis of *The Crimson Kimono* obviously stems from the prominent role the Korean War plays in its plot, its significance also lies in how the gestures of remembering it engages in entail a kind of forgetting as well, for although the film largely pivots around Joe's struggle with internalized racism, it makes no specific reference to the experiences that may have produced it. It might be plausible for viewers to assume, on the basis of the character's age and since he is presumably from Los Angeles—suggested by his easy familiarity with the Japanese Americans who live in Little Tokyo, where much of the film was shot—that he and his family had been interned when he was a child. Yet the film makes no reference to his early years, except in reference to the love of painting he inherited from his father. The lack of any allusion to this event is especially striking given the prominent attention paid to the internment in Fuller's earlier film, *The Steel Helmet*.

The absence that seems to emerge in the intervening years between 1950 and 1951, the release dates of Fuller's two films, lends credence to arguments that Marita Sturken and Caroline Chung Simpson have made concerning the seeming erasure of the internment experience from American cultural memory that took place during the first half of the Cold War era.[40] Simpson asserts that representations of Japanese

Americans from this period actually offered a "proliferation of information" about the event that "ironically furthered the nation's avoidance of the deeper challenges of the role of internment in our understanding of postwar and cold war national history," eventually moving toward its virtual disappearance until the rise of Japanese American activism in the 1970s.[41] Simpson argues that this history "is articulated within a simultaneous containment of its meaning, as an 'absent presence,' to cite Sturken's compelling term, which remains irretrievable."[42]

Simpson's theorization of a kind of mnemonics that works through erasure is applicable to the other "absent presence" that *The Crimson Kimono* illuminates, which concerns the Korean War, for the film memorializes not just the war itself but also its forgetting. What Joe must leave behind in order to enter fully into the American manhood that awaits him is, in a sense, his memory of the Korean War, an event that is figuratively entombed in the interracial intimacy he enjoys with Charlie. What the film ultimately issues is a kind of Nisei farewell letter to the memory of the Korean War, one that has been sealed with a kiss.

The Crimson Kimono also intimates, though only with the scantest detail, that as Joe leaves behind the interracial relationship that had, in a sense, memorialized the war, he will also engage in the forgetting of another kind of intimacy: the one he enjoyed with Korean civilians. That such bonds had even formed is only hinted at through a detail that is quite difficult to detect: a framed photograph on the wall of Joe and Charlie's apartment that is barely visible in a scene in which Chris is looking at mug shots. It is a picture of the two men in their military uniforms standing next to two Korean civilians, an elderly woman and a child she carries on her back. That this image is included in a way that essentially occludes it is in fact symptomatic of the exclusive focus that military Orientalism places on Japanese American subjects. This absence is even more dramatic in the *Pacific Citizen*, which offered absolutely no commentary during the Korean War concerning the country—its inhabitants or its history—in which Nisei soldiers were performing so valiantly, an aspect of that paper's reporting that is all the more striking when contrasted with the attention given to Korea's "sordid" colonial history with Japan by black journalists like Lucius C. Harper.

In the next chapter, I turn my attention to cultural works that, in contrast, center on the Asian subjects most affected by the violence of that war: Koreans themselves. As we shall see, the reporting of mainstream journalists and Hollywood films that addressed "the refugee problem" underscored that Korean civilians were due objects of humanitarian care, foregrounding their suffering in ways that also made them objects of sentimental attachment. In so doing, however, such works, which exemplify the humanitarian Orientalism that emerged during the conflict, also affirmed that despite whatever sympathy Americans might muster for such subjects, they nonetheless comprised a population whose accidental deaths, and even those directly caused by US military actions, were a tragic but necessary consequence of war.

4

Picturing Koreans

The Age of the World Target and Humanitarian Orientalism

One would like to imagine that the American public would not have been so unanimous in its acquiescence to the Korean War if it had been confronted with photograph evidence of the devastation of Korea, an ecocide and genocide in some respects even more thorough than those inflicted on Vietnam a decade later.
—Susan Sontag, *On Photography*

Writing to an audience in the mid-1970s that would have been aware of how the circulation of images depicting the devastation that US military intervention had brought to the Vietnamese people and their country had helped galvanize the antiwar movement, Susan Sontag suggests that the similarly destructive effects of the Korean War had been largely invisible to Americans in the 1950s: "No one brought back photographs of daily life in Pyongyang to show that the enemy had a human face."[1] Sontag's comparison of the two conflicts underscores the disparity in how Americans think of them—one has been remembered for catalyzing the divisions that threatened to tear the country apart and the other has been simply forgotten—while asserting certain underlying similarities: they both involved "ecocide and genocide."

Sontag's reflections suggest how productive the Vietnam War analogy can be for opening a window onto a conflict much less familiar to most Americans, inviting us to see the Korean War as a kind of dress rehearsal for the tragic and absurd drama that would take place a decade later. The aptness of this analogy is captured by Bruce Cumings in his description of the Korean War journalism of Reginald Thompson: "Here was the Vietnam War we came to know before Vietnam—gooks, napalm, rapes, whores, an unreliable ally, a cunning enemy, fundamentally untrained

GIs fighting a war their top generals barely understood, fragging of officers, contempt for the know-nothing civilians back home, devilish battles indescribable even to loved ones."[2] Such parallels make it tempting to believe that if the American public had only seen how terrible and absurd the Korean War was, it would have galvanized the kind of protest that the Vietnam War did, perhaps even obviating US participation in that second conflict.

While in the epigraph to this chapter, Sontag seems to entertain this counterfactual fantasy, her larger point is that context is everything in terms of how people respond to images of war: "A photograph that brings news of some unsuspected zone of misery cannot make a dent in public opinion unless there is an appropriate context of feeling and attitude."[3] Whether or not such images of the Korean War were brought before the American public is beside the point, she insists, "because there was, ideologically, no space for them."[4] Sontag offers a straightforward and plausible explanation for the Korean War's forgotten status: the fervent anti-Communism of the 1950s made it impossible for Americans to confront what their military forces were doing to a country they were ostensibly trying to save or to take in images that revealed such actions.

While Sontag's larger point is unimpeachable—that visual images of war only gain purchase if "an appropriate context of feeling and attitude" exists—the tactics deployed by US military forces in Korea, which prefigured those used in Vietnam, were in fact visible to the American public. Historian Steven Casey has demonstrated that the press was given "a wide degree of latitude" in the early months of the war, as General Douglas MacArthur was initially reluctant to impose any military censorship, which may explain why journalists were able to report on incidents of civilians being killed by US air and ground forces and on the use of napalm.[5] Perhaps more surprisingly, as we shall see, such deaths became a key plot element in Hollywood films about the war. However constrained the ideological space of the 1950s was, it was nonetheless roomy enough to accommodate the kinds of images *and* narratives that Sontag suggests were nonexistent.

If journalists and filmmakers did not exactly "show that the *enemy* had a human face," to use Sontag's formulation, they did draw attention to the plight of Korean civilians caught in the cross fire as they fleshed out what I term a *humanitarian Orientalism*. Indeed, the two films I will look at in this chapter—*One Minute to Zero* (1952) and *Battle Hymn* (1959)—actively elicit viewers' sympathies for such victims. Moreover, these films foreground that their suffering was at times a direct result of US military actions. However, they do so in ways that encourage a somber acquiescence rather than dissent. The sentimental responses such works evoke, which might incline viewers against the war, are *contained* in these films—neutralized by conjuring the specter of the Communist menace but also by a rerouting of affective energy. The sentimental attachments that such depictions encourage are rechanneled in ways that center attention on the ethical and epistemological dilemmas faced by soldiers who, in trying to save Korean civilians, end up killing them. Their affective focus is thus on Americans who feel deeply about the civilian lives lost in the conflict and who consequently emerge as more fully human in the depth of that feeling than the Asians whose deaths they mourn.

"The Case of the Mysterious Koreans": The Meaning of *Life* and the Korean War

One significant cultural site from which Americans learned about the effect the fighting was having on Korean civilians was *Life* magazine. As is well known, *Life* was a highly influential periodical, the most popular title in Henry R. Luce's publishing empire. By the late 1940s, the magazine's circulation had reached 22.5 million, which represented roughly one-fifth of the adult population in the United States at the time.[6] In his 1936 prospectus for the magazine, Luce described its mission as enabling readers "to see life; to see the world; to eyewitness great events" and "to see and to take pleasure in seeing; to see and be amazed; to see and be instructed."[7] Reflecting this emphasis on visual pleasure and education, the magazine Luce introduced to the world later that year depended heavily on photographs, and its dominant genre was the photo essay. He sought to influence not only popular opinion, however, but also foreign policy. In the words of Robert E. Herzstein, one of the primary forces that shaped Luce's life "was a fervent faith in America's God-ordained global mission in Asia."[8] While US foreign policy at midcentury was centered on Europe, Luce was a fervent "Asia-firster" who engaged in a virtual crusade "to involve the United States deeply in the battle against Communism in China and Korea and Vietnam."[9]

Herzstein's *Henry R. Luce, Time, and the American Crusade in Asia* offers a comprehensive account of Luce's efforts—through his publishing,
personal, and political networks—to fortify the US resolve to thwart the
spread of Communism in Asia. This agenda is more apparent in *Time*'s
coverage of the war, as Herzstein demonstrates, than in *Life*'s, which was
not extensive. The articles from *Life*, which I focus on here, are illuminating, however, for their foregrounding of the visual as a kind of
technology, their pedagogical mission, and the emotional registers in
which they operate.

Rather than offering an exhaustive analysis of the depictions of the
conflict in *Life*, I offer close readings of several pieces that illuminate
two different modalities through which Koreans were made knowable to
readers. The first concerns the ability to discern which Koreans are the
proper objects of military violence: to better know our enemy. The second, however, focuses more on feeling—on the emotional attachment
that Americans should form toward those Koreans who are friendly to
our cause.[10]

The first modality of knowledge production is epitomized by a linked
series of articles and photo essays that appeared in *Life* on August 21,
1950. This issue came out as United Nations (UN) forces struggled to
maintain the perimeter they had established around Pusan. The ten-
page, multipart photo essay on the fighting is replete with tropes that
should now be familiar from previous chapters: the taking, losing, and
retaking of hilltops; an enemy impossible to discern in the surrounding hills that is best taken out by devastating artillery barrages and air
attacks; and multitudes of white-pajama-clad refugees, which include a
significant number of "Communists in disguise." Of particular significance here are the final two pages of this ten-page spread, titled "Refugees Get in Way" (figure 4.1). Its first page includes three photographs
that convey the plight of the refugees. One pictures a father smiling
rather incongruously at the camera and carrying a heavy "load of bed-
mats on his back," guiding his naked son in front of him.[11] Another
shows the anguish and worry of three female refugees who are also carrying their belongings. That the war has nearly reduced these Koreans to
beasts of burden is suggested by the third photograph, of an ox freighted
down with household goods. These images are arrayed around a short

Figure 4.1. The refugee problem as pictured by *Life*. Carl Mydans, "Refugees Get in Way," *Life* 29, no. 8 (August 21, 1950): 22–23.

essay by Carl Mydans that focuses first on their plight: "Refugees are handled hit or miss by the Americans. In some areas they have been removed successfully, in others they remain to be a problem when the battle begins. Fleeing the North Koreans, they stream southward in sad hordes, cluttering highways and getting in the way of the war. *And always among them are Communists in disguise who turn around and shoot Americans in the back*."[12] The full-page photograph that takes up the facing page shifts the focus to the dire predicament in which US fighting men are placed as they attempt to manage these masses of civilians. The photo has been taken from a vantage point behind the two soldiers in the foreground, who look into the distance, guns at the ready, at the mass of civilians crossing the river. Visible behind the refugees are, the caption explains, "enemy-held hills."[13] This photograph enlists the viewer to experience what it must be like to fight an enemy who uses both the landscape *and* refugees as camouflage.

The problems posed by such an enemy come in for an extensive analysis in the second article in this issue, "Report from the Orient: Guns

Are Not Enough." Written by John Osborne, this piece reverses the ratio between picture and text characteristic of *Life* and seems more like one that would have appeared in *Time*, for which he served as foreign news editor.[14] Though it is accompanied by several photographs, this lengthy essay offers an extended analysis of how the enemy makes use of the refugee population and the responses it has provoked in US forces. In it, Osborne highlights the fact that American soldiers have started to fire on Korean civilians, a tactic that would obviously constitute a liability in the war of hearts and minds so crucial to achieving victory in the Cold War.

After first testifying to the high level of preparedness and training apparent in the soldiers who have been sent to Korea, Osborne asserts that they are fighting "an ugly war, perhaps the ugliest that Americans have ever had to fight."[15] Conditions there

> force upon our men in the field acts and attitudes of the utmost savagery and not the usual, inevitable savagery of combat in the field, but savagery in detail—the blotting out of villages where the enemy may be hiding: the shooting and shelling of refugees who may include North Koreans in the anonymous white clothing of the Korean countryside, or who may be screening an enemy march upon our positions, or who may be carrying broken-down rifles or ammunition clips or walkie-talkie parts in their packs and under their trousers or skirts. (77)

The exceptional kind of "savagery" into which US soldiers are descending stems from the fact that, as Osborne asserts, "this is a guerrilla war, waged amongst and to some extent by the population of the country." To illustrate this point, he invites his reader to "see with me some of the scenes that I have witnessed or heard of at firsthand" (78).

The first incident he describes takes place on a street in "an important headquarters city in South Korea." The jeep he is riding in is forced to stop when it meets "a long, long file of refugees from the fighting areas" (78). He notices that the young men "seem to outnumber the others" and that "most of them carry packs, apparently of extra clothing." "Watching them march by without escort of any kind," he recounts, "I knew the constricting doubt and fear that every American in Korea comes to know as he watches those silent strangers, to whom he cannot speak, filing down the roads." He adds that several days later, he would think of this particular column of refugees upon hearing "that North Korean guerrillas have unaccountably turned up far behind our lines and are fighting within a few miles of the city" (80).

He next ushers his readers to "a hilltop in southwest Korea," where a US command post housed in a schoolhouse had just been subjected to two attacks "by hundreds of North Koreans who emerged without warning from the hills." From that very same hilltop, Osborne writes, US soldiers had watched as North Korean soldiers retreated out of range and "calmly change[d] from the green uniforms of the North Korean army to the white trousers and blouses of Korean peasants" and joined a column of refugees (80).

A third scene takes place in "a village at the foot of a valley" in the early morning as a small group of GIs confronts another throng of civilians moving toward them (81). The soldiers are nervous because they had earlier faced a similar situation only to find out that the refugees had been driven forward by members of the North Korean Army "to confuse our men and tempt them to hold their fire as the enemy rises from the deep grass of the paddies." Osborne pauses in this fraught moment: "For what seems to be a full minute, but must have been a matter of seconds, the thin file of soldiers and the still, dumb hundreds of refugees stand in the road facing each other across the chasms of language and tradition that divides them" (82). What prevents carnage from ensuing is that one of the GIs gestures to the old man who seems to be the group's leader to take a different road, which they do.

In describing a fourth encounter, however, which takes place in an outpost at midnight, Osborne suggests that the "savagery" of firing on civilians has become a military necessity. A radio report comes describing a column of refugees making its way toward a company of US soldiers. A major tells his colonel that the civilians should not be allowed through. "And of course the major is right," Osborne intones. With reluctance, the colonel formulates a series of orders in consultation with his staff, telling them to first fire over the heads of the refugees and then, if they don't disperse, to "fire into them if you have to. If you have to, I said." He goes on to reveal that similar orders are now being implemented throughout

Korea. He reports the anguished outcry of one officer who is speaking on the radio to one of his men, "My God, John, it's gone too far when we are shooting children" (84).

Osborne also asserts that US soldiers have already been engaged in "savagery by proxy" because they are forced to work closely with South Korean military and police forces who routinely "murder to save themselves the trouble of escorting prisoners to the rear; they murder civilians simply to get them out of the way or to avoid the trouble of searching and cross-examining them. And they extort information—by means so brutal that they cannot be described. Too often they murder prisoners of war and civilians before they have had a chance to give any information they may have" (77). These South Koreans embody a fully enacted version of the "savagery" that American soldiers risk exemplifying themselves.[16]

Osborne's ultimate aim in registering the exceptional violence of this war—a violence that targets the very civilian population that Americans are ostensibly there to protect and save—is to argue for a set of strategic and personnel changes that would lessen civilian casualties and thus make this war winnable. He argues for a more robust ideological campaign, which would mark a departure from current planning. The United States needs to stop "think[ing] of war and 'politics' as two separate things . . . of political warfare as something to be practiced by rear-area pamphleteers and tolerated by the fellows doing the real fighting." What "our military organizations in Korea and elsewhere do not have, as integrated parts or even as detached complements to the regular staffs," are "sufficient personnel equipped to deal with the people of the country, to explain to them and to our own men why we happen to be fighting there" (78).

Some of the resources for developing the army of experts required for this kind of "political warfare" already exist, Osborne points out, a product of the period directly following the end of the Second World War: "We occupied [Korea] for nearly three years and in this time we should have accumulated a considerable staff of military and civilian officials who came to know the country, the people, the language." Osborne stresses another aspect of the post-1945 period that is little known to most Americans—that, in Bruce Cumings's words, "the United States occupied Korea just after the war with Japan ended, and set up a full military government that lasted for three years and deeply shaped post-war Korean history."[17] "Report from the Orient" suggests that realloca-tion of personnel from Japan would also ameliorate the situation faced by troops on the ground, noting that South Korea's prior colonization by Japan is actually a boon in this context, since as a result, "Japanese is the second language of the country" (78).

Osborne's overall point is that more accurate and comprehensive knowledge about Korea is of vital strategic interest. Ironically, a dis-ciplinary apparatus of the very sort he calls for, one that would create knowledge about places like Korea imperiled by Communism, would soon materialize in the United States. Rey Chow, Bruce Cumings, Harry Harootunian, and of course, Edward Said have argued that the emer-gence of area studies at midcentury was spurred by the exigencies of the Cold War struggle against Communism.[18] As Cumings has observed, "The American state and especially the intelligence elements in it shaped the entire field of postwar area studies, with the clearest and most direct impact on those regions of the world where communism was strongest: Russia, Central and Eastern Europe, and East Asia."[19] Osborne's article suggests the military value of the information such intellectuals could provide. But while a cadre of such experts does not currently exist or at least has not been set in place, the epistemological authority with which he invests his virtual tour of the fighting in Korea suggests that *journal-ists* might serve, in the meantime, in their stead.

Indeed, the full-page photograph and accompanying caption at the very beginning of this article exemplify the kind of weaponized knowl-edge that journalism is capable of producing (figure 4.2). Apparently taken from atop a US tank, the barrel of its gun visible in the lower right foreground, this photograph shows three identically clad Korean men striding toward the left of the camera. That this photograph is intended to invite readers to experience the same worried unknowing that soldiers in Korea regularly face is clear from the accompanying text, which cites an intelligence officer who points out three details suggesting these men are actually "North Korean infiltrators": "1) these horsehair hats are worn only by heads of families and it is unusual to see three of them together; 2) the men are marching in perfect mili-tary step; 3) the traditional white robes are bulging with what could be hand grenades" (77). Readers are here given the kind of information

Figure 4.2. *Life* shows readers how to distinguish between friendly and hostile Koreans in 1950. John Osborne, "Report from the Orient: Guns Are Not Enough," *Life* 29, no. 8 (August 21, 1950): 76–78+.

that would be so useful to US troops but that many currently lack: how to tell the difference between "harmless patriarchs" and "North Korean infiltrators."

The final scene Osborne recounts—in which a group of US GIs once again confronts a mass of refugees, though more successfully this time—also allegorizes the point made by this photograph: "A Marine is passing a mine detector over the clothing and packs of the refugees. Any metal—a rifle barrel, a pistol, a clip of ammunition, maybe the parts of a radio—will presumably be spotted by the detector. Anyhow it is better than guns and policemen whom I have seen at work." This extemporaneous repurposing of a mine detector signifies "something of an advance in American communication with the people of the country" (85). This Marine's inventive use of technology is able to make something previously illegible about Koreans legible: namely, their intentions. In enabling US soldiers to determine whether any particular Korean body is hiding "a rifle barrel, a pistol, a clip of ammunition, maybe the parts of a radio," this improvised detection device produces an objective knowledge that makes visible a formerly invisible subjective intent. The metal detector thus symbolizes the technology of information retrieval and knowledge production that the article asserts is necessary for the winning of the war.

This device also functions as an allegory, I would suggest, for the kind of journalism concerning Asians and Asian Americans that *Life* typically offered. During the Second World War, as Christina Klein notes, Luce had specifically used *Life* and its sister magazine *Time* "to disseminate positive stories about America's Chinese allies."[20] Among scholars of Asian American history, however, *Life* was also infamous for the ways in which it purported to teach its readers about how to discriminate between Asians and Asian Americans who were allied with the American cause and those who were hostile. The December 22, 1941, issue, published soon after the attack on Pearl Harbor, included a photo essay titled "How to Tell Japs from the Chinese" (figure 4.3).[21] This one-page photo essay comprised three annotated photographs and an accompanying essay that promised to identify for readers the facial features that reveal the subtle differences between the members of those ethnic groups that give us the ability, as does the Marine's metal detector, to distinguish between hostile and friendly Asians.

In returning to Osborne's 1950 article, we should note a second piece of American military technology it highlights on its final page: a helicopter. As with the mine detector, the article draws attention to a secondary use to which it can be put—one that signifies "something of an advance in American communication with the people of the country." The final scene he describes takes place in the port city of Pusan, where Osborne sees two US helicopters flying overhead. What draws his attention is "a boy of perhaps 7 or 8" who "stares upward at the monstrous things with a gaze of fixed and bright fascination. His eyes shine, his lips are parted, and I think of an American boy gazing at his first bicycle on a Christmas morning." This spectacle reminds Osborne of the earlier scene, and he concludes, "The mine detector, the helicopters, the boy on the roadside—here, after a fashion, was communication between the American West and the people of South Korea" (85). What gives this reporter a sense of hope are two pieces of American military technology and a young Korean. In light of the article's overall thesis, each component of this triad takes on a symbolic significance. I have already

Figure 4.3. *Life* shows readers how to distinguish between friendly and hostile Asians in 1941. "How to Tell Japs from the Chinese," *Life* 11, no. 25 (December 22, 1941): 81–82.

explored the meaning of the mine detector, but the value of the helicopters in this instance is also tied to the potential effect they can have on Korean bodies—not militarily but ideologically. The helicopters—which, through a kind of soft dissolve in Osborne's imaginative vision, transform themselves into the gift of a bicycle—are notable for their effect on the young boy, who looks up at them with "a gaze of fixed and bright fascination" that makes him resemble an American boy on Christmas morning. His expression—"his eyes shine, his lips are parted"—and the desire it clearly conveys suggest that certain technological objects can function as technologies of integration, instilling in Asian subjects that most American of sentiments, the desire for consumer goods.

The mine detector and the helicopters and the relationship to Asian subjects they enable articulate a fantasy about the technologies capable of winning the war of hearts and minds. In celebrating the forms of transnational and interracial intimacy such technologies can thereby enable, the conclusion to "Report from the Orient" provides a metacommentary, I suggest, on what the magazine is itself doing—on how media like *Life* can function as vital components in the apparatus of war. If this essay argues that technologies of military destruction (guns) must be supported by a technology of detection that will enable its users to tell the difference between hostiles and friendlies (the metal detector) and it also points out the military necessity of a technology of representation that educates its viewers and readers in the ways of American consumer desire (the helicopters), then what's being described here as well is *Life* itself.

To see how this is the case, simply consider the physical layout of the pages in which the article appears. This photo essay weaves its way through often colorful advertisements that describe the luxurious rest that Pullman sleeper cars can provide, that promise dog owners a way of cleaning their dogs without bathing them, and that extol the virtues of Oneida silverware, New Williams shaving cream, and Best Foods prepared mustard. This layout is typical of *Life* and other magazines of its type. As Erika Doss observes, such periodicals are "often organized as jumbled assemblages of images, text, features and advertisements whose miscellaneous graphics, words, and intended effects are intermingled and often intentionally inseparable."[22] Bearing in mind the multiple aims of *Life* laid out in Luce's prospectus—"to see and to take pleasure in seeing; to see and be amazed; to see and be instructed"—we can see how the magazine's message was carried not only by the content of its photo essays but also by the advertisements that appeared on its pages, the juxtaposition of which were key to its aesthetic: "This juxtaposition of 'instructive' articles and photo essays in monochrome hues and 'pleasurable' advertisements in color gave the magazine a certain rhythm and flow, and guided readers between what to think about . . . and what to buy."[23] What this magazine is selling in this and every issue—in the advertisements as well as in the photo essays—is the American way of life.

That the promotion of such ideologies can serve a military purpose is evident from a full-page photograph that appeared a mere two months later (figure 4.4), in the October 23 issue, which rather uncannily recalls Osborne's evocation of the youth entranced by US helicopters. Accompanying this picture of a Korean boy happily sucking on a Popsicle, seated in a jeep next to a smiling GI, is a caption that reads, "The faces of these companions, taken by Mydans, reflect mutual satisfaction with the war's progress in Korea and the promise of better things to come—for the lieutenant, more victories as U.N. forces move north; for the South Korean boy, more Popsicles as victors grow more free with largesse."[24] In contrast to Osborne's dire prognostications just two months earlier, this photograph reflects how much better the prospects for victory seemed by late October. The US soldier's smile suggests that things look better militarily, as UN forces had recently crossed the thirty-eighth parallel, commencing the war of rollback that would eventually push the front line nearly to the southern bank of the Yalu River, a period of optimism that would be shattered in less than two months by the entry of Chinese forces. The young boy's expression suggests that things are looking better ideologically as well—that the war for the hearts and minds of Koreans is also being more successfully waged. Like the child Osborne describes, the one pictured here also has his lips parted with desire, but in this case, he is more literally partaking of American "largesse" in the form of a Popsicle, and the pleasure and gratitude imparted by this gift seem to have made him unambiguously loyal to the American cause.

In this picture, we see the dominant modality through which Koreans came to be constructed as objects of knowledge in US depictions of the Korean War: as the grateful recipients of American generosity and protection, as the privileged objects of a humanitarian Orientalism. The

THINGS LOOK BETTER IN KOREA

The faces of these companions, taken by Carl Mydans, reflect mutual satisfaction with the war's progress in Korea and the promise of better things to come—for the lieutenant, more victories as U.N. forces move north; for the South Korean boy, more Popsicles as victors grow more free with largesse.

37

Figure 4.4. *Life* asserts that "things look better in Korea." Carl Mydans, "Things Look Better in Korea," *Life* 29, no. 17 (October 23, 1950): 37.

duo pictured in this photograph has numerous counterparts, and we have already encountered one filmic example in the friendship between Sergeant Zack and Short Round in Samuel Fuller's *The Steel Helmet*. This photograph also captures the more lasting impression that most Americans have of their role in the Korean War, which renders their military intervention in salvific terms. It is wryly captured by Chang-rae Lee in his 1996 novel *Native Speaker* in a comment that his Korean American protagonist, Henry Park, makes to his white wife about an implicit message he sees in his father-in-law's body: "It's that coloring those old guys have about the face and body, all pale and pink and silver, those veins pumping in purple heart. It says, 'I saved your skinny gook ass, and your momma's too.'"[25] Henry's reflections speak to what Jodi Kim has termed the "Cold War racial optics" through which Americans have come to view the Korean War, which often figures Asians as children or women who needed to be saved from a Communist menace.[26]

Before I turn to two films that situate these optics within melodramatic narratives that involve the killing as well as the saving of Korean civilians, I want to turn briefly to Rey Chow's *The Age of the World Target: Self-Referentiality in War, Theory, and Comparative Work*. Its central argument—which draws on and supplements Martin Heidegger's contention that in the age of modern technology, the world has become a "world picture"—is that we should conceptualize the post-1945 era as "the age of the world target." Drawing on the work of Michel Foucault, Chow asserts that the dropping of the atomic bombs on Hiroshima and Nagasaki engendered a "great epistemic shift" that fused knowing, seeing, and targeting together, and as a result, "the world has . . . been transformed into—is essentially conceived and grasped as—a target. To conceive of the world as a target is to conceive of it as an object to be destroyed."[27]

The scholarly disciplines that emerged in the United States during the Cold War years to produce knowledge about Asian countries like Korea exemplify a militarized mode of knowledge production that defines the age of the world target: "Despite the claims about the apolitical and disinterested nature of the pursuits of higher learning, activities taken under the rubric of area studies, such as language training, historiography, anthropology, economics and political science, and so forth, are fully inscribed in the politics and ideology of war."[28] Chow's contention resonates with the message conveyed in Osborne's "Report from the Orient" concerning the role that an army of experts must play in waging not just the Korean War but the Cold War overall. In the "virtual worlding" that such knowledge produces, Chow elaborates, "the United States always occup[ies] the position of the bomber, and other cultures are always viewed as the military and information targets."[29]

However, the militarized knowledge that *Life* produces about Korea as an "information target" has another dimension to it, which suggests how Chow's argument requires some supplementation. Knowing Korea as Luce's magazine invites us to does not entail the demarcation of areas to be carpet-bombed or subjected to nuclear annihilation or seeing the country as a whole or all its people as military targets. Rather, it entails a certain capacity for discernment: a more granular ability to distinguish between those subjects deemed to pose a threat and those who do not. Korean civilians in the latter category, moreover, are rendered as targets for a different kind of intervention—an integrative and humanitarian one, the first component of which is the development of an emotional sense of connection.

As a number of cultural critics and historians have noted, the figure of the orphan played a pivotal role in defining Asians as singular objects of sympathy and humanitarian intervention during the Cold War period.[30] The Korean War, moreover, served as a watershed event in the emergence of the discourse and practice of transnational adoption, which reflected the Cold War Orientalism of the United States. As Christina Klein notes, "The hybrid, multiracial, multinational family created through adoption" served as "a way to imagine U.S.-Asian integration in terms of voluntary affiliation."[31]

Klein's analysis thus offers a crucial supplement to Chow's assertion that Cold War–era knowledge production took shape as a targeting of those regions of the world in which "the United States competed with the Soviet Union to rule and/or destroy the world"—areas "that required continued, specialized super-*vision*,"[32] for another key element of this martial episteme was the capacity to distinguish between (as *Life* claimed it could) those Asian subjects who could be integrated into the American sphere of influence and should thus be saved and those who could not and should thus be targeted and killed. Chow's work helps us confront aspects of the US Cold War project that Klein does not always fully consider—for example, that it involved the killing of some Asians and the sentimental integration of others. Klein's work likewise calls attention to the more granular aspects of the world-targeting form of knowledge production that Chow anatomizes: the distinction it makes between those subjects who should be annihilated and those who should be brought into the fold and made the proper objects of our sentimental and humanitarian care, nestled within the folds of humanitarian Orientalism.

"In Order to Save, at Times We Must Destroy"

I turn now to *Battle Hymn*, a 1959 melodramatic biopic directed by Douglas Sirk and starring Rock Hudson. This film encapsulates, to borrow Robyn Wiegman's phrase, the canonical architecture through which Korean civilians were made knowable during the Korean War as both the targets of US humanitarian care and the, at times, accidental victims of US military violence. Through its sentimentalism, *Battle Hymn* invites US viewers to know Koreans as people who deserve our sympathy and are worthy of whatever sacrifice our military forces might make in defending them but also to realize that some of them will die, tragically but necessarily, as a direct result of our efforts. Sirk's film was based on an event much heralded in the United States that dramatically highlighted the humanitarian dimensions of its military intervention. In December 1950, a thousand orphans from Seoul were airlifted in US military planes to a newly established orphanage on Cheju Island just as the capital was about to be taken for the second time by Communist forces. Much more successful and heartwarming than the disastrous and tragic airlift that took place in Saigon as American forces left Vietnam, "Operation Kiddy Car," as the Korean undertaking came to be known, was orchestrated by Dean Hess, a former minister and air force colonel who achieved fame during the Korean War. He became known not only as a kind of patron saint of orphans but as an accomplished fighter pilot who successfully completed 250 missions during his tour of duty. Hess played a significant role in building support for Korea's war orphans in the United States and himself adopted a six-year-old Korean girl in the 1960s. He worked in concert with organizations like the Christian Children's Fund (CCF), which was founded in 1938 to help Chinese children orphaned during the Sino-Japanese war, and by 1955 it was working in fifteen Asian countries. As Eleana Kim and Arissa Oh have demonstrated, organizations like the CCF helped popularize and institutionalize the practice of transnational adoption, which helped frame how Americans came to see their humanitarian *and* military endeavors in Korea and elsewhere in Asia.[33]

Like Fuller's *The Steel Helmet*, *Battle Hymn* occupies a relatively marginal status in the oeuvre of a director revered by many critics and theorists—and this despite the fact that it is redolent with the filmmaker's signature high melodrama and stars his preferred leading man, Hudson.[34] One reason may be that Sirk's typical sentimental excess—which can be viewed as a subtle critique of the repressive norms of midcentury American culture—is put to overtly propagandistic purposes in *Battle Hymn*: it is used to frame a moral and, indeed, religious justification for the civilian deaths that are an inevitable consequence of how modern wars are waged. Sentimentalism is, in this film, militarized.

While *Battle Hymn* is, like many Korean War films from Hollywood, a generic hybrid, it is first and foremost a biopic. It centers on a striking duality in the figure of Dean Hess. As Hye Seung Chung notes, Sirk seems to have been fascinated by this "ordained minister-turned-combat pilot who flew hundreds of missions during World War II and the Korean War."[35] Hess—known as "the flying parson" and "Killer Hess"—was the focus of "The Pious Killer of Korea," a profile that appeared in the *Saturday Evening Post* written by Harold H. Martin (who also penned the controversial profile of the all-black Twenty-Fourth Regiment I examined in the second chapter). It stresses the apparent incongruities of a deeply religious man who is also "one of the deadliest killers of the Korean war, a lean, gaunt, but strangely tireless pilot wholly dedicated to blasting Chinese and Red Koreans with bombs and bullets, rockets and napalm."[36] Hess possesses "a deep fear of killing a noncombatant—an old man, a woman or child"—but he is also relentlessly engaged in "experimenting, trying to find more deadly ways to hurt the enemy."[37]

What Martin describes as Hess's "deep fear of killing a noncombatant" is presented in Sirk's film as stemming from an incident that took place during the Second World War, when he accidentally bombed a German orphanage. (This is based on an event that actually happened and is recounted by Hess in his memoir, though he expresses no sense of guilt over it.) Early in the film, Hess's peacetime vocation as a minister in Ohio has not eased his conscience, which is still troubled by the children he unintentionally killed. After hearing that war has broken out in Korea, he immediately resigns his ministry and reenlists. His primary duty is to train South Korean pilots for the fledgling ROK Air Force. He is unsure, however, of whether he will be up to the killing required by war, haunted as he is by his past mistake. He begins to find atonement when he awakens to the plight of the many Korean orphans who have come to the air base scrounging for food, and he devotes himself to helping them. He is particularly taken with a boy named Chu, who takes to calling Hess "Father" in Korean. With the help of two Koreans—the beautiful En Soon Yang (Anna Kashfi) and the elderly Lu Wan (Philip Ahn)—he transforms a bombed-out Buddhist temple into a makeshift orphanage. When the orphans are imperiled by an enemy advance, he searches for a way to transport them to Cheju Island, which happens to be where Miss Yang (as she is called throughout the film) is from. Hess, Miss Yang, and Lu Wan lead the children on a trek to an airfield, but they arrive to find it deserted. There they come under attack from enemy planes, and Miss Yang is killed as she shields a child's body with her own. Shortly thereafter, five transport planes arrive to save the day. The arc traced by the film's protagonist is a simple and straightforward one: by saving the orphans created by the Korean War, Hess is able to move past the guilt he had felt for the ones he killed in the prior war.

Hess is presented to American audiences as an exemplary figure, as a template for how they might come to see Koreans as objects of sentimental attachment and humanitarian care. As is evident even in the name of the film, Christianity frames much of what takes place, and the film depicts Hess's development as a kind of pilgrim's progress. Its title references not just any hymn, however, but one that became famous during the US Civil War. By aligning itself with the "Battle Hymn of the Republic," which identified the Union cause with the righteous wrath of an angry God, the film suggests a parallel between the Korean orphans that Hess saves and the enslaved Africans who were emancipated in the prior century. This analogy is highlighted by the crucial role played by Lieutenant Maples (the African American actor James Edwards in yet another Korean War film role), who helps Hess lead the orphans to the airfield, where their deliverance will come. Maples carries supplies, lifts up children who tire, and sings "Swing Low, Sweet Chariot" to help them sleep. Maples's presence among these children suggests a resonance between their perilous trek and the journeys from bondage that his grandparents might have attempted a hundred years earlier.

The integrationist power of Christianity is also apparent in the figure of Lu Wan, the elderly patriarch who, along with Miss Yang, plays a key supporting role in Hess's mission. He first comes across Lu Wan at roughly the film's midpoint. Hess gently implores him to help run the temporary orphanage. Many of Lu Wan's lines have the sound of fortune-cookie Confucianisms, casting him as an exemplar of an ancient Eastern wisdom, and his exotic otherness and approval of Hess's actions give them a kind of indigenous sanction.[38] His cryptic-seeming statements are not Zen koans, however, but expressions of an explicitly Christian mysticism. This mixture of qualities is evident when he tells Hess, "First impressions are nets to catch the wind, but I have a persistent one about you. That you might be a man of God."

The character who plays an antithetical role to Lu Wan's is Captain Skidmore (Don DeFore), a pilot who had served with Hess during the prior war and who articulates a cynical realism that recalls the grizzled Sergeant Zack in *The Steel Helmet*. After returning from a mission that resulted in the deaths of Korean civilians, Skidmore insists, "Wars are full of accidents. You know that yourself. You know how everything looks alike from the air." Skidmore is also skeptical when he learns that Hess is a minister: "Once I thought you knew what war was about, but not anymore. Just keep this one thing in mind. All that counts is who wins. Not how nice a guy you are. You win or you die. You go soft and you're one step from being dead."

Unlike Skidmore, however, Maples, exhibits a "softness" in that he responds emotionally to the consequences of the military acts he commits in combat. During the mission that he attempts to justify to Hess, Skidmore had ordered Maples to take out a truck that was believed to be carrying Communist troops but was instead full of refugees, including women and children. Maples's actions directly resulted in civilian deaths, much as Hess's had in the prior war.[39] After landing and disembarking from his plane, Maples pours out his anguish, pounding his fists on the fuselage and crying, "Those kids. Oh, those poor little kids." Hess makes his way to Maples's tent, intending to offer words of comfort, but he ends up being comforted himself. Maples calmly but sadly says to his commanding officer, "It's the way of things, I guess. I figure it's all God's making and will. Doesn't the Book say it? No sparrow shall fall to the earth unless He first gives His nod. . . . We have to trust Him, sir. How can we live without that?" What mitigates Maples's guilt is his devout belief that everything that happens, even during war, is a manifestation of "God's making and will." He tells Hess that since "God and all His reasons are invisible to the eyes of man," all we can do is trust that we are given "light enough to take our next step, do our next chore." The consolation Maples finds in his religion and the fervency with which he soon devotes himself to the orphans make an impression on Hess. Through his own efforts on behalf of the orphans, Hess, like Maples, seems to find a way of atoning for the killings from the past war that haunt him.

The killings that the current war requires, however, are another matter. In a parallel scene later in the film, Hess struggles with his guilt after another training flight: he had shot down an enemy fighter that had targeted Maples's plane and is disturbed by the death he has caused. He is consoled by Lu Wan, who begins by conceding that "yes, war is evil." But after asking Hess to allow "a poor carver of ivory [to] babble for a moment," he clarifies that during war, it comes down to "a choice of two evils" and that "to accept the lesser sometimes can be our only choice." "In order to save," he continues, "at times we must destroy." Lu Wan's words thus give a religious veneer to the truism that whatever lives are taken in this war by men like Hess, they are justified by the ones that are saved.

Additionally, Lu Wan asks, "In times like these, can a man of good conscience ask others, 'Protect me, kill for me, but do not ask me to stain my hands'?" He thereby suggests that all who are protected by the violence of war are in a sense implicated in it as well. Insofar as Lu Wan stands in for the Korean people, this exchange suggests that they understand and sympathize with the Americans who came to their defense and regard the deaths they cause as the lesser of two evils, the greater of which would have been to allow the Communists to bring even more destruction to the country. Lu Wan cites the following from Lamentations 3:59, "Oh Lord, Thou hast seen my wrong. Judge Thou my cause." While this passage identifies God as the only subject who can determine whether the "wrong" Hess committed is justified by its "cause,"

Lu Wan nonetheless seems to speak for the divine when he says to Hess, "I see what is in your heart."

The religiosity imbued by Maples and Lu Wan as Hess's trusted advisors suggest a softer and more spiritual version of the military Orientalism expressed by grittier films. It is deployed in this film, however, to provide a religious sanction for the inevitable killing of civilians by US soldiers. In one telling sequence, however, *Battle Hymn* acknowledges the more instrumental and necropolitical dimensions of the humanitarian Orientalism it articulates. Early in the film, an older Korean female character is introduced who presents herself as an informal caretaker of the orphans but is revealed to be a Communist guerrilla fighter. She is shot and killed by one of the Korean airmen just as she is about to throw a grenade into the ammunition dump. The next day, Hess receives an intelligence report detailing this woman's history, and he is disturbed by the expedient use she made of the children under her care: "She picked up those poor starving kids to make her look good." When Hess is advised by one of his officers to make the base off limits to all civilians, he asks, "Including the little civilians? Think there might be guerrillas among them too?" The officer explains that what makes the orphans "dangerous" is that their presence in and among the airfield has made the pilots nervous about taking off and landing. Hess's ominous reply is that they may indeed be dangerous in another way: "for what they might become someday. If they live long enough."

The dark calculus revealed here suggests that the alternative to adoption is extermination, that if Korean children are not integrated, literally or symbolically, into the American family, they are at risk of becoming enlisted by the enemy. In order to win this war and the larger conflict of which it is a part—and underlying all of Sirk's melodramatic excess in the film is still a message about the necessity of defeating the Communist menace—it will be necessary to be both "the flying parson" and "Killer Hess." It will require rejecting the stark binary Skidmore offers ("All that counts is who wins. Not how nice a guy you are.") and embracing the proposition that "niceness," like napalm, must be weaponized in order to win this war.

Thus Hess's Korean counterpart is as much the Communist guerrilla who posed as the caretaker of orphans as it is Lu Wan. Like her, Hess may take an altruistic interest in the children, but both of them also share the same military objective of defeating the enemy. Hess's disparaging comment that she had "picked up those poor starving kids to make her look good" points toward the strategic aspects of his own altruism. Saving orphans is not just a matter of feeling good about yourself; it may also be the best means of preventing them from growing up to become Communists.

"We Sometimes Cut Good Tissue along with Bad Because We Can't Take the Chances"

The sentimental and religious mournfulness with which *Battle Hymn* acknowledges the civilian deaths resulting from US actions in the Korean War is also apparent in the film I look at next, *One Minute to Zero* (1952). This film, however, also uses a medical analogy to frame such deaths, emphasizing the biopolitical and necropolitical dimensions of the humanitarian Orientalism that bridges both works. The affective palette of *One Minute to Zero* has much different emphases, partly because it rests more comfortably within the genre of the combat film but also because of the qualities of its lead actor, Robert Mitchum, who plays Colonel Steve Janowski. Directed by Tay Garnett (best known for the noir classic *The Postman Always Rings Twice*), this film begins just before the outbreak of the war and mainly takes place in the first few weeks of fighting.[40] In contrast to Hudson's gentle and sensitive Hess, Mitchum's Janowski is a tough and seemingly cynical character. While Hess's defining act is the rescue of orphans, Janowski's will involve the slaughtering of dozens of Korean civilians. This film does, however, contain a heavy dose of sentimental melodrama in the love story it also features, which involves Janowski and UN aid worker Linda Day (Ann Blyth). The tension between the military and humanitarian impulses in Sirk's protagonist is split in Garnett's film between its two romantic leads: the hard-boiled military man who cracks wise and the caring UN functionary who passionately expresses her emotions. The relationship of these two characters to Koreans is diametrically opposed—one kills them while the other tries to save them—which poses the primary obstacle to their romance. Ultimately, however, the tension between them is resolved as Linda learns to accept the gritty realities of war as her sense of Christian faith is rekindled.

The climactic scene in *One Minute to Zero* depicts Janowski ordering his men to fire repeatedly into a group of Korean civilians, and it is quite reminiscent of the scenarios Osborne reports in *Life*. The remarkable inclusion of a scene that essentially depicts a massacre perpetrated by US soldiers seems to reflect the film's overall aim of projecting a sense of verisimilitude and also weaves in what seems to be documentary footage. These elements suggest that this film is shaped by a "torn-from-the-headlines" sensibility akin to the one Fuller ascribes to his film *The Steel Helmet*. Indeed, the movie's purported authenticity is highlighted in some of RKO's publicity materials. The poster Robert J. Lentz reproduces in his *Korean War Filmography* promotes its thrilling realism: "THIS IS THE REAL THING! Big . . . Tense . . . here's the inside-the-lines story of the most exciting guys in all the world!"[41]

The film begins with a series of scenes that seem to have been shot by journalists or perhaps members of the US military (the source is never identified) that have been spliced together into a newsreel-like montage, and similar sequences appear throughout the film. The one that opens *One Minute to Zero* functions as a kind of extended establishing shot. These repurposed images have an ethnographic quality, depicting the lives of ordinary Koreans on the eve of the war: girls jumping rope, boys playing baseball, an open-air market, scenes of village life, a lone farmer in a rice paddy. Blyth's voice-over identifies her character, Linda, as someone who can speak with authority about the events the film portrays because she was a witness: "South Korea in the spring of 1950, a gentle land whose people wanted only to live as one. At peace with the world. I know. I was there. My name doesn't matter." While miming the conventions of the newsreel, however, it is not a voice from nowhere that speaks, for Blyth soon identifies the film's authority with domestic femininity ("I'm any wife, any daughter, any sister, mother, or sweetheart") and an international humanitarianism: "I was serving with the United Nations. Not a big wheel. Just a tiny cog in a huge machine. Thirty-second Assistant Observer on a Health and Sanitation team." The opening frames the combat film we are about to see within a woman's film, suggesting that we are being offered a kinder, gentler, and more intimate perspective on the war.

The image of a crude sign designating the thirty-eighth parallel in English, Russian, and Korean marks a pivot point between this opening sequence and the next, which is clearly cinematic. We watch a training exercise in which South Korean recruits attempt to destroy a tank with a bazooka and fail miserably. Blyth's voice-over explains, "The South Koreans were preparing themselves against invasion. Their methods were primitive. Their equipment pitifully crude. But they were trying." The first diegetic dialogue is uttered by Mitchum's Janowski in response to the Korean soldiers' feeble performance: "No. No. No. Cease fire." He has been observing this exercise with a group of ROKA officers and the obligatorily gruff Sergeant Baker (Charles McGraw). Janowski and Baker then demonstrate "how to kill a tank," and the South Korean soldiers are duly impressed. The dialogue between Janowski and Baker establishes the camaraderie that comes instantly to the men, who are both revealed to be "retreads."

A jeep carrying UN workers arrives, and they speak in French to the Korean officers. Janowski and Baker react dismissively to their conversation, characterizing it as the "yak yak yak" that UN workers and "dames" typically use. Linda introduces herself to Steve Janowski, explaining that she is conducting a health survey, and asks if it is safe to cross into North Korea. When he replies that it is not, since Communist armies directed by Moscow are in the midst of mobilizing for an invasion, she is skeptical. She asserts, "They wouldn't dare; they'd be taking on the whole world." His rejoinder is "That didn't stop Hitler."

This scene establishes Steve and Linda as opposites who take an immediate dislike to each other, identifying the polarities that will have to be mitigated as their inevitable romance blossoms. For the two lovers to come together, it is Linda who must undergo the most dramatic transformation, and Lentz accurately captures how she is depicted: "Linda possesses a naive, holier-than-thou attitude. Later this softens, but at the beginning of the story, she is quite irritating."[42] Steve's attitude will also change during the course of the film, at least in reference to Linda. The film establishes at the outset that he is not only a career military man but a confirmed bachelor. Their initial personal differences are also couched as political differences. Steve is skeptical of the UN's role in the conflict, while Linda espouses a sincere belief in its humanitarian ideals. Seen within the context of the film's romance narrative, the killing of refugees by soldiers under Steve's command poses the primary obstacle to their relationship. Overcoming it will require a "softening" of Linda's initial horror at what Steve orders his men to do in that pivotal scene.

The two are on a collision course through the early part of the film: while Steve's orders are to evacuate all US civilians, hers are to remain in Korea. She angrily refuses to leave, even after she is almost killed in a strafing attack: Steve saves her, which is when a glimmer of attraction first appears. He eventually carries out his orders by literally carrying Linda into a plane.

Soon thereafter, as Steve is recuperating in a hospital in Japan from injuries sustained during the invasion, he receives a visit from a chastened and grateful Linda, who asks if she can make amends for her earlier behavior. He invites her to dinner, and she prepares a romantic candlelit meal for him at her apartment. She reveals that she is a widow without providing any real details. Their date concludes with the two trading verses of a Japanese love song playing on the phonograph, he in Japanese and she in English.

This cozy domestic sequence comprises a roughly fifteen-minute interlude in what is still a war film. Though this scene makes no use of local color, it reinforces the image of Japan that would emerge out of numerous Korean War films and novels as a site of rest, recreation, and romance, though the dalliances usually involve white servicemen and Japanese civilian women. The gender codes through which the desire between Steve and Linda are communicated—inflected as they are by the Japanese setting—convey a sense that something is askew in the shape of their relationship, for in their improvised duet, it is Steve that sings in Japanese and Linda in English, as if he were playing Butterfly to her Pinkerton. After a few dates, moreover, he impulsively asks her to marry him, and in responding, she sounds more like a reluctant groom than a breathless bride-to-be: "Look, we're having fun. Why rush into something that we both may regret?" She explains soon thereafter, however, that her first husband had died in combat and posthumously received the Congressional Medal of Honor, leading Steve to understand her hesitance to become a military wife once again.

When the two return to Korea, their different careers again set them on opposite paths. Linda is assigned to a UN humanitarian mission, and Steve is given command of a unit whose responsibilities will involve managing "the refugee problem" dramatized in *Life*'s early coverage of the war. In the pivotal scene that will rupture their relationship, the men under his command have established a roadblock, monitoring the flow of refugees to ensure that their ranks do not include North Korean soldiers in disguise.

The night before the massacre, Steve offers words of advice to Ralston (Richard Egan), his second-in-command who has recently been promoted to major, a commentary that will prove relevant to the actions he will perform the next day: "It's those decisions that scare you. Most of them are easy, but sooner or later comes the big one. That's the roughest. Because it's a decision that rightfully belongs to God, and we've just taken it in our own hands. It's life or death. But the decision has to be made whether we like it or not." Though Steve is not presented as a man of faith, his reasoning is shaped by a religious framework similar to the one in *Battle Hymn*, echoing that of Maples.

The scenes that depict Linda's actions before the massacre, however, invite viewers to regard what they are about to be shown from Linda's perspective, setting her up as both a humanitarian witness and a proxy for the audience. She has been tending to injured and dying refugees at a UN aid station and has become particularly drawn to an unnamed orphan who had plaintively asked her to take care of his infant sibling, apparently unaware that the bundle he has been carrying holds only the smallest of corpses. When refugees suddenly stop appearing, another aid worker informs Linda that this is due to the roadblock Steve's men have established. Puzzled that he "would make war on the refugees," Linda and her supervisor, Dr. Engstrand (Edward Franz), drive off in a jeep to investigate.

Meanwhile, at the roadblock, Steve's men are searching refugees who are making their way to the UN aid station. As he and Steve are watching from a command post, Major Ralston comments, "About half of them are refugees by day and soldiers at night." Several clips of documentary footage are spliced into a sequence that seems as if it had been directly drawn from Osborne's "Report from the Orient." One woman, who claims through a translator that her baby is sick, is actually hiding a machine gun in the carriage—a discovery made by a soldier using a metal detector. Another female civilian turns out to be a male guerrilla fighter in disguise. These discoveries lead Steve to order that no more refugees be allowed through. Steve's friend Colonel Parker (William Talman) is flying reconnaissance over the roadblock and radios that more civilians are arriving. A message in Korean is broadcast from the plane, telling the refugees that if they move back, food and medical supplies will be dropped to them and warning that they will be shot if they continue moving forward. In response, the guerrillas become more forceful in pushing people toward the roadblock, prodding them at gunpoint.

An excruciating sequence follows in which Steve calls in successive rounds of artillery fire, each landing closer to the front of the column. The refugees continue to move forward as shells land in front of them. Each time they pause, they are forced forward by the gun-wielding guerrillas. The refugees become increasingly distressed, as do the soldiers who fire upon them, but Steve is resolved and the firing continues. Just as Linda and Dr. Engstrand arrive at the command post, Steve orders a final artillery barrage that directly targets the civilians. Dozens of them are killed, but the barrage continues until they scatter, and Steve finally gives the command to cease fire. Shots of Linda's horrified reaction as well as the stricken expressions on the faces of some of the soldiers mirror the response that the film is clearly seeking to evoke in the audience. Linda runs up to Steve and shrieks, "You killed them! Those helpless people! You killed them! I saw you! I saw!" Steve responds by slapping her and orders his men, "Get those civilians out of my sight." However, Steve is also upset by what he has done. His words to Ralston the night before—that men in command are sometimes called up to make decisions that rightly belong only to God—had been tragically prescient.

As far as Linda is concerned, the final third of the film depicts the process through which she comes to accept what she has witnessed as a necessary part of war. At first, she is simply horrified, rendered nearly prostrate when she returns to the aid station. As she is ministered to by Dr. Engstrand, he insists that she immediately sign a statement he has authored. As she reads the following words aloud, she is incredulous: "As an eyewitness of the entire episode, and in full knowledge of the conditions which caused it, I wish to record my fullest approval and admiration for the action of Colonel Janowski." When the outraged Linda resists, Engstrand presses his case, couching his explanation within the language of medicine: "War is the most malignant disease of the human race. It is an infection. It is contagious. When we doctors amputate, we sometimes cut good tissue along with bad because we can't take the chances. That is exactly what Colonel Janowski did today." Linda, however, still refuses: "Doctor, how can any words justify what we saw today? I can't sign this."

Linda does, however, have a change of heart about Steve's actions soon thereafter. Colonel Parker comes across her as she is leading a group of orphans riding in a mule-drawn cart down a city street. After hugging Linda, Parker admonishes her for judging Steve's actions as harshly as she has. To explain why she was wrong to do so, he escorts her down an alley and takes her to a makeshift morgue containing numerous corpses of US soldiers with their hands still tied behind their backs. These images seem to have been taken from documentary footage. Parker explains, "This is what the guerrillas in those refugee columns have been doing to our men every night." She is immediately regretful about her reaction to Steve and implores Parker to tell Steve she is sorry. In the next scene, Linda goes to a bombed-out church at night and prays not for Koreans like the ones who perished in the massacre but for her beloved Steve: "Dear Father in Heaven, I've been so wrong. So unjust. I've hurt him so deeply, and I love him so much. Forgive me. Forgive me. Oh please, Dear God, watch over him. Protect and guide him. Lead him to victory. Spare him to know a lasting peace. And in thy infinite mercy, Dear God, bring him safely back to me."

The remaining half hour of the film dramatizes a stealthy nighttime attack led by Steve's unit that successfully disrupts the Communist supply route but leaves the unit stranded behind enemy lines. The men make a heroic final stand through the next day and night, but only Steve and three other soldiers survive. Colonel Parker also dies during the fighting when his plane is shot down during an airdrop of much-needed supplies and ammunition. When General Thomas (Roy Roberts) finally arrives with reinforcements, he commends Steve and affirms the significance of the men's actions, as they coincided with MacArthur's successful landing at Inchon. Steve is informed that the tide has now turned and that he will be promoted to general for his actions. Steve and the other three survivors drive off by jeep to be integrated into a new unit. They come across Linda as she is again tending to a group of refugees. She runs up, embraces Steve, begs his forgiveness, and agrees to marry him. They kiss and he drives off.

The film ends with Linda, tears streaming down her face, watching as Steve's jeep drives away, part of a long convoy of US military vehicles. Her concluding voice-over is a prayer, a revised version of the one she had offered for Steve, enlarged now to include all the men headed off once again to meet the enemy: "Oh please, Dear God, watch over them. Protect and guide them. Lead them to victory. Spare them to know a lasting peace. And in thy infinite mercy, Dear God, bring them safely back to us." This ending makes clear that *One Minute to Zero* and *Battle Hymn* are—despite the obvious differences between them—cut from the same cloth ideologically speaking. Christianity in both films has a powerful integrative function, pulling together the two diametrically opposed aspects of the US role in Korea: its humanitarian and military dimensions. As Klein's persuasive account of the integrationist cultural logic of Cold War Orientalism would lead us to expect, these films do emphasize the good that can come from the incorporation of Asian populations into the American sphere of influence, sentimentalizing the affective ties that can be built through the literal or symbolic adoption of Koreans and celebrating the enduring friendships that can emerge among whites, blacks, and Asians. They also reveal, however, the bloody underside of this integrationist discourse: the violence that is an integral part of the humanitarian Orientalism they also articulate. To cite once again Dr. Engstrand's analogy, the civilians whom American soldiers must sometimes kill constitute "good tissue" that must at times be cut out "along with bad because we can't take the chances." And Hess's cynical aside in *Battle Hymn* points to the military as well as the moral imperative that underwrites the adoption of Korean War orphans, which is to ward off the "danger" of "what they might become someday. If they live long enough."

* * *

These films illuminate the biopolitical and necropolitical dimensions of the twin endeavors of war-making and humanitarian aid foregrounded in US depictions of the Korean War—depictions framed by the structure I call humanitarian Orientalism. While the cultural artifacts examined here stress the necessity of being able to distinguish the populations who can be legitimately targeted for death and those who should be recognized as objects of humanitarian care, they also reveal that this distinction can be overridden by military necessity. While civilians are thus consigned to what I have termed a racial demilitarized zone (DMZ) that renders them all killable subjects—as exemplars of bare life—these depictions make use of a Christian framework that imbues their deaths with a sacrificial aura and manufactures as their central drama the heroic anguish of American subjects who either engage in the killing of civilians or acquiesce to its necessity. Indeed, the melodramatic and sentimental excesses with which *Battle Hymn* and *One Minute to Zero* highlight the suffering of its humanitarian protagonists effectively overshadow the experiences of the Korean civilians whose deaths at the hands of US soldiers these films grieve and memorialize: hence Linda's prayers are for Steve and men like him, not for the civilians who die in the fighting.[43]

The humanitarian Orientalism articulated in the works examined in this chapter is restaged and disfigured in the novels taken up in the next, which remember this war in ways that extend the reframing of the mid-century depictions of the conflict that part 1 of this study has sought to accomplish. As we shall see in part 2, Jayne Anne Phillips's *Lark and Termite* and Chang-rae Lee's *The Surrendered* set in motion a dynamic of empathetic reading that reiterates how Americans were invited in the 1950s to "know" the people their military forces had been sent to Korea to protect and save. However, rather than delivering us to an emotional safe haven of complacent grief and pity, these novels plunge us into a much more discomfiting position, opening out to a view of the longer histories of war in which that conflict is embedded—histories that extend further into the past than 1950 and continue to the present.

PART II

Assemblages of Memory

5

Angels of Mercy and the Angel of History

The Disfiguring of Humanitarian Orientalism

Part 2 of this study moves forward in time to the turn of the millennium and takes up an emergent tradition of novels that look back to the Korean War. While together they compose an exemplary archive of cultural memory that illuminates the interlocking racial and transnational histories of empire in which that event was embedded, none of these works, as I suggest in the introduction, takes the form of conventional historical fiction. In ways that range from subtle to extravagant, each troubles the realist idiom in which they also operate. These novels catch readers in the draft of the historiographical imperatives they unleash, dragging them into a much more expansive view of the spatial and temporal contexts in which the Korean War is embedded. As I elaborate more fully in the introduction, the mode of cultural memory I hope to evoke here has affinities with what Michael Rothberg terms "multidirectional memory," which stresses the intimacies of the various racial and colonial histories that these novels bring together.[1] They also forward a corrosive critique of what Alexander G. Weheliye calls "the racializing assemblages"[2] that took shape during the Korean War, the emergent version of military multiculturalism that framed mainstream depictions of the newly integrated US Army, as well as of the humanitarian Orientalism that structured representations of Korean civilians caught in the cross fire, the refugees who were consigned to the status of bare life even as their deaths were plaintively mourned. These works do so by plunging readers into the *affective* dimensions of the intimacies engendered by the Korean War in ways that wreck the simple grammar of integrative and familial connection privileged by the sentimental modes of Orientalism that took shape during the 1950s.

I begin with two novels that reframe the interracial intimacies that lie at the heart of the two films analyzed in the previous chapter: the

bonds that emerged among US servicemen, humanitarian aid workers, and Korean civilians. The eponymous protagonists of Jayne Anne
Phillips's *Lark and Termite* are a young white working-class woman in
West Virginia and her severely disabled half-brother whose lives have
been shaped by the violence of the Korean War; Termite's father, Bobby
Leavitt, had perished while trying to protect a group of Korean civilians
as they were massacred by US troops. Chang-rae Lee's *The Surrendered*,
arguably the most ambitious American novel about the Korean War to
have been published to date, tells the intertwined stories of three protagonists: June, a Korean woman whose family perished during the conflict; Hector, a US soldier who comes across June when she is a child and
leads her to an orphanage; and Sylvie, a US missionary who, along with
her husband, runs the orphanage in which June finds refuge. Both works
trouble dominant narratives of humanitarian Orientalism, suggesting
how US efforts to protect and aid Korean civilians from the violence of
war engendered forms of intimacy that imposed a brutality of their own.

Lark and Termite: "A Timed Bloodletting with Different Excuses . . . a Long Music"

According to Robert J. Lentz, the 1952 film examined in the previous
chapter, *One Minute to Zero*, became "notorious" among South Koreans
in the early 2000s because its depiction of US soldiers firing into a crowd
of Korean civilians bore an eerie resemblance to an event that had been
uncovered by a team of AP reporters.[3] Lentz is referring to the reporting
of Charles Hanley, Sung-Hung Choe, and Martha Mendoza, who in 1999
broke the story of a massacre that took place near the village of No Gun
Ri during the early months of the Korean War. Their multipart series of
reports, which was awarded the Pulitzer Prize, was based on interviews
with Korean survivors and US soldiers who were there. The Korean witnesses estimated that roughly one hundred villagers were killed during
an air attack by US fighter planes and another three hundred in the tunnels under a railroad bridge where they had sought shelter afterward.
Their assertions were corroborated by several veterans, some of whom
had taken part in the violence. The numbers of civilians killed "would
make No Gun Ri one of only two known cases of large-scale killings
of noncombatants by U.S. ground troops in this century's major wars,

military law experts note. The other was Vietnam's My Lai massacre, in 1968, in which more than 500 Vietnamese may have died."[4] This reporting prompted an investigation by the US Department of the Army that culminated in President Bill Clinton issuing a statement of "deep regret" on January 11, 2001. What led the president to stop short of an apology, however, was a report prepared by US Army investigators suggesting it was an isolated incident. In an article published in *Critical Asian Studies*, Hanley, one of the AP reporters, itemizes the flaws in this report. He points out that army investigators ignored written evidence that US commanders had explicitly authorized firing at civilians, that they deemed both the survivors and the veteran witnesses to be unreliable, and that they downplayed the number of deaths that resulted.[5] Hanley characterizes the findings of the Truth and Reconciliation Committee of the Republic of South Korea, which were released in 2007, as much more plausible, based as it is on "the accounts of the most reliable sources, the surviving Korean witnesses," and cites this report's summary of what took place:[6]

> On July 25th, 1950, Korean villagers were forced by U.S. soldiers to evacuate their homes and move south. The next day, July 26, the villagers continued south along the road. When the villagers reached the vicinity of No Gun Ri, the soldiers stopped them at a roadblock and ordered the group onto the railroad tracks, where the soldiers searched them and their personal belongings. Although the soldiers found no prohibited items (such as weapons or other military contraband), the soldiers ordered an air attack upon the villagers via radio communications with U.S. aircraft. Shortly afterwards, planes flew over and dropped bombs and fired machine guns, killing approximately one hundred villagers on the railroad tracks. Those villagers who survived sought protection in a small culvert underneath the railroad tracks. The U.S. soldiers drove the villagers out of the culvert and into double tunnels nearby. The U.S. soldiers then fired into both ends of the tunnels over a period of four days (July 26–29, 1950), resulting in approximately 300 additional deaths.[7]

The white Southern author Jayne Anne Phillips based her novel *Lark and Termite* partly on this massacre. While its primary focus is on the echoes of the Korean War that resonate in the lives of a white working-class family long after its ostensible end, the novel also high-lights the violence US forces had inflicted on Korean civilians. Phillips's work could credibly be described as magical realist, as it is populated by entities and forces that traverse the two locales and timelines that compose its primary settings. Parts of it take place during the four-day massacre in late July 1950 and center on Bobby Leavitt, a corporal in the US Army who ends up being shot by his fellow soldiers in Korea and perishes along with hundreds of Korean civilians, though he tries vainly to save them and himself. Most of it takes place, however, on the very same dates but nine years later in West Virginia, relating how the lives of those he left behind were irrevocably shaped by his death.

The emotional focus of *Lark and Termite* is on how the war's violence inexorably travels from No Gun Ri to West Virginia, taking the lives of not only Bobby and the Korean civilians with whom he is trapped in the tunnels but also Lola, who commits suicide soon after hearing about her husband's death. The war's afterlife also takes shape in the secrecy and sadness that afflict the next generation. *Lark and Termite* itemizes the toll exacted by a faraway war on Americans, and even on those who would seem barely proximate to its reach. Its central theme is pithily encapsulated by Elise, a friend of the family, who says to Lark, "People forget that a soldier's death goes on for years—for a generation, really. They leave people behind."[8]

In Bobby Leavitt, Phillips invents a figure who seems an imaginary forerunner to Hugh Thompson Jr., the helicopter pilot who intervened during the My Lai massacre. Leavitt also recalls a figure like Dean Hess, another example of what should be apparent by now as a familiar Korean War archetype: the US soldier as an angel of mercy. As we shall see, however, while Leavitt is depicted sympathetically by a narrator who records his thoughts and memories, the novel ultimately dismantles the notion that he and other US soldiers who ostensibly came to the aid of Koreans were acting as their protectors.

The memories that come to Leavitt as he shuttles in and out of consciousness after having been shot reveal aspects of this character that make him an amenable figure within the parameters of contemporary racial liberalism. For one thing, Leavitt is revealed to be not only working class but a secular urban Jew and therefore, in the novel's reckoning, not quite white. His memories fill in his backstory: a rough-and-tumble upbringing in Philadelphia shaped by an alcoholic and abusive father and a loving mother who died suddenly from an aneurysm when he was a teenager. His ethnicity is underscored by his memories of bantering with his closest friend, Tompkins, who is proud of the fact that his mother was Seminole. As Tompkins tells Leavitt, he thinks of himself as "white like you white, Philly Jew Boy. No Florida cracker tell you I'm white, or you neither" (15–16). Leavitt's memories also reveal that Leavitt, a jazz trumpeter, had "liked playing the black clubs, where he learned more and made less, and the pros called him Whitey with tacit affection" (9). By giving Leavitt this background, the novel also suggests why he might feel a kind of affinity for the Korean civilians he is escorting along the railroad tracks, since "he's a refugee in his own life, sans family or possessions. Like the Koreans, he owns what he carries" (11). His connection to them is further emphasized by the fact that he is able to speak some Korean, having volunteered for a unit that received training in the language. Overall, Leavitt is presented as not only comfortable with diversity but embodying a version of it as well. He is, as it were, a rebooted version of the protagonist of humanitarian and military Orientalist narratives that took shape in US midcentury depictions of the Korean War: Dean Hess 2.0.

That Leavitt is a more modest version of the archetype monumentalized in films like *Battle Hymn* is suggested by the fact that his altruistic actions shortly before and during the massacre are not driven by some lofty religious or humanitarian sense of mission but emerge almost accidentally. This likely makes him a more palatable character to contemporary readers, but it also marks a significant alteration of the salvific scenario the novel plays out. For one thing, Leavitt's actions are not the expression of a spontaneous burst of compassion but, rather, a response to a Korean girl who confronts him with "a demand, not a request" for his assistance (28). He recognizes that she is "the child's guardian, the old woman's protector," which is why she "glares at Leavitt, enraged that she needs help, angry at herself" (30). He accedes to her demand to help her with her great aunt, who is quite elderly, and her younger brother, who is blind and mentally disabled, and in doing so finds himself trapped with them in the tunnels. The driving agent in Phillips's restaging of the humanitarian Orientalist scenario is thus a Korean subject, one who is not grateful for the presence of US soldiers but angered by it.

While the novel does not delve into the consciousness of any of its Korean characters, what is notable about their depiction is that it refrains from imbuing them with the pathos so evident in the popular representations from the 1950s examined earlier. This is evident even when Leavitt is leading the refugees along the tracks: "Leavitt heard the hatred and distrust, the discomfort, the resentment in their voices, as warning and knowledge. They were angry and their country was defenseless; everyone would pay" (14). The Koreans' hostility toward him—and by implication toward the American presence overall—is epitomized by the girl's frail and elderly great-aunt, whom Leavitt hears "curse him under her breath, like a whisper or chant," and who then "spits on him." At one point, the old woman "croons a kind of dirge," which leads Leavitt to speculate that "she might be a shaman, a practitioner of what the country people called Tonghak, the Heavenly Way" (128). He knows enough Korean to realize that she is calling him a "demon," "a murderous spirit wandering among the dead" (129). Soon thereafter, the old woman takes Leavitt's gun and shoots herself in the head.

This old woman's curse reverberates through the entirety of the novel, and she ultimately emerges as a kind of angel of vengeance. Within the terms of the Korean spiritual cosmology evoked here, what happens to Leavitt and to his family back home is the enactment of a kind of poetic justice. Her revenge is enacted by proxy: it is meted out by his fellow soldiers when they shoot him in the back and paralyze him, which results in the girl carrying him to the tunnel, and again when he dies along with the civilians in a final volley of gunfire. His son emerges, moreover, as a kind of secondary object of the old woman's curse, his disability the collateral damage of her rage. The congenital deformities that are the source of Termite's condition—"his spine hadn't closed right" (50)—mirror the injury that had left his father paralyzed. After being shot, Leavitt awakens to find that "his legs are dead and his guts torn apart but his spine opens up like a star" (243). Finally, there is Lola's suicide. She, too, shoots herself with a gun that had belonged to Leavitt. Through such symmetries, the novel presents Termite and Lola as distant casualties of the Korean War. The bullet that took the life of Leavitt's widow a year after his death seems the ricochet of a shot fired nine years earlier by an old woman wracked with rage over what US soldiers had brought to her country.

Moreover, the novel reveals an unsettling memory of Leavitt's that troubles whatever sense of identification readers might come to feel for him. When he is first confronted by the girl demanding his help, "he wonders if he knows her," thinking she might be one of the prostitutes he frequented in Seoul, though he soon realizes she is not (29–30). Nonetheless, he sees her as "a village girl, beautiful, petite like most of them, dressed in the usual white garments" and as "the incarnation of those ritual dances whores never forgot" (30).

Earlier passages recount his experiences with such women. Unlike Tompkins, who accompanies him to these brothels and simply seeks "the youngest, most petite girl he [can] find" (16), Leavitt searches for another kind of experience:

> Leavitt closed his eyes, allowed an angel to kneel before him. He wouldn't put himself inside them: he adhered to this small fidelity like religion, like another charm, enjoying the control itself, the tension and the heat. . . . In Korean, he'd tell her what to do, how to dance, moist in the little room, not dancing as she did in the bars but as she had in her village, slow ceremonial dance that was ritual and folklore. They'd all come from a village, years back or not so long ago, all the women and the girls. . . . She'd dance then, as they all did, slowly, a prayer beyond language, a shape moving in afternoon light or near darkness. (16–17)

What Leavitt appears to want at first is simply to stand witness while providing these women an opportunity to experience again the bodily pleasures they had enjoyed before becoming sex workers catering to the whims of US servicemen—to regain a sense of their innocence, as it were. His form of interaction seems to provide them an opportunity to grieve but also incites his voyeuristic desire: "Sometimes she would cry and Leavitt would ask her to lie down, open toward him in his chair, touch herself until the crying stopped or turned to sighs and whispered gasps." While he wonders if they had "shared their privacy"—their self-pleasuring and their tears—with him "as a gift," his memories reveal that his lingering on what might seem to be an attitude of respectful restraint was more a form of foreplay: "Regardless, *when the performance seemed genuine enough* and time was nearly gone, he'd stop the girl and pull her to him, *so aroused* he was shaking. Finally she'd minister to him with her mouth, both of them listening as Tompkins rammed himself again and again into the youngest, most petite girl he could find" (17). That the sound of what Tompkins is doing in the next room accompanies the girl's performance of oral sex on Leavitt underscores the parallel between the seemingly disparate forms of pleasure the two men are taking. While Tompkin's fetish is "the youngest most petite girl he could find," what incites Leavitt's desire is the genuineness of a prostitute's performance of self-pleasuring and sorrow over the prewar innocence she has lost. It is her capacity to embody momentarily her prior unsullied self that makes him want to sully it.

In her depiction of these exchanges, Phillips offers a radically desublimated view of the pleasures white subjects take in the scenarios of humanitarian Orientalism, for the manifest altruism expressed by Leavitt's gestures, the affective aid he seems to be providing these girls, belies the fact that their latent content has been sexual. The fantasy he plays out suggests the voyeuristic and pornographic dimensions of humanitarian Orientalism: how arousing the performance of Korean innocence and innocence lost can be for a white spectator who wants to see himself as engaged in an exchange of gifts.

In light of these revelations, it is difficult to feel an unalloyed sympathetic identification with Leavitt, though he, too, will perish in the fusillade of gunfire that will take the lives of the civilians with whom he is trapped in the tunnel. As such, it becomes hard to see him or, by implication, any of the US soldiers who fought in Korea as entirely innocent victims. That he is guilty, at least by association, of an unwanted intervention is suggested by "the hatred and distrust" and "resentment" he hears in the voices of the refugees as he leads them along the tracks (14). Indeed, he realizes that "the refugees need no urging; it's *their* civil war, their homes and lands lost, he's merely a conductor. *No savior here*" (20; emphasis mine). His inadequacy to this role is evident from the fact that he is unable to save the Korean girl and her disabled brother—or any of the hundreds of other civilians hiding in the tunnels—from being massacred.

Leavitt, or at least a spectral echo of him, does seem to reemerge in West Virginia in 1959 to save another sister and brother: his son, Termite, and Termite's half-sister, Lark, who resemble the pair he could not save nine years earlier in Korea. He appears in the person of Robert Stamble, a social worker who arrives unannounced at Lark and Termite's house, bringing with him a child-sized wheelchair. Stamble has an instant rapport with Termite, and he seems like some kind of apparitional trace of Leavitt. The two share the same first name, Robert, and the same pale complexion and white-blonde hair. Moreover, when Lark meets him, she immediately detects his good intentions, which to her are almost like a "smell": "I hate that smell. Dads wear it in Dadville" (47). When a massive flood comes to Winfield and the two titular characters find themselves trapped in their attic, Stamble materializes once again and helps rescue them by coaxing the terrified Termite onto the boat that will take them to safety. Soon thereafter, Stamble dives into the rising waters and disappears without a trace.

In the aftermath of the flood, however, the two siblings face a second threat. Nonie, the aunt who has been raising them, has been jailed for her involvement in an accidental death and awaits trial. Since Lark is seventeen, she cannot serve as Termite's legal guardian, and he risks being institutionalized. However, a number of fortuitous developments take place that point Lark and Termite toward a hopeful future. As the novel ends, the two of them are on a train headed to Florida, accompanied by Solly, a childhood friend whose relationship with Lark has blossomed into a romantic one. They will live in a cottage that Lola and Bobby had originally intended for them. Once Lark turns eighteen, she will be able to assume guardianship of Termite, and Solly will accept a football scholarship and attend college.

The tidiness of this ending is unsettled, however, by a historical irony Michael Dirda astutely points out in his admiring appraisal of the novel: "And so happiness would seem to await this young couple. But then one remembers the date: 1959. In just a few years the American involvement in Vietnam will start to claim a whole new generation of young men—and the women who loved them and the families they might have had."[9] Attentive readers like Dirda will thus realize that another generation of young working-class men like Solly will soon find themselves conscripted to fight in another Asian civil war, and another civilian population will be caught in the cross fire.

Through its depiction of Termite's mental disability and the clairvoyance that accompanies it, *Lark and Termite* suggests a historiographical explanation for why US soldiers of Solly's generation will end up making the same mistakes as those of Leavitt's—of why No Gun Ri will be recapitulated in My Lai—for the readers' access to the events of the massacre comes through Termite, who experiences them as a kind of eternal present: "Pictures that touch him move and change, they lift and turn, stutter their edges and blur into one another. Their colors fall apart and are never still long enough for him to see, but the pictures inside him hold still. . . . The pictures tell their story that repeats and repeats again and stays inside him until it ends. He sees them without trying" (63–64). Termite's consciousness houses a kind of indexical record of what happened to his father and to the civilians in the tunnels at No Gun Ri. Encrypted in his body—a code that nobody around him can crack, not even the sister who understands him best—are events that would only be made known to Americans five decades later. He is thus an apt emblem of not just historical memory but also the amnesia surrounding that conflict that has afflicted the American consciousness.

Ultimately, the novel's rendering of Termite as an inaccessible repository of historical memory opens up to the kind of counterfactual speculation that Susan Sontag entertained in her essay *On Photography* and voices a similar wistful question: *If Americans had known what their soldiers had done during the Korean War in places like No Gun Ri, would they have been able to prevent similar events from happening decades later in the Vietnam War?* As we know, however, the history encrypted in Termite is doomed to unfurl in a repetition that is poetically conveyed in the following passage: "The planes always come . . . like planets on rotation, a timed bloodletting with different excuses. Part of a long music" (244).

The Surrendered: Angels of Mercy and the Angel of History

Chang-rae Lee's *The Surrendered* similarly invites readers to see the Korean War as "part of a long music." In addition to that conflict, which leaves one of its protagonists an orphan, this novel also directly references the Second Sino-Japanese War. More indirectly, it alludes to another forgotten conflict—the Austro-Sardinian War, or the Second War of Italian Independence—the brutality of which catalyzed the emergence of modern humanitarianism. Finally, in the Homeric provenance of its third protagonist's name, Hector, *The Surrendered* also evokes a much deeper historical context that stretches back to classical antiquity. Given the panoramic vista of human history he evokes in *The Surrendered*, Lee does risk simply using the Korean War as an occasion to issue a grand literary statement about how war disfigures the most selfless of human aspirations and delimits the possibilities of authentic intimacy. While Lee's universalizing aims can reduce present-day South Korea to just another nation forged out of the savage crucible of war, his novel's evocation of a vast temporality that makes contemporary conflicts part of a historical continuum that begins with the Trojan War enables him to level a devastating critique of the *ideals* that are routinely evoked as justifications for military conquest. The history of the West is conjured as an endless cycle of wars waged in the name of civilization, often suffused with ostensibly humanitarian aims, and the best that characters can hope to wrest from that legacy are fleeting, seemingly ineffectual bonds of intimacy that can be as destructive to the self as they are to the other.

The Surrendered does, however, have a more historically specific target: the kinds of humanitarian representations examined in the previous chapter. After all, its three primary characters recall ones already encountered: Hector is a US serviceman, Sylvie a female missionary/aid worker, and June a Korean orphan/refugee.[10] Through its repurposing of these stock figures of humanitarian Orientalism, moreover, *The Surrendered* performs a genealogical analysis of the salvific narratives used to justify the US intervention in Korea through the prominent role played by a copy of Henri Dunant's *A Memory of Solferino*. This book, which is a kind of ur-text of modern humanitarianism, metonymically links its three protagonists: originally given to Sylvie by her missionary parents, it comes with her to Korea, where June and Hector both notice her reading it at the orphanage and become curious enough to look into it themselves; it is later given to June and travels with her to the United States and then, after her son Nicholas steals it from her, comes with him to Italy; it is finally returned to June shortly before she dies. The prominence of this intertextual link asks us to consider how Lee's novel both resembles and departs from the kind of humanitarian narrative exemplified by Dunant's memoir (as well as the films examined in the previous chapter). It is also suggestive of why reading *The Surrendered* can be a painfully daunting if not unbearable experience, for the novel reanimates the empathetic impulses that such narratives provoke only to disfigure them.

To understand how *The Surrendered* does this, it is instructive to turn to Joseph R. Slaughter's essay "Humanitarian Reading," which provides an incisive account of how such narratives work and how some readers have wanted to think they work. His argument is based on a careful analysis of *A Memory of Solferino*, which he describes as "one of the most objectively successful of humanitarian interventionist narratives in history, precipitating both the incorporation of the Red Cross and the first Geneva Convention for the Amelioration of the Condition of the Wounded and Sick in Armed Forces in the Field."[11] The memoir itself recounts how Dunant and a number of the other tourists with whom he had been traveling, along with members of the local population, provided what care they could to the nearly thirty thousand soldiers injured during the Battle of Solferino during the Austro-Sardinian War.

Slaughter takes issue with a paradigm of humanitarian reading premised on readers developing a direct emotional intimacy with the suffering subjects identified as the due objects of humanitarian care, a dyadic model of identification that underwrites the work of Richard Rorty and Martha Nussbaum. This model of humanitarian reading, Slaughter argues, emphasizes "the cultivation of a *noblesse oblige* of the powerful (rights holders) toward the powerless (those who cannot enact their human rights) that ultimately reconfirms the liberal reader as the primary and privileged subject of human rights and the benefactor of humanitarianism."[12] Readers of such works actually end up assuming, he asserts, a "patronizing sense of moral superiority and cosmopolitan largesse."[13]

Slaughter discloses a preemptive criticism of such a perspective and a more modest model of how humanitarian fictions route readers' sympathies in *A Memory of Solferino*. This work, he writes, "invites us to *empathize* with the humanitarian, with one who, indifferent to nationality, seeks to relieve the torments of the *défigurés*."[14] The humanitarian protagonist is thus the "third actor" in such narratives, who serves as "an intermediary between ourselves and the ones who suffer, acting as a conduit for our emotional investments in the scene of suffering."[15] This third actor does not exemplify an exceptional heroism in Slaughter's account but "becomes simply a position in a grammar of relief that may be occupied by anyone who disregards nationality in the face of human suffering."[16] This substitutability leaves open a relay to the reader who can more easily imagine herself in the position of humanitarian protagonists, each of whom is substitutable for the other. He suggests that a "sense of ethical obligation perhaps develops not in response to an other's tragedy but as a sense of responsibility to the moral integrity of one's own class of humanity."[17]

While Slaughter's schema theoretically lacks the patronizing and self-congratulatory dimension of a dyadic model of sympathy, as we have already seen, US popular narratives that have sought to justify military intervention on humanitarian grounds tend to elicit sympathy for protagonists who are rendered as exemplary not in the sense of being ordinary but in the sense of being exceptional and heroic. This is certainly the case in US cinematic and journalistic narratives about the Korean War like those examined in the previous chapter, which lionized US soldiers and United Nations (UN) aid workers as the saviors and protectors of civilians, often orphans. Nonetheless, Slaughter's analysis is quite useful for understanding Lee's novel not only because *A Memory of Solferino* plays such a prominent role in it but because it helps clarify what makes reading this novel such a discomfiting, even excruciating, experience, for the catharsis that readers might achieve by identifying with protagonists who seem "the humanitarian extension of our better angels" is precisely what Lee's novel promises and then brutally denies to its readers.[18]

To see how that takes place, I will first take up the characters the novel explicitly presents as exemplars of Dunant's principles, Sylvie's parents. The Binets, Francis and Jane, are presented as deeply earnest, viewing humanitarianism as "the most urgent calling in this life" and having devoted themselves to "educating children, feeding the poor, ameliorating suffering"; they have brought their daughter with them as "they traveled from destitute place to destitute place, from the Amazon to West Africa and now to Asia."[19] Though nominally Christian, their true devotion was to the humanitarian vision Dunant articulated in his memoir, evident in a pilgrimage they had once made with their daughter to the Cappella-Ossario Di Solferino, a church that serves as a reliquary in which the bones of the unknown soldiers who had died during the battle have been laid to rest. The Binets were, the narrator asserts, "two people who over the years had honed themselves into ideal instruments of mercy" (177).

Their efforts in Manchuria and the awful events that bring them to an end are recounted in chapters 7 and 8 of *The Surrendered*. The mission the Binets have established there provides medical care, food, and schooling to the civilians caught between the Japanese soldiers who have invaded Manchuria and the Communist insurgents who are trying to repel them. Their humanitarian endeavors are brought to a violent close when a group of Japanese soldiers, led by a particularly sadistic young officer, commandeers the schoolhouse in which their mission is housed. These men are part of a counterinsurgency effort attempting to root out members of the resistance. Their brutal interrogations result in the deaths of two Chinese missionaries, and they soon discover that one of the teachers who works there, Benjamin Li, is a Communist agent. When Li refuses to divulge the names of his co-conspirators despite being tortured and beaten, they direct their violence at the Binets and the other missionaries to coerce him into talking. They force Li to copulate with Sylvie's mother at gunpoint and bayonet Sylvie's father when he tries to intercede—he dies shortly thereafter. When they turn their sights on Sylvie, her mother tries to intercede, and she herself is shot dead. It is only when Benjamin's eyelids are cut off and he is forced to watch as Sylvie herself is about to be raped that he relents and begins to scream the names of his compatriots.

It is impossible to overstate how horrific the novel's depiction of these events is. If readers are drawn to identify and empathize with the Binets as instantiations of Dunantian humanitarianism, they are forced to confront how inadequate the ideals they exemplify are to the context of an ongoing war, especially an asymmetrical one, in which an invading army is engaged in a brutal counterinsurgency campaign. While Dunant arrives on the field of battle after the fighting has ended, the Binets have journeyed into the heart of an ongoing conflict. Their desire to maintain their neutrality—their cosmopolitan indifference to nation—proves to be untenable within this context. Indeed, Francis's humanitarian devotion to extending the principle of mercy *to all* has led him to harbor a sense of loyalty to Benjamin, whom he knows to be an insurgent. His adherence to Dunant's tenets results in not only his own death and the rape and murder of his wife but also the possible sexual assault of Sylvie—the novel leaves unclear whether the soldiers' intended rape of her is carried out.

Sylvie is presented as having inherited her parents' humanitarian values, and thus her spiritual lineage also traces back to Dunant. She had accompanied them on their pilgrimage to Solferino, and her copy of his memoir bears her parents' inscription: "To our steadfast daughter. May you be an angel of mercy" (249). This legacy leads her to help her husband run an orphanage in postwar South Korea. By highlighting Sylvie's humanitarian genealogy with such specificity, the novel connects the dots, as it were, between the nineteenth-century war that led Dunant to launch the humanitarian crusade that established both the Red Cross and the Geneva Conventions and the Korean War. In so doing, the novel reminds us that the latter was, as Sar Conway-Lanz puts it, "the first armed conflict in which the United States attempted to live up to the human rights and humanitarian standards newly institutionalized in the late 1940s" and that it began just one year after "forty-five nations signed the four new Geneva Conventions."[20]

The novel offers a compassionate portrait of Sylvie—whom we might think of as hearkening back to a humanitarian Orientalist figure like Linda Day, the UN aid worker played by Ann Blyth in *One Minute to Zero*—by revealing the devastating trauma that fundamentally shaped her. It does so, however, without wholly making her an object of sympathy. The flashbacks that describe her young adulthood—which leave unclear how she survived the massacre or made her way to Seattle, where her parents were originally from—reveal the addictive behaviors that are her response to the trauma she endured.[21]

In college, she volunteers in a soup kitchen and begins an affair with Jim, a fellow volunteer in his forties who is a veteran of the First World War. Despite the genuine comfort the two seem to find from each other, her desire for him has an exploitative dimension to it. Sylvie is the one who initiates the relationship, and she comes to it from a position of relative power. While Jim is nearly destitute, Sylvie is comfortably middle class. While Sylvie is regarded as "a beautiful, somewhat aloof, scholarly girl who had so quickly righted herself after such a lamentable family tragedy" (217), she sees Jim as "frail, if not somehow wrecked," and senses "something ruined about him" (215, 213). He suffers from a bad back, an injury from the war. She soon discovers that he also lost his genitals in the fighting, but this revelation seems to stoke her desire, as if she had simply found a physical manifestation of the psychic wounding she has been hoping to touch. The pleasure she takes from Jim—he performs oral sex on her—seems to enable her to erotically luxuriate in his past pain, a pain that provides a dark mirror to her own. She also learns from Jim how opiates might ease the suffering caused by war. Their relationship becomes sexual immediately after she steals a drink from a bottle of laudanum he always has nearby, and it unleashes her own addictive proclivities, enabling her to "feel whole again" and "no more substantial than ether and light" (215).

These addictive tendencies do not, however, originate from her time with Jim, for she had been recalling her experiences in Manchuria with an obsessive mixture of pleasure and pain: "For a long time afterward, for the rest of her years in fact, her grasp of that day would function more as an ill fantasy than a memory, a dark figment she could screen for the purpose of self-torment, letting herself view it over and over until it became a kind of homily, a saying in pictures, until she lost herself within it completely" (205). Sylvie returns to this event in her mind with a masochistic repetitiveness, and the talisman of this trauma's persistence is the volume of *A Memory of Solferino* that her parents had given her. Sylvie's nearly obsessive rereading of it seems to keep alive the bond to her parents that was severed by the violence of war. In the orphanage, June notices "how Sylvie handled the book, with indeed a kind of enjoyment, a certain somber savoring" (247).

The novel's characterization of Sylvie resembles a Freudian case study, for her troubling psychic tendencies—her "neuroses"—are presented as having their origins in a traumatic event that occurred just as her sexuality had started to emerge: she had begun to feel attracted to Benjamin Li not long before he was violently disfigured in front of her. The fusion of sexual desire and horrific violence, the loss of her parents, the savage rapes she witnessed and was perhaps a victim of herself—their intermingling seems to account for the "perverse" pleasures she takes from Jim, her addictive tendencies, and the "enjoyment" and "somber savoring" she derives from her obsessive reading of *A Memory of Solferino*.

However compassionately it may be executed, the psychological portrait of Sylvie does suggest that there is something amiss in her—that her commitment to Dunant's principles is absent the unalloyed altruism of her parents, as it has become grafted to her memories of the violence she witnessed and endured and of the sexual awakening that had taken place shortly before. Her missionary efforts are driven by the unmourned loss and the unresolved trauma that haunt her, and the only relief she finds from them comes through an eroticized masochism and an addiction that she satisfies by making use of others.

Not long after Sylvie arrives in Korea with her husband, Tanner, she finds substitutes for what she had lost in Jim. She begins an affair with Hector, who is in certain ways as "wrecked" and "ruined" as Jim had been and who helps her shoot up with what appears to be morphine. The figure to whom she is most intensely drawn, however, is June. The two soon develop an intense bond, which leads the girl to believe that she will be adopted by the Ameses. Tanner admonishes his wife for disregarding the humanitarian principle of indifference in her desire to adopt June, noting that "none of them has a more profound story than any of the rest." He reminds her that their colleagues had warned them, "So many pretty stones in the river, but you can't pick them all up" (165). But because Tanner actually has plans to adopt "three infants in Seoul," the problem with June seems to be that she's not a pretty enough stone, as it were. As he says to Sylvie, "She's not a nice girl. She's not a kind girl. Maybe she was once, but she isn't anymore" (164).

Despite her husband's warnings, Sylvie's bond with June deepens. It further intensifies when Tanner, aware that Sylvie is falling into a deep depression, tells June to watch his wife closely when he is gone. What June feels for Sylvie is both poignant and understandable—she thinks of their bond as one of "comrades who by the curse of war had been sentenced to be alone" (326). But in honoring Ames's request, her intimacy with Sylvie takes a disturbing turn.

June becomes voyeuristically enmeshed in Sylvie and Hector's relationship, spying on their covert couplings in a seldom-used storeroom, after which Hector helps Sylvie shoot up "with the medicine that made her shiver and then go slack, turn a ghastly bone-blue" (333). These voyeuristic episodes exacerbate feelings in June that already had an erotic component to them. When June glimpses Sylvie changing out of her clothes one day, she realizes that the nausea she felt was actually "the expression of a desire" (324).

June and Sylvie also develop a habit of reading passages of Dunant's book together: "Sometimes June would ask Sylvie to read *A Memory of Solferino* to her and she'd refuse at first but always eventually yield, *the passages entering them, June thought, with both pain and bliss like the medicine in the kit*, and making them cling more tightly to each other" (333–34; emphasis mine). The two end up sleeping in the same bed while Tanner is gone, with Sylvie shooting up one last time before joining the girl and falling asleep. One night, June fondles Sylvie's breasts and takes her nipple into her mouth. As she does so, she is "poised for Sylvie to protest, to stir. But she did not. Nor did she when June's hand slid down and nestled in the burning cup of her long legs, not moving, nor stirring, neither wanting the other to wake" (334). That this sexual contact is of a piece with the strange intimacy they experience through their mutual devouring of Dunant's memoir is signaled by the narrator's description of June "pull[ing] back the blanket *as if it were the frail leaf of an antique book*" as she begins her explorations of Sylvie's body (334; emphasis mine).

To the extent that readers are moved to identify with Sylvie as a humanitarian figure, what they find reflected back to them is an angel of mercy who acts not out of a kind of Dunantian disinterest but in response to her own childhood trauma of war—one who seeks some measure of solace and pleasure in the "pain and bliss" she and June share. Her relationship to the girl is aptly conveyed by Slaughter's description of the self-congratulatory conception of humanitarian identification he finds problematic, which involves "imagining ourselves in an *adoptive* relation with the agonies of another."[22] While Sylvie's motivations are legible psychologically, they are also compromised by the desires and trauma that fuel them. Her interest in others is shot through with a damaged and damaging narcissism, which was apparent in her relationship to Jim but emerges fully blown in the one she develops with June.

That such forms of sympathy pose a threat to both its objects and subjects is the larger point that *The Surrendered* makes about the humanitarianism that Sylvie exemplifies, for Sylvie—after having fueled and then frustrated June's fantasy of becoming adopted by her (she does acquiesce to Tanner's disapproval)—gives the girl, as meager recompense, the copy of *A Memory of Solferino* that her parents had given her and that they had devoured together. Rather than engendering June's gratitude, however, it provokes a suicidal and homicidal rage. In being denied the possibility of becoming a grateful orphan, she becomes a figure of wayward vengeance. June sets fire to the orphanage in an attempt to kill herself and Min, another seemingly unadoptable orphan. While June survives, Min, Sylvie, and Tanner all perish in it. Disturbingly, there is a kind of poetic justice to Sylvie's death, for it underscores how her humanitarian intimacy was driven by a self-immolating narcissism.

The other non-Korean protagonist of *The Surrendered*, Hector Brennan, also attempts in his own way to be an angel of mercy. Like Phillips's Leavitt, Hector recalls the figure of the US GI as a savior of Korean children. When he first encounters June, Hector is making his way to the orphanage run by Sylvie and Tanner. He has been dishonorably discharged and has no interest in returning to the United States, and Reverend Hong, who established the orphanage, had offered him a job there. When they first meet, June is close to dying of hunger and thirst. Despite her desperate state, she is immediately fearful of him: she resists his overtures of help, and he has to knock her unconscious to keep her from running off. When she awakens, she checks to make sure she has not been sexually assaulted, and the only thing that keeps her from fleeing is Hector's offer of water and chewing gum. He does convince her to follow him, but she does so with significant trepidation. Their initial exchange significantly revises the scenarios we have come across in the previous chapters. Hector's offer of aid is initially met with fear and suspicion because, it would seem, June's prior experiences with US soldiers have led her to see them as sexual threats. And while she does accept the customary candy, June does not become the meet recipient of his altruism—an orphan grateful for the refuge to which he leads her. Instead, she ends up killing the woman both of them love when she sets fire to the orphanage.

Hector makes a second gesture of altruism when he marries June and brings her with him to the United States. He mistakenly holds himself responsible for the fire that took Sylvie's life: he hadn't checked the stoves in the orphanage that night as he usually did because he was so distraught by Sylvie's announcement that they had to end their affair. He also erroneously believes that Sylvie would have adopted June, and his proposal of marriage to June is, he reflects, his "lame mode of apology" (366). By taking June as his wife, he seeks to bring to fruition a semblance of the dream Sylvie had encouraged in June of a future life in America. June, however, is hardly the eager and appreciative war bride: "He never touched her, except that final night before their agreed-upon separation, when she had plied him with more liquor after he'd come home from a night's drinking and then later startled him from his dead man's sleep, straddling him as he spasmed awake. She left their flat right then, leaving him with the feeling that he'd been not so much used as robbed" (305).

Some three decades later, Hector is conscripted into more acts of altruism when he is approached by the adult June, who is now dying of cancer. She reveals to him that the product of their single coupling was a son, Nicholas, who has been living in Europe for the past eight years and from whom she has become estranged. She implores Hector to help her find him so that they can be reconciled before she dies. He reluctantly agrees to come with her to Italy, where Nicholas's last postcards were sent from. While anticipating their meeting kindles in Hector a paternal curiosity and even longing, he soon meets a young man who turns out to be "a liar and a cheat, a world-class shit" (350). But in fact, the Nicholas he tracks down is an imposter—"an Asian-British man" rather improbably "named Nicky Crump" (302). It turns out that Nicky and Nicholas had been small-time criminals, grifters who had partnered in various scams. Nicholas had died in an accident, and Nicky had been impersonating him in postcards he sent to June asking her for money. Nonetheless, through the threat of violence, Hector forces Nicky into a final imposture by paying final respects to June. He thereby enables June to die with a measure of peace, but only by stage managing a wholly fictitious familial reconciliation.

Hector performs a final act of mercy for June in the novel's closing pages. He carries the dying June to the chapel in Solferino, allowing her to take her last breath in a site that she knew held a quasi-sacred meaning for Sylvie and thus for herself; he does this even after June confesses that she had set the fire. It is telling, however, that Hector's ultimate gestures of generosity entail a good dose of deception, even a sense of betrayal—that he only succeeds in being the kind of angel of mercy who eases the suffering of a dying woman by lying to her. But in the moral universe Lee depicts in this novel, this is as good as it gets. Not only are all motivations—even altruistic ones—shown to be impure, but so are the gestures in which they culminate.

To return then to the issue of the identifications that humanitarian narratives elicit, we are left with the question of what kind of reactions are invited by the two figures who resemble the typical protagonists of such fictions produced during the Korean War. Hector and Sylvie ought to function as versions of the "third actor" that is, in Slaughter's account, the decisive feature of humanitarian dramas: "the humanitarian figure who is an exemplary extension of our better angels."[23] But while they invite the reader's sympathy, they offer no place of psychic refuge. They do not allow the reader to indulge vicariously in an experience of humanitarian goodwill and beneficence. The disturbing power of Lee's novel stems from the fact that it offers up humanitarian protagonists with whom readers cannot *help but* identify—the soldier and the missionary—and then disfigures the sympathies it elicits. It also features a victim—the war orphan—who turns out to be not the grateful object of humanitarian largesse but a subject of vengeful violence.

Ultimately, the figure from the novel whom readers come to resemble most is Benjamin Li, the Communist insurgent who is tortured by his Japanese captors in an exceptionally sadistic way:

When the [Japanese] officer stepped back Benjamin's eyes were bloodied; they looked as if they had been gouged out. But the officer roughly wiped them with his sleeve and it was clear what he had done: he had cut away only the eyelids. The eyes themselves were intact, the orbs monstrous, for being so exposed. His was a fleshy skull. They retied his hands so that they were secured behind his back.

"Watch now, you son of a bitch."

The officer sharply gave an order and one of the soldiers stood over Sylvie and began unbuckling his belt.

It was then that Benjamin began screaming again. He was screaming bloody murder, all the names of his compatriots, screaming them in a litany, most loudly his own. (230–31)

In the family name given to this figure—Li, which is a homonym for the author's own—the novel suggests his own positionality. However, his first name, Benjamin, suggests a sardonic reference to another author, the one whose essay, referenced earlier, contains this famous description of the angel of history: "A Klee painting named 'Angelus Novus' shows an angel looking as though he is about to move away from something he is fixedly contemplating. His eyes are staring, his mouth is open, his wings are spread. This is how one pictures the angel of history. His face is turned toward the past. Where we perceive a chain of events, he sees one single catastrophe which keeps piling wreckage upon wreckage and hurls it in front of his feet" (257). In the end, I argue, the great power of Lee's *The Surrendered* derives from the fact that the only viable ethical position it allows US readers to cling to is one that is *historical* and resonates with this passage. Through this novel, readers come to resemble not only Benjamin Li but also the angel of history evoked by Walter Benjamin.[24] In turning our faces to the past to confront a largely forgotten war, we come to see the chain of events that leads from then to now as a single catastrophe. In confronting the wreckage resulting from the United States' attempt to function as an angel of mercy in the multiple wars it has engaged in since 1950, we come to recognize that whatever humanitarian justifications have been made for such interventions, they have brought the most tragic of unintended consequences to those the country has ostensibly tried to save—breeding in them not gratitude and love but their opposite, making them into wayward angels of vengeance.

* * *

In the next chapter, I continue the analysis of Lee's *The Surrendered* and also examine another novel written by a Korean American author—Susan Choi's *The Foreign Student*—for the ways in which they both reverse the gaze of the Korean War humanitarian Orientalism examined in part 1 of this study. Through the Korean protagonists of these works—examples of what Josephine Park terms "the friendly," whose survival depends on being enfolded within US military and humanitarian formations—Lee and Choi explore not only the complexities of the traumas that haunt immigrants who are survivors of war but also the profound and ferocious ambivalence that structures their orientation to the interracial and transnational intimacies that enabled their putative rescue from the violence of war. These novels are also significant, as we shall see, for the ways in which they both refract and ultimately destabilize a Korean diasporic cultural politics that would wholly conflate identity with the injurious trauma of the war.

"Bled in, Letter by Letter"

Postmemory and the Subject of Korean War History

As may be discernible from the account of Chang-rae Lee's *The Surrendered* in the previous chapter, significant elements of the novel make it difficult to characterize it as a realist work—at the very least, they force readers to confront its artifice. Take the character of Hector, for instance, who is from a town in upstate New York rather implausibly named Ilion, which happens to be the home of the Remington Arms company. Moreover, as the novel slowly reveals, Hector is quite literally an immortal—impervious to age and injury. In addition to wearing its Homeric allusions on its sleeve, *The Surrendered* is structured by turns of event that are contrivances of the highest order. For instance, the son Hector never knew he had turns out to be an imposter who happens to share the same name and biracial background. Throughout the novel, characters appear and die in extraordinarily convenient moments as far as the plot is concerned, often in ways that meld together the operatic and the banal, high tragedy and bathos.

I want to begin this chapter by considering how the antirealist elements of Lee's novel might be interpreted as an attempt to thwart the expectations readers might bring to a Korean American novel about the Korean War. Those assumptions are suggested by Lee himself in his account of the motivations behind the writing of *The Surrendered*. In the short essay on the novel's Amazon.com webpage, Lee recounts that its origins lay in conversations he had with his father. These were prompted by a seminar in modern Korean history that Lee was taking in college at the time: he had wanted to write a final paper that would be "a reporter-at-large-type piece that would offer personal testimony and narrative set against a historical backdrop." During their discussions, his father revealed that he had watched his own brother die during the war. Lee writes, "The kernel of what had happened grew to become the first chapter of *The Surrendered.*"[1] While I will return later in this chapter to the story told by Lee's father, I want to add that Susan Choi, the other Korean American author whose writings will be the primary focus of this chapter, tells a comparable story about how she came to write her Korean War novel, *The Foreign Student* (1998).

In a profile in the *South Bend Tribune,* Choi recounts that part of her motivation was simply a desire to know more about her father's life and particularly about his experiences in Korea, which he left in the 1950s to attend college at Sewanee, The University of the South. She began with an "eight-page fragment" based on these early conversations, which she produced while pursuing a master of fine arts degree at Cornell in 1994.[2] As she started to work in earnest on *The Foreign Student* some time later, she began to ask her father for more details. She quickly realized that understanding her father's experiences in Korea would require remedying her own ignorance about the war that shaped them: "I was very conscious that even Americans who are up on history are remarkably ignorant about the Korean War. . . . I consider myself American—I was born in Indiana and raised here—but I didn't know a thing about this war."[3] As she began conducting her own research into the conflict, she experienced "amazement and discomfort" over the fact "that not only did our nation fight this war, but it was responsible for the causes for the war." She began to feel a sense of "indignation" and developed a political belief "that this war shouldn't [have] occurred."[4]

Lee and Choi both speak of a longing for a greater personal knowledge about an obscure family history shaped by the Korean War as a motivating factor in the novels they wrote. In learning more about these familial pasts, both authors developed a greater historical awareness of an event that shaped the lives of so many immigrants who began arriving in the United States in significant numbers after the 1965 immigration reforms. For Choi at least, this historical knowledge produced an "outrage" directed, at least in part, at the United States. Both *The Foreign Student* and *The Surrendered* are thus animated by a desire to make these two levels of memory—one familial and the other national—available as objects of a wider cultural knowledge: to make this conflict and its effects on Koreans and Korean Americans part of American historical memory. The stories of how these novels took shape affirm Grace M. Cho's contention that "the Korean diaspora in the United States has been haunted by the traumatic effects of what we are not allowed to know—the terror and devastation inflicted by the Korean War, the failure to resolve it, and the multiple silences surrounding this violent history."[5]

That having been said, it is worth taking seriously how insistently these authors underline the fictional nature of their works. While Choi acknowledges that many of her protagonist's experiences were based on events that had happened to her own father, she insists that she was only able to produce her novel once her father briefly mentioned a white woman who had befriended him when he first arrived at Sewanee. This small detail led Choi to create the character of Katherine Monroe, a white woman whom the fictional Chang Ahn falls in love with. As she explains in an interview, "Katherine was never meant to be such a principal character; she was originally meant to be just one of many people Chuck meets in the U.S. But she was very aggressive. She kept annexing more and more of the book."[6] However, once this character emerged, the Choi's manuscript "became a novel and stopped serving as biography."[7]

So, to state the obvious, *The Foreign Student* and *The Surrendered* should not be treated as if they were nonfiction accounts of what took place, as if they were witness statements, biographies, or oral histories. Choi wryly notes that her father was quite aware of the kind of work she was producing: "When I told him that the novel would be different, that I was changing it to make the story better, he said, 'I know what fiction is.'"[8] Lee offers a similar caveat when he discusses how he reshaped his father's anecdote in his novel: "Naturally the details changed quite drastically as I began to write, the story expanding in every direction, developing its own world and aims, and *soon enough it was not my father's story at all*."[9] While such statements might seem like generic pronouncements one often hears from authors, they take on a vital and particular significance in terms of how these novels engage with what we might think of as the literary politics of identity.

Given that Lee and Choi are both Korean American, we might expect their novels to be driven by a desire to generate a sense of imagined community among Korean American subjects by positing a shared history of traumatic loss—one that promises an intergenerational reunification, breaching the gap of silence that separates survivors and their descendants through the entanglement of their memories. However, the sense of intimacy these novels seek to engender is not primarily based

on ethnicity or familial connection. Both authors take pains to emphasize in their novels that being the children of immigrants who survived
this conflict does not grant them the epistemological or ethical authority to definitively say what their parents endured, and Choi's novel
in particular, as we shall see, engages in a rather expansive politics of
identity.

"Authenticity Ultimately Lay in the Story You Could Tell": *The Surrendered*

In returning to Lee's novel, I first want to take up the story the author's
father told him that served as the "kernel" that "grew to become the
first chapter of *The Surrendered*." In the early days of the war, the elder
Lee's family, which was from Pyongyang, "had joined the throngs of
refugees who were heading south in an attempt to get behind the line
of American forces." They had been forced to leave behind a "favorite
older cousin" because she was pregnant and had gone into labor just as
they were about to depart. "Telling that story of his cousin," Lee recalls,
"seemed to break the grip of something on my father," and he went on
to recount how

> his brother had been killed . . . by a boxcar of a train full of refugees. They
> were among the hundreds who filled the cars. The car holding the rest of
> their family was packed tight, so he and his brother had to sleep on top
> of the boxcar. In the middle of the night the train halted violently, and his
> brother, who was eight years old, fell off, the train then lurching forward
> for a short distance. My father jumped down and went back and found
> his brother, whose leg had been amputated by the wheels of the train.
> My father carried him back to the car, to the rest of their family, as the
> blood—and his life—ran out of him.[10]

Lee writes that this story "haunted" him not only because of "the horror
of the accident" but also for the altered perspective it gave him of his
father. It put before him "the picture of my father as a boy, a boy who
had to experience his brother's death so directly and egregiously. I was
struck, too, by how unperturbed my father had always seemed to me,
this cheerful, optimistic man who certainly didn't appear to be haunted

by anything. But of course this was not quite true. The events of the war had stayed with him, and always would."[11] Lee's anecdote speaks to the experiences of many Korean Americans whose parents were part of the first wave of Koreans arriving in the United States. It suggests that the "model minority" identity that many took on—the "cheerful, optimistic" demeanor they may have assumed—is nonetheless haunted by the horrific experiences of war they had witnessed and lived through, experiences they may well have refrained from sharing with their US-born children. Discernible as well in Lee's essay is a familiar Asian American narrative of intergenerational reconciliation in which the second generation comes to a greater understanding of the immigrant generation by gaining a sense of the traumas they had suffered in the home country. In fact, an incipient version of this narrative of intergenerational intimacy serves as a central plotline of *The Surrendered*. It does not, however, reach the conclusion we might expect.

Unlike Chang in *The Foreign Student*, who clearly invites comparisons with the actual person on whom he is based, June, Lee's protagonist, is presented as a more explicitly fictional creation. If Hector's name calls to mind the Trojan War, June's suggests the conflict that has shaped her existence, for it is also the name of the month in which the Korean War is officially considered to have begun. The basic outline of her life in the United States further suggests her symbolic function as a kind of synecdoche for the generation of Korean immigrants that came to the United States in the years after the war, for she assumes a kind of model minority life after her emigration, rising from humble origins to attain financial success as an antiques dealer in New York City and raising a high-achieving son, Nicholas.

What happens to her in the first chapter, moreover, is suggested as a microcosm of the horrors that many ordinary Koreans endured as refugees. It introduces us to June at age eleven or twelve and relates the events that left her orphaned. She is traveling with her two surviving siblings, a younger brother and sister who are fraternal twins. Their father had been executed by an anti-Communist militia and their older brother forcibly conscripted into the Republic of Korea Army (ROKA). Their older sister and mother had been accidentally killed during a US air attack that had, ironically, saved the older sister from being raped by South Korean soldiers. Lee's narrator suggests that the randomness with which survival and death are meted out have been indelibly stamped on June's psyche: "You could never anticipate what might happen next, the earth-shattering and the trivial interspersing with the cruelest irony. You could be saved by pure chance, or else ruined. That was the terror of it, what kept June awake at night and stole her breath through the day, though *it was the terror that was also forming her into her destined shape, feeding the being of her vigilance until it had grown into the whole of her, pushing out everything else.*"[12] June views herself and her two younger siblings as "the last of their kind," and she watches over them "in a state of animal vigilance" (24). Only in dreams is her relentless watchfulness suspended, and she can become again the girl she had once been:

> She cast a stony front to the world but in her sleep's throes it was for the moment vanquished and she was once again the child she had been on the eve of the war, a too-tall, soft-spoken girl of eleven who was content to play with much younger children, who was still too shy to look the village boys in the eyes, who wanted nothing more than to sit in her father's lap and hum along with his records while he drew on his corncob pipe, the smoke hanging fatly and sweetly about them. (26)

June loses her remaining siblings when the two of them are thrown from the top of a boxcar they had climbed on as part of a mass of refugees fleeing the fighting. June jumps down from the car to discover that her younger sister, Hee Soo, is dead and that her younger brother, Ji-Young, is mortally wounded, one of his legs having been amputated by the train. She is faced with the wrenching decision to either stay with her dying brother or abandon him in order to survive. While he initially asks her to stay with him, he soon tells her,

> "It's okay. You don't have to."
>   She let go his still-warm hand, kissed his still-warm face. She stayed with him as long as she could. But when the last car of the train passed her she rose to her feet and steadied herself. And then she ran for her life. (30)

The novel goes on to suggest how such events established the basic shape of June's personality.

Indeed, the qualities that enabled her to survive—the "stony front" and "animal vigilance"—persist in her American life. They make her a formidable businesswoman, but they also impede the forms of intimacy she is able to enjoy with her loved ones. "Her talent, her gift," the narrator offers, "was an instantly patent resolve, so that both longtime acquaintances and strangers . . . encountered an equally intransigent edifice, this deep-rooted stone" (44). Later in the novel, the narrator recounts June reflecting on this capacity: "Even before they [her family] had all perished, or vanished, she had had a heart that craved more readily than it accepted, she could look upon the face of a beloved with no ill reason or malice and in an instant cleave herself from the bond. It was an effortlessly monstrous ability, as if she could simply pluck from her heel a spur called love, her own cool blood the quickest antidote" (323). Significantly, June thinks of this "monstrous ability" as something she has always possessed, even before the war, but the first chapter suggests that the personality traits she has come to view as an intrinsic quality of her "heart" were are a product of its violence.[13]

As the dying June reflects on her relationship with her son, she seems to believe that their estrangement is a consequence of these qualities, which she has passed on to her son. Her memories of Nicholas reveal a boy with a preternatural gift for independence and self-reliance—a virtual mirror of the qualities that define his mother: "He never appeared to be cowed by her, or demoralized. He always seemed happy enough. Aside from his scholarly ability, his teachers always told her in conferences that he was one of the more popular boys. But perhaps in the face of her, the sheer steep wall, he had receded like any child would, measure by imperceptible measure, until one day he must have seen the distance to be startling, and acceptable" (45). The "sense of independence" Nicholas develops concerns June, for she "couldn't help but wonder if it was a quality of his that was already too evolved" (49). Her memories of how she responded when awakened by the sounds of him crying in his sleep when he was a young boy suggest how she might have inculcated this quality in her son: "He wasn't deeply distressed—it was the softest crying, self-muffled, if that was possible—and although it would have been the simplest thing to wake and comfort him, she inexplicably stood over him in the dark, staring at his racked mouth and the tight, quivering shrug of his shoulders, and it took everything in her to renounce the thought that here was a boy she would have to carry about forever" (240). By establishing the war as the shadowy cause of the fractured intimacy of this Korean mother and her American-born son, Lee's novel sets in motion a narrative trajectory that readers might expect to culminate in the intergenerational reconciliation June longs for, one that would heal the hidden wounds of a long-ended conflict. The more immediate source of her guilt toward Nicholas as she faces her death is her response to a call she had received not long after she began cancer treatments. Nicholas went to Europe after high school, but this gap-year trip had extended to eight years. During this time, their only contact had been occasional postcards from various locations, often asking for money. One night she answers the phone to hear "an Englishwoman's voice on the other end, saying that her son was badly injured." June, however, "was still mostly asleep and terribly sick, perhaps out of her mind at the time with a third round of treatments, and she'd somehow blurted out that she had no son and hung up" (50). June devotes the short remainder of her life to seeking out her son. And the reunion that eventually takes place is a sham: it is with a con man who has been impersonating her son and has been stage-managed by Hector.

By rather ostentatiously withholding the expected resolution of the narrative of intergenerational reconciliation it partially unfolds, *The Surrendered* suggests that it is not a novel primarily seeking to make the trauma inflicted by the war on immigrants, which travels into the next generation, foundational to a Korean American or Korean diasporic identity. A key passage explaining how the murky provenance of the antiques that June sells becomes imbued with a sense of authenticity highlights the fabricated status of the novel: "Fakes abounded in every era, most of them poorly done, but there were always a few masterfully executed works. Of course, for the vast majority of non-auction-house items there was only the experienced eye and what one could say about them without simply lying or even sounding like a prevaricator. Authenticity ultimately lay in the story you could tell, a tale most effective when it was at once fanciful and mundane" (246). This passage invites readers to see *The Surrendered* as a "masterfully executed" fake, a Korean American novel about the Korean War whose aura of authenticity derives most from the story Lee is able to tell, a story "at once fanciful and mundane" but that should not be assumed to be the real thing.

That the novel seems to renege on its promise to provide a story that would culminate in the emergence of a Korean American intergenerational intimacy might reflect its author's recognition of certain ethical pitfalls that attend works of cultural memory that return to a formative moment of historical trauma in order to construct an "authentic" sense of minority identity. This critique, which is implicit in Lee's Korean War novel, emerges more explicitly in Choi's.

The Foreign Student and the Subject of Korean War History

On the surface, *The Foreign Student* hews much more closely to readers' expectations than *The Surrendered*, especially in regards to the author's story of its composition. Its protagonist, Chang Ahn, is modeled on her father, and its third-person narrator fleshes out a relatively extensive historical account of the war that seems to be based on Bruce Cumings's scholarship. Nonetheless, as I will demonstrate, Choi's is also a self-reflexive novel, one that calls attention to its own fictive status in more subtle though pervasive ways. Through these metafictional elements, *The Foreign Student* strives to make its readers aware—most dramatically through the motif of translation that permeates it—that it seeks to disrupt the literary identity politics in which it is also necessarily engaged.

The Foreign Student is mainly set in 1955 in Sewanee, Tennessee, where Chang has arrived to start his new life as a student at the University of the South. As the beneficiary of a Christian charity that has arranged for his immigration and a scholarship to the university, he assumes the American name Chuck and soon falls in love with Katherine Monroe, a local woman. Katherine, however, is already romantically entangled with the much older Charles Addison, an affair that began when she was fourteen. Despite their mutual attraction, neither Katherine nor Chang is initially willing to begin a relationship. Through a fortuitous turn of events, Katherine breaks off her engagement to Charles, and the two star-crossed lovers, as it were, act on their desire for each other. When the novel ends, Chang has lost his scholarship but continues to attend college, supporting himself by working as a member of the domestic staff. Interspersed throughout are flashbacks to Chang's and Katherine's earlier lives, and the novel as a whole is recounted by a third-person narrator.

While the novel's title refers to its protagonist, Chang, it has another implicit referent as well: its American readers, who become increasingly immersed in a history that is likely quite foreign to them. This pedagogical imperative of *The Foreign Student* is announced early in a highly self-conscious scene in which Chang gives a slide-show presentation to an audience of churchgoers as a gesture of gratitude to the Christian charity for funding his scholarship. In the presentation, Chang acts as a kind of informal historian and native informant, providing his audience with what would seem to be an insider's view of Korea and the Korean War. The predicament Chang faces in this scene mirrors the author's own.

In giving such presentations, Chang "always felt hopeless, called upon to deliver a clear explanation of the war. It defied explanation."[14] He resorts to using terms that will resonate with his Southern audience, however inapt the analogies might seem to be: "'Korea is a shape just like Florida. Yes? The top half is a Communist state, and the bottom half are fighting for democracy!' He would groundlessly compare the parallel to the Mason-Dixon line, and see every head nod excitely. 'In June 1950, the Communist army comes over the parallel and invades the South. They come by surprise, and get almost all to the sea.'" Chang offers another related analogy when he describes how the US-led coalition was nearly defeated in the early days of the war: "The Communists go fast, until the UN force is crowded into a very little space at the bottom of Korea, around the city Pusan. . . . This is like, if the war is all over Florida, and our side are trapped in Miami" (51). Chang's narrative concludes with an account of how MacArthur's landing at Inchon turned the tide of the war.

Koreans—or, at least, those in the South—do figure prominently in this account of the war, for it was their freedom and their loyalty to the West that American military intervention secured. Chang begins his lectures with "I'm not here, if this doesn't happen," his way of saying that, in the narrator's words, "his presence before them was the direct result of MacArthur's Inchon landing" (50). He is apparently regarded as someone who, in coming to America, has been saved not only from Communism but from the primitivism that would have otherwise been his birthright. As his audience is "only fascinated by Oriental things" (54), his lectures venture into ethnography, as Chang "generally explained that Koreans were farmers, that they enjoyed celebrating their holidays clad in bright costumes, that they were fond of flowers and children." He also presents slides he had made "from a set of National Archive photographs of Korea" (39) and finds that his audience responds especially well to ones captioned "Water Buffalo in Rice Paddy" and "Village Farmers Squatting Down to Smoke": "Everyone murmured with pleasure at the image of the farmers, in their year-round pajamas and inscrutable Eskimo faces" (52). These Americans want to see Koreans as a simple, gentle people worthy of their military protection and to see themselves as belonging to a nation powerful and benevolent enough to have provided it. Chang's presentation answers both of these desires.

Overall, Chang's narrative conforms to the larger ones in US culture encountered earlier in this study, and the narrator refers to it as "a potted history of the war" (39). At the most basic level, the historiographical mission of *The Foreign Student* is to highlight the complexities that dominant depictions of the war subordinate or leave out. Chang's presentation covers only a period of three months: from the invasion of North Korean forces on June 25, 1950, to MacArthur's landing at Inchon on September 15. Later chapters fill in the basic details of what took place over the next three years: the entry of the Chinese in November, the counterattack that pushed the United Nations (UN) force south of the thirty-eighth parallel, and the stalemated trench warfare and fitful negotiations that marked the remaining years of fighting, which officially came to an end on July 27, 1953. This is the Korean War as it is generally known to Americans.

Choi's novel, however, breaks out of the usual temporal frame of reference (1950–53) and narrates events dating back to the period of Japanese colonization, a reperiodization crucial to *The Foreign Student*'s historiographical project. In so doing, the novel locates the origins of the Korean War in the period of Japanese colonial rule, which began in 1910. Chang was born in 1930, and his family actually thrived within the power structure installed by the Japanese, which tended to reinforce the hierarchies of the feudal order it ostensibly replaced. He and his father were model colonial subjects. A member of the scholar, or *yangban*, class, the elder Chang "had been one of the small class of Koreans selected for the Japanese Imperial University in the 1920s" (69); Chang himself would have been sent to Tokyo to study had the liberation not intervened. With the end of Japanese rule in 1945, Chang begins to mingle with working-class students for the first time. He forms a close friendship with one of them, Kim, who becomes part of the Communist insurgency. Chang, by contrast, is drawn to the Americans, who are presented as the new colonial power in Korea. Through the divergent political allegiances formed by these two friends, Choi renders the tensions that would eventually pull the country apart, suggesting that the "groundless" parallel Chang had drawn between the thirty-eighth parallel and the Mason-Dixon line contains a kernel of truth, for the Korean War was also a civil war.

Indeed, the novel's historical view of the conflict is largely in accord with the perspective outlined in the first chapter of this study, which is based on Bruce Cumings's scholarship. Choi herself seems to have drawn heavily from Cumings's work. For one thing, her novel brings attention to the crucial five years between the end of World War II and the official beginning of the Korean War, which marked the transition from the colonial order imposed by the Japanese to the one established by the United States south of the thirty-eighth parallel. In its account of the decision to partition the peninsula, the novel emphasizes, much as Cumings does, the offhandedness with which US military commanders reached the decision to partition the Korean peninsula: "With two atom bombs days before having leveled Japan, the problem of how to administer Japan's former possession was not the most absorbing, and the time at the table was brief. They chose the thirty-eighth parallel, latitude north. It was on everybody's map" (63).

The Foreign Student does not actually have much to say about the regime that took shape in the North, only noting that the leader the Soviets installed was "a great people's hero, a revolutionary who had fought the Japanese throughout the thirties" (51). A sympathetic portrait of Koreans who allied themselves with the Communist cause emerges through the character of Kim: because he is presented as principled, the political position he represents is granted a certain legitimacy.

It is the United States and the government it had propped up in the South that receive the brunt of the novel's criticism. In a virtual gloss of Cumings's account, the novel describes Syngman Rhee, the man installed as the president of South Korea, as "bellicose, paranoid, and so undiscouragably determined to declare war on the Communist North that the United States deliberately underequipped his security forces" (64) and the government he leads as "repressive, incompetent, and stupendously unpopular," generating an upsurge in "peasant uprisings" and "antigovernment, proleftist insurrections" (65). To quell these, General John Hodge turns first to the hated National Police, whose ranks were filled with Koreans who had collaborated with the Japanese, and he then creates the ROKA. By 1949, the novel suggests, a low-grade civil war was already well under way in the South.

Choi's novel exposes the counterinsurgency tactics used by the National Police and the ROKA, the violence with which they conscripted civilians, the torture they inflicted on prisoners and on anyone deemed disloyal, and the mass executions. And since the illegitimate and repressive regime that committed such atrocities had been created and supported by the United States, the history of the Korean War is not actually a foreign history, the novel insists, but one in which Americans are fully implicated. Moreover, the novel also documents the devastating air war US military commanders unleashed that sought to turn the North into a "wasteland": "Anything that could be located, within a generous margin of error, was intensively bombed. 'Sinuiju,' the information office announced, 'has been removed from the map.' Towns and factories were bombed flat, burned out, plowed under, removed from the map" (186).

To a significant extent, *The Foreign Student* offers a literary elaboration of Cumings's postcolonial historiography of the Korean War. However, I would also point out that only four of the novel's fourteen chapters are set in Korea. The bulk of the narrative is actually devoted to the new life Chang builds in the United States and highlights his status as a racialized immigrant trying to find his way in the racial landscape of the United States. In this respect, *The Foreign Student* is also driven by a second historiographical imperative shared by my book as well: it asks its readers to ponder the Korean War's relevance to US domestic histories of race.

"They Don't Know What to Make Me": The Fictive Parallels of Race

The central domestic drama in the novel pivots around the interracial romance between Chang and Katherine, and Choi's use of its Southern setting asks readers to consider the position her Korean protagonist occupies in the black-white racial landscape of that region at midcentury.

An early scene describes Chang and Katherine stopping by a gas station attached to a small café. While she had been there many times before without arousing any interest, this time she and Chuck draw the focused attention of the employees and customers, who are all white. The reader's expectations of how such a scene might culminate are drawn out, but nothing actually happens: "They might have been watching a ship come in, Katherine thought. For a moment she could feel it. The arrival in a strange land, and stepping onto the gangplank as the whole harbor paused in its work and turned a single gaze toward you. She stood there with him in a half circle of constant, unshy observation until she had paid the boy and they had emptied their glasses and slowly walked back to her car" (37). Katherine's vision of a stranger disembarking from a ship calls to mind the immigrant masses who enjoy a privileged place in American mythology, but it also evokes the forced migration that brought Africans to these shores by slave ship. An ambiguity thus emerges as to whether white Southerners will associate Chang with blacks or see him as simply a curious kind of foreign newcomer. That the scene ends without violence suggests that the latter is the case, but what he says to Katherine as they drive away underscores the racial inscrutability that shrouds him: "They don't know what to make me" (37).

The question of whether the violently enforced taboo against black-white miscegenation applies to Chang is raised in several other scenes, most of which involve his college roommate, Crane, whose father is a Grand Dragon in the Ku Klux Klan. Crane hopes to provoke an incident by inviting Chang home for Thanksgiving, though he is unsure of what his father's reaction will be. As it turns out, the elder Crane is unperturbed, eminently polite if condescending. In offering his guest a serving of turkey, he seems to be offering something else as well: "When you look back, Mr. Ahn, on your first years in America, on your first lessons in things American, you will think of the Cranes. I am giving you white meat and dark. You will develop a preference in time. You may develop a preference right away. If you do, exercise it" (60). The ironic sexual symbolism of this gesture is hard to miss. Rather than being affronted by the appearance of this nonwhite guest at his dinner table, Mr. Crane, an elder in the Klan, seems willing to grant this "emissary from a distant land" an honor that his organization would forcibly reserve only for white men: the prerogative to choose freely between white meat and dark (59).

Despite the honorary whiteness that Mr. Crane and some other white Southerners appear willing to grant him, Chang keeps himself at a remove from the racial privilege they enjoy.[15] This is due to his seemingly intuitive sense that his position is somehow more comparable to that of the black staff of the college. "In his first week," the narrator recounts, "he'd shaken hands with the colored table servant at formal Friday dinner" (15). Later he addresses a "negro busboy" at a posh restaurant "as if they were both guests at a surprising and solemn affair" (146). Over the Christmas break, however, when he is the only student left in the dormitory, Chang realizes the extent of the distance that separates him from the black men who work for the college. As he enters the dining hall to join them for dinner, he finds them eating together in the kitchen, listening to jazz and talking. His presence makes them uneasy, however, and he realizes that to these men, "the desolate interval between the fall and spring terms was a time of simplicity and freedom, and he embodied the force of observation from which they'd expected a reprieve" (167). To them, Chang is aligned with a whiteness "embodied" primarily as a "force of observation" even though he, too, has been subjected to its discriminating gaze. Chang is thus located in a domestic version of the racial demilitarized zone (DMZ), stranded in the borderlands between black and white but a citizen of neither realm.[16]

By the end of *The Foreign Student*, however, Chang does come to occupy a position that places him alongside blackness without being incorporated into it. When he is accused of theft, Chang is stripped of the scholarship that enabled him to come to Sewanee. He is able to continue his studies, however, by becoming part of the college's domestic staff, a change in status that results in his being accepted, albeit partially, by this community of black working men: "He got along well with these men. They never peered into his thoughtful silences, but they accepted him with humor, and their company sheltered him" (324).

A related and somewhat comparable set of issues concerning Chang's racial location are explored in the tenth chapter of the novel, which marks a striking departure. It takes place in the summer after Chang's first year of college, when he temporarily joins a community in Chicago's Little Tokyo, an ethnic enclave in which Asians from various homelands have begun to transform themselves into Asian Americans. His sojourn there is precipitated by the news that Katherine has become engaged to Charles. Through the assistance of a dean, he finds a job in Chicago in a bookbindery. In this chapter, *The Foreign Student* seems to transform momentarily into a different kind of novel in which its protagonist is reconstructed as a prototypical Asian immigrant subject.

In contrast to the American South, Chang seems to take on a coherent racial identity from the moment he embarks on the bus ride that will take him north. A young white boy, who claims to know about "gooks," is immediately drawn to him. The boy has gained this knowledge from a brother who fought in the war, but he also seems to think that Chang is a "Chinaman" headed to Chinatown, "where they've got a place where they've got sharks and giant snakes and monkeys hung in the windows to eat" (229). Soon after his arrival in Chicago, Chang is approached by "an Oriental man" who gives him a card advertising a massage parlor on "North Clark Street, Little Tokyo." He makes his way to that neighborhood and takes a room in a "boardinghouse occupied entirely by Japanese men" (241). He is soon "adopted" by "the neighborhood people" (243), joining in poker games and going with them to Cubs games. What happens to Chang is happening to other Asians across the city: "If these people knew he was Korean, they didn't seem to care. Arriving Filipinos were eagerly courted by Japanese massage-house proprietors, and Japanese teenagers rode the El to Chinatown to work in the restaurants. Old prejudices were irrelevant and unprofitable" (244). All of these newcomers are becoming subjects of a nascent Asian America, an identity predicated on the blurring of ethnic distinctions. His new Japanese American friends take to calling Chang "Sensei Einstein," because they "took him for the thing he dreamed of being, a scholar. At the Belmont Noodle House he was allowed to sit for hours with his books, his empty bowl shoved aside, his teacup kept endlessly full, although the restaurant had just a handful of tables" (247).

While Chang comes to feel at home in Little Tokyo, the novel depicts his assimilation into the Asian American community in Chicago as temporary. "He had known," the narrator tells us, "at the back of his intoxicating happiness here, that he would never really stay" (250). Chang's sojourn concludes with a jarring turn of events: he receives a letter informing him that Katherine and Charles have set their wedding date and that she has gone to New Orleans to visit her dying mother. Soon thereafter, he happens to find a hundred-dollar bill in one of the books he is processing, which he uses to purchase a bus ticket to New Orleans. (For this he will be accused of the theft that will result in his losing his scholarship.) After this chapter, the narrative returns once again to its Southern setting.

In contrast to the confluence of distance and proximity that structures Chang's relationship to the black service staff at the University of the South, the bond that emerges between him and the Japanese American men he befriends in Chicago is a more intimate one. He seems to feel genuinely at home in Little Tokyo, and the question that thus emerges is why Chang's incorporation into an emergent Japanese American and Asian American community is presented as an ultimately untenable option. The answer may lie in the fact that the terms of his assimilation involve the reemergence of the Japanese he had learned as a boy—the language that all Koreans were compelled to learn under the Japanese. His integration into this American interethnic community thus recapitulates the reeducation Koreans underwent when their country was violently integrated into the Japanese Empire—an empire as racist and brutal as any devised by the West. Because this history is referenced by the novel to explain Chang's fluency in the language, it is difficult to view his absorption into this community in purely positive terms despite the fact that it consists of Japanese *Americans*.

However, *The Foreign Student* does not place Chang in juxtaposition to African American and Japanese American characters simply to underscore his difference from them—to emphasize that he cannot simply be slotted into these other racial categories, whether long-standing (black) or newly established (Asian American). In placing these characters alongside Chang, the novel invites readers to consider the *intimacies* of the histories that shape them. So, for example, the novel places Chang in a region of the United States in which profound and tumultuous changes are about to unfold. He arrives in the American South in 1955, the same year Emmett Till was lynched in Money, Mississippi, and Rosa Parks refused to give up her seat to a white man on a bus in Montgomery, Alabama, and one year after the Supreme Court's landmark *Brown v. Board of Education* decision. While none of these events are explicitly referenced by Choi's narration, I would insist that they implicitly hover

around the edges of the frame. By setting the story of a Korean War survivor in an American South about to be transfigured by such events, *The
Foreign Student* invites its readers to consider the sorts of issues I have
examined in part 1 of this study: to explore connections between a civil
war that took place on an East Asian peninsula and a movement for
civil rights that would erupt in earnest in the American South a few
years later. What the novel leads readers to think about, in other words,
is how this domestic history of race is contemporaneous with the transnational history of the Korean War.

While it does not theorize *how* these distinct histories may be related,
it does underscore their contiguity. Readers are thus left with the task of
considering the connection between them. What thus makes *The Foreign Student* such a significant novel for the purposes of this study is
that it, in a sense, launches so many of the historiographical trajectories
I have sought to trace, the kinds of linkages that Lisa Lowe illuminates in
The Intimacies of Four Continents. As such, it "does not foreground comprehensiveness and teleology . . . but rather emphasizes the relationality
and differentiation of peoples, cultures, and societies" and "unsettles the
discretely bounded objects, methods, and temporal frameworks canonized by a national history invested in isolated origins and independent
progressive development."[17]

The "Fact of the Secret" and the "Depth of the Rift"

The *affective* axis of intimacy around which *The Foreign Student*
revolves, however, is the one that emerges between its protagonist and
Katherine. The blurb on the back cover of the paperback edition of the
novel accurately, if melodramatically, highlights this aspect:

> In 1955, a new student arrives at a small college town in the Tennessee
> mountains. Chuck is shy, speaks English haltingly, and on the subject of
> his earlier life in Korea will not speak at all. Then he meets Katherine, a
> beautiful and solitary young woman who, like Chuck, is haunted by some
> dark episode in her past. Without quite knowing why, these two outsiders
> are drawn together, each sensing in the other, the possibility of salva-
> tion. Moving between the American South and South Korea, between an

adolescent girl's sexual awakening and a young man's nightmarish memories of war, *The Foreign Student* is a powerful and emotionally gripping
work of fiction.

The parity suggested here between the two lovers who are "haunted
by some dark episode in [their] past" is reflected in the novel, which
devotes as much attention to Katherine as to Chang. Although their
personal histories are both traumatic, there is nonetheless a tremendous disparity between the forms of suffering each has been afflicted
by—between "an adolescent girl's sexual awakening and a young man's
nightmarish memories of war."

The amount of space that a novel ostensibly about the Korean War
gives to Katherine and the fact that it seems to place her past experiences
on the same plane as Chang's might trouble or frustrate some readers.
However, Katherine's function in the novel is quite crucial. She is, I will
argue, a kind of foil or mirror for the reader, and in that respect, she
serves a vital pedagogical function. If the complex constellation of histories that *The Foreign Student* places before readers is meant to bring
us to a greater critical awareness of the Korean War's historical significance, Katherine models for us the affective response the novel seeks to
engender its readers—she schools us, in other words, on what it means
emotionally to be a "foreign student" of this war.

Read on its own terms, Katherine's narrative is a moving coming-of-
age story about a sensitive and intelligent girl in the American South at
midcentury who transgresses the mores of the conservative community
in which she has been raised, engaging in a quietly tragic act of sexual
rebellion—a more privileged version of Jayne Anne Phillips's Lark, if
you will. She is part of an affluent family from New Orleans, the Mon-
roes, that summers in Sewanee: their social circle there includes Charles
Addison, a popular professor of Shakespeare at the University of the
South. When she is fourteen, Kathleen begins an affair with Charles.
She initiates the relationship, perhaps as an escape from the tedium
and emptiness of her social world: "She had been for so long, it seemed
then, . . . moving within narrow grooves, over familiar surfaces, test-
ing the very few things she had power to do and the very few ways she
could do them" (31). Mrs. Reston, the matronly housekeeper to the vice

chancellor who adores both Chang and Katherine, offers this perspective on their relationship: "She was just a child when he started with her. And he ruined her" (162).

One result of this affair is that it deepened her already present sense of isolation. In high school, "Katherine became a beautiful, conspicuous girl who was subtly avoided," and a "cool space hung around" her that "nobody entered" (130). She remained a solitary figure as she started college, which she attended just for a year, and also in Boston, where she moved thereafter. When her ailing father writes asking her to look after their summer house in Sewanee, which has been vacant for many years, she agrees. Only with the prospect of returning there does she realize how lonely she has been. And soon after her arrival, her relationship with Charles is renewed, but this time he seems to be the subordinate and dependent partner, pathetically seeking in her a sense of compensation for the disappointments and bitterness of a life less than fully realized. Despite the damaging effect it has had on her, Katherine resumes the relationship that has been the defining force in her life, because "she always felt indebted to him, although she knew he'd exacted a price" (136).

When Katherine meets Chang, she is in a state of ascetic resignation: "She was still thin and small-breasted. Her bones seemed too evident, as if to provoke the thought of breaking them, so that the thought would be admitted impossible. She was uninjurable" (136–37). However, the novel does not wholly present her as a victim based on its depiction of events, and neither is Charles depicted as a villainous rapist; in fact, both are treated sympathetically. Her affair with Charles destroyed her chance at a more conventional life of affluent domesticity that was to be her legacy, but it is a life she had already perceived as empty. She is the kind of character we might expect to see in a contemporary novel set in the United States at midcentury—leading a life of quiet desperation, as it were, but not quite "ruined," as Mrs. Reston would insist.

The reasons the novel offers us for why Katherine is drawn to Chang are significant, however, for they turn out to mirror the ones that might lead readers to pick up a work whose central protagonist is, as the blurb puts it, by "nightmarish memories of war." Katherine's attraction to him derives in part from his novelty. "You're the first new thing here in a while," she tells him (35). But as she reflects on her fascination with him, her thoughts are largely absent of the conventional tropes of Oriental-ism: "He had come from a distant land, and to her that was lighter than air. He always looked as if he'd briefly dropped out of an airplane, stand-ing thin and transient in his dark suit, a glaring interruption in the back-ground of the unremarkable. She had wanted to step inside that circle" (256). While the phrase "a distant land" is also used by Crane's father in reference to Chang's origins, Katherine frames the distance he repre-sents in notably abstract terms—as something "lighter than air"—and Chang's otherness as "a glaring interruption." Similarly, when Katherine first notices her attraction to him, as the two are having dinner in a res-taurant in Nashville, she thinks of it in linguistic metaphors that have nothing to do with an inscrutable East, but in relation to a more homely memory of the French she likely learned in high school or college. In seeing Chang as attractive she experienced a "shearing through all her ideas of what a handsome man should look like, and then, as abruptly as it had come, it was gone again" (147). The sudden unexpected appear-ance and disappearance of her desire recalls for her "the first time she had ever dreamed in French" and how afterward when "she tried to re-capture that unconscious fluency, she always failed. Looking at him was like this. She'd found him beautiful; then something intervened" (147.)

But what seems to draw Katherine to Chang more concretely are qualities that are related to his wartime experiences. She confesses to him in early on: "I've always wondered what a war really looks like. There's no way to tell, reading the papers" (34). And during their con-versation at a Nashville restaurant, she points out a second quality of Chang's that draws her in—"Do you know how easily you dodge ques-tions? As if questioning were a pressure that drove you straight back-wards" (148)—and afterward considers its effect on her: "She had the idea that you might reach behind moments. She wanted to reach behind this one and say, Listen: give me whatever you're holding apart from me, just so I know there's a rift. I don't want the secret itself, only the fact of the secret, so that I can measure the depth of the rift—but she wanted the secret as well" (151). The subsequent unfolding of the romance plot suggests that the "secret" alluded to here has a specific referent—the contents of a recurrent dream Chang has about the war.

Readers are given an initial sense of this secret in a scene that takes place on New Year's Eve, when Katherine pays a visit to Chang, who is staying alone in the dormitory, avoiding her because he has found out she is engaged to Charles. She makes him dinner and he becomes quite drunk from the brandy they have shared. She puts him to bed in his room while she goes to sleep in Crane's, but she is soon awakened by his crying out in the middle of a nightmare. He rejects her comforting gestures and sends her away. Afterward she reflects, "Sometimes she was sure that the distance she felt between them wasn't difference, but a wariness they both turned toward the world. That they turned it toward each other was mistaken, the thing they shared camouflaging itself. She was oppressed by her inability to know what she wanted and say what she meant, but now she saw that he might be the same. He was only able to speak in the throes of his dream. And then she answered, and he made her go away" (216). Such passages set the reader up to expect that when the two lovers do finally given in to their desires the "rift" between them will dissolve—that they will be able to let go the "wariness they both turned toward the world" and "toward each other" and reveal to each other the pasts that haunt them. If Chang's dream condenses the horrors of the war that he experienced, then the revelation of its contents will enable her, we might assume, to a full understanding of who he is and lead to a romantic union premised on the utter transparency of each to the other.

The intimacy that finally emerges between them arrives, however, without any such revelation. There is no heartfelt sharing of traumas that would render their two histories emotionally equivalent. The closest the novel comes to offering such a moment occurs quite late, soon after Chang and Katherine finally consummate their desire in a hotel room in New Orleans. She finally asks him about the dreams that haunt him and Chang gives an astonishingly sparse answer: "Mostly I am running. Soldiers come behind me and I run, run, run. . . . Then I hear a shooting. . . . I feel the bullets come in me" (287–88). When Katherine follows up with "Did this happen to you?" he replies, "No. This is never what happened to me" (288). This dream—which has been alluded to in ways that make Katherine and the reader assume that it holds the key to understanding the suffering he lived through during the war—houses a memory that is false, records a trauma that isn't even his. For as the novel later elaborates somewhat on the dream, it turns out to record an event that never happened: his being shot by North Korean soldiers as he made his escape from Seoul.

What makes their intimacy exemplary, I would argue, is that it retains and honors the alterity of their experiences, the "rift" between them. Their connection does not entail the total transparency of each to the other nor a revelation of their respective histories of trauma, though it remains suffused with affective power. By valorizing the strange intimacy that joins Katherine to Chang, one that acknowledges the distance between the vastly different and incomparable histories that have shaped them, the novel specifies the terms in which readers should think of whatever affective investment we end up making in its protagonist's story. Whatever pain of Chang's it makes us feel, the novel subtly reminds us that his experiences remain, in the end, foreign to us. To the extent that Choi's novel makes us into students, as it were, of Chang's war trauma, we must honor the insuperable "rift" that likely separates our own histories of suffering and his.

This has additional ramifications for how we should regard the novel's framing of the events that happen to Chang. For a version of the "rift" that cements Katherine's relation to Chang is also integral to the intimacy that connects the novel's third-person narrator to its protagonist. The novel highlights this gap through a recurrent motif of translation.

In certain crucial moments, the narrator marks the limits of her omniscience and invites readers to see the novel as an extended act of *translation*. These highlight that Chang's interiority is conveyed in a language that is not really his but that belongs instead to the narrator. This is made clear in the depiction of Chang's very first conversation in America. He is greeted by Mrs. Reston, the housekeeper who asks how long his flight from Korea took. He replies:

> "Eighteen hours and—" He wanted to add something to answer her kindness as well as her question. "And we stop to take fuel in Alaska."
>
> "Alaska! First time in this country and you've already been to Alaska. I don't think I will ever see Alaska in my life. Was it beautiful?"
>
> This did not seem the word. It had been a gloaming, purple and vast. Past the end of the world. *But he didn't have these words, either.* (8; emphasis mine)

Chang understands that the English word "beautiful" is not quite right. The narrator provides two phrases that would offer a more adequate description—"a gloaming, purple and vast" and "past the end of the world." But in pointing out that "he didn't have these words, either," the narrator highlights a certain set of uncertainties that are both linguistic and narratological. Are these two phrases an interpretation—a literal translation into English of Chang's thoughts, which are in Korean? Or are they an interpolation—*her* description of what Chang saw? In moments like this, the narrator foregrounds her mediating presence, not only suggesting the limits of her own seeming omniscience but also underscoring a linguistic gap between herself and the character whose experiences she recounts.

What is registered in this brief but vital passage from the novel's opening pages reverberates through the rest of the novel—an acknowledgment that the narrator is providing a *translation* of what Chang went through during the war, one that may involve both interpretation and interpolation. This alerts readers that we should remain aware of a linguistic "rift" between the narrator and her protagonist—that past the end of her linguistic world is a realm of experience that she can only map through approximation, "a gloaming, purple and vast." In highlighting the gap that haunts her transcription of Chang's thoughts and emotions, the narrator underscores how her account of events—even within the novel's own diegetic terms—is a mediated one, a translation of memory across time, nations, generations and subjects.[18]

Readers should thus bear this in mind even as the narrator probes more deeply into the source of Chang's trauma, experiences of such cruelty that they do not even surface in his dreams. The thirteenth and penultimate chapter describes his arrest and interrogation on Cheju Island by the National Police who suspect him of being a Communist spy. The repeated torture to which he was subjected during a detainment that lasted weeks is described in excruciating detail. The violence through which his false confession is finally extracted seems to have had a disfiguring effect on his capacity to remember. Echoing Elaine Scarry's observations about the unmaking of the world that torture effects, the narrator describes how Chang's "memory was flattened and distorted, like the globe of the world unpeeled and forced onto a map" (311).[19] The narrator is left to recount events that Chang no longer clearly recalls—to offer her interpolation, her translation of events that lie beyond the borders of her protagonist's memories.

Later passages make explicit that Chang's recovery from this experience has entailed a kind of process of psychic scarring and splitting. He actually carries two memories of the war, which he experiences as almost wholly distinct. The first concerns the country estate where his family spent summers located in what is now North Korea. "That memory," the narrator asserts, "of that place, was sealed like a globe within him" and she then lists various features of the landscape and the atmosphere of the place that Chang will forever recall (317). In contrast, the other memory, of the weeks of torture endured, had "obliterated itself and took part of him with it, like the injured tissue surrounding a wound, fusing together where it shouldn't, and shrinking the body. He could not remember the pain he had felt, as if all that had happened to him had been enacted on another" (317). Healing from that trauma entailed the scarring over of a painful memory, a disfiguring encryption that "obliterated" it. Chang's psyche has undergone a kind of self-division, as if the partitioning of the peninsula had manifested as an internal psychic rift between these two memories and his past and present selves. Since Choi's narrator has compensated for Chang's obliterated memory by telling his story, offering a translation of an original that has been erased, her rendering of events cannot be authoritative. To the extent that the readers are able to remain aware of the narrator's mediation of this experience, we remain cognizant that what we are reading is a fiction, however compelling it to be.

Without wanting to solder this narrator too tightly to the author herself, her relationship to her protagonist does mirror something of Choi's to her father, upon whom Chang was modeled. Through the long conversations she had with her father in the course of writing her novel, she attempted to close a "rift" roughly comparable to the one that both divides and joins her novel's narrator and protagonists. These exchanges were attempts by a second-generation Korean American to understand the experiences of a previous generation that may have lived through events of immense trauma that they have passed on only through what King-kok Cheung has described an articulate silence.[20]

A useful concept for illuminating the position that Korean American authors like Choi and Lee occupy as they address the topic of the

Korean War comes from the work of cultural critic Marianne Hirsch: "postmemory." She originally developed this term to describes the positionality of Jews who were born after the Holocaust but for whom that event constituted an indelible part of their living memory. Put in more generalized terms, postmemory refers to a situation in which "children of survivors of cultural or collective trauma" are haunted by "stories and images" of that trauma "that are so powerful, so monumental, as to constitute memories in their own right."[21] It refers, then, to a virtual memory of a past event, the prefix underscoring its "temporal and qualitative difference from survivor memory, its secondary or second-generation memory quality, its basis in displacement, its belatedness."[22] Its emotional power, however, derives precisely from the fact that "its connection to its object or source is mediated not through recollection but through projection, investment, and creation."[23]

The stories that Choi and Lee both tell about the origins of their Korean War novels speak to a situation that seems in one important respect antithetical to the one that Hirsh describes: for the traumatic event that was formative for their parents is one that has remained shrouded in silence. Grace M. Cho has described this scenario, which is common for second-generation Korean Americans, as a "transgenerational haunting" in which "the haunting effect is produced not so much by the original trauma as by the fact of its being kept hidden."[24] What Korean American subjects in this position therefore confront is not a "powerful" and "monumental" archive of memory but its absence.

To a significant extent both *The Foreign Student* and *The Surrendered* attempt to rectify this situation by constructing a visceral and perhaps even monumental Korean American archive of cultural memory—for whatever else they might be, these are works they convey the horrors of what ordinary Koreans experienced during the war with immense emotional power. However, even as they engage in this affective labor, both novels highlight the artifice and mediation through which they have sought to materialize the trauma of that event. In other words, *The Surrendered* and *The Foreign Student* take pains to present themselves as self-conscious works of postmemory.

In her novel, Choi negotiates in an exemplary way a certain ethical danger skirted by authors who write about an experience of historical trauma that is not, properly speaking, their own—that belongs instead to an earlier generation. "The challenge for the postmemorial artist," as Hirsch alerts us, is "to find the balance that allows the spectator to enter the image, to imagine the disaster, but that disallows an overappropriative identification that makes the distances disappear, creating too available, too easy an access to this particular past."[25]

The Foreign Student negotiates this danger by asserting a necessary "rift" between the memories of those who lived through the war and the second-generation postmemory of those who hope to undo its forgetting—that the latter are inevitably a translation of the former. It also highlights how survivor memory might itself be scarred or even "obliterated" by the trauma it records. In so doing it seeks to banish the fantasy that one could somehow revisit and rectify a violent and traumatic past solely through a compensatory act of narration, for the novel's primary aim is not to engage in a narrow version of literary identity politics: to fill in the absence that is the war with an existential sense of injury, identifying a wound that might be fetishized as the origin and source of a singular and coherent ethnonationalist identity.[26]

How we are to understand Choi's postmemorial novel as an interpretation and interpolation of a trauma—as a translation—is suggested in a passage where it explicitly theorizes the practice of translation, a craft that Chang learned from his father. What he came to understand was the impossibility of arriving at a one-to-one correspondence between words in different languages. Instead, "every equivalence of terms was arrived at by taking an indirect route, as if by shooting slightly wide of the mark they could compensate for the inevitable shifting of meaning, the drift of a thought from its mooring once the word that had housed it was gone" (81). While "equivalence" is the aim, "an indirect route" must be followed to achieve it. Moreover, the connection between the two terms cannot be precisely mapped out: it must be dynamic, able to "compensate for the inevitable shifting of meaning." But while there is an inexactitude, even a messiness to the process, there is a singularity and certainty to the moment when the perfect translation has arrived: "The thing would emerge and begin to grow buoyant, as if it could read only just as it was. This was what his father wanted: for the original to vanish. Then you knew it was actually there, bled in, letter by letter" (81). This suggests that while translation expresses a desire to make two disparate things fit seamlessly together, it can only really take place when that desire is frustrated: "You wanted one thing to equal another, to slide neatly into its place, but somehow this very desire made the project impossible. In the end there was always a third thing, that hadn't existed before" (67). Like the ideal translation, the novel presents itself as "a third thing that hadn't existed before," underscoring the experience of suffering it hopes to convey not as a memory but as a postmemory—one that marks the vanishing point of an original that is nonetheless "actually there, bled in, letter by letter."

Racialized Assemblages as Translation

This notion of translation also speaks to the messy and dynamic relation of interracial contiguity *The Foreign Student* establishes between Chang and the Asian American and African American characters he encounters. As the novel ends, the itinerary of Chang's journey through the US racial landscape remains somewhat open ended, though an honorary whiteness has been removed as a possible destination. Additionally, the novel leaves upon the question of how we might conceptualize the relationship between the various racialized histories it references.

I would contend that the ways in which *The Foreign Student* juxtaposes these histories and makes them contiguous translations is resonant with Alexander G. Weheliye's conceptualization of "relationality," which I cited in the introductory chapter, as well as with his notion of "racializing assemblages." In proposing this latter concept he draws on Gilles Deleuze and Felix Guattari's concept of "assemblages," which imagines social formations as "inherently productive, entering into polyvalent becomings to produce and give expression to previously nonexistent realities, thoughts, bodies, affects, spaces, actions, ideas, and so on" and "do[es] not assume change to adhere in full, self-present, and coherent subjects."[27] Weheliye modifies this analytical paradigm by drawing on the work of Stuart Hall: specifically his reworking of the Marxian concept of "articulation," which enables a better engagement with "historically sedimented power imbalances and ideological interests, which are crucial to understanding mobile structures of dominance such as race or gender" and how those hierarchical modalities of difference are integral to "the modus operandi of assemblages."[28]

As I asserted in my introduction, what is particularly germane about Weheliye's work both to Choi's novel and to my project overall is how it draws from fields like Asian American, Latinx, and postcolonial studies from a particular vantage point—in his case black studies—to evoke an assemblage of racializing histories should not be seen as comparable but rather a kind of "relational" translation. What is exemplary in this respect about *The Foreign Student*, is that it ultimately resists the exceptionalist pull of a traumatic history that might form the basis of a Korean American or diasporic identity, in part by placing it alongside other histories shaped by marginalization and violence. It does so in ways, moreover, without resorting to what Weheliye terms a "grammar of comparison."

From the vantage point provided by Weheliye, we can grasp the significance of the irresolution that characterizes Chang's racial identity as it has taken shape on the cusp of the momentous changes that will transform the racial landscape of the United States in the 1960s: for he is presented not so much as having become a specific kind of Asian American subject but rather in a state of becoming. Similarly, we can apprehend how the various racialized and colonial histories the novel places before us are presented not as discrete and finished but in an interrelated state of becoming: an ongoing transformation of "racializing assemblages" that, like the version of translation the novel theorizes, are about the "shifting of meaning," "the drift of a thought from its mooring," and a tending toward "a third thing, that hadn't existed before" (67).

We will turn in the next chapter to three novels that explore different racialized and colonial dimensions of the assemblage of cultural memory has taken shape around the Korean War, works that offer African American, Chicano and Chinese/American perspectives on the conflict, expanding upon and multiplying the historiographical trajectories that Choi sets into motion in her novel.

7

The Racial Borderlands of the Korean War

I turn in this chapter to what might be termed a racializing assemblage of Korean War works that explore that conflict's significance for African Americans, Mexican Americans, and Chinese Americans. I want to begin by returning to a figure mentioned in chapter 2, Clarence Adams. In 1965, Adams broadcast a message on Radio Hanoi addressed to black soldiers fighting for the United States in Vietnam, telling them, "You are fighting the wrong war. Brothers, go home. The Negro people need you back there."[1] As I suggested, Adams mobilizes a historiography of a race war to cast both the Korean and Vietnam Wars as ones waged by a white empire against a colored population, much as a more well-known figure, Muhammad Ali, did two years later in his statements explaining his refusal to register for the draft. Both men, in stating their opposition to the Vietnam War, made use of what Bill Mullens terms Afro-Orientalism, positing a solidarity among, as Ali put it, "the darker people the world over."[2]

The idea of such an alliance is both elaborated on and complicated by the works taken up in this chapter, novels by Toni Morrison, Rolando Hinojosa, and Ha Jin. While all the works examined here do point to the devastating effects of the Korean War on Koreans themselves, that is not their primary concern. In looking back at the conflict, these authors are most interested in illuminating its significance for the racial and ethnic communities of which they are a part—what the war meant for African Americans, Mexican Americans, and Asian Americans on the one hand and for the Chinese on the other.

Placing these works alongside one another, however, enables us to engage with the tensions between exceptionalist and potentially competitive currents of cultural memory and those generative of a more relational articulation of an event's myriad meanings. As Michael Rothberg notes, given "the inevitable displacements and contingencies that mark all remembrance," it is also inevitable that "competitive scenarios" will arise from such "restless rearticulations" of cultural memory.[3] Since the primary concerns of the works taken up here are with the Korean War's significance for black, Chicano/a, and Chinese subjects, they register "the inevitable displacements" of issues that are the most pressing to Korean American authors. However, they also contain elements that enable us *as readers* to see them as "visions that construct solidarity out of the specificities, overlaps, and echoes of different historical experiences."[4]

All the novels share an impetus to engender in readers a pointed skepticism about the official narratives foreign powers used to justify their intervention in what was, at bottom, a Korean civil war as well as the narratives about soldiering they sanctioned. These works convey the perspectives of US and Chinese combatants who grew progressively disillusioned by their governments' role in the conflict as they came to recognize how ordinary soldiers were treated as "war trash," to use Ha Jin's metaphor, by those in command and as they increasingly registered how devastating their actions were to Korean civilians, whom they had ostensibly come to protect and save. This latter aspect draws attention to what humanitarian Orientalist accounts attempt to shroud with pieties. In their novels, Morrison and Hinojosa highlight the hypocrisies of US ideologies of military multiculturalism by focusing on the racism that soldiers of color continued to experience on the battlefield and on their return home; they also draw attention to how African and Mexican American servicemen were complicit in the destruction brought to the Korean people.

Jin's *War Trash* broadens the transnational scope of the assemblage of cultural memory explored in this chapter, for it illuminates how the Korean War marked a great victory from the vantage point of the People's Republic of China (PRC), which sent the greatest number of troops into the fighting. In the PRC nationalist narrative, its People's Army came to the heroic aid of a sister regime, helping the North Koreans successfully repel a foreign invasion by US imperial forces. Jin's novel punctures this triumphalist mythology, however, by evoking the war as "an enormous furnace fed by the bodies of soldiers," but one that consumed a vast number of Korean civilian lives as well.[5] Moreover, this novel, along with Hinojosa's Korean War writings, suggests how that conflict is embedded within longer colonial histories of empire that involve not only the United States, China, and Japan but also Mexico.

While the primary focus of this chapter is on novels, I first turn briefly to Clarence Adams's posthumously published memoir *An American Dream: The Life of an African American Soldier and POW Who Spent Twelve Years in Communist China* (2007), which is notable not only for its trenchant critique of the military multiculturalism of midcentury US representations of the Korean War but also for the astonishing range of Afro-Orientalist identifications to which it gives expression, some of which provide a more unvarnished view of the civilian deaths that humanitarian Orientalist accounts gloss over with platitudes.

Race War, Afro-Orientalism, and Clarence Adams's *An American Dream*

While Adams had been a largely forgotten figure when he issued his statement on Radio Hanoi in 1965, he had achieved a level of notoriety a decade before as one of twenty-one American prisoners of war (POWs) who refused repatriation at the end of the Korean War and chose instead to go to the People's Republic of China. In *Name, Rank and Serial Number*, Charles S. Young offers a comprehensive account of how the mass media in the United States as well as its government not only pathologized the twenty-one who refused repatriation but also cast suspicion on all POWs, specifically about the effects Communist "brainwashing" might have had on them during their incarceration.[6] The journalistic smear campaign waged against the defectors is epitomized by Virginia Pasley's *21 Who Stayed: The Story of the American GIs Who Chose Communist China* (1955).[7] Like most other reporters, Pasley assumes that no *rational* American would have chosen a Communist nation over his own. In the portraits she offers of Adams and two other African American defectors, she insists that their experiences of racism played no significant role in their decisions, asserting instead that they, like their eighteen white counterparts, were alienated loners who exhibited neuroses produced by deficient family structures that rendered them vulnerable to manipulation by their Communist captors.

Adams's memoir primarily rebuts this characterization by comprehensively anatomizing the racism that had been the determining structure of most of his life decisions. One of its more striking aspects is that the chapters covering the Korean War and his incarceration in a POW camp arguably contain less violence than those that recount his earlier years growing up in Tennessee and his peacetime deployments to Fort Dix, Korea, and Japan before the outbreak of the conflict. He describes the segregated Memphis he grew up in as existing in a state of virtual race war: young black men faced the perpetual threat of racist violence that was most often meted out by white policemen. He only left his hometown and enlisted in the US Army in fall 1947 because he feared being arrested and abused by cops for his involvement in the beatings of a white vagrant and a black neighborhood bully.

Adams recounts versions of this same racism during basic training from white officers and during his peacetime deployments to Japan and Korea. Although he was initially enthusiastic when war broke out and was deployed to the peninsula, he recalls that he and other African Americans quickly became "disillusioned," partly because being in combat did little to lessen the racism they had become accustomed to confronting; they also began to "understand that the North Koreans had not done anything to us, so why were we there trying to kill each other?"[8] Adams soon "gained respect" for North Korean soldiers because of how fiercely they fought (31). He registers a critique of the military multiculturalism examined in earlier chapters, one that will be echoed in the novels examined next.

Additionally, his sparse but pointed acknowledgments of the civilian deaths caused by US military actions also dismantle the humanitarian Orientalism that shaped mainstream depictions of the conflict. He recounts that the multitudes of Koreans he came across, living and dead, closed the door on any belief that this was a war worth fighting: "As we moved further north, we saw more and more civilian refugees. They were dragging along all their belongings, and many women had babies on their backs. I frequently saw young kids and old women lying dead alongside the roads. Sometimes tanks would just run over them. More and more I asked myself, What kind of war is this where such things happen? Should we really be here killing innocent civilians?" (33). The horror of what US military forces were doing to ordinary Koreans is crystallized for Adams by an event he witnesses during his brutal trek to the prison camp after his capture by North Korean soldiers. Although he is unstinting in describing the horrific conditions he and other POWs face during this march, he pauses at one moment to highlight the even greater violence to which Korean civilians were subjected—and at the hands of US military forces. He watches as several US fighter jets napalm a unit of Chinese soldiers and inadvertently set fire to a Korean hut: "A woman with a baby on her back came running out of the house, engulfed by orange flames and thick black smoke. She ran several yards before crumbling to the ground. She and her baby burned to death before my very eyes. I was not more than a hundred yards away, and I could see the imprint of the baby on her back after both were dead." "This incident," he recalls, "made me see the horror of war like nothing else," and he sees the rage on the face of the North Korean guard as justifiable: "If this guard shoots us, well, we deserve it because we should not be here in Korea" (40).

The Afro-Orientalism Adams expresses thus takes shape through its depictions of both the Communist soldiers he fights and comes to respect and the Korean civilians whose suffering so greatly affects him. These aspects of his memoir affectively deepen the identification with Koreans as a colored and colonized people that is evident in some of the black press's early reporting on the war. A version of this Afro-Orientalist identification also forms around the Japanese civilians he meets when he is stationed there before the war. He recalls how he once intervened when he witnessed another African American soldier assaulting an elderly Japanese man for no reason: "I yelled at him, 'What in the hell are you doing?' He mumbled something about 'slant-eyed Japanese,' and he hit him again. I told him, 'Hey, stop that! Would you want somebody to do you like that?' *I was thinking of what happened so often to blacks back home. 'That's the way we've been treated.* If you do that again, I'll kill you.' I threw a round in my carbine and told him, 'Aggie, I'm not playing. If you do that again, I'm going to shoot you'" (28; emphasis mine). Adams is motivated here by a recognition of a structural similarity between the relationship of Japanese civilians to US state power under the occupation and that of black boys in Memphis.

The relationships he forms with his Chinese captors and the country in which he lives for twelve years after the Korean War is a different one, less affectively laden and somewhat more instrumental. He refuses repatriation to the United States not because of any deep attachment he has formed with his Communist captors or because their ideology appeals to him emotionally. Instead, what he sees in the People's Republic of China is similar to what the "Tan Yanks" glimpsed in the lives they were able to build with their "musume" lovers in Japan. Adams hopes "to be treated as a human being" and "to live a better life" (59). More concretely, he wants "an education, a job, and to get married," and he decides that he stands a better chance of achieving these basic aspirations by emigrating to China (64).

If he had returned to Memphis in 1953, he writes, "I would have been a twenty-four-year-old African-American high school dropout, with few opportunities to create a successful life. . . . I might have made it as a boxer, but only the few who reach the top make any kind of living. More likely, I would have gone back to hustling tips as a hotel porter or room service boy" (141). By emigrating to the People's Republic of China (PRC) instead, Adams is able to attend college and earn an advanced degree in Chinese literature. He has a rewarding career as a translator working in a major publishing house and marries a Chinese woman, Lin Liu, with whom he has two children. He socializes with working-class Chinese families but also with foreign diplomats and high-ranking party functionaries. He even meets W. E. B. Du Bois.

The China that emerges from Adams's memoir is not unlike the Japan depicted in the black press in the 1950s: it is a site in which black men could imagine themselves achieving a version of the good life that white men at midcentury could simply claim as a kind of birthright. Ironically, the middle chapters of An American Dream that recount Adams's twelve years in China resemble a classic immigrant narrative, telling the story of a newcomer of humble origins who makes himself anew, finds a satisfying career, marries a local girl, starts a family, and ascends the ranks of society. So, too, do its final chapters, which recount how Adams recreates himself once again after returning to Memphis. He initially takes a series of menial jobs but is eventually able to save enough money to open a Chinese restaurant, which enables him to achieve financial security for his wife and children.

The title of Adams's memoir, An American Dream, is thus apt because its rendering of this remarkable life story is very much in the American grain.[9] Indeed, he takes pains at several points to reiterate that he remained an American throughout his life: "I never became a Communist or a Chinese citizen, not even after my many years in China" (59).

It is worth noting, however, one particular way in which Adams's memoir imbues the entrepreneurial ethos it celebrates with a certain

Afro-diasporic and postcolonial coloring. Toward the end of *An American Dream*, as Adams looks back on what he values most about his time in China, he highlights the experience of meeting "African diplomats who made such a profound impression on me," referring to friendships he formed with men and women who worked at the Ghanaian embassy (141). From them, he gains a sense of pride and knowledge about "the magnificent African kingdoms of antiquity" and the fact "that Africans had developed civilizations long before the Europeans did" (98). He is particularly impressed by the Ghanaian ambassador's proclamation that "we have our own flag, and we're our own boss. . . . We Africans have driven out the British, French, Dutch, and German imperialists. We may not much economic wealth, but at least we control ourselves, and that is very important!" He translates this man's description of an anticolonial nationalist desire for self-determination into the "concept of being one's own boss," which "would later become a guiding principle in my life. Very few blacks in the America of my youth ever considered not working for someone else. This was simply an alien concept, but it was precisely what later motivated Lin and me to open up our first Chop Suey House in Memphis" (99). What thus enables Adams to become a kind of model minority subject after his return to Memphis is an interracial and transnational legacy that includes both the education he receives in China and the cultural influences he absorbs through the diasporic connections he develops with an ancestral "homeland."

In returning to this forgotten figure from a forgotten war and retracing the multiple trajectories of his extraordinary life, we gain a sense of the complex and contradictory forms that the Afro-Orientalism engendered by the Korean War could take. On the one hand, the intimate relationship Adams forms with China and the Afro-diasporic connection to Ghana it facilitates are made compatible with an ethos of self-determination and entrepreneurialism—"being one's own boss"—that has been enshrined in American culture as a core value. On the other, Adams's statements on Radio Hanoi in 1965 and certain aspects of his memoir deploy a historiographical narrative of race war that suggests a continuity between the racist violence to which African Americans were subjected at home and the US military and imperial violence to which the people of Japan and Korea were subjected at midcentury and to which the Vietnamese would be subjected a decade later.

In this latter aspect of Adams's perspective, and especially in his 1965 statement, we find affirmation of Daniel Widener's assertion that "the unease, anxiety, and opposition generated between 1950 and 1953 produced lasting impressions among a critical swath of black Americans, including several who would play critical roles in the radical era that accompanied the Vietnam War."[10] Toni Morrison, whose Korean War novel I take up next, has asserted, like Widener, that the Korean War's effects on African Americans played a crucial role in their political mobilization in the following decades.

"They Rose like Men": Bringing the 1950s Back Home

Toni Morrison's *Home* (2012), her tenth novel, elaborates in fictional terms Adams's contention that the America to which he would have repatriated in 1953 would have been pretty much the same white supremacist country he had left. Its protagonist, Frank Money, is a returning veteran who finds that the military service of black men like himself during the Korean War has secured little in terms of racial progress at home. He discovers that lynchings persist and that medical experimentation on unwilling black subjects, like the men at Tuskegee who participated in a study that left their syphilis untreated, continues to take place. He discovers the latter when he learns that his younger sister, Cee, is being subjected to medical "treatments" that leave her unable to bear children.

Because the novel is set in the United States, as is usually the case with Morrison's writing, the primary significance of the memory of the Korean War she evokes stems from the critique it offers of the military multiculturalism examined in chapter 2. Her primary aim, as she has described it in various interviews, was "to take the scab off the '50s, the general idea of it as very comfortable, happy, nostalgic."[11] Along with the war's effect on African American men, she wanted to suggest other aspects of the decade that also revealed the persistence of antiblack racism, including the lynching of Emmett Till and the revelation of the Tuskegee experiments. In addition, she wanted to demonstrate how such events were "among the seeds that produced the '60s and '70s. I wanted to look at that, so I chose a man who had been in Korea who was suffering from shell shock. He goes on this journey—reluctantly."[12]

As in much of Morrison's work, *Home* refracts its account of a specific historical moment through the lens of gender—more specifically through an account of how antiblack racism is effected through what Hortense Spillers has described as an ungendering brutality.[13] As Morrison elaborates, "A lot of the book confronts the question of how to be a man, which is really how to be a human, but let's say 'man.' And [Frank is] struggling with that, and there's certain pro forma ways in which you can prove you're a man. War is one."[14] His journey over the course of the novel entails his growing realization that the vision of manhood to which he aspired—the one that led him to enlist in the army and fight in Korea—is bankrupt and his search for an alternative.

Morrison deploys a striking narrative device in this novel: Frank directly addresses the author and recounts his memories in several italicized chapters. At times he hectors her about what she could not possibly understand, and at others he reveals secrets he had previously withheld. These give the impression that her telling of her protagonist's story has emerged out of a collaboration that is, at times, contentious. In these chapters, Frank most clearly articulates the conceptions of masculinity that shaped his life choices.

Flashbacks reveal Frank as a young man growing up in Lotus, a small town in Georgia. When he thought of what awaited him as he grew older, he believed that "*there was no future, just long stretches of killing time . . . no goal other than breathing, . . . nothing to survive or worth surviving for*" (83–84). The emptiness of what awaited him in Lotus led him and his two friends to enlist, because they "*couldn't wait to get out and away, far away*" (84).

The vision of the manhood that he could not achieve by staying in Lotus was crystallized for him in a spectacle that he and his younger sister had come upon one night when they had been sneaking around a nearby horse farm. His memory of this childhood event is recounted in the first italicized chapter, which opens the novel. He and Cee had been mesmerized by the sight of two stallions in combat: "*They rose up like men. We saw them. Like men they stood. . . . They bit each other like dogs but when they stood, reared up on their hind legs, their forelegs around the withers of the other, we held our breath in wonder.*"[15] This scene seemed to have imprinted upon Frank the idea of manhood to which he would aspire, a "*secret picture of myself,*" which was also connected to protecting his younger sister:

> She was the first person I ever took responsibility for. Down deep inside her lived my secret picture of myself—a strong good me tied to the memory of those horses and the burial of a stranger. Guarding her, finding a way through tall grass and out of that place, not being afraid of anything—snakes or wild old men. I wonder if succeeding at that was the buried seed of all the rest. In my little-boy heart I felt heroic and I knew that if they found us or touched her I would kill. (104)

This passage also alludes to the other event they witnessed that night—"the burial of a stranger"—which I will come back to later.

Since this memory implanted in Frank's "little-boy heart" what it meant to be "heroic," he imagined becoming a soldier as a way of living up to that vision. The dark cost of doing so, however, is evident from the debilitating hallucinatory episodes that are the symptoms of the post-traumatic stress disorder (PTSD) he struggles with upon his return. His hallucinations contain fragmentary memories of the war, which appear to him as "pictures" that "never went away": "He saw a boy pushing his entrails back in, holding them in his palms like a fortune-teller's globe shattering with bad news; or he heard a boy with only the bottom half of his face intact, the lips calling mama" (20).

Significantly, these memories also reveal that he targeted civilians in his misplaced acts of vengeance for the death of Mike, a boyhood friend: "And all of that killing you did afterward? Women running, dragging children along. And that old one-legged man on a crutch hobbling at the edge of the road so as not to slow down the other, swifter ones? You blew a hole in his head because you believed it would make up for the frosted urine on Mike's pants and avenge the lips calling mama. Did it? Did it work? And the girl. What did she ever do to deserve what happened to her?" (21–22). While the girl he refers to here, as I will discuss later, will actually turn out to be the crucial figure in these memories, initially the most significant detail seems to be Mike's death: "With Mike gone, he was brave, whatever that meant. There were not enough dead gooks or Chinks in the world to satisfy him. The copper smell of blood no longer sickened him; it gave him appetite" (98). Frank became

THE RACIAL BORDERLANDS OF THE KOREAN WAR | 213

part of an efficient killing trio during the war, which included Stuff, another friend from home, and also a white Southerner, Red. He recalls, "Those two, Stuff and Red, were especially close. 'Neck' was dropped from Red's nickname because, hating northerners more than them, he preferred to associate with the three Georgia boys—Stuff most of all" (98–99). Stuff and Red were also killed in action, and Frank witnessed their deaths.

Through these flashes from Frank's memory, Morrison provides a brief but critical vision of what the integrated army that took shape during the Korean War actually did, highlighting the violence inflicted not only *on* black soldiers but also *by* them. The view of black military service in the Korean War that emerges from *Home*—though sparsely rendered—is thus opposed to the laudatory depictions of "Tan Yanks" that appeared in the popular representations of the conflict examined in chapter 2. Frank's "bravery" took shape as a promiscuous and racist violence that targeted "gooks and Chinks" alike, civilians as well as soldiers (98).

While Frank has come to realize that the war did not enable him to rise up like a man, he seems to have a second chance at that aim when he discovers that Cee is essentially being held prisoner by a white doctor who is performing medical experiments on her: he learns of this from a letter sent by an acquaintance of hers. When he sets his sights on rescuing her, he is once again drawn in by a belief in the restorative power of violence. As it turns out, however, he is able to deliver his sister to safety without much resistance. When he shows up at the doctor's house, the man draws a gun on him, but it misfires, and the doctor runs away in fear. As Frank leads Cee out of the house and into a cab, he notices "the deep satisfaction that the rescue brought, not only because it was successful but also how markedly *nonviolent* it had been" and realizes that "not having to beat up the enemy to get what he wanted was somehow superior—sort of, well, smart" (114; emphasis mine). In this moment, Frank prefigures the black men in the next decade who would exemplify a version of manhood predicated on a "smart" use of nonviolence, which would demonstrate their moral superiority over the racist white men with whom they battled.

That Frank's conception of masculinity has altered is further conveyed by the fact that after arriving in Lotus with Cee, he turns the care of his sister over to Miss Ethel, who bans him and all men from the house in which her healing will take place. He accepts that he can do nothing for her injured body or psyche. Cee emerges from her ordeal as a stronger, more independent woman who no longer looks to her brother or any man for protection.

The culmination of what Morrison characterizes as Frank's reluctant journey to a new conception of manhood comes in the final act he performs in the novel: accompanied by Cee, he excavates the bones of a man the two of them had watched being buried and reburies them. They had witnessed this burial as children just before seeing the two stallions that had so captured their attention. Early on, Frank had alluded to what he had repressed in his memory of that event: "*Whatever you think and whatever you write down, know this: I really forgot about the burial. I only remembered the horses.*" (6).

Upon his return to Lotus, Frank had become curious about the man who was buried, whose ghost seems to haunt him. He hears from a group of elderly men that the farm he and Cee had sneaked onto as children had been the site of repeated acts of racist violence. Pairs of black men would be abducted and forced to fight one another to the death—spectacles that comprise a dark mirror of the majestic vision of stallions rising in combat that so arrested Frank as a boy. Frank discovers the identity of the man he and Cee had witnessed being buried: a father who had been forced to fight his son. This man had demanded that his son kill him, a request that was finally and tearfully honored. Frank also learns that after a fire had burned down the farmhouse, the stallions he had so admired had been sold off to a slaughterhouse, a fate similar to that of so many black soldiers who had been sent off to Korea.

These revelations cause Frank to reevaluate this formative memory: to reconsider who had actually "stood like men," the horses or the dead man whose identity he now knows. The novel's penultimate chapter begins with Frank imploring Cee to accompany him as he tries to locate the remains of the body they saw being buried, which they succeed in doing. After reburying them in a more prominent location, under a "sweet bay tree—split down the middle, beheaded, undead"—Frank places a makeshift marker on the grave that reads simply, "Here Stands a Man" (143).

The black masculinity the novel ultimately memorializes is not the one captured by the "secret picture" of himself Frank revered in boyhood, of beings magnificently rising in violent combat, a version of the "Tan Yanks" memorialized by the military multiculturalism that emerged during the Korean War. Rather, the manhood that stands at the end of *Home* is exemplified by a father who was willing to make himself an object of racist violence—indeed, to make the ultimate gesture of self-sacrifice—in order to save his son. Morrison's stated aim of disclosing "the seeds that produced the '60s and '70s" manifests itself in her protagonist's ultimate embrace of a black masculinity predicated not on violence but on its renunciation.[16] It is exemplified not only by the man whose bones Frank and Cee finally give a proper burial but also briefly by Frank himself, who realizes after rescuing his sister that "not having to beat up the enemy to get what he wanted was somehow superior—sort of, well, smart" (114). Moreover, the form of manhood Frank finally embraces leaves space for black women like his sister to find their own way rather than reducing them to objects in need of male protection. Befitting the elegant concision and sparseness of the novel, the message of *Home* seems quite straightforward: that the toxic ideal of martial masculinity to which African American men aspired through their service in the Korean War would need to be replaced in the following decades by one predicated on nonviolence, self-sacrifice, and a recognition of the autonomy of black women.

"The More One Looks, the More That Is Revealed"

Somebody was hiding something—and by somebody, I mean the narrative of the country, which was so aggressively happy. Postwar, everybody was making money, and the comedies were wonderful . . . And I kept thinking, That kind of insistence, there's something fake about it. So I began to think about what it was like for me, my perception at that time, and then I began to realize that I didn't know as much as I thought. *The more one looks, the more that is revealed that's not so complimentary.*

—Toni Morrison (quoted in Bollen and Winter; emphasis mine)

The closure that arrives at the end of *Home* is haunted by the figure of a dead girl, a ghost who never achieves corporeal form as Beloved does in the novel that bears her name but who exerts considerable force nonetheless—embodying a story that should not be passed on but that must be passed on. Frank reveals who this spectral figure is in two italicized chapters, 9 and 14, the second of which drastically revises the first. That this mysterious figure is the key to understanding Frank's PTSD is suggested by the fact that his episodes are triggered by the sight of young girls.

In chapter 9, Frank seems to explain why. While on guard duty in a Korean village, he had noticed a girl scavenging for food from the garbage that US soldiers had dumped. He recalls that she *"reminded me of Cee and me trying to steal peaches off the ground under Miss Robinson's tree"* (94). He then recounts that this Korean girl was killed by a fellow soldier when she had offered to exchange sex for food. Reflecting on why, Frank offers, *"I think the guard felt more than disgust. I think he felt tempted and that is what he had to kill"* (96).

This revelation turns out to be a misdirection, however, which is made clear in chapter 14, when Frank confesses,

> *I shot the Korean girl in her face.*
> *I am the one she touched.*
> *I am the one who saw her smile.*
> *I am the one she said "Yum-yum" to.*
> *I am the one she aroused.* (133)

He then explains his reasons for killing her through a series of rhetorical questions:

> *How could I let her live after she took me down to a place I didn't know*
>   *was in me?*
> *How could I like myself, even be myself if I surrendered to that place*
>   *where I unzip my fly and let her taste me right then and there?*
> *And again the next day and the next as long as she came scavenging.*
> *What type of man is that?*
> *And what type of man thinks he can ever in life pay the price of that*
>   *orange?* (133–34)

What most disturbed the "secret picture" of himself, it turns out, was not what the army had done to him or the war to his friends but what he had done to a young Korean girl who had reminded him of his own sister.

Whereas Morrison's fiction typically excavates historical crimes that whites have committed against blacks or the semihidden violence that circulates within African American communities, the event that emerges from *Home* as a kind of primal scene of racial and sexual violence is a war crime in which the victim was a Korean girl and the perpetrator an African American man who is the novel's protagonist. It is Frank who is the primary subject of guilt in this novel, and the question of what acts of reparation toward that Korean girl would be warranted remains unresolved throughout.

The final chapter, immediately following his confession to "Morrison," is written from the perspective of the novel's third-person narrator and recounts Frank remembering what he had done to the girl and trying to come to terms with it: "He had spent a sleepless night, churning and entangled in thoughts relentless and troubling. How he had covered his guilt and shame with big-time mourning for his dead buddies. Day and night he had held on to that suffering because it let him off the hook, kept the Korean child hidden. Now the hook was deep inside his chest and nothing would dislodge it. The best he could hope for was time to work it loose. Meantime there were worthwhile things that needed doing" (135). Frank does go on to do the "worthwhile things that needed doing"—he excavates and reburies the remains of the black man who had sacrificed himself for his son and had thus stood up in his own way against the racist violence that had been directed at him and his family. These acts do not, however, provide any redress for the horrific act of violence he had committed against a young girl in Korea. And although Morrison's narrator takes care of the "worthwhile things that needed doing" by bringing Frank's journey to its close, she nonetheless leaves readers with the knowledge that this resolution does nothing to compensate or atone for the war crime her protagonist has committed.

In the end, *Home* is a novel that subtly alerts readers to their own expectations of what a Toni Morrison novel about the Korean War might look like; however, in so doing, it draws attention to and risks becoming marginalized by the conventions she has established in prior works.

The storytelling machinery we have come to associate with Morrison is brought to bear on the Korean War, and what emerges front and center is how this American conflict—like every other—did not deliver on the promise of manhood it offered to the men of color who fought in it. There is, however, a ghost in the machine, as it were—a discomfiting reminder that as members of a military that committed unspeakable acts against the civilian population they were ostensibly there to protect and save, black servicemen have been not just complicit bystanders of such deeds but perpetrators as well. As Morrison herself puts it, "The more one looks, the more that is revealed that's not so complimentary."

Being a Good Soldier: Rolando Hinojosa's *Rites and Witnesses*

I turn now to a trilogy of Korean War novels by Rolando Hinojosa that offers a similarly complex perspective on men of color who served in that conflict and how their experiences affected their communities back home. As I will show later, one of these works spotlights, as *Home* does, the fact that Korean civilians were killed by US soldiers. However, the central focus of these novels—*Korean Love Songs* (1978), *Rites and Witnesses* (1989), and *The Useless Servants* (1993)—is on the experiences of Rafe Buenrostro, a Mexican American soldier from South Texas who serves as a spotter, identifying targets for artillery attacks. Perhaps because of his position, Rafe does not seem to have much direct interaction with Korean civilians. The enemy soldiers he encounters consist primarily of Chinese forces, and these he engages only at a distance as he identifies them as targets. While Koreans are thus largely absent from these novels, Rafe does evince a sense of connection to other Asians—to the Chinese soldiers he fights and also the civilians he becomes friendly with in Japan, where he is stationed before he is sent to Korea. In addition to articulating a kind of Chicano counterpart to the Afro-Orientalism theorized by Mullen, these works also invite readers to explore connections among a number of seemingly disparate histories, including a domestic history of race relations that centers on Mexican Americans in South Texas and a postcolonial history of the two Koreas.

The novels considered here are part of Hinojosa's multivolume work *Klail City Death Trip* (*KCDT*), the vast majority of which takes place in

Belken County, a fictionalized version of the South Texas community in which Hinojosa was born and raised. He characterizes the sense of history that shapes his work as beginning "in 1749 when the first colonists began moving into the southern and northern banks of the Río Grande. That river was not yet a jurisdictional barrier and was not to be until almost one hundred years later; but, by then, the border had its own history, its own culture, and its own sense of place: it was Nuevo Santander, named for old Santander in the Spanish peninsula."[17] Hinojosa evokes here the community that sprang up on both banks of the Rio Grande as a discrete entity, one that was fractured by the establishment of the border instituted in 1848 as a result of the US-Mexico War, a century before a similar partition would divide the Korean peninsula. *KCDT* as a whole explores the long history of this region by following a cast of characters across much of the twentieth century. Rafe Buenrostro, Hinojosa's primary protagonist and fictional alter ego, like the author himself, joins the US Army and sees action in the Korean War.

Mexican American soldiers were generally not featured in the kinds of popular representations of Cold War military multiculturalism I examined in part 1 of this study. The reason might be that since they were racially classified as white and thus not consigned to segregated units in prior conflicts, the integration of military forces during the Korean War would not seem to have the same degree of significance for Mexican Americans as it did for African and Japanese Americans. Nonetheless, as Hinojosa's writings reveal, military service seemed to offer the same promise to Mexican Americans as it did to other men of color: providing them with a way to demonstrate their loyalty to the United States and to gain access to greater opportunities for upward mobility. They also faced similar forms of racism from white soldiers. These novels thus provide insights into the part that Mexican Americans—particularly those in the military—played in the transformations in the US racial order catalyzed by the Korean War.[18] Additionally, Hinojosa's Korean War trilogy invites readers to situate that conflict within a wider and deeper historical context that encompasses an awareness not only of the role played by the People's Republic of China but also of a longer history of US empire that stretches back to the nineteenth century.

Each of Hinojosa's Korean War works is an experiment in genre. *Korean Love Songs* is a series of poems that together approximate a novelistic narrative, and *The Useless Servants* takes the form of a journal written by Rafe himself. I begin with *Rites and Witnesses*, which is by far the most challenging of the three. It consists almost entirely of dialogues that resemble a screenplay or dramatic text and first-person testimonies or witness statements. Readers are plunged into events in medias res and must engage in tremendous interpretive labor to arrive at even a provisional understanding of the events they are reading about. However, only by engaging with the novel's immense formal challenges can readers grasp the elusive connections it invites one to make between the two seemingly disparate historical sites it brings into intimate contact—Korea in 1950 and South Texas in 1960—and the specific point it is making about the participation of Mexican American soldiers in the Korean War.

Rites and Witnesses features two protagonists: Rafe, the central figure in the 1950 timeline, who must overcome not only the threats posed by enemy soldiers but also the incompetence and racism of white commanding officers, and Jehú Malacara, who lies at the heart of events that take place ten years later in South Texas and negotiates the class and race hierarchies of Belken County as he begins working for the KBC, a kind of syndicate composed by members of the richest Anglo families in the region: the Klails, the Blanchards, and the Cookes. The connection between the Korean and Texan plotlines of the novel centers on the comparable positions the two protagonists find themselves in vis à vis the two institutions they serve. This sense of doubling is emphasized by Hinojosa's use of acronyms to identify both organizations: the KBC and the AUSA (Army of the United States). The first part of the book is titled "The Rites," suggesting as its focus the rites of passage that Rafe and Jehú must negotiate as they serve the AUSA and the KBC, respectively.

The chapters that depict the Korean War are easier to follow and very much of a piece with the other works in Hinojosa's trilogy. They center on a military action Rafe is involved in and its aftermath. He and his men identify a large group of Chinese soldiers in the valley below, call in an artillery attack that decimates hundreds of them, and then are themselves subjected to a devastating barrage of enemy fire. Rafe is badly injured and knocked unconscious as he tries to bring a wounded soldier to safety. He awakens in a hospital in Japan and learns that the man he had tried to rescue has died. He is visited by three white soldiers: Lieutenant Phil Brodkey commends Rafe for his bravery and informs him that he's been recommended for a Bronze Star; Sergeant Frank Hatalski relays the news that Charlie Villalon, one of Rafe's friends from home, has been killed and offers to arrange for a visit to his grave; and finally, the racist and duplicitous Captain Ted Bracken declares the affinity he feels for the injured Rafe as a fellow Texan but has actually been trying to get him court-martialed.

Overall, the portrait of the US Army that these chapters paint is of a bureaucracy in which most of the men, Anglo and Chicano, attempt to do their best but are undermined by and indeed killed as a result of mistakes made by white officers like Bracken, who are incompetent as well as racist. These parts of the novel constitute something like a Mexican American memorial to the Korean War—paying witness and administering last rites, as it were, to the collective sacrifice of US soldiers who died in that conflict. *Rites and Witnesses* does not offer, however, the kinds of nationalist platitudes one finds in US memorials to the veterans of the Korean War: their deaths are not rendered as the necessary price of freedom.[19] Rather, the novel critiques the notion that the participation of Mexican American soldiers in the war brought an end to the racism they faced at home. The juxtaposition of "the two settings and the two time-frames (1960 in Klail City and 1950 in Korea)," as Rosaura Sanchéz argues, "expresses the futility of the deaths of many American boys, among them many Chicanos whose bodies were fished out of the river by fellow soldiers so that the Klails, Blanchards and Cookes of the world could continue to profit, scheme, manipulate, fornicate and destroy the Valley of their forefathers. The Rites are for the dead in Korea and for the decaying Valley, in the hands of Anglo capitalists and their Chicano lackeys."[20] Sanchéz accurately conveys the continuing machinations of the KBC families who rule Belken County. The conversations depicted in the first half of the novel reveal two Machiavellian schemes the KBC are putting into motion in 1960. One involves their search for "Chicano lackeys," as Sanchéz puts it, whom they hope to install in various positions of relative power. The other involves the Fredericka Cooke Institute, a nonprofit organization established ostensibly to honor one of their own who dies of cancer early in the novel. The KBC devise the institute as a kind of shell company that will enable them to reap the profits from a leather factory without having to pay the US government any taxes: it is an entirely legal scam.

Insofar as the KBC families remain the dominant power in the region, the South Texas that Chicano veterans find themselves negotiating in 1960 seems much like the one they left in 1950 to fight in Korea. Indeed, Ramón Saldívar insists that Hinojosa's writings demonstrate how "the Texas home to which the Korean War veterans will return is no different from the one to which the World War II veterans returned."[21] This assessment, however, is only partially correct, for the novel stresses the discontinuities as well as the continuities in South Texas before and after the Korean War.

Rites and Witnesses reveals a fundamental shift in the tactics and strategies Anglo elites rely on in 1960 to maintain their hegemony. In the early part of the twentieth century, the KBC amassed their wealth and power by stealing land from Mexicans and through orchestrated acts of racist violence. Their lead enforcer in this respect was George "Choche" Markham, who was a member of the Texas Rangers. Readers become acquainted with the egregious acts that Markham and the Rangers had committed during the first part of the twentieth century from chapters in the second half of the novel—titled "Witnesses"—that read like statements given in a legal proceeding. These include Markham's lynching of Mexican prisoners in his custody in 1915 and his murder of Ambrosia Mora, a returning World War II veteran in the 1940s. By 1960, however, Markham has outlived his usefulness. In one conversation, members of the KBC discuss the need to ease Markham into retirement. Moreover, the now elderly Markham himself denies the violence he perpetrated as a young man against Chicanos, protesting, "I'm their friend. What the hell do they know. . . . Why, I married a Mex, didn't I?"[22]

The Fredericka Cooke Institute, the nonprofit that functions as a covert tax shelter, reflects the kinds of schemes in which the KBC is now engaged in 1960. Significantly, Jehú—Rafe's best friend and the other primary character in the *KCDT* as a whole—plays a key role in establishing the institute through his position as a bank officer. That he clearly understands what this stratagem entails is evident from his observation that "the KBC didn't have to put it to the Mexicanos anymore; they now went after bigger game; the U.S. Treasury, for one" (54).

The novel thus registers how life in South Texas has changed for Mexican Americans as well—or at least for some of them, for the overall impression given by the novel is that Klail City in 1960 was a community that was slowly and unevenly becoming integrated. Several of the chapters in the "Witnesses" section provide evidence of these changes. In one, a retired schoolteacher voices her racist nostalgia for a time when "the Mexicans didn't go to school with us" and complains, "Now, they go on to school and even graduate sometimes," despite the fact that "they *still* speak Spanish" (97, 98). Another Anglo woman, a storeowner with more moderate views on race, recounts, "[I] traded with Mexicans all my life, and got three of them working for us," and she approvingly observes that "times've changed and for the better in many ways," relating how Vicente Vizcarra Jr., a used car and insurance salesman, was able to open an office in a section of town formerly denied to Mexicans (77).

Though readers must work to arrive at an explanation for the changes that have taken place between 1950 and 1960, *Rites and Witnesses* provides a clue by juxtaposing the comparable positions occupied by its two protagonists in the two organizations they serve: Rafe's service as an artillery spotter for the AUSA and Jehú's work as a bank officer for the KBC. Readers should eventually recognize how the latter is, historically speaking, partially a consequence of the former—that the service of Mexican American men in the Korean War paved the way for some of them to rise into the middle class. Though this is fleshed out in other volumes of the *KCDT*, Rafe and Jehú both served in Korea and were subsequently able to receive college educations as beneficiaries of the GI Bill.

The historical dilemma *Rites and Witnesses* brings into focus is the one faced by subjects like Rafe and Jehú at midcentury—one they confront precisely because of their participation in the Korean War. *Rites and Witnesses* accentuates that its protagonists and other middle-class Mexican Americans were the potential beneficiaries of the racial order that emerged after the war. The Jehús, Rafes, and Vicente Vizcarras represent a Mexican American middle class whose ascent was facilitated by a Cold War welfare state that brought a legal end to segregation and enabled some members of some minority groups to reap the benefits of the GI Bill. In identifying the opportunities that opened up to some Chicano men, *Rites and Witnesses* calls attention to the fact that one tangible outcome of the Korean War was to enhance *their* life chances, even if the same was not necessarily true for other people of color or even other Mexican Americans. Readers also should be aware, though this aspect of the decade is not foregrounded by the novel, that 1954 marked the beginning of Operation Wetback, a militarized program of mass deportation that ostensibly targeted Mexicans who had immigrated illegally but actually targeted US citizens as well.[23]

With some Mexican Americans' greater capacity for choice came a greater possibility of complicity and cooptation. Insofar as Jehú acts as a good soldier, as it were, for the KBC, he risks becoming reduced to one of their "Chicano lackeys," as Sanchéz puts it.[24] Hinojosa's depiction of the region in the *KCDT* overall resonates with José Limón's assertion that "since the 1830s, the Mexicans of south Texas have been in a state of social war with the 'Anglo' dominant Other and their class allies," and Jehú thus finds himself allied with a social and racial class that has been victimizing his community for well over a century.[25] This deeper historical context leads us to see Rafe's service for the AUSA in a critical light as well, for the US military force he serves has played a central role in the race and class war that defines the border region. While several statements in "Witnesses" identify the Texas Rangers as being responsible for the worst acts of anti-Mexican violence that took place in the early twentieth century, they also make clear that members of the US Army—like John F. Goodman, a retired US cavalryman whose last name has a ring of irony—were allied with the Rangers, even if they self-servingly distanced themselves from the excessive brutality of men like Markham.

The issue of what Rafe and Jehú will do later on in the century with the middle-class status they have achieved by 1960 is explored in other volumes of the *KCDT*. In them, readers learn how these protagonists negotiate the invitation to collaboration offered to them by the KBC elites. What matters here is that *Rites and Witnesses* illuminates how the historical origin of their ethical dilemma lies in the Korean War.

Being a Good Reader: Hinojosa's Asias

Hinojosa's Korean War writings are also significant for their intermittent and partial but nonetheless significant expressions of transnational and cross-racial solidarity with the various Asian populations with whom Rafe and other Mexican American soldiers come into contact—primarily civilians in Japan, where they are stationed before the conflict, and the Chinese soldiers they fought.

Several chapters of *Korean Love Songs*, Hinojosa's first Korean War novel, recount how Rafe and other Chicano soldiers become romantically involved with local civilian women in Japan. The friendships and romantic relationships they form with the Japanese suggest a kind of interracial affinity. One of Rafe's friends from home, Sonny Ruiz, has deserted the army and assumes a Japanese identity as Kazuo Fusaro, a schoolteacher who is engaged to be married. He has been able to pass because "to Americans he looks Japanese."[26] In a chapter titled "Brief Encounter," two MPs have stopped Rafe and are inspecting his papers when they notice a figure stroll by whom they assume is Japanese:

> Just then, Sonny Ruiz passes by and tips his hat, showing,
> As he carries, the biggest, the loudest, the most glorious bouquet
> In the whole of Honshu.
> One of them grunts and says:
> "Pipe the gook and them flowers, there.
> Damndest place I've ever seen." (102)

Linking Japanese and Mexicans is a seeming physical resemblance that can make them indistinguishable to the racist gaze of the white MPs. In the preceding passage, the indiscriminate nature of this racism is rendered in comedic terms. The motivations for Sonny's racial masquerade, however, are treated quite seriously when he provides an answer to Rafe's question in the following exchange:

> And home?
> "*This* is home, Rafe, why should I go back?"
> He has me there, Why indeed? (100)

Sonny's decision to go AWOL and pass as Japanese makes sense to Rafe because it enables an escape not only from the horrors of war but also from the racism that defines life in South Texas. As Ramón Saldívar has observed, "The cultural affinity between Japanese and Mexican

American life" that Sonny finds so congenial "allows for this assimilation and its resulting turn away from an oppressed, self-negating home in South Texas."[27] "Objects of prejudice and exploitation at home, dying in Korea," Saldívar continues, "it is no wonder that they are charmed by the allure of Japanese self-sufficiency, integrity and family solidarity in the face of an occupying American army."[28] As Saldívar suggests, Rafe and his friends seem to see a reflection of their own community in the Japanese—who have sought to retain a sense of "integrity" despite the presence of a racist occupying army—because their people confronted similar circumstances during and after the US-Mexico War.

The many Chinese soldiers whose deaths Rafe causes or witnesses also become visible as objects of sympathy and respect in Hinojosa's Korean War writings, though at a distance. When Rafe first describes the mass killing of such soldiers in a chapter titled "Chinaman's Hat," he does so dispassionately:

> From Kujang-dong, we had supplied the fire
> Which, along that of armor.
> Rid the Chinese and cut them to pieces. What we didn't kill
> The Air Force did, and those who were left,
> Up they scurried to Chinaman's Hat. (26)

But later, in a chapter titled "The January–May 1951 Slaughter," it is clear that these actions have taken a psychic toll:

> No one talks about the cold anymore, nor about the dead,
> Theirs or ours, but mostly theirs.
> Also, we never seem to run out of shells. . . .
> I don't want to look at the Chinese dead.
> There are hundreds of them out there. They died in the city,
> They died in the fields and in the hillsides.
> They died everywhere. (42)

This lament for the multitudes of Chinese soldiers Rafe has killed is expanded in Hinojosa's final Korean War novel, *The Useless Servants*. Over the course of that work, which is written as if it were a journal,

Rafe comes to feel first a growing numbness and then a mute outrage over the vast loss of life he has witnessed and caused. He ultimately draws on a kind of universal discourse of soldiering in order to evoke an interracial and transnational brotherhood of war. In these passages, we see a reworking and expansion of the military Orientalism of midcentury American depictions of the Korean War: instead of incorporating loyal Japanese American soldiers into the "exclusive club" that the US military exemplifies, however, Hinojosa's vision evokes a virile fraternity of fighting men whose service and sacrifice should be honored, one that includes Asian enemy combatants. In the final pages, Rafe dedicates his writing not only to his fellow US soldiers but also to the Chinese soldiers he had fought: "And it's for all the other useless servants, the CCF [Chinese Communist Forces], who also fought for their masters in a foreign land."[29]

However, virtually absent from Hinojosa's Korean War novels, and especially the first two, is any significant mention of Korean civilians or soldiers. This absence is particularly striking given that the title of the first is *Korean Love Songs* and that Hinojosa has suggested an interview that the experience of seeing multitudes of dead civilians had a lasting impact on him: "The strongest memories of all these years remains the same: the weather (monsoon and freezing winters), the desolation (burning of forests and scarring of the countryside), *the refugees (dead men, women, children, and their bones)*, and fear (the unknown, pain, and death)."[30] His third novel, *The Useless Servants*, rectifies this absence to a certain degree, for a spectacle of civilian deaths caused by US military forces figures prominently in it; indeed, it haunts Rafe for the remainder of his tour of duty. Moreover, his reaction and that of the other US soldiers who witness this mass killing of Korean refugees takes on a crucial significance in that novel, as it models for readers how they should respond to the events they are reading about.

Rafe describes this event, which took place in July of 1950, early in the novel. He and Joey Vielma, a friend from home, watch as "columns of refugees (in the hundreds, maybe thousands: people, carts, oxen, etc.)" walk across a bridge that has been slated for demolition (35). While some effort is made to clear the refugees, the bridge is blown up while many are still on it:

The Gen (don't have his name yet) gave the order himself. And then, the bridge was destroyed. Blown up. Hundreds died on it: kids, families, animals.

Joey and I turned our backs to avoid seeing the bodies. The bridge was blown up in all kinds of pieces. A roar, a geyser of water and who knows what else went up in the air. All the time, our vehicles revving the motors, but we could still hear the screaming and the crying. The Engineers had set the charges and were waiting for all units to get across.

This was worse than any hand-to-hand fighting we had had in Chuchi-won. (35; emphasis mine)

Rafe is generally a stoic character, and this is one of the few moments in the novel in which he expresses any emotion, however muted it may be. Despite the fact that he and Joey turn away, he underscores the singularity of the horror that took place as he registers the violent loss of civilian life in a series of sounds that incite his imagination: a "roar," the "revving of motors," "the screaming," the "crying."

Notably, Rafe's response is a desire to make sense of what he has witnessed, which motivates a series of conversations among the soldiers in his unit. Three days after the demolition of the bridge, Rafe is "shooting the shit with the guys and the Old Guys [the more experienced soldiers]," and they find themselves talking about the refugees who perished at the hands of US Army engineers:

Old Guys say that the majority of refugees (back to that again) are city people. From as far away as Seoul, some of them. K[orea] is mostly a land of farmers, and peasants tend to stay put. The Communists treat them better than city folk, too. After all this talk got back to blowing up of bridge.

Still living with it. What can I do? (40–41)

While this talk does little to mitigate Rafe's guilt and horror, it does produce in him a greater contextual awareness of the nature of the war in which they are embroiled. Several similar conversations subsequently take place that mirror to readers how they should respond to the novel overall—that they, like Rafe and the other soldiers, should engage dialogically with what they have witnessed and strive to situate it in a historical context.

Again, Rafe's sense of guilt is unassuaged—"Still living with it. What can I do?"—which resonates with how Frank feels about the Korean girl he shot in *Home*: "The best he could hope for was time to work it loose."[31] The best that readers of Hinojosa's novels can hope to do is to register the unease that Rafe feels—which deepens over the remainder of the novel until he experiences a kind of mental breakdown—while also asking the kinds of questions he and the other men do. As we watch Hinojosa's protagonist go about the business of being a good soldier, his journal also alerts us to how we might become good readers, which involves focusing on those details that invite us to supplement what we are witnessing by developing an understanding of the wider and deeper historical trajectories that have shaped those events.

Reading in this way entails dwelling on the ramifications of a certain detail Rafe and the other soldiers note: that most of the civilian refugees are "city people," while Korea itself is "mostly a land of farmers." What is to be made of that fact is left unsaid. But since reading Hinojosa always entails connecting details across various works, those who supplement their analysis of *Rites and Witnesses* with an awareness of what takes place elsewhere in *KCDT* will glimpse a resemblance between the North Korean Communists and Rafe's own family. After all, the Buenrostros, while they are members of the Mexican American aristocracy, represent its "good face" (as the English translation of this surname would suggest), as they have tried to act in the interests of the working-class farmers and ranch hands threatened by the predations of the Rangers and the KBC. Their antithetical rivals are the Leguizamóns, who collaborate with Anglo elites in exploiting other Mexican Americans.

To be clear, Hinojosa never offers any explicit commentary about either of the Korean regimes. But insofar as the Buenrostros-Leguizamón conflict is rendered as a kind of civil war that plays out in the context of a colonial war between the United States and Mexico and then a race war between Anglo elites and working-class Chicanos, his writings invite readers to glimpse the parallels between these two warring clans and the two states claiming sovereignty over the Korean peninsula. Readers are also encouraged to see that modern Korea has been shaped by the legacy of Japanese imperialism, to recognize that "Koreans don't like the Japs one damned bit," as some of Rafe's fellow soldiers put it, because "both Korea and Manchuria were under Jap domination for years" (78).

If we move, as Hinojosa's writings impel us to, beyond the events that they actually depict, but from an angle that retains an after-image of South Texas, we arrive at a view of the two regimes that emerged north and south of the thirty-eighth parallel that accords with the perspective Bruce Cumings consistently outlines in his scholarship. Cumings persuasively argues that only one of the two Koreas should be seen as emerging out of a legitimate decolonizing struggle for national self-determination.[32] The political movement that took shape as the Democratic People's Republic of Korea, whatever its obvious and ample shortcomings, seems to resemble the heroic Buenrostros; the counterpart to the villainous Leguizamóns would seem to be the men who came to power in the Republic of Korea, for the latter regime was replete with figures who had collaborated with a prior occupying power, the Japanese, and was largely installed in power by a second, the US government.

Another line of historical inquiry that Hinojosa's KCDT encourages its readers to pursue concerns the parallel outcomes of the Korean War and the US-Mexico War in the partitions established at the ends of both conflicts. He evokes the community that had resided on both sides of the Rio Grande as one that possessed "its own history, its own culture, and its own sense of place" and that had been cut in two at the end of the US-Mexico War with the signing of the Treaty of Guadalupe Hidalgo.[33] The river was turned into a national border by an occupying colonial power, the United States. Hinojosa's writings invite us to follow the path of the Rio Grande and see its figurative continuity with another partition established at the conclusion of a much later US war.

Nearly a century later on the other side of the globe, the United States created another political border that would also divide a community that had long existed as a single entity. "The initial decision to draw a line at the thirty-eighth parallel was wholly an American action," Cumings writes, "taken during a night-long session of the State-War-Navy Coordinating Committee (SWNCC), on August 10–11, 1945."[34] And the line that divided the two Korean states that erupted in war in 1950 was "not an international boundary like that between Iraq and Kuwait, or Germany and Poland; instead it bisected a nation that had a rare and well-recognized unitary existence going back to antiquity."[35] While the United States initially treated the thirty-eighth parallel as a wholly legitimate international border when it intervened, it was actually a partition that nation had played a key role in establishing. In highlighting this fact, Cumings argues against the legal rationale that the United States relied on in its decision to intervene (explored in chapter 1): that it was defending the sovereign integrity of one nation that had been subjected to an illegal attack by another. Rather, the North Korean invasion of the South was the first battle in what was, at bottom, a civil war.

Hinojosa's Korean War writings implicitly invite readers to imagine how the history that shaped modern Korea might connect to the one that shaped the US borderlands. If the annexation of Texas made manifest the colonial aspirations of an emergent hemispheric power in 1848, the decision to send nearly two million soldiers (among them Rolando Hinojosa) to Korea a century later reflected the imperial aspirations of what had become the leading global power. No longer content to simply draw a line in the sand between itself and its neighbor to the south, the United States partitioned off a massive portion of the globe, claiming the First and much of the Third World as its bailiwick. This brought into being, as Cumings describes, "an archipelago of empire": "In the second half of the twentieth century an entirely new phenomenon emerged in American history, namely, the permanent stationing of soldiers in a myriad of foreign bases across the face of the planet, connected to an enormous domestic complex of defense industries. For the first time in modern history the leading power maintained an extensive network of bases on the territories of its allies and economic competitors. . . . an archipelago of empire."[36] Much of the power of Hinojosa's Korean War writings derives from how they invite us to see 1848 and 1945 as part of a continuous history, to see the Rio Grande and the thirty-eighth parallel, now the demilitarized zone, as associated segments in the borderlands of US empire.

War Trash: Neutrality with an Edge

As I turn now to the Chinese and Chinese American perspective on the Korean War that emerges from Ha Jin's *War Trash* (2004), I should attend first to the absence in Hinojosa's writings of any mention of *North Korean* military forces: they are not counted as among "the useless servants" his third novel memorializes. While this may seem a curious elision, it might reflect the enormous size of the military force that the PRC sent to Korea. The number of Chinese soldiers who were killed or went missing during the conflict (600,000) is comparable to that of North and South Korean soldiers combined (406,000 and 217,000, respectively) and far smaller than that of US soldiers (36,568).[37] These numbers suggest how significant the Korean War was to the Chinese. The name used to refer to it in the PRC—the War to Resist US Aggression and Aid Korea—encapsulates how the country has framed it as a decisive victory in which its military forces successfully thwarted an imperialist invasion that sought to bring regime change to an ally whose leaders had joined its People's Army in their fight against the Japanese in Manchuria.[38] However, *War Trash* issues a critique of this triumphalist narrative from the perspective of Chinese POWs who were treated as outcasts—as "war trash"—upon their return home.

In focusing on their plight, Jin's novel also highlights, as does Adams's *An American Dream*, the issue that became the primary point of contention in the peace talks that took place during the final two years of the war: whether POWs would be summarily repatriated or allowed to choose which country they would be sent to upon their release.

Moreover, *War Trash*'s depiction of the POW camps—as sites in which the violence of the Second Chinese Civil War (which ended with the Nationalists fleeing the mainland) reemerged in conflicts between cadres of prisoners loyal to the PRC and those loyal to Taiwan—underscores the historical intimacy of the Chinese Civil War and the Korean War: the former formally ended one year before the latter officially began. Additionally, as several reviewers observed when it was published in 2004,[39] *War Trash* suggests how the incidents of prisoner abuse in Abu Ghraib and Guantánamo Bay that had recently become public had a precedent in the conduct of US military prison guards during the Korean War.

Formally, *War Trash* somewhat resembles Hinojosa's *The Useless Servants*, as it is presented to the reader as a journal or memoir written by a soldier—or in this case, a veteran. Jin's narrator and protagonist is Yu Yuan, who served in the Chinese People's Army. In the opening pages, Yuan, who is now seventy-three, explains that he will be writing his memoir during an extended visit with his son, who works as an engineer in Atlanta, is married to a Cambodian American woman, and is raising two American-born children. His aim is "to tell [his] story in a documentary manner so as to preserve historical accuracy," suggesting that his will be an objective, nonpartisan account.[40] However, readers soon learn that Yuan has no real respect for either the mainland Chinese or Taiwanese governments. He offers a rather straightforward documentation of his life experiences, beginning briefly with his life in China before the Communist victory and continuing with his experiences in battle and his capture in the summer of 1951. While the bulk of *War Trash* describes Yuan's time in a series of prison camps, it concludes with an account of the quiet life he has led in China after the war.

The first half of the novel offers a scathing portrait of the Nationalists. The camp to which Yuan is initially sent—Compound 72 on Koje Island—while nominally under the control of the US military is actually run by POWs fervently loyal to the Nationalist regime Chiang Kai-shek had established in Taiwan. These overseers engage in a campaign of violent intimidation, seeking to coerce members of the People's Army into refusing repatriation. Their efforts are in no way curbed by the US guards. Yuan draws the attention of the Nationalist leaders because of his fluency in English. At one point they invite Yuan to a meal and implore him to choose Taiwan, warning him that he will always be regarded with suspicion in the PRC. When Yuan refuses, they knock him unconscious and tattoo "FUCK COMMUNISM" in English onto his stomach. They have tattooed many others with similar slogans, though in Chinese, that would be sure to cause difficulties upon repatriation to the PRC.[41]

The most ruthless of the Nationalist leaders is Liu Tai-an. Shortly before the initial screening, Liu and his men round up all the prisoners who have been tattooed. Those who still insist on returning to the PRC have their tattoos carved out of their skin. Some are beaten and killed. One particularly vocal Communist, Lin Wushen, is stabbed and disemboweled by Liu's men in front of the other prisoners. Despite the intense pressure exerted by the Nationalists, Yuan declares his intent to return to the mainland, and he is transferred to Compound 602, which is run by Communists.

While Yuan mainly wants to return home to be reunited with his mother and his fiancée, Julan, he does hold a higher opinion of the Communists than he does of the Nationalists, at least initially. He recalls that the cadets at the military college he attended—even though it had been founded by Chiang Kai-shek and functioned as his version of West Point—"had been disgusted with the corruption of the Nationalists, so they readily surrendered to the People's Liberation Army when the Communists arrived" (6). He also remembers the sense of hope he then felt: "In every direction I turned, life seemed to smile upon me. It was as if all the shadows were lifting. The Communists had brought order to our country and hope to the common people. I had never been so cheerful" (7). In the camps, Yuan is struck by the cohesiveness of prisoners from the PRC, which he describes to Commissar Pei through a simple arithmetical analogy: "I believe there must be a power much larger than an individual, like a multiplier. If you tap that power, you can multiply yourself. You can become one hundred or one thousand, depending on what the multiplier is" (125). Pei offers that he has found that "multiplier" in Marxism.

In Compound 602, Yuan is drawn into the orbit of Pei and the Communist leadership. He plays a small but significant role in a plot devised by the North Korean POWs to abduct General Bell, the US Army officer in command of the camps on Koje Island, which they successfully carry out on May 7, 1952, with the assistance of the Chinese prisoners. (This episode is based on an actual event, the kidnapping of General Francis Todd by POWs on Koje Island.) Yuan becomes an active participant in the ensuing negotiations, serving as a translator and testifying to the abuses he and other People's Army POWs have experienced. Their gambit proves successful, as the imprisoned North Korean and PRC soldiers are able to extract from General Bell a promise to investigate such abuses and to improve the conditions in the camp. This turns out to be a significant propaganda victory, as the event receives international attention, giving the North Korean and Chinese leadership leverage in their negotiations.

This victory is short lived, however, for the men are soon shipped off to Camp 8 on Cheju Island, which has been specifically constructed to prevent such acts from taking place again: Commissar Pei is held in a small hut away from the other men, and the layout of the other barracks prevents large groups of prisoners from congregating. Yuan plays a key role in overcoming these barriers to communication when he helps devise a code that enables Pei to continue issuing commands to his men. Pei orders them to construct flags and raise them on October 1, 1952, which marks the three-year anniversary of the Communist victory in the Chinese Civil War. The men carry out these orders with enthusiasm, but their rebellion is violently quelled by US soldiers. Dozens of POWs are killed and hundreds injured.

As Pei continues ordering his men to sacrifice themselves in such actions in order to prove his loyalty to the leadership in Beijing, however, Yuan becomes increasingly disillusioned with him and the Communists overall. In fact, when the conceit contained in the novel's title is first cited in Yuan's narrative, it references how soldiers are treated by the Communist leadership. Wang Yong, one of the Nationalist leaders, asserts that the Communists "use men like ammo," referring to the "human wave" tactics used by the People's Army that were aimed at taking enemy positions by assaulting them with multitudes of infantry without air or artillery support—these attacks would result in thousands of men giving their lives in order to take one hill (176). A version of the titular image comes to Yuan after listening to Wang's commentary: "His words conjured up the horrible image I hadn't been able to shake off—that the war was an enormous furnace fed by the bodies of soldiers" (76). The final pages of the novel, which recount the POWs' homecoming, convey how they were treated as "war trash" at home as well. "With a few exceptions," Yuan recounts, "we were all discharged dishonorably, which meant we had become the dregs of society." Hundreds of POWs "were imprisoned again, labeled as traitors or spies," and "placed under special control for the rest of [their] lives." Pei is demoted and lives out his days as a rice farmer, leading Yuan to reflect that "he too had been a mere pawn, not much different from any of us. He too was war trash" (345).

The deeply critical view of the PRC leadership that emerges from the novel aligns with the sentiment expressed by the tattoo the Nationalists had carved into Yuan's skin: "FUCK COMMUNISM." This extends a line of political critique apparent throughout Jin's writings and repeated in his interviews, unsurprising for a writer who had decided to stay in the United States after the Tiananmen Square massacre. The typical antagonist in most of Jin's works, as Michelle Kuo and Albert Wu observe, is "the Chinese state," which is always rendered as "spineless, manipulative, untrustworthy, and corrupt, . . . treat[ing] ideology as provisional and people as disposable." In *War Trash*, this critique targets Taiwan as well as the PRC.[42]

In contrast to blunt statements he has made about the repressiveness of the Chinese government in Beijing, Jin has been relatively silent concerning any similar actions taken by the government of his adopted country. In regards to *War Trash*, this silence is all the more striking, since many favorable reviews of the novel in 2004 saw it as commenting on the mistreatment of prisoners by US soldiers. Russell Banks, for example, applauded the novel's "significance and inescapable relevance to events being played out in the world today, from Abu Ghraib to Guantánamo Bay."[43] Linda Jaivin similarly noted that the novel's depiction of abuses inflicted by US guards suggests how "Abu Ghraib could be tradition, not aberration."[44] When Dwight Garner pointed out these contemporary resonances of *War Trash* to Jin in an interview, however, the author simply replied, "Yes, it is quite mysterious. But when I started this novel in 2000, I didn't expect anything like this would appear in the news."[45]

Despite Jin's seeming hesitation to draw a parallel between the POW camps it depicts and the detention centers administered by the United States and thus between the Korean War and the so-called War on Terror, it is virtually impossible for readers to avoid making such connections.[46] Indeed, like many of the novels taken up in this study, *War Trash* was published in an era when Americans were becoming increasingly aware of the morally and legally dubious strategies US military forces and intelligence organizations had been pursuing in the ongoing struggle against Al Qaeda, ISIS, and the like. In looking back to the Korean War and inviting readers to see similarities with the present, these works lend support to a historical understanding of the Cold War's greatest significance as stemming from its putting into place what Mary Dudziak terms "a new logic of governance" and the development of "the national security state" that necessitates the existence of detention centers.[47]

There is, moreover, the novel's dramatic opening sentence: "Below my navel stretches a long tattoo that says 'FUCK . . . U . . . S . . .'" (3). We later learn that a sympathetic People's Army doctor had altered it from "FUCK COMMUNISM" to shield Yuan from suspicious party officials. While the original version would seem to better convey the perspective of the novel overall, the novel also includes a scene in which Jin's phlegmatic protagonist angrily voices sentiments that are close in spirit to the redacted version of the tattoo. Yuan's outburst takes place during the kidnapping of General Bell as he testifies about the abuses he has suffered: "I spoke in English, describing the persecution in Compound 72—how Liu Tai-an had disemboweled Lin Wushen and how my former schoolmate Yang Huan had been cudgeled and strangled to death. After giving an account of how the pro-Nationalist officers in that compound had cut some men to collect the tattoos they themselves had inflicted on them by force, I pulled up my shirt and displayed the words on my belly—FUCK COMMUNISM." General Bell laughs when he sees the tattoo and diminishes it as a "prank." The incredulous Yuan points out that the tattooing constitutes a war crime that "took place in one of the compounds under [Bell's] charge" (178). Moreover, he asserts, "Those prison chiefs were trained in Japan and Taiwan, and then sent back by your government to help you run the camp. They murdered and beat us at will. Isn't the American government responsible for their crimes?" (179). Bell's noncommittal responses engender this reaction in the ordinarily stoic Yuan:

> I lost self-control, shouting at him hysterically, "Stop dodging! You think you're clean? Let me tell you, you too are a criminal whose hands are stained with Chinese and Korean blood. You think you can pretend you don't know what crimes your men committed? You think you can bend our will and force us to betray our motherland? Do you know what the true Chinese spirit is? Let me tell you, if we're alive, we're Chinese men; if we're dead, we're Chinese ghosts. Those bastards under your protection can never change us by mutilating our bodies. Let me say this to you—"
>
> Ming grabbed me by the shoulders and dragged me out of the tent to cool me down. "Boy, I never thought you could be so emotional," he said. (179)

Yuan's outburst allows readers to see the POW camps and the anti-Communist overseers who run them as metonyms for the states that emerged in countries like Taiwan and South Korea, emphasizing how the repressive leaders there were propped up by the US military. Compound 702 on Koje Island is depicted as very much a miniature of Taiwan, ruled as it is by a strongman, Liu, who "hated the Communists so much that he often publicly flogged men who wanted to return to Red China. The Americans had adopted a let-alone policy and didn't care what happened in the compounds as long as the POWs remained behind the barbed wire, so *Liu ruled this regiment like a police state*" (68; emphasis mine). While *War Trash* directly targets Asian fanatics from both sides, it also holds Americans responsible for the egregious acts committed by such strongmen, who enjoyed the full support of the US government. If what rages in the prison camps are civil wars in miniature, their violence is inflamed by the conditions of their enclosure. From this vantage point, the positioning of the US military forces who stand guard behind the barbed-wire fences that surround the camps emerges as an allegory for the policy of containment that shaped US foreign policy in Asia during the Cold War years, which enabled anti-Communist strongmen like Chiang Kai-shek and Syngman Rhee to exert their authoritarian power over their own people.

The Ultimate Object of the Novel's Critique: Us

As should now be evident, Yuan's stated aims as a narrator—"I'm going to tell my story in a documentary manner so as to preserve historical accuracy" (5)—do not result in an account devoid of critique or affect. Instead, like the two versions of the tattoo inscribed in his skin, his story expresses a rage directed not only at the Communists but also at the United States. Ultimately, the easy substitutability of the referents of the epithet expressed by the tattoo—the "U . . . S . . ." and "COMMUNISM"—suggests an equivalence between the US and the PRC, the global powers responsible for the bulk of the devastation that took place during the Korean War. A mirroring of these two entities is suggested in the following passage, in which Yuan reflects on how *all* military leaders engage in an identical calculus in regards to the men under their command:

To be able to function in a war, an officer was expected to view his men as abstract figures so that he could utilize and sacrifice them without any hesitation or qualms. The same abstraction was supposed to take place among the rank and file too—to us every American serviceman must be a devil, whereas to them, every one of us must be a Red. Without such obliteration of human particularities, how could one fight mercilessly? When a general evaluates the outcome of a battle, he thinks in numbers—how many casualties the enemy has suffered in comparison with the losses of his own army. The larger a victory is, the more people have been turned into numerals. This is the crime of war: it reduces real human beings to abstract numbers. (192)

At the most general level, the primary object of critique in *War Trash* is the militarized nationalism that led both the United States and the PRC to intervene in Korea. In the calculus shared by commanding officers on both sides, the soldiers who lost their lives in the fighting had only registered as "abstract figures," making it easy for them to be treated as "war trash."

Like the other works examined in this chapter, *War Trash* is primarily concerned with memorializing the soldiers who came to Korea to fight in a war their countries should not have entered. The primary reparative gesture these novels perform is to restore a sense of dignity to those "useless servants" (to use Hinojosa's phrase) who were treated as "war trash" (to use Jin's) by the governments that sent them to intervene in a Korean civil war. These works compose a literary archive of cultural memory of the Korean War that highlights the traumas endured by African American, Mexican American, and Chinese soldiers. In so doing, however, all of them, though to varying degrees, testify to the fact that any exclusive focus on what *soldiers* suffered during the Korean War threatens to obscure those who suffered the most. Hence the resolution of Morrison's novel is troubled by the specter of a Korean girl who had been murdered by her African American protagonist, and Hinojosa's novel similarly features a protagonist who is haunted by a memory of hundreds of Korean refugees who had been blown up on a bridge by the US Army. Jin's novel concludes with a suggestion that the people who might be the ultimate referents of its title are the Koreans themselves. He voices his understanding of "why occasionally some Korean civilians were hostile to us": they viewed Chinese troops as "com[ing] here only to protect China's interests" and "by so doing, we couldn't help but ruin their homes, fields, and livelihoods." He points out that, moreover, while "it was true that the Koreans had started the war themselves, . . . a small country like theirs could only end up being a battleground for bigger powers. Whoever won this war, Korea would be a loser" (301). As Yuan later adds, "We thought we had come all the way to help the Koreans, but some of us had willy-nilly ended up their despoilers" (303). The ultimate finger of blame is thus pointed at *all* the foreign soldiers who had brought destruction and ruin to Korea, for the "us" indicted by the tattoo on Yuan's chest includes not just the US and PRC governments who victimized their own soldiers but the soldiers themselves, the "war trash" and "useless servants" who victimized the people they had ostensibly come to save.

* * *

All the works examined in this chapter call attention to, as *War Trash* ultimately does, the devastation brought to the Korean people by foreign military forces. In their brief but pointed references to the civilian deaths caused by such forces, they provide a necessary corrective to the humanitarian Orientalist narratives examined in chapter 4. As *War Trash* suggests, such losses within a biopolitical accounting were simply fleshly ciphers—the necessary expenses that are simply part of the business of war-making. Although readers might want more from these authors in terms of humanizing the civilian victims of the violence unleashed by foreign military forces, the novels at least avoid imbuing those deaths with an aura of sacrifice, sanctifying them as martyrs to a divine cause. While I have already engaged with more complex explorations of Korean subjectivity in the Korean American novels examined in chapters 5 and 6, in the final chapter I will turn to a South Korean novel, Hwang-sok Yong's *The Guest*. As we shall see, this work paints a sympathetic and discomfiting portrait of Korean civilians caught up in the war's violence, which humanizes them as not only its victims but also its perpetrators.

8

The Intimacies of Complicity

I want to preface this final chapter, which offers an analysis of a novel that provides a South Korean perspective on the Korean War, with an acknowledgment of how the overall aim of this study has been shaped by the national location from which it has been written: namely, the United States. It is important to underscore that while this conflict has customarily been thought of in this country as "the forgotten war," an erasure that this project seeks to help undo, this label would be irrelevant to Koreans on either side of the demilitarized zone (DMZ). To understand the aims of Hwang Sok-yong's Korean War novel *The Guest* (2000), it is first necessary to step outside of the US context and situate the work in relation to the domestic framing of the war it addresses. As such, the bulk of this chapter will focus on this work's significance for Koreans, which will entail some historical understanding of the transformations that took place in South Korea in the 1990s. However, I will ultimately resituate this novel in the US context in which it began circulating in translated form in 2005, exploring how *The Guest* actually takes on additional meaning when we attend to the unexpected connections it makes between the colonial histories that shaped the Korean War and US histories of race pertaining to Korean immigrants and African Americans.

While it should be self-evident to US readers that the Korean War is, in many ways, the foundational event in the histories of both the Republic of Korea and the Democratic People's Republic of Korea, they might be unaware that it is not the only one, for that event, as far as Koreans are concerned, is also intimately connected with two others: the annexation of the peninsula by Japan in 1910 and its partitioning upon its liberation from the Japanese Empire in 1945. The essential historiographical gesture performed by Bruce Cumings's foundational scholarship, it could be argued, is to situate 1950–53 in this wider temporal framework and to view it through a postcolonial lens attuned to the particular histories of empire that have shaped East Asia.

South Koreans generally call the Korean War the *yugio chŏnjaeng*, or the 6/25 War—referring to the date of the Northern invasion. They are obviously aware that, despite the cessation of hostilities in 1953, it remains an unended war. Its persistence is apparent not only from the DMZ that divides the two Koreas but in the very shape and structure of the states that have developed on either side of it. Paik Nak-Chung—a South Korean literary critic who has developed a public profile in his country somewhat akin to that of a Noam Chomsky in the United States—has coined the term *division system* to capture the symbiotic relationship that has emerged between the two Koreas, one predicated on maintaining the peninsula's divided status. In Paik's analysis, the division system occupies an intermediary position between the capitalist world system in which it is enclosed and the systems of the two Koreas. This concept aims to help us "understand more clearly the complicated (and structured) way the two different systems—that is, sets of social institutions—of the North and the South reproduce themselves in a curious entanglement with each other."[1] "To say that the social reality of division has taken on a systemic nature," he explains, "is to say that with the solidification of the division this particular social structure has literally taken root in the daily lives of Koreans on both sides, and it thus has acquired a considerable level of self-reproducing power."[2]

The repressive regimes that governed South Korea from 1953 through the 1980s were characterized by a fervent anti-Communism, and they justified their authoritarian measures by continually stressing the threat posed by North Korea. Sheila Miyoshi Jager and Jiyul Kim argue that the dominant narrative promoted by these governments was one of "continuous war," calling on South Koreans to be ever vigilant in the face of an always-imminent attack. This Cold War narrative "had placed the North Korean invasion and brutality at the center of the story, precisely in order to prevent the wounds of the war from healing."[3] In somewhat comparable ways, Jae-Jung Suh argues that hegemonic understandings of the war in the South have been framed by "a *yugio* (6/25) narrative," which "lifts the Korean War out of a complex history, and places it in the realm of state-sanctioned myth, a realm much more conducive to policing and cyclical rituals of anticommunist patriotism."[4] This framing identifies South Koreans "first and foremost as the victims of the violence committed by communists and their puppets" and "implicates the North Korean military in unconscionable acts of violence and crimes committed against innocent and defenseless civilians, as it swept through most of South Korea in the first months of the war, as well as the looting, killing, and abductions perpetrated by the retreating North Korean military after the United Nations forces landed in Inchon."[5]

The "continuous war" narrative had begun to lose its hegemonic force in South Korea by the time it elected its first civilian president, Kim Young-sam, in 1992. Kim was an activist who had been in a prominent leadership role in the democratization movement that had challenged the autocratic rule of Presidents Park Chung-hee and Chun Doo-hwan. While Kim's predecessor, Roh Tae-woo, was a general in the South Korean Army whom Chun had groomed to be his successor, he initiated certain policies of reform—including overtures to the North—in an attempt to preserve the authoritarian core of the government he presided over while mollifying the significant opposition he faced. While the prospects for reconciliation with the DPRK have waxed and waned in the decades since and a potent anti-Communism still animates those on the right, a more complex orientation toward North Korea has emerged in the South.

Indeed, Jager and Kim argue that a different narrative of the Korean War emerged in the 1990s, prompted by the end of the era of military dictatorships, the collapse of the Soviet Union and the seeming end of the Cold War, and South Korea's growing awareness of how much it had economically surpassed its increasingly isolated rival to the North. Such developments required, according to Jager and Kim, a "new story of the Korean War" to be written, one that could "mobilize South Koreans in 'tacit forgetfulness' of North Korea's 'criminal responsibility' for the war, while simultaneously holding North Korea accountable for the nation's family tragedy."[6] This narrative would also place emphasis on an attitude of "'forgiving' North Korea's wrongs by incorporating them into a narrative of pan-Korean familial tragedy allowed South Koreans to exclude the negative aspects of the war while commemorating the war as a national calamity for both sides."[7]

Hwang Sok-yong's *The Guest* first appeared in serial form in 2000, a time when hopes for reconciliation were particularly high. This novel looks back at a massacre that happened in the early days of the conflict in Sinch'on, a town located in what is now North Korea. *The Guest* insists that the acknowledgment of such atrocities, which Koreans themselves perpetrated during their civil war, is a necessary precondition for a more peaceful and unified future.

The Guest at Home: "The Atrocities We Suffered Were Committed by None Other Than Ourselves"

The Guest was first published during the presidency of Kim Dae-jung, another prominent opposition leader, who launched a series of initiatives he termed the "Sunshine Policy." These included "approving large shipments of food aid to the North, lifting limits on business deals between the North and southern firms, and calling for an end to the American economic embargo against the North in June 1998, during a visit to Washington."[8] Moreover, Kim "explicitly rejected 'unification by absorption' (which was the de facto policy of his predecessors) and in effect committed Seoul to a prolonged period of peaceful coexistence, with reunification put off for twenty or thirty more years."[9] Such was the atmosphere in which Hwang's novel, as Youngju Ryu puts it, "made its timely, and critically acclaimed appearance."[10]

While the impetus of the novel is a desire for reconciliation, at its core it is an account of a horrific episode from the early days of the Korean War. In her brilliant and illuminating account of *The Guest*, Ryu offers this summary of the events it dramatizes:

> For nearly two months in late 1950, residents of Sinchon, a major district in South Hwanghae Province just north of the 38th parallel, slaughtered one another, leaving an estimated thirty-five thousand dead. Neither the perpetrators nor the victims of the violence were soldiers in the strict sense. The killings occurred not as a part of some tactical battle maneuver, essentially a confrontation between strangers, but as a series of reprisals within a well-established community with a long shared history. As such, the massacre bore the intensely personal character of violence articulated at a close range on the bodies of people intimately known. Some of the killers were equipped with modern firearms, but many others with only simple farming implements; slitting throats and hacking off limbs with hoes and sickles, these men literally bathed themselves in the blood of their neighbors or childhood friends.[11]

While violence was committed by both sides, the most egregious and systematic killings came at the hands of anti-Communist youth groups made up primarily of Protestant men from well-to-do families, land-owners whose properties and way of life were threatened by the land reforms the local People's Committee sought to implement. The People's Committee, primarily composed of peasants and laborers who had worked the farms, was supported by the Communist government, whose hostility toward Christianity had become increasingly apparent. This incident had been, for obvious reasons, little known in the South, though "a right-wing view" of it had circulated in the 1950s, authored by Christians who had taken part in it. According to Ryu, these men had insisted that "the 'incident' was 'patriotic' in nature and 'defensive' in origin" and that the "violence was an uprising rather than a massacre, a heroic attempt to liberate Sinchon from the communists and prepare the way for the northward advance of the US forces."[12] North Kore-ans, in contrast, have referred to the event as the "Massacre of Sinchon Civilians by American Imperialists" and have "long claimed that a mass murder took place at the hands of US soldiers acting under the order to obliterate the popular base for communist support."[13] A museum that the North Korean government has erected on the site, referenced by Hwang's novel, monumentalizes precisely that narrative.

The Guest, like many of the novels examined in this study, does not offer a straightforward account of what took place. Instead, in his "Author's Note" to the novel, Hwang employs a magical realist mode of narration that he explicitly characterizes as having been inspired by the work of Gabriel García Márquez.[14] Memories of what took place are relayed to the reader by various ghosts who appear to the protag-onist, a Korean American minister named Yosŏp Ryu, an immigrant and naturalized US citizen. Yosŏp's journey back to his hometown in Sinch'on forms the novel's narrative spine. Though he was not a per-petrator of any war crimes, his older brother, Yohan, was. Among the people Yohan killed were Ichiro, a village servant, and Uncle Sunnam, who had worked as a handyman, both of whom the Ryus had regarded as intimate friends of their family. Yohan dies in his sleep shortly before his younger brother's departure for their hometown. Throughout Yosŏp's journey, the ghosts of those who perished in the massacre and that of his recently deceased older brother appear to him. Through the testimonies of these figures, readers learn what transpired during those two months and gain an understanding of the larger historical trajectories that culminated in that violence.

For Koreans to move toward the goal of reconciliation, Hwang's novel asserts, they must acknowledge that such events took place and accept responsibility for them. The point Hwang hammers home in each ghost-memory he puts before his readers is that the violence that took place in Sinch'on was of the most intimate kind—that friends and neighbors were tortured, raped, and killed by friends and neighbors. *The Guest* explicitly exhorts its Korean readers, North and South, to come to terms with the fact that the Korean War was and is, first and last, a civil conflict—a fratricidal war in which the perpetrators of the most appalling atrocities shared a common language, ethnicity, and blood with their victims. The concluding paragraphs of the Author's Note speak directly to this agenda:

> As it turns out, the atrocities we suffered were committed by none other than ourselves, and the inner sense of guilt and fear sparked by this incident helped form the roots of the frantic hatred that thrives to this day. Less than five years ago, when I first completed *The Guest*, I received fierce attacks from both Southern and Northern statists.
>
> The scars of our war and the ghosts of the Cold War still mar the Korean peninsula. I can only hope that this particular exorcism helps us all move a step closer to a true, lasting reconciliation as the new century unfolds. (9)

The Guest thus challenges the dominant narrative of South Korea, which paints Christians who perished or slaughtered their countrymen during the war as either pious martyrs or righteous crusaders as well as the official state narrative of North Korea, which casts US military forces as the perpetrators of the war crimes that were committed at Sinch'on.

Despite the evenhanded inclusiveness suggested by the "we" in his Author's Note, the novel depicts Christians as the primary perpetrators of the horrific acts that took place. This is conveyed through its depiction of Yohan, which unambiguously paints him as a war criminal. When readers are first introduced to Yohan, he is a bitter, lonely, and paranoid immigrant living in New Jersey, seemingly unrepentant about the acts he committed. He defensively asserts to his brother, "We were the Crusaders—the Reds were the sons of Lucifer! The hordes of Satan! I was on the side of Michael the archangel, and those bastards were the beasts of the Apocalypse!" (24). The atrocities fueled by this self-righteous wrath are cataloged through the memories that the ghosts of Ichiro, Sunnam, and Yohan himself recount to Yosŏp. Yohan had been a leading member of an organization that the novel refers to as the Taehan Youth Corps.[15] During the massacre, Yohan had ordered men under his command to drag Ichiro to an air raid shelter where hundreds of other alleged Communist sympathizers were also incarcerated, pour gasoline into it, and burn them alive. Yohan had also shot and killed Uncle Sunnam after his men had hung him from a utility pole. He had also shot and killed Ms. Yun, a beloved schoolteacher accused of being a Communist sympathizer. And he had hacked to death two adolescent female North Korean soldiers who were actually just musicians whose only duties were to "go around from troop to troop and perform for them to cheer them up" (212).

Astonishingly, however, and without mitigating the horror of the murders he committed, the memories he and other ghosts recount humanize Yohan to a certain extent by revealing that two of them were mercy killings of a sort: Sunnam had asked Yohan to kill him in order to be spared from the brutal torture that he knew would preface his eventual execution; Yohan had shot Ms. Yun as she was being subjected to a gang rape by other members of the youth corps, thereby shortening the suffering and degradation that would have only ended with her eventual execution. Additionally, he committed the third set of murders—of the two girl soldiers—to protect himself and Yosŏp, who had helped them hide. If this had been discovered, both Ryu brothers would likely have faced incarceration, torture, and execution.

What enables this more complex portrait of Yohan to emerge is the novel's compositional form, which Hwang characterizes as being inspired by not only García Márquez's *One Hundred Years of Solitude* but also a native cultural and spiritual tradition: "This twelve-chapter novel is modeled after the Chongwi exorcism of Hwanghae Province. . . . As is the case during an actual exorcism, the dead and the living simultaneously cross and recross the boundaries between past and present, appearing at what seem like random intervals to share each of their memories" (7). This structure allows the ghosts of both Christians and Communists to offer their memories of the massacre while obviating the issue of punishment, since it has no meaning to those who have passed over. Because the ghosts thus recount their truths about the massacre in a spiritual proceeding in which juridical concerns of reparation, compensation, or punishment are precluded, the novel's form seems to anticipate the Truth and Reconciliation Committee of the Republic of Korea (TRCK), which was established in 2005. Formed under the administrations of Presidents Kim Dae-jung and Roh Moo-hyun, the TRCK's mandate was to investigate "most wrongdoings committed by the state in the past," which included "illegal massacres before and after the Korean War." Like many similar bodies, its primary aim was "truth-verification rather than judicial prosecution of perpetrators as a means of rectifying past wrongdoings."[16] While the TRCK did not focus on the Sinch'on massacre, it did investigate a number of similar events in which the preponderance of violence was enacted by anti-Communists. Like the testimonies given to such bodies, the recounting of personal memories in *The Guest* is uncoupled from questions of reparation or punishment.

The ghost-witnesses in the novel recall what happened with sadness and some anger but without a burning desire for vengeance. As Yohan's ghost reveals to Yosŏp, "Hey, hey, there isn't an iota of resentment left in me. Life itself is a curse, isn't it? Damned if I know why the hell we were so frantic about everything back then" (57–58). And the ghost of Uncle Sunnam explains, "There aren't any sides over there—no my-side-against-your-side" (28). For the dead, it would seem that a reconciliation has already taken place.

The novel's spiritual and ethical focus, then, is on the living. What they need to do is modeled by its protagonist, Yosŏp, a devout Christian whose journey back to Sinch'on and confrontation with what happened there becomes legible as a kind of spiritual pilgrimage of atonement. That he too shoulders a burden of culpability for atrocities that he himself did not commit and did not even witness is forcefully articulated during a conversation he has with Uncle Some, a Christian who never left Sinch'on and to whom ghosts have also been appearing. When Yosŏp voices his confusion about why the two of them have been the recipients of these hauntings, since "you and I, we weren't to blame," Some's reply is emphatic: "Show me one soul who wasn't to blame!" (162).

By making Yosŏp the protagonist of his novel, Hwang explores the forms of culpability that attach not only to the perpetrators of atrocities but to those who were their direct beneficiaries. Yosŏp is, in other words, a particular kind of *bystander*—not one who witnessed a criminal act and did nothing to prevent it but one whose survival and ability to enjoy a comfortable life were facilitated by it. Most pointedly, the responsibility he bears for what took place in Sinch'on stems from the fact that he was a direct beneficiary of Yohan's brutal execution of the two girl soldiers he had helped hide from the Christian mob. As a consequence of their murders, Yosŏp was protected from the violence of the youth corps and was able to flee to the South. Hwang thus offers Yosŏp as a proxy for his novel's South Korean readers, imploring them to recognize that they too bear no small measure of responsibility for the horrors that occurred in places like Sinch'on even if they were not directly involved in them, for they too were the beneficiaries of such acts. *The Guest* thus evokes South Korea as a kind of bystander nation, as it were, that was able to survive and rise from the ashes of war because of the heinous deeds committed in its name.[17]

Yosŏp's Christianity is integral to this allegorical function, and to understand why, it is necessary to attend here to that religion's formidably complex history in Korea and how it is conveyed by the novel. The brief chronicle of the Ryu family history that *The Guest* provides is used to unfold a larger account of Christianity's role in the region. While Hwang's novel does trace the itineraries of the Western missionaries who first brought their religion to the peninsula (the most successful of whom were Protestants), it makes plain that Korean converts were responsible for its popularization. One of these was Samsŏng Ryu, Yosŏp's and Yohan's grandfather. Samsŏng's conversion and how his family amassed its wealth are revealed by childhood memories that come to Yosŏp early in the novel, mostly of conversations he had with his great-grandmother and with Samsŏng himself, her son, that took place shortly after the end of Japanese rule. These passages open a window into not only the colonial period (1910–45) but also the social order that existed in Korea prior to its annexation by Japan, offering a glimpse of life during the final decades of the Chosŏn dynasty, the sinocentric and monarchical regime that reigned for more than five centuries (1392–1910).

Under Chosŏn, the Ryus had worked, as Yosŏp's great-grandmother admits, as "agents for the landowners—we farmed the land that belonged to the palace," and as such, they "even managed to buy a bit of land" (42). Yosŏp himself reflects that by the end of this dynasty, his family "owned acre upon acre of rice fields, fields they had hoarded for untold generations, a little bit at a time, as they managed the land in the name of the royal family" (56). Samsŏng came to Christianity through the efforts of Cho Pansŏk, a childhood friend whose family shared the same class designation as the Ryus. Christianity's attraction for Pansŏk and Samsŏng derived from the access to modernity it promised. From the missionaries, Pansŏk learned new farming methods and how to read and write, and in studying the Bible, "he came to realize that the world outside of Chosŏn was enormous, not to mention enlightened and civilized," and this "impressed Yosŏp's grandfather immensely" (55–56).

Samsŏng's attraction to Christianity also stemmed, however, from a certain class resentment. Despite his status as a landowner, there was a limit to how high he could hope to rise within the Chosŏn social order because of the government's bias against the northwestern region of Korea in which the Ryus lived. Samsŏng had been a diligent student and hoped to pass a provincial exam enabling him to "earn a low-level government position some day—a dream born of the fact that the Ryus had lived in servitude for generations upon end, harboring resentment and envy of anyone with a government post of any kind" (56). Through Christianity, Samsŏng could envision his family pursuing much loftier ends. He recounted to Yosŏp that after being baptized by a US missionary, he had returned home "and smashed our ancestral tablet, the false idol your great-grandmother worshipped. I graduated from the Pyongyang Seminary and became a minister. Your mother is the daughter of a minister who went to school with me—both the families of your mother and your father are people who have been chosen by God" (57). Samsŏng's conversion to Christianity was thus an act of rebellion, enabling him to leave behind his precarious dream of attaining "a low-level government position" in the Chosŏn government and to see himself and his family instead as part of a chosen people.

Significantly, in the novel's telling, when that regime fell as Korea came under Japan's colonial dominion, it actually proved to be a windfall for the Ryus and other Christians. While Japanese authorities seized the land that had belonged to the monarchy, the Ryus were able to not just maintain but increase their wealth. "By the time we were liberated from Japan," Yosŏp recalls, "we were one of the richest families in the village" (44).

What emerges from these memories is the lore that the Ryus had established about their centuries-long rise from humble origins. They were able to become "one of the richest families in the village" not only because they were such "diligent workers," as Yosŏp's great-grandmother was so proud to insist (42), but also because they recognized that their careful management of land (their own and that of others) and their incremental but steady gains in property would pay dividends for later generations.

This mythology of self-sufficiency is punctured, however, by Uncle Sunnam's revelations. The Japanese, Sunnam's ghost tells Yosŏp, had seized his family's land, and they had thus been forced to become tenant farmers. The Ryus had been able to keep their property because Yosŏp's father had worked as an agent for the Japanese colonial authorities. Sunnam explains what such an agent does: "He raises the taxes that tenants have to pay and he makes them pay for his own tax, and if the tenants don't obey, he just terminates the contract and transfers their tenant rights to another farmer. The Oriental Development Company and the Financial Union, not to mention the landowners—*they liked the go-getters you know*" (73; emphasis mine). The Ryu family wealth, it turns out, was not entirely self-made. It required the assistance of the Japanese colonial authorities, who were always on the lookout for "go-getters"—subjects like the Ryus, diligent workers ever seeking opportunities to get ahead. What set the Ryus apart was that regardless of their circumstances, they aspired to something better and were willing to make themselves useful first to the Chosŏn government and then to the Japanese colonial authorities to increase their wealth, even if it meant colluding in the subjugation of other Koreans. That they found Christianity along the way is no coincidence, for as Max Weber famously observed, this quintessentially capitalist ethos is deeply compatible with Protestantism.

In fundamental ways, the account of Korean Christianity offered by *The Guest* departs—most emphatically in aligning the religion with the Japanese—from South Korean nationalist mythology, which Cumings characterizes as follows: "Christian opposition to the Japanese is both a fact and a legend. The churches were sanctuaries in times of violence, like that of the 1919 independence movement, and many Western missionaries encouraged underdog and egalitarian impulses. But the post-1945 image of Syngman Rhee and other pro-American politicians as great Christian leaders and resisters to colonialism is false."[18] We can gain a sense of the partiality of the novel's account of the religion's role in modern Korean history by comparing it with the one forwarded by Chung-Shin Park in his study *Protestantism and Politics in Korea*.

Park identifies the northwestern provinces like P'yŏng'an and Hwanghae (where the Sinch'on massacre took place) as regions where the Christianity originally introduced by Protestant missionaries spread with astonishing rapidity in the latter part of the nineteenth century. Elite families like the fictional Ryus embraced this religion because, despite their wealth, "residents of this region had been subjected to a discriminatory policy that restricted opportunities for upward social mobility by appointment to regular government posts and rapid promotion."[19] However, the Koreans drawn to that religion were, Park writes, "for the most part *sangmin* (commoners)—drawers of water, hewers of wood, tillers of soil, and artisans of cheap, everyday ware—and *chŏnmin*—butchers and other social outcasts, including some slaves."[20] They were drawn to Christianity because "it preached equality and freedom in a hierarchical Confucian society."[21] They were attracted, for instance, by the egalitarianism that defined Protestant congregations, in which "nobles and commoners, men and women, old and young sat together in one place as equals to hear sermons, sing hymns, read the Bible and discuss matters of religion."[22]

Park conveys the leading role that Christians played in the independence movement that emerged during the early colonial period. Between 1905 and 1919, when all overtly political organizations were banned by the Japanese, Park writes, "the Protestant church came to serve as a place for solace, a political forum, a communication network, and an organizational base for Korean nationalist activities."[23] He points out that 16 of the 33 signatories to the Declaration of Independence that was the documentary centerpiece of the March 1 Movement of 1919—a nationwide set of carefully planned demonstrations that were brutally disrupted by Japanese colonial forces—were church leaders, and 1,719 of the 7,835 major participants in the demonstrations, or 22 percent, were Protestant Christians.[24]

While these more progressive and nationalist elements of Korean Christianity as it took shape in the early decades of the twentieth century are left out of *The Guest*, its rendering of the Ryus' collaboration with the Japanese does harmonize with Park's account of how the church transformed in the 1920s and 1930s as the Japanese imposed less draconian measures to impose their power: "There was a metamorphosis of the Protestant church from a religion of the alienated, the poor, the maltreated and the oppressed to a religion which was separating itself from these groups," and it "now tended to avoid controversial issues in society and in nationalist politics."[25] Beginning in the 1920s, Park writes, "many prominent Christians . . . became active collaborators with the Japanese": though some "were forced to" do so, "others collaborated so that they could continue to operate their churches and schools; and still others to protect their wealth and position."[26] As such, the Ryus do bear a resemblance to the generally conservative Christians who assumed leadership positions during the latter part of the colonial period.

Timothy S. Lee's *Born Again: Evangelicalism in Korea*, as well as Park's study, illuminates the role that Christian refugees who fled south before and after the war would play in the government that took shape there. Lee estimates that of the 1,014,000 to 1,386,000 Koreans who fled south between 1945 and 1953, 70,000 to 80,000 were Christian.[27] They brought with them reports of massacres of Christians perpetrated by the Communists. "Northern evangelical refugees," he asserts, "became a force to reckon with" in the South.[28] As Park elaborates, the real-life counterparts to Hwang's fictional Ryu brothers would have lasting effects on the peninsula, as they played a leading role in "the emergence of an anticommunist Christianity and church-government collusion in the south. The migrant Christians and the refugees who became Christians not only became anticommunists themselves, but also made anticommunists of their fellow Christians in the south by revealing their painful experience under the Kim Il-sung regime. To combat communism, these Christians cooperated with the anticommunist regimes of Syngman

Rhee, Park Chung-hee, Chun Doo Hwan, and Roh Tae-woo."[29] These Christians would go on to enjoy what Park describes as a "symbiotic relationship" with the authoritarian governments that ruled South Korea through much of its history.[30]

The persecution Christians had faced in the North is not a fiction, though it is somewhat downplayed in Hwang's novel, for they were certainly among the groups subjected to increasingly repressive measures by Kim Il-Sung's regime even before the start of the war. Cumings notes that between 1945 and 1950, the Communists "eliminated all nonleftist political opposition with a draconian thoroughness" and that "Christians were particular targets of the regime."[31] Kim's program of land reform seized property from well-to-do Koreans, many of whom were Christian, and the government also made it illegal for churches to own property and nationalized all Christian schools.[32] Church leaders were jailed, and Christian rallies and revivals were violently broken up by vigilantes aligned with the government. The exodus of Christians to the South thus began in the five years before the war broke out and only intensified afterward.

It is within this context that we can understand the appeal that Hwang's novel makes to its readers in South Korea and the polemical nature of its rendering of the role of Christianity in the peninsula's history. The story of the Ryu family chronicled by *The Guest* holds up a difficult mirror to a nation in which Christianity has become, according to Lee, "the most influential religion of South Korea" as well as the most popular one.[33] Hwang's novel calls on readers in South Korea to recognize in evangelical refugees like Yohan the origins of the fusion of vehement anti-Communism and Christianity that had served as the ideological engine that enabled a series of autocratic regimes and military dictatorships to rule South Korea for much of its history. The brutality with which Yohan and other "crusaders" gave expression to their Christian beliefs and their hatred of Communists provides such readers with a dark genealogy, troubling a nationalist mythology content merely to highlight the leading role that Christians played in the independence movement. The popularity of *The Ghost* with South Korean audiences in 2001 suggests that this was a legacy that they were finally willing and able to confront.

The Guest in the Diaspora

While, as I have been arguing, *The Guest* aims primarily at dismantling both North and South Korean nationalist mythologies that have papered over the atrocities committed by Koreans themselves, its critique also has a collateral target, for it also intimates that US forces did play a role in the massacre even as it directly challenges the North Korean narrative that identifies US soldiers as the perpetrators of the war crimes that took place. As such, Yosŏp's allegorical function is also tied to the nation to which he emigrated after the war, the United States, which serves as the novel's literal point of departure. As such, *The Guest*—especially in its incarnation as a translated and transnational text—also asks its readers to reflect on the ethical obligations that accrue to those who are, like Yosŏp, US citizens.

An indirect critique of the United States' role is apparent in the novel's careful delineation of the movements of US forces before and during one of the most heinous acts that took place: the burning alive of hundreds of civilians in an air-raid shelter. The narrator describes how a platoon of US soldiers, who had been ordered to determine the status of a "Rightist uprising" that had erupted after the Communist withdrawal, enters Sinch'on and is relieved to find no evidence of violence and to see it under the control of anti-Communist leaders. The soldiers are treated to a welcome rally during which they notice that "only about a thousand" of the fifteen hundred Korean men there are armed. They subsequently "contact the regimental headquarters in Chaeryong and request that rations, some medicine, and, most importantly, munitions such as bullets and grenades be brought to Sinch'on." The matter-of-fact description of the two hours that these US forces spend there is followed by a chilling account of the machinery of mass slaughter clicking into motion: "After the welcoming rally, it is announced that the defeat of Communism and the unification of Korea has become a reality. In the county hall, the Taehan Youth Corps and the new Autonomous Police are established, and a ceremony is held the following morning in the front yard to celebrate. Once the festivities are complete, the men return their attention to the air-raid shelter and the trench. The executions begin" (203). While the narration makes plain that no US forces were directly involved, it also implies that it was the departure of US soldiers and the provisioning of the local paramilitary forces with weapons that preceded and perhaps served as the catalyst for the violence that ensued immediately afterward. While the text does not issue a direct indictment of US forces, this omission mirrors the nature of their crime. Their guilt stems not from something evil they did but from the catastrophe they enabled by doing nothing—a sin of omission rather than of commission, as it were. In this way, the novel quietly underscores that they, like Yosŏp, were unknowing bystanders who thus bear a proximate form of culpability for what took place. While Hwang's novel obviously highlights that the Korean War was, at its heart, a civil war, it also gestures toward how the fratricidal nature of the violence that took place was intensified by the intervention of outside powers such as the United States.[34]

Another insight that emerges from contextualizing *The Guest* as a translated work that now circulates in the United States concerns certain transnational resonances that are an effect of its protagonist's identity as a Korean American, for Hwang's novel also imparts a specific message to readers to whom Yosŏp is linked by ethnicity *and* citizenship, as it introduces the Ryu brothers in ways that highlight their status as representative Korean immigrants:

> Despite the twenty years, however, Yosŏp still lived in a humble Brooklyn apartment. His brother Yohan, on the other hand, had long since moved to a white residential area in New Jersey, as befitted *a true immigrant of the sixties*. It was an unremarkable place—a small, wooden house of the kind commonly found in the suburbs of New York: it had a garage, a deep basement, a living room, and bedrooms of indifferent size, a backyard just spacious enough to hold a barbecue, and a white wooden fence out front. (12–13; emphasis mine)

Hwang's novel goes on to highlight a discomfiting quality in these two brothers and the community of which they are a part: a quintessentially middle-class anxiety about crime that takes shape as a fear of African Americans. This is first suggested by the complex security system, complete with security monitors and intercoms, that Yohan has installed in his house. The racial dimensions of this anxiety seem to emerge in

Yohan's fearful response to the ghost of Sunnam, who appears to him as a "*black* thing," and that of Ichiro, whose face "float[s] up out of the *black* blankness of the screen" (19; emphasis mine).

Yosŏp's fears are also revealed as taking on this racialized shape, and even more explicitly, in the novel's description of his drive to his brother's house, where he will tell Yohan about the trip to Korea he plans to make. It is oppressively hot that day, and since the air conditioning is not working, his windows are rolled down. He rolls them up, however, any time he hits a red light because of what members of his congregation had told him: "If you simply stood at an intersection with your windows open, they'd say, a black man would be sure to materialize, gun in hand, and hop in" (13). To some degree, *The Guest* explains this racism by fleshing out the Ryu brothers' past, which suggests that it is the manifestation of a paranoia that is the product of their wartime experiences—the unfortunate expression of a generalized anxiety about security and a fear of violence.

The novel does more than simply suggest that Korean Christian immigrants' antiblack racism might be an unfortunate symptom of a war trauma that haunts the diaspora. *The Guest* also hints that the fear and antipathy toward the black underclass are a continuation of a pattern that originated in the homeland, one that has emerged as a consequence of the tensions that have shaped modern Korean society for centuries. In calling attention to the fear of African Americans that Korean churchgoers in the US harbor, the novel invites readers to consider the relationality of the Korean history it unfolds and a US history in which antiblack racism has played a significant part.

Such a linkage might be found in the novel's account of the peasant and tenant farmer classes and their treatment by wealthy Christians like the Ryus. As seen earlier, *The Guest* depicts Christians as comprising a kind of comprador class that gained its wealth by colluding with first the Chosŏn regime and then the Japanese colonial apparatus in exploiting the lower classes. In contrast, the novel portrays Marxism in far more positive terms. In Marxism, Koreans like Sunnam and Ichiro found a powerfully illuminating understanding of the repressive conditions under which they and their families had lived and labored for generations as well as hope for a better future. Their sympathetic portrayal is deepened by an implicit analogy to African Americans, a transnational connection foreshadowed by the allusions to antiblack racism on the part of Korean Americans pointedly made in the opening chapter.

The character who emerges from *The Guest* as the representative of the Korean underclass is Ichiro, the village servant whom Yohan sent to his death. Ichiro's story is recounted by the ghosts of Yohan and Uncle Sunnam, who relate in contrasting ways the growing tensions that emerged between Communists and Christians after liberation. While sporadic incidents of violence had erupted between the two sides, the catalyst for its escalation was the program of "land reform" that the Communists sought to impose. In giving voice to how this initiative was viewed by the members of the landowning class, Yohan raises the specter of a crime similar to the one Korean American Christians fear will be perpetrated by black men: "If it had been total strangers or some foreign bastards who showed up and tried to rob us of our land at gunpoint, well, then we might have just cried our hearts out, been mortified at our own helplessness, and given in—but that wasn't how it happened" (114).

What particularly galled wealthy families like the Ryus was that the demands were being issued not by strangers but by "our friends, the kids we grew up with, the ones we'd known from babyhood" (114). Yohan claims that wealthy families treated the men whom they hired to work in their orchards or as servants with a kind of noblesse oblige and even regarded them in familial terms. As evidence of this, he recalls how he, Yosŏp, and their other boyhood friends would address Ichiro—who had been hired as a kind of village servant who took care of whatever menial tasks were required in exchange for wages that "were paid to him in rice"—"as if he was one of them" (124). Because they had viewed Ichiro in such intimate and familial terms, Yohan recalls that they were both baffled and enraged when he reappeared in Sinch'on after an absence of several months as "Comrade Pak Illang," wearing an armband that read "Rural Village Committee Chairman" and issuing a demand to the Ryus and other wealthy families to turn over their land to be redistributed to the people.

From Sunnam we learn that Pak Illang was actually Ichiro's given name—the latter had been given to him by a Japanese foreman—as well as the details of the tragedy that had shaped his life before he came to work as a village servant in Sinch'on. When Illang was a boy, his father had been killed while working as a logger, and Illang was abandoned by his mother shortly thereafter. For a time, he and his grandmother engaged in slash-and-burn farming to eke out a meager existence, and he married when he was eighteen. But after that form of farming was criminalized by Japanese colonial administrators, he was jailed for ten months. Upon his release, he learned that his home had been burned down, his grandmother had died, and his wife had disappeared. He worked for a while at various construction sites until he came to Sinch'on.

When the People's Committee established an education program for men like Sunnam and Ichiro, the two became close friends. Both of them found in Marxism a way of understanding their lowly status as the consequence of an oppressive feudalist system predicated on forcibly extracting labor from men like themselves. Ichiro also gained a newfound sense of dignity and self-worth. Sunnam offers this passionate description of how being taught to read and write by the Communists effected a dramatic transformation in his friend:

> Ichiro, the same Ichiro you all thought was a brainless half-wit, the same Ichiro you talked down to—just think about it for a second— that same Ichiro learned to read and write. He learned to write his own name. Pak Illang. If that's not what the liberation was all about, I don't know what is. Comrade Pak Illang, who used to carry firewood and work like a cow while you people ate white rice, slept under warm blankets, learned at schools, sat in churches, read Bibles, prayed and sang hymns—well, he learned too, and now he could read and write words like *land reform*. (128; italics in original)

The poignancy with which this chapter renders the promise of liberation that Illang found in Marxism privileges the version of modernity that the Communists sought to instantiate in Korea, for they sought to eradicate a deeply oppressive class structure, one that had predated the Japanese occupation but had also been fortified by it. While *The Guest* finds nothing to glorify in the present shape of the North Korean state, it does convey the sincerity and ethical legitimacy of those like Illang who found in the ideology of Marxism tools for understanding and overturning their oppression.

Moreover, the evocation of the United States' own long history of racial oppression works in concert with the novel's sympathetic rendering of a Korean underclass that toiled for generations in conditions akin to slavery. The condescending paternalism that shaped the affection with which young Yohan viewed the middle-aged man he called Ichiro is evident in his fond memory of how they all spoke to him: "No one in the village used the polite form of speech to Ichiro, but he would use the high honorific form to all the married men, regardless of whether they were older or younger than himself—he only spoke the low form of speech to young children. The children, in turn, spoke it right back to him, as if he was one of them" (124). Korean is a language in which one uses an honorific form of address when speaking to elders and strangers and a familiar form with friends or subordinates. Yohan's statement reveals that while Ichiro was regarded as an intimate of the Ryus, he nonetheless assumed in their eyes the status of a boy despite the fact that he was a man in his forties. In his servitude, Ichiro shares something in common with adult black males in the United States who have been addressed by racist whites as "boy." Also, the insistence of the Ryus and other landowners that they regard men like Ichiro and Sunnam as family recalls the paternalism of US slave-owners who offered similarly self-serving characterizations of how they regarded the blacks who were their property as family. Finally, Sunnam's account of the sense of dignity and empowerment that Illang gained from his encounter with Marxism resonates with the pivotal event that lies at the heart of many slave narratives: the achievement of literacy as enabling an unprecedented sense of self-worth and the first imaginings of liberation from bondage. Because Sunnam's memories flesh out a humanizing and sympathetic understanding of Comrade Pak Illang and the class he typifies, he would seem to be the primary subject of the chapter in which his life story is related, which is titled "A Pure Spirit: Clarification before Reconciliation."

Bearing all this in mind, we can now specify more precisely the message that *The Guest* carries to readers who are, like the Ryu brothers, "true immigrant[s] of the sixties" who have built new lives in America. Its *diasporic* pull, which is enacted through Yosŏp's journey home, calls on Korean Americans to recognize their implication in and their responsibility for the kinds of horrific acts that were committed during the Korean War in places like Sinch'on—not necessarily as perpetrators but as beneficiaries.[35] Given that all of those who were able to emigrate to the United States did so, with rare exceptions, from the Republic of Korea (even if they were originally from the North) and that the majority of them are Christians who harbor a deep antipathy toward Communism, *The Guest* implores them not only to see Communists in a humanizing light but also to acknowledge the connection they have to the Koreans north of the DMZ, some of whom might be family.

In *domestic* terms, however, *The Guest* also implicitly calls on Korean Americans to confront how the anxiety and racism they might feel toward African Americans could have been shaped by their experiences in the Korean War. One explanation for such an antipathy might originate from encounters with African American soldiers or exposure to the racism of their white counterparts. *The Guest* suggests, however, that its origins might lie in their awareness of how some of the most intimate forms of fratricidal violence that took place during the Korean War were the expression of a kind of class warfare—one that has resonances in the tensions that they have experienced with African Americans.

Hwang's novel thus asks such readers to consider, as Hoenik Kwon suggestively does in *The Other Cold War*, how the racial color line that places Korean Americans and African Americans in tension with one another might interact with an "ideological color-line" that was operant within Asian countries like Korea and Vietnam during this period, in which an allegiance to Communism took on a quasi-racial significance to those allied with the West: "Civil war–generation Koreans are familiar with similar idioms, such as 'red blood line.' For people whose genealogical backgrounds include ancestors once classified as Communist subversives, sympathizers of communism, or defectors to the Communist North, 'red blood line' has been a terrifying idea associated with the memory of summary killings and mass murder, surviving family members' experience of social stigma, and the restriction of their civil rights."[36]

In suggesting how both an intermingling of these color lines, one racial and one ideological, might partially explain the antiblack racism of Korean Americans like the Ryus, *The Guest* voices a quiet critique of how they—insofar as they regard working-class African Americans with fear and anxiety—have reconstituted a version of the class privilege they benefited from in their homeland and how they risk once again contributing to the oppression of those whose lives and security may be significantly more precarious than their own, who may in turn regard them with suspicion and hostility.

* * *

By first situating *The Guest* in the context in which it initially circulated—South Korea at the turn of the millennium—and then exploring the dimensions of that novel that take on greater historical resonances within the context of its recirculation as a translated work in the United States (particularly in the relationality it suggests between African Americans and Korean peasants), I have thus come full circle in a sense, for I have suggested how this South Korean novel might also speak to concerns that have conventionally been thought of as the particular province of Asian American and African American literature, dramatizing once again the intimacies of the various histories of race and empire that converge around the Korean War.

I have also tried to suggest how, in their totality, the works I have brought together in part 2 of this book evoke a multivalent web of complicity, the expansiveness of which is conveyed by Uncle Some's assertion in *The Guest*: "Show me one soul who wasn't to blame!" The novels taken up point to the culpability of Chinese, American, and Korean subjects in the devastating violence of the Korean War. Given all of this, we might give the epithet expressed in Yu Yuan's redacted tattoo in *War Trash* its most expansive reading—as, in other words, "Fuck *Us.*" For it is all of us, these works collectively assert, who must claim a sense of ownership of what took place in Korea—not only for what was done to us but for what we did to each other and ourselves.

Conclusion

"The Delicate Chains of War"

As I bring this book to a close, I would like to acknowledge a personal dimension to my interest in its topic, for I have my own version of the story that Chang-rae Lee and Susan Choi tell about how they became curious about the Korean War. When I was in my early forties, my mother mentioned to me that her father, my grandfather, might still be alive. This came as a surprise to me, since it had always been said that he had died sometime before my parents emigrated to the United States in the late 1960s. I had always assumed this must have happened during the war. As it turns out, he had apparently abandoned his wife and two daughters to fight for the North and was not heard from again. As I now understand, given that South Korea had become virtually a police state during the war and remained so for decades afterward, to admit such a fact could easily have resulted in my grandmother, mother, and aunt being brought in for questioning or worse. And so a family story was born. I know that much heartbreak and pain lies behind the veil of secrecy in which this story has been shrouded. I have found myself not wanting to pierce it entirely, though I know my own life has been shaped by the aftereffects of this event. At the same time, I suspect that part of the reason I have been drawn to Korean American and Korean novels like *The Foreign Student*, *The Surrendered*, and *The Guest* is that I perhaps discern in them a shadowy and oblique mirror of what my parents and my grandmother, who raised me, must have endured.

But what I have also learned from such works—and whatever else it is, this book has been an attempt to elaborate on that lesson—is how the affective labor that goes into honoring a trauma that has shaped a generation of Korean immigrants who are also survivors of war might also become part of a more collaborative and open-ended endeavor of cultural remembrance, one that might open up a politics of identity different from that enacted by the war itself.

As I suggest in my analyses of *The Surrendered* and *The Foreign Student*, I find these works to be exemplary Korean American expressions of postmemory in that they attest to the Korean War as a foundational trauma for much of the immigrant generation while refraining from making that injury the basis of an essentialist notion of Korean diasporic identity. Both novels do this by highlighting a necessary gap between the tragic experiences suffered by one generation and the attempts by the next to translate them into literary form. Even as they acknowledge the gravitational pull exerted by a desire to fuse identity and injury, they are not wholly structured by it. Instead, they make an array of histories of loss and migration intimately contiguous. *The Foreign Student* does so without trying to establish a neat symmetry among the histories that have shaped various US communities of color, rendering them comparable, or highlighting any particular one as absolutely exceptional. In drawing attention to the Korean War's significance for African Americans, Japanese Americans, and Mexican Americans, my own book has sought to extend and add to the historiographical trajectories that shape Choi's novel. What I have explored here, however, is intended as provisional, and it would certainly be gratifying for me to see scholarship that would extend and expand such lines of inquiry or open new ones: to take up, for instance, the war's significance for Native Americans, especially given the small but significant part played by Chief in the film *All the Young Men*.

That having been said, there remains a particular if not singular problematic that refracts the Korean American postmemorial novels taken up here and that might also engender a hesitation about treating the trauma of the war in exclusively ethnonationalist terms: namely, that Koreans in the United States have tended to be constituted as a model minority and their country of origin as "a model minority nation-state," to use Jin-kyung Lee's formulation.[1] For whatever injuries were inflicted on Koreans in the past by US military intervention and however darkly the experiences of Korean Americans have been shaped by the trauma of the war, both are assumed to occupy positions of relative comfort and privilege. The Korean and Korean American novels examined engage the complexities of this problematic in exceptionally illuminating ways.

Lee, Choi, and Hwang suggest how the seeming resilience and entrepreneurial wherewithal of their immigrant protagonists might be seen not so much as the expression of essential Asian or Korean values but rather as survival mechanisms forged in the crucible of war. Additionally, *The Foreign Student* and *The Guest* address the uneasy position that Korean immigrants who are also survivors of war have come to occupy in regards to other communities of color and to African Americans in particular. Rather than positing a history of victimization comparable to that of, for example, blacks in the United States, these works suggest a messy contiguity—a sense of relationality that leaves unresolved the issue of how they might be placed alongside one another. Hwang and Choi do, however, invite a consideration of how Korean Americans' histories of victimization in the war may shape the ways in which they have been complicit in maintaining the hierarchies that structure the racial formation of the United States. Their works do so, however, without either naturalizing or justifying this complicity.

While this project's trajectory has been transnational, it is worth acknowledging that it has only begun to address Korean perspectives in the final chapter through its analysis of Hwang's *The Guest* and does not venture at all into North Korean perspectives.[2] I would like to end this book by elaborating a bit more on how South Koreans have begun to retell the story of the conflict since the end of the Cold War, through the ups and downs in the prospects for reunification that have characterized this recent era. I will do so first by discussing the War Memorial of Korea, a monumental site that houses several official nationalist narratives concerning the Korean War, and then by exploring how the growing international prominence of South Korean films unfolds trajectories of remembrance that interact in complex ways with the American ones examined in this study.

My analyses are complicated by an aspect of contemporary South Korea noted by many specialists, which is the breakneck pace of change that defines life there. The exigencies of neoliberalism are felt with a particularly intense sense of acceleration in Seoul, and the nature of the political system means that each new presidential administration can dramatically alter the shape of the country and its relationship to North Korea.[3] While the postmilitary dictatorship era began with three presidents who adopted a conciliatory posture to the North—Kim

Young-sam, Kim Dae-jung, and Roh Moo-hyun—the government took a reactionary turn when Lee Myung-bak took office in 2008 and Park Geun-hye in 2013. The fact that Park was the daughter of Park Chung-hee, the autocrat who ruled the country from 1963 to 1979, and proudly claimed her father's legacy and was elected nonetheless indicates how far to the right much of the population had swung. The resurgence of the Cold War–era posturing that defined the Lee and Park administrations largely came to an end with the election of Moon Jae-in in 2017. With a new presidential administration coming into office in the United States as well that year, the relationship between the two Koreas and the United States has seen further dramatic shifts, suggesting how quickly the prospects for reconciliation can be altered.

This volatility is reflected in the cultural artifact I turn to now: the War Memorial of Korea, in which at least three dominant narratives concerning the Korean War have been literally monumentalized—narratives that are, at least to some degree, contradictory.

The War Memorial of Korea and Virtual Nationalism

The memorial, which opened in 1994, is an epic structure: it comprises an enormous main building, which occupies roughly twenty thousand square meters and houses a museum and ceremonial spaces, and the expansive plaza surrounding it, which features more ceremonial spaces, several imposing memorial sculptures, and a field of military equipment, including tanks and aircraft. It first opened during the presidency of Kim Young-sam, the country's first civilian leader, though it was planned by his predecessor and stands as "one of the showpieces of Roh Tae Woo's presidential legacy."[4] It is through a careful analysis of this structure that Sheila Miyoshi Jager and Jiyul Kim elaborate on what they term the "new story of the Korean War," which I discussed in chapter 8.[5] "One of its striking features," they note, "is its downplaying of anti-North Korean rhetoric"; as such, "its treatment of North Korea's role is largely abstracted from the brutal history of that conflict," and notably absent are "any reference to known North Korean atrocities committed during the war."[6] This more conciliatory orientation to the North central to this post–Cold War narrative is resonant, as I argued in the previous chapter, with the one adopted by Hwang Sok-yong in *The Guest*.

Exemplifying the memorial's conciliatory stance toward the North is the immense Statue of Brothers (figure C.1), which—despite the clear hierarchy it establishes between the two Koreas—hardly vilifies a Communist menace. This sculpture, which visitors encounter when they first enter the grounds, symbolizes South Korea as an adult male soldier, North Korea as a boy, and the hope of their reunification through their loving embrace. Also exemplifying this post–Cold War narrative is the Korean War Monument, which was unveiled in 2003. Its centerpiece is the June 25 Tower, which resembles a gargantuan bullet or artillery shell that has been bisected vertically. According to the visitor's pamphlet, however, it is actually "the embodiment of the bronze sword and the tree of life. The bronze sword represents the rich history and martial spirit, and the tree of life symbolizes the peace and prosperity of the Korean people." According to Jager and Kim, the sword is linked with the earliest Korean "race," the Yemaek people who migrated from Manchuria in 1000–700 BC. The June 25 Tower resignifies that date not as one in which a villainous enemy invaded from the North but as one in which an immense *tragedy* visited the Korean people as a whole, severing a nation that has existed since time immemorial and giving expression to a "hope for the rebirth among brothers that union would bring."[7]

As I have elaborated elsewhere, however, while Jager and Kim's analysis convincingly highlights how this newer conciliatory narrative is enacted through the exhibits on the war and especially in the sculptures that are a dominant feature of the grounds of the memorial, they do not quite capture the ways in which the Cold War–era "continuous war" narrative is actually embedded in the museum itself.[8] While the exhibition rooms devoted to the Korean War were not populated with vilifying depictions of the North Korean or Chinese invaders (at least in their original form), this earlier narrative is to a certain extent hardwired, as it were, into the very structure and layout of the museum, for visitors come to the Korean War exhibitions only after having walked through room after room depicting five millennia of Korean history as one of repeated invasions. As visitors thus retain a vivid memory of the various armies that have imperiled the nation over this long history, the most recent "invaders" need not even be depicted in order to conjure the existential threat they pose to the nation—they have been spectrally implied by those prior threats.

Figure C.1. *The Statue of Brothers*, the War Memorial of Korea. Photograph by author.

Tessa Morris-Suzuki suggests that Jager and Kim's emphasis on the newer, more conciliatory narrative imparted by the memorial might reflect the fact that their essay was published in 2007. As she points out, it was "written during the presidency of the late Roh Moo-Hyun, at a time when the Sunshine Policy of engagement between North and South was at its height"; when Morris-Suzuki visited the memorial in 2009, "the pendulum of politics had swung to the other side of the divide: the Lee Myung-bak administration had renounced the Sunshine Policy, and tensions on the Korean peninsula had reached a new peak," and her own essay reflects on how this shift had shaped her experience of it.[9]

The South Korean government had swung further to the right by the time I myself made two research visits to the war memorial in 2013. (My first had taken place two years earlier, in 2011.) I was surprised to find that the exhibition rooms devoted to the Korean War had been completely renovated, presumably to accord better with the more hardline approach to the North adopted by Lee Myung-bak when he became president in 2008 and by his successor, Park Geun-hye, who had assumed office earlier that year. The new incarnation of the Korean War rooms reflects the Cold War perspective on North Korea that had resurged during these administrations. The revamped exhibits advance an essentially right-wing narrative: they draw a good deal of attention to North Korean atrocities, for example, and point to documentation of communications between Kim Il Sung, Joseph Stalin, and Mao Zedong that prefaced the invasion, thereby reiterating what Jae-Jung Suh has termed a *yugio* (6/25) narrative identifying South Koreans "first and foremost as the victims of the violence committed by communists and their puppets."[10] They also engage in a revanchist celebration of Syngman Rhee, who had long been discredited for his authoritarianism and establishing a template that his successors would follow.

The rather retrograde ideological narrative the memorial now forwards has been soldered to a new one, which is manifest in the extensive use of immersive digital and cinematic technologies throughout the exhibition rooms.[11] Whereas the paradigmatic representational medium in their original versions had been the diorama and a color scheme comprising mainly subtle earth tones, the new displays are extremely high tech, drawing extensively on computer graphics and featuring immersive 3D spectacles accompanied by thunderous and crystalline musical soundtracks and state-of-the-art sound effects. The lighting throughout is now quite dramatic—often bathing visitors in glaring light and suddenly submerging them in darkness—and the color palette mainly consists of a spectrum of grays interrupted by sheets of red. While the old exhibits encouraged a deliberative, even meditative response, the new ones aim at a more dynamic, gripping, and immersive experience—presumably tailored to younger generations accustomed to the blockbusters that are now a staple of the Korean movie industry, PC bangs (arcades for multiplayer online computer games), HD/4k televisions, and Samsung smartphones and tablets. The kind of computer-generated graphics familiar to anyone who has played (or watched someone playing) computer games are found throughout the exhibit. It is impossible not to think of the ascendance of corporations like Samsung and LG—companies that have arguably surpassed Sony and Microsoft and are now capable of going toe-to-toe with Apple—when one walks through the new version of the War Memorial of Korea. The medium is indeed the message in the new version of the war memorial.

Encoded into this extravagant display of digital and cinematic technologies is what we might call a virtual nationalism tied to the broader theme of technology that many of these dazzling exhibits address. For example, military technology plays a decisive role in the account of why South Korean forces were defeated in the early days of the conflict offered by the exhibitions. Instead of exploring how poor training or a lack of conviction about the cause may have played a role, the inability of South Korean forces to repel the invasion is explained as stemming from a pronounced technology gap: the Republic of Korea Army (ROKA) was simply outmatched by the Soviet T-34 tanks possessed by the North Korean People's Army. This disparity in military technology is dramatized in an especially bombastic way by a new display portraying the beginning of the war. The side hall visitors enter to watch a short documentary depicting the invasion seems like a conventional screening room, but in fact, the floor trembles and shakes. The film's central message—that the Soviet T-34 tanks possessed by the North Koreans played a decisive role—is enhanced by the floor's rumbles and vibrations that seek to mimic what it was like for ROKA soldiers to feel the proximity of such devastating technology. As it the film ends, lights come up behind the screen—actually a translucent scrim—and one sees that hidden in front the whole time was a Russian T-34 tank with a small contingent of North Korean soldiers arrayed around it.

Highlighting the nearly disastrous consequences of this technology gap in the early days of the war lays the foundation for an argument conveyed throughout the rest of the memorial: that such a disparity is a relic of the past. The sheer mass of all the military equipment displayed in the main building and arrayed across the grounds amply reassures visitors of that fact. Moreover, the media used in the new version of the memorial also highlight another technology gap that has emerged in recent years—one that also decidedly tilts toward South Korea's advantage.

In the new incarnation of the war memorial, one can discern a mashup, if you will, of a Cold War–era nationalism touting South Korea's military power and what I term a virtual nationalism that showcases the country's technological and corporate power—one that will presumably enable the country to thrive within an era governed by the structures of globalization and neoliberalism. These now threaten to overshadow the more conciliatory narrative identified by Jager and Kim, though that one remains permanently seated, it would seem, in sculptures like the Statue of Brothers or the 6/25 Tower. What also remains is the fact that the primary purpose of this site is, obviously, to memorialize the Korean soldiers who have sacrificed their lives in defense of their country. Many of the ceremonial spaces both in the building and on the grounds are clearly intended to allow visitors to reflect on members of the ROKA who perished during the Korean War.

Indeed, as Sheila Miyoshi Jager argues in the final chapter of her book *Narratives of Nation Building in Korea* (2003), "The idea that Korea's war heroes, from the establishment of the ROK Army during the Korean War era to its deployment overseas during the Vietnam and Gulf wars, could be traced back to a single 'patriotic' (male) warrior lineage, beginning with the Three Kingdoms period, lies at the very core of the memorial's significance as a state monument and national museum."[12] Jager notes, moreover, that while the memorial provides the ROKA with a resplendent genealogy linking it to the various armies that have defended Korea throughout its history against multiple Japanese, Chinese, and Mongolian invaders, the soldiers of the North Korean People's Army are not included in this virtual bloodline.

At the broadest level, in positing a distinct cultural identity that has existed for millennia, the memorial gives expression to a distinctly Korean ethnonationalism that is, as Jin-kyung Lee points out, a product of colonial modernity, a "resistive assertion of ethnic purity that performatively helped create unity and solidarity around a single ethnicity" that emerged in "reaction to the Japanese empire's production of Koreans as an ethnicized or racialized collective."[13] This ethnonationalism became further elaborated and integrated into the "militarized modernity," to use Seungsook Moon's phrase, that Park Chung-hee established during the eighteen years he ruled the country, from 1961 to 1979.[14] As Lee notes, the anti-Communist nationalism Park fostered fused economic developmentalism to a "militarization of South Korean society that penetrated deeply into the everyday life of the villages and cities, accomplished through dissemination of militarist nationalist ideologies in schools, factories, and companies, through various programs and policies at all levels and venues of South Korean society."[15] As such, the memorial's positing of the South Korean soldier as the model citizen-subject of the nation extends a legacy that begins with Park's authoritarian rule.

In exhibits that honor the actions the nation's military has engaged in since the end of the Korean War, the memorial points toward an aspect of the Vietnam War that US visitors will likely find surprising. As Charles Armstrong notes, "Between 1965 and 1973 the Republic of Korea contributed a cumulative total of more than 300,000 combat troops to the American war effort, second only to the United States itself and far exceeding all other Allied contributions combined."[16] These soldiers, who comprised what were termed "expeditionary forces," arguably functioned as mercenaries, developing a reputation among both allies and enemies for their brutality: in exchange for their participation, the United States provided significant aid to Park's dictatorship. Indeed, Armstrong writes, "Vietnam was a goldmine for South Korea," since "War-related income in the form of direct aid, military assistance, procurements, and soldiers' salaries amounted to over $1 billion. In 1967 alone war-related income accounted for nearly 4 percent of South Korea's GNP and 20 percent of its foreign exchange earnings."[17] Indeed, he asserts, "South Korea's economic takeoff in the mid-1960s would not have been possible without the profits gained by fighting for the United States in Vietnam."[18]

The memorial frames this history within a triumphalist narrative, which is neatly encapsulated in a placard in front of a small diorama depicting a scenario that will be familiar to US visitors: soldiers disembarking from a Huey helicopter. However, in this case, the soldiers are members of the ROKA: "Through the dispatch of armed forces to Vietnam, we gained confidence and experience in building a more self-reliant defense force. It also increased the momentum of our economic development, strengthened the US commitment to the defense of the Republic of Korea, and solidified South Korea's politico-military status vis-à-vis the United States. Furthermore, the impressive performance of the Korean forces in Vietnam enhanced our international reputation."[19] In trumpeting the endeavors of Korean "expeditionary forces" in Vietnam, this exhibit harkens back to the message Park Chung-Hee imparted in various ceremonies honoring soldiers who were leaving for or returning from combat. As Jin-kyung Lee notes, "The idea that the Vietnam War was the very first occasion where Korea, in its long, five-thousand-year history, sent its troops overseas is emphatically reiterated in the state publicity discourses as a historical achievement that should 'deeply stir all Koreans.'"[20]

In the memorial, one can see how the Vietnam War analogy mobilized by Jayne Anne Phillips, Bruce Cumings, and Susan Sontag to criticize the US role in both Asian civil wars functions in a South Korean nationalist narrative of ascent: while in their own civil war ROKA forces were initially overwhelmed and were only able to prevail with the assistance of US-led forces, in the Vietnam War they were able to gain "confidence and experience in building a more self-reliant defense force" that was capable of bringing the fight against Communism to another country and provide crucial support to its most important ally.

Military Orientalism Redux

To reframe in countervailing terms the nationalist celebration of the soldier as a model citizen-subject in which the memorial engages and to draw a different kind of connection between the Korean and Vietnam

Wars, it is useful to turn to Jin-kyung Lee's *Service Economies: Militarism, Sex Work, and Migrant Labor in South Korea* (2010). In this book, Lee details how the public discourse orchestrated by Park Chung-hee to justify sending South Korean troops to Vietnam and echoed in the memorial worked to "associate[e] the prestige and status of the nation with the enhancement of collective masculinity," and this proved to be "enormously effective in the context of a South Korean patriarchy that had suffered political, economic, and military subordination to the United States since 1945, when the Korean peninsula was liberated from Japanese colonialism and the southern half was inserted into the United States' sphere of influence."[21] In other words, this rhetoric defined Korean military involvement in Vietnam as a project of remasculinization, reversing an emasculation effected by the subordinate status the country had assumed vis-à-vis the United States and, prior to that, Japan. However, as Lee incisively illuminates, this fiction covered over the fact that South Korean soldiers actually functioned in Vietnam as "a subimperial force," providing a cheaper outsourced supply of military labor that had essentially been purchased by the United States in order to help maintain its neocolonial presence in East and Southeast Asia.[22]

As such, South Korean troops constituted what she terms, drawing from the language of military strategists, a "surrogate army," which refers to "a military 'arm' that is part of joint operations but is not part of coalition forces," and "filling the gaps created by U.S. strategic choices and necessities."[23] They were assigned the most "dangerous and difficult" tasks, as were other Asians (Hmongs, Filipinos, Laotians, and Cambodians) and were, it would seem, eager to perform them: "Members of the younger generation of South Koreans, who grew up in the aftermath of the Korean War, were indoctrinated as staunch anticommunists, willing soldiers to fight for the cause. Hungry and poor, they were eager to prove their masculinity."[24]

Of particular relevance to this study is the linkage Lee makes between ROKA soldiers, who served from the US perspective as a foreign surrogate force, and what she terms "domestic surrogates": as she notes, "The inequitable draft system [in the US] allowed deferments for white middle- and upper-class draftees, leaving predominantly African Americans, Latino Americans, immigrants, and the white working class to fill the ranks of Vietnam service."[25] As such, "both the 'domestic' racialized and working-class force and the 'international' force formed a continuum as a state-produced, state-controlled transnational migrant labor."[26] Lee's analysis enables us to grasp how the military Orientalism I examined in earlier chapters is not simply a mode of representation that seeks to elicit the affective attachment of Asians and Asian Americans to the American cause; it also manifests as a military labor force that is segmented and stratified both domestically and transnationally. It names a formation into which such populations are conscripted, and sometimes willingly so, as essential cogs in the machinery of US warmaking. In this respect, military Orientalism seems a rather appropriate term for how South Korea and other Asian nations that served as allies during the Cold War—South Vietnam, the Philippines, Thailand, and Japan—came to function as, in Lee's words, "a colossal military-industrial complex for the United States,"[27] or, to use Chalmers Johnson's formulation, "an empire of bases."[28]

Rescreening the Korean War

Given that South Korean forces have been such a crucial component in the military Orientalist form of empire that the United States would establish in Asia by the end of the Korean War, it is rather striking how invisible South Korean military forces are in the Hollywood films examined in the first half of this study. Of the movies surveyed thus far, only *Battle Hymn* and *One Minute to Zero* picture South Korean military men at all. In the latter, ROKA soldiers appear only in the very first scene, as the pathetic recruits for whom Robert Mitchum's Steve Janowski demonstrates how to "kill a tank," and in the former, South Koreans also appear as trainees—the overeager fledging pilots that Rock Hudson's Dean Hess has been commissioned to lead. Their meager presence in these films and their absence in the others are in keeping with the premise that the conflict in Korea was a proxy war, suggesting that its real actors were the more powerful foreign nations that intervened.

It seems appropriate, then, to conclude this study with an analysis of *Taegukgi: The Brotherhood of War*, a South Korean blockbuster that premiered in 2004 and the first major production to address the topic in the postmilitary dictatorship era. This film's focus is *exclusively* on Korean characters, and the only Americans to appear onscreen are two reporters who only show up briefly in a small but significant scene. As such, *Taegukgi* provides (as do other contemporary South Korean films on the conflict) an obvious corrective to the humanitarian Orientalism of US representations that reduced Korean civilians to objects of care. It also departs from the military Orientalism of such representations in that it centers on Asian combatants who are not Japanese American but Korean. Additionally, in its complex highlighting of Korean perspectives, this film moves beyond the essentially symbolic function to which Koreans are reduced in even the more progressive depictions encountered in this study: as we have seen, US works that are critical of the role played by that country's soldiers, whether white or of color, nonetheless leverage Orientalist tropes even as they disrupt prevailing historical narratives. Finally, by highlighting its status as a civil conflict, *Taegukgi* disrupts the commonplace understanding in the United States of the Korean War as a proxy war and of the Cold War as cold.

That having been said, as my analysis of the film will make clear, it would be a mistake to overstate the subversiveness of *Taegukgi* in relation to either the US or South Korean nationalist understandings of the conflict. When placed in its domestic context, the film's value stems from the illuminating contradictions that emerge from its attempt to disentangle viewers' affective investment in the familial intimacies that lie at its core from Korean nationalist ideologies and not from a thoroughgoing or coherent critique of the war itself. Additionally, positioning it as a transnational work leads to related but distinct criticisms about the US role in the conflict, but this does not necessarily lead to a delegitimizing of the necessity or fortuitousness of President Truman's decision to intervene.

To further temper expectations about the transgressive potential of a film like *Taegukgi*, one should be mindful of the developments that have made such works widely available to the English-speaking world. Since the 1990s, a primary strategy South Korean culture industries have developed to grapple with globalization has been to create translated versions of their products that will better enable them to penetrate foreign markets. Such corporations have been greatly assisted in these efforts by the South Korean government.[29] *Taegukgi* is among the big-budget South Korean films that have composed a vital cinematic component of what has come to be known as *hallyu*.[30] This term, often translated as the

"Korean wave," refers to the astonishing rapidity with which South Korean movies, television series, and popular music have become popular since the 1990s in other Asian countries and, increasingly, in the English-speaking world. This development can be credibly characterized, as Viet Thanh Nguyen does in *Nothing Ever Dies*, as marking "the triumph of Korean soft power, enabled by Korea's economic transformation."[31] Indeed, the ethnonationalist potential of *hallyu* is evident in the cinematic technologies that are marshaled to such great effect in the renovated Korean War rooms in the war memorial. Given how immense and contradictory these increasingly global forms of South Korean culture are, however, the potential remains for them to be more than just propagandistic expressions of a triumphalist nationalism.

The complex political significance of films like *Taegukgi* is suggested by the fact that it—as well as two other films that helped establish the Korean blockbuster as a staple of that country's film industry—engages in various ways with the Korean War and its complex aftermath in the tensions that remain between North and South. The films I am referring to are *Shiri* (1999) and *JSA* (2000), which along with *Taegukgi* and *The Host* (2006) are regarded as having established this genre and Chungmuro, the Korean film district that is that country's counterpart to Hollywood, as a force in world cinema.[32] While the aesthetic mastery, technical skill, and high production values evident in these films make clear that they are quite serviceable as expressions of South Korean soft power, as Nguyen asserts, these films also, as Jinhee Choi notes in her study *The South Korean Film Renaissance*, "question and doubt the legitimacy of the militaristic nationalism and ideology advanced and advocated by the Korean government for the last couple of decades during the era of military dictatorships."[33] Choi suggests that a partial explanation lies in the fact that the filmmakers who wrote and directed these movies all came of age during the politically turbulent 1980s. While they "were not directly involved" in the democratization movement, she writes, they "did witness the political turmoil in the 1980s, and their experiences, even as bystanders, seeped into their work."[34] Moreover, as I will discuss, even cursory accounts of these films are evocative of how they emerged out of essentially the same cultural moment as Hwang's *The Guest*, a period when the government in the South had been making gestures of reconciliation to the North.

Shiri, an action thriller and romance directed by Kang Je-gyu and released in 1999, represents the first of the Korean blockbusters. The rather improbable romance at the heart of this film involves Yu, a male South Korean intelligence officer, and Lee, a female sniper who is a member of a rogue North Korean special forces unit that regards the willingness of its government to enter into talks with the South as a betrayal. These North Korean soldiers have infiltrated the South in a plot to assassinate the leaders of both Koreas and murder thousands of civilians by setting off a bomb in a stadium during a soccer match between the North and South Korean teams. Yu is ultimately able to thwart their plan. In so doing, he learns that his fiancée is actually a member of the renegade North Korean unit who has undergone plastic surgery and assumed another identity: she has been passing along secret information and assassinating South Korean targets. He ends up having to shoot and kill Lee. In the film's denouement, however, we learn that Lee had actually fallen in love with Yu and was pregnant with his child: she had even left a voice message, which failed to reach him in time, declaring her undying love but also revealing the details of the plot so that he might thwart it even though it will lead to her death.

While North Koreans are the villains in this action thriller—which owes as much to the work of Hong Kong director John Woo as to Hollywood—they are depicted as acting against their own government, which is in the process of responding positively to the South's gestures toward reconciliation. Moreover, Lee, the North Korean sniper and love interest, emerges as a kind of allegory for North Korea itself in that the violence she directs toward the South is presented as a product of the war and the division of the country—the expression of a purely political identity, in other words—while her personal and thus more authentic identity is conveyed by the love she feels for Yu. Their star-crossed romance, which comes to a tragic end in the film, casts the desire for reunification as an anti- or postpolitical impulse.

The next South Korean blockbuster, *JSA*, came out a year later, in 2000 (the same year *The Guest* was published), and was directed by Park Chan-wook, who would come to be internationally acclaimed as an auteur four years later with the release of *Oldboy*.[35] Structured loosely as a murder mystery, *JSA* focuses on four soldiers who stand guard at the demilitarized zone (DMZ)—two North Korean and two South

Korean—who secretly visit each other and become friends over an eight-month period. Though the film ends tragically with the deaths of all but one of the men, the North Korean Sergeant Oh, the film marked a landmark moment in South Korean cinema for its humanizing portrait of North Korean soldiers. Song Kang-ho's remarkable performance as Sergeant Oh helped establish him as one of South Korea's leading male actors. The film evokes the possibility of reconciliation through its depiction of the innocent and joyous camaraderie the four men enjoy. The antagonist to their intimacy is the division system itself, and particularly the political and military leaders who would see the friendship of these four men as treason.

Choi does not ultimately ascribe much political significance to the focus of these films, characterizing them as exhibiting what she terms only an "*apparent* historicity."[36] She asserts, moreover, that their engagement with "the North-South issue should be considered as product differentiation from Hollywood blockbusters and other national cinemas," a way of "utiliz[ing] the unique aspects of Korean culture and history for commercial gain."[37] Even so, she acknowledges that "such blockbusters provide[d] an occasion or a site for audience and filmmaker alike to revisit and reconsider issues specific to Korea through cinematic means."[38] Given their popularity (as well as that of Hwang's novel *The Guest*), it would seem that South Koreans had become willing at the turn of the millennium to move beyond the confines of the *yugio* narrative that invited them to see themselves "first and foremost as the victims of the violence committed by communists and their puppets,"[39] for these films all emphasize, in various ways, that the ongoing tensions are the result of a conflict that was a civil war, thereby downplaying the role that foreign actors play in maintaining those tensions.

The framing of the war in this way serves an important purpose, for in highlighting the civil nature of the conflict, these films depart from a historiographical narrative promoted in both the North and the South that is encapsulated, as Jini Watson Kim writes, in the "well-known Korean proverb: *korae ssaum e saeudŭng tŏjinda*—in a fight between whales, it's the shrimp who gets his back broken," which positions Korea as a victim of the foreign nation-states who have influenced its fate.[40] From this perspective, "it is Japan, the United States, Great Britain, China, and the Soviet Union who are the real historical actors, and North and

South Korea their arbitrary creations," and such a rendering of history bespeaks a "myth that both North and South have long agreed upon: the indisputable unity of the Korean people [*minjok*] forged out of a collective history of suffering caused by external invasions."[41] As such, these films (as well as Hwang's *The Guest*, which is Watson Kim's focus) provide Koreans with an opportunity to reckon with their agency in the violence that took place during the war and afterward as well as their complicity in the atrocities.

Depicting the war exclusively as a fratricidal affair, however, does not necessarily lead to a critique of the myth of an ethnically pure and singular Korean nation that had remained intact for millennia before the division of the peninsula—the ethnonationalist mythology that both Watson Kim and Lee critique. Indeed, the desire for reunification these films express certainly operationalizes this mythology, and arguably Hwang's novel does as well.[42] Moreover, by largely placing off-screen the actions of foreign powers who did in fact play a devastating role in the conflict and who continue to exert an outsize influence on the fate of the two Koreas, these films obscure South Korea's *sub*imperial status.

My discussion of the film, as did my analysis of *The Guest*, will begin by situating the film domestically, highlighting how it addresses itself to South Korean audiences, before turning to how we in the United States might read it as a transnational work. In that second context, I will underscore how *Taegukgi* in small but significant ways invites US viewers to recognize their country's complicity in the tragic events it depicts—to adopt the stance of a Benjaminian witness to this history of catastrophe and to recognize it as also partly their own.

Taegukgi and the Intimacies of Division

When considering why the film might have resonated so strongly with South Korean audiences, we might begin, ironically, by taking up its English-language title, *Taegukgi: The Brotherhood of War*, which actually speaks more directly to its central concerns than the Korean title, which a more literal translation would render as "Waving the Korean Flag." The two parts of the translated title highlight a primary tension in the film between the ideologies of nationalism symbolized in flags and the fraternal bonds that connect its two protagonists, Lee Jin-tae and Lee Jin-seok. Directed by Kang Je-gyu, who also directed *Shiri*, this film invites its viewers to invest more fully in the latter than the former, and one of the most intriguing aspects of the film are the gaps and tensions that emerge between filial bonds and the imagined community conjured by the modern nation-state.

At the emotional heart of what is in many ways a very conventional two-and-a-half-hour war film is a very Korean family saga that memorializes the heart-wrenching sacrifices made by an older brother to ensure that his younger siblings would be able to pursue their studies and enjoy a better life, a legacy that has been passed on to the next generation. As the film renders it, the essential tragedy of the Korean War was that the governments on both sides conscripted ordinary people into a civil conflict that led to the fracturing of the most sacred of human bonds, which it ultimately presents as familial. *Takegukgi* connects the authentic self of Jin-tae—the older brother who fully embraces his role as a soldier—not to the opposing ideologies he successively and feverishly adopts but to his filial devotion, which he is able to regain as he heroically sacrifices himself and enables his brother to survive the war.

Taegukgi does little to convey North Korean perspectives of the war, though it does reiterate, as South Korean depictions generally do, that Korean People's Army (KPA) forces committed significant atrocities. Nonetheless, the only war crimes actually presented onscreen are ones perpetrated by South Korean soldiers—and in several instances by one of its protagonists, Jin-tae. Overall, the injustices the film emphasizes are ones enacted by those fighting for the South Korean cause. The ROKA first appears in the film not as patriotic defenders of Korean citizens but as agents of a ruthless state that forcibly conscripts them. The younger brother, Jin-seok, is apprehended by South Korean soldiers, as he and his family are among a throng of refugees attempting to flee Seoul shortly after the invasion. When Jin-tae forces his way onto the train where Jin-seok is being held, he is beaten by military guards, and both brothers become part of an army that neither sought to join: they simply wanted to stay with their family.

Idyllic scenes set on the eve of the invasion offer a highly romanticized portrait of the family that Jin-tae and Jin-seok are forced to leave behind—a mother and several younger siblings—and of their intimate bond as brothers. Even though their father has passed away, the family is quite close and happy. Jin-tae shines shoes but hopes one day to become a shoemaker and open his own shop. He has abandoned his studies in order to help support the family, whose collective hopes for a better life are pinned to Jin-seok, a college student. Young-shin, Jin-tae's loving fiancée, is presented as an appropriate match for him, someone who can gently smooth his rough edges, and her potential as a good daughter-in-law is illustrated by the valuable assistance she provides to her future mother-in-law, who runs a food stall that serves noodles.

Jin-tae's devotion to his younger brother, not any allegiance to the Southern cause, leads him to become a formidable soldier. Soon after being conscripted, he strikes a deal with his commanding officer that if he can distinguish himself by earning a medal, his brother will be discharged. He volunteers for the most dangerous missions. When Jin-tae is later promoted to sergeant, his zeal for combat results in the death of Yong-man, a fellow soldier with whom both brothers have become quite close. This also creates a rift between the brothers. After one particularly brutal battle, Jin-seok angrily asserts he will refuse to leave the army if his older brother receives a medal, because his freedom will have been purchased by the lives of the other men Jin-tae has been so willing to sacrifice.

In the course of the fighting, Jin-tae does begin to feel a genuine hatred of the enemy, inflamed by evidence of the atrocities the Communist forces have committed: the corpses of civilians who have been slaughtered. He orders his men to execute captured North Korean soldiers. He comes to view all of them, even a boyhood friend from home who had been forced to join the North Korean Army at gunpoint, as "commie bastards" who should all be killed. *Taegukgi* depicts his internalization of this rabid anti-Communism as a kind of corruption. Jin-seok pointedly insists in several exchanges that even if the violence Jin-tae directs with increasing brutality toward enemy soldiers had initially been motivated by a desire to protect his younger brother, it has been overtaken by a naked ambition and patriotic bloodlust.

By the time Jin-tae has performed enough heroic actions to receive his medal, his platoon is stationed just north of Seoul. They had been with the bulk of the South Korean forces as they pushed their way to the verge of the border with China and were then forced into a chaotic retreat with the entry of Chinese forces into the fighting. During their march south, their commanding officer, who had promised to free Jin-seok from service, had been shot and killed. Jin-tae is under arrest when he first meets his new commander. Jin-tae had been taken into custody by "the Anti-Communist Federation," a paramilitary organization of thugs who round up and summarily execute any civilians suspected of disloyalty, which is working in concert with the South Korean Army. His fiancée, Young-shin, had been shot and killed by members of this militia, though she had only joined the Communist Party in exchange for food to feed her family, not out of any political allegiance. Jin-tae and Jin-seok had been arrested for trying, unsuccessfully, to save her. When Jin-tae requests that his new commander honor the deal his predecessor had made and discharge Jin-seok, the commander refuses, saying he is not bound by it. Their conversation, which takes place at a command post shared with the militia, is interrupted by an enemy attack. Realizing that they will soon be overrun, the new commander orders his men to set fire to the building in which Jin-seok is being held with other soldiers suspected of being Communists and to burn all the prisoners alive. In the aftermath of the fire, Jin-tae comes across what he believes to be his younger brother's remains, and when he sees the man who caused Jin-seok's death being led away by North Korean soldiers, he brutally beats the man to death with a brick.

As a result of this complicated turn of events, Jin-tae switches sides and becomes a formidable fighter for the North, promoted in its propaganda as the commander of an elite contingent of soldiers that has been dubbed "Flag Unit."

Jin-seok has actually survived the fire, however, and in the ferocious battle that comprises the final half hour of the movie, he surrenders to the KPA, hoping to be taken to his brother. He believes that if Jin-tae can be made to realize that his younger brother is still alive, he will switch sides once again. During a frenzied battle that descends into the most savage hand-to-hand combat, Jin-seok succeeds in getting his brother to recognize him. The two brothers had been engaged in a brutal fight, which is interrupted when both end up being injured by other soldiers. Only then is Jin-seok able to shake his brother out of the battle frenzy that had overcome him. As they tearfully embrace, Jin-tae demands that his younger brother retreat with the other South Korean soldiers, promising that he will surrender after the war and rejoin his family. He further implores Jin-seok to stay alive and to live the life that he and their parents had sacrificed themselves for—to continue his education and fulfill the dreams of their family. As Jin-seok reluctantly limps away with other ROKA soldiers who are trying to escape the withering attack unleashed by the men of Flag Unit, Jin-tae begins firing on his former comrades, changing sides once again. He is ultimately shot and killed while covering Jin-seok's escape.

All of the above is framed by scenes set in the present that bookend the film, establishing that most of it is an extended flashback. In these framing scenes, we learn that Jin-tae's bones have been discovered in the course of a South Korean government project to collect the remains of fallen soldiers and identify them so that they might be given a proper burial by their families. In the penultimate scene, Jin-seok kneels in front of the excavation site that holds Jin-tae's bones and offers a moving address to the brother who had sacrificed so much for him. His grand-daughter stands beside him, moved to tears by his outpouring of grief.

The very final scene in the movie returns to the earlier timeline and captures the homecoming of the younger Jin-seok and his reunion with his mother and siblings amid a devastated Seoul. Signaling this family's resilience, his mother seems to have already reestablished her noodle business even though the city itself has largely been reduced to rubble, and one of his younger siblings tells him how excited she is that classes will be starting again. In the final lines of dialogue, another sibling asks Jin-seok, "I want to go to school too. How about you?" He replies, "Of course I do."

By the end of *Taegukgi*, the film has memorialized the fallen Jin-tae not so much as the model citizen-soldier lionized in the war memo-rial but as an exemplary familial subject. Although in the course of the war he has passionately asserted and violently enacted his hatred of first "commies" and then "Southern bastards," Jin-tae's primary motivation always stemmed from his love and devotion to his younger brother: he killed North Koreans in order to protect Jin-tae and then killed South Koreans out of vengeance for what he believed had happened to his younger brother.

It is the primacy given to the familial that enables a critique of cer-tain elements of South Koreans' conduct during the war to emerge: the forcible conscription that first severs the Lee family, the incitement of a virulent anti-Communism in Jin-tae that spurs him to commit atrocities, the senseless murders committed by anti-Communist thugs working in concert with the South Korean military, and commanding officers so obsessed with killing the enemy that they will order their men to kill both their fellow soldiers and civilians whose loyalty is suspect. The actual object of Jin-tae's allegiance is articulated in a scene in which Jin-seok is questioned by South Korean intelligence officers who are suspicious of his loyalties as well. Jin-seok insists that his brother "doesn't know what communism or democracy is" and that "the Jin-tae I knew was just an innocent shoeshine boy who loved his family, especially his brother." "The decorated man leading Flag Unit," he continues, "is not my brother." The film overall affirms Jin-seok's assertion that the true Jin-tae was exemplified not by the military uniforms he donned but by his identity as a devoted brother.

That having been said, *Taegukgi* does seem to draw a pointed contrast between the injustices committed by the South Korean government during the war and its current endeavors to address that legacy, for the film opens with South Korean civilian workers and soldiers who are engaged in the forensic excavation project that will enable the elderly Jin-seok to be reunited with his brother's remains. They are toiling at a site identified as the "Memorial Site for the Souls of the Korean War." All of them wear white gloves and handle with the utmost care the various artifacts they uncover—which include personal items like a journal and a harmonica—placing white flowers beside them, and they gently put the remains they disinter into varnished coffins, which they then cover with South Korean flags. They also bow down respectfully before the flag-draped coffins, paying belated respect to these men who died during the conflict. The worker who first telephones Jin-seok identifies himself as working with "the Korean War Excavation Department," and he is calling from a military base. These framing scenes thus underscore the notion that the South Korean military and government of today are quite different from the entities that committed such terrible actions against their own people in the past.

Because of this contrast, it is possible to interpret the film as suggesting that this difficult past was a horrific *but necessary* prologue to a more peaceable and comfortable present, for it was out of the ashes of that horrific conflict that the Republic of Korea was able to make its phoenix-like emergence. This point is conveyed by the final images of the film: a long shot of Jin-seok and his young siblings walking away from the camera, which cuts to a panoramic shot of the war-torn cityscape of Seoul accompanied by dialogue in which they proclaim their eagerness to resume their studies. Korean moviegoers who walked out of multiplex theaters after seeing this film would presumably register that what they had just watched was a moving account of the sacrifices that have enabled them to enjoy their current prosperity and to live in the glittering metropolis that Seoul has become. To such viewers, the atrocities committed by men like Jin-tae might be viewed as tragic mistakes that can be forgiven, since they were made in the name of family.

Having evoked how *Taegukgi* invites its South Korean audience to view their country's turbulent and traumatic past, I want now to highlight certain elements of it that are particularly important for US viewers to notice, for these point to *their* country's role in the events they have witnessed even though US soldiers never actually appear onscreen.

I want to retrace how the film conveys the transformation that Jin-tae undergoes as he begins to inhabit more fully his role as a heroic ROKA soldier. A crucial shift in his personality takes place roughly an hour into the film, after a brutal battle near the Pusan Perimeter just before MacArthur's landing at Inchon. In it, Jin-tae had singlehandedly destroyed the bunker serving as the headquarters of the North Korean soldiers his platoon had been battling. He is made the standard bearer of his unit for those actions, and his exploits earn him a measure of international attention. A press conference is held to honor his deeds. Playing to the cameras and press, he claims that he had *volunteered* to join the army to "prevent my family from suffering under the oppression of the communists."

While Jin-tae is flanked by South Korean generals as he speaks and is prompted by questions shouted to him in Korean, noticeable in the throng of reporters because of his shock of blonde hair, though visible only momentarily, is an American who is speaking rapidly to another white man sitting beside him, furiously scribbling notes. These two men are briefly visible in the very next shot, which tracks Jin-tae walking away from the press conference as the men in his platoon hoot and howl.

The presence of these two white characters, who are presumably journalists, suggests that the performance of South Korean soldiering that Jin-tae offers—which viewers know is false—has been tailored to reach a US audience: presumably his words will reassure Americans that their military has been fighting alongside men like him, patriotic and filial Koreans who enthusiastically took up arms to prevent their families from falling under the yoke of Communist domination. US viewers *today*, however, are alerted not only to the untruthfulness of that narrative but also to the fact that the South Korean subjects who parroted it might have been doing so for strategic purposes.

While the persona Jin-tae adopts in the press conference is one he has self-consciously performed for the cameras, subsequent scenes suggest that it is one that he has started to internalize. That something has changed in him is evident in the tracking shot that immediately follows. As he is walking away from the press conference, Jin-seok asks him to help him find someone who might deliver a letter to their family, letting them know the two of them are safe. Jin-tae declines, however, as he is eager to attend a reception being thrown in his honor. The next scene shows the men eating and joking about the new version of "Private Lee" they witnessed at the press conference, the "hero" who will soon appear on television. One of them asks, "Didn't you see Private Lee with the American officers and the cameras flashing?" They sardonically note the newfound patriotism and anti-Communism Jin-tae had ventriloquized in his performance.

That the persona Jin-tae has adopted has a specifically *American* provenance is conveyed shortly thereafter, when he appears with a duffel bag stuffed with candy that he empties before the men, who scramble immediately after the treats he has presumably secured from the "American officers." Flush with his newfound fame and drunk from the alcohol he consumed at the reception, he presents his younger brother with a gigantic Hershey's chocolate bar. These details make a rather on-the-nose reference to the archetypical image of American GIs in the Korean War who bestowed gifts of chewing gum and candy on grateful Korean children.

Further allusions to the US role in the fighting are evident in the very next battle scene. While no American soldiers appear onscreen, the tanks and other armored vehicles that support the platoon prominently feature the white star that suggests the presence of such men inside.

These references to the off-screen presence of the US military directly preface Jin-tae's transformation in the next section of the film into a soldier whose hatred of Communists is so inflamed when he finds evidence of the atrocities they have committed that he starts ordering the killing of the North Korean soldiers he and his men take prisoner. As such, they suggest that as Jin-tae throws himself into the role of rabid cold warrior, he is engaging in a kind of transnational racial mimicry.[43]

Additionally, while US infantry are not involved in the final battle depicted in the film, in which the two brothers are reunited, Americans play a significant role in how events turn out in addition to providing the tanks and fighter plans that support the ROKA infantrymen in their attack, for the South Koreans had apparently devised a rather time-intensive and complex plan, though the details of this are quite vague, that would involve Jin-tae joining a unit of soldiers that would somehow engage with the enemy in a way that would allow him to make himself visible to his brother and, hopefully, influence him to switch sides. This plan is scrapped, however, because US military commanders have ordered ROKA soldiers to move up the time of the attack by twenty-four hours. While its prospects for success are presented as murky at best, this gambit might have enabled both brothers to survive the final battle. As it turns out, because the movement of South Korean soldiers is dictated by a timeline imposed by the Americans, Jin-seok must resort to more drastic measures, which involve disobeying direct orders and surrendering to the enemy. And even though he succeeds in reuniting with his brother and getting him to fight for the South, his actions, which were partly determined by those of the US military, will result in Jin-tae dying at the hands of North Korean soldiers.

*　*　*

As I hope I have conveyed, a delicate balancing act is involved as we take up South Korean works like *Taegukgi* and *The Guest*. In addressing them, it is necessary to be attentive both to their meanings for South Koreans and to the additional and different resonances they take on as works that now circulate in the United States in translated form. Including such works in the archive of cultural memory I have put before the reader helps reiterate that this archive is intended not as singular but as open ended and potentially deterritorializing—as part of an increasingly expansive racialized assemblage of remembrance. I have tried in this study not to ascribe a discrete eventfulness to the Korean War or to highlight its significance for a single community but rather to trace its seepage into an array of multiple historical trajectories that stretch back at least to the beginning of the twentieth century and extend to the present.

The persistent afterlife of the conflict is attested to by Hwang Sok-yong in his Author's Note to *The Guest*, which points to the resonances his novel took on shortly after its publication, in the wake of the 9/11 attacks. For Koreans, he writes, "the onset of this new 'Age of Terror,' along with the inclusion of North Korea in the so-called Axis of Evil, and the beginning of a whole new war, made the fragility of our condition clearer than ever. It was a chilling experience to be so reminded that despite the collapse of the Cold War infrastructure, our small peninsula is still bound by the delicate chains of war."[44] That the peninsula remains "bound by the delicate chains of war" is suggested not only by the connection Hwang draws between the Korean War and current conflicts but also by its ongoing status. His comments invite us to recognize that we remain within, as Christine Hong eloquently asserts, "the *longue durée* of the unending Korean War," which is best understood "as a protean structure, at once generative and destructive, whose formations and deformations, benefits and costs, truths and obfuscations, can be traced on both sides of the North Pacific. Naturalized as 'forgotten' in the United States yet seared into national consciousness in both Koreas, the Korean War, as a differentiated and multisited structure of feeling, perception, memory, knowledge, and historical ruin, has persisted some six decades after the signing of the Armistice Agreement."[45] In evoking a multidirectional memory of a war that persists and is part of a larger ongoing complex of war-making, I have sought to resist the notion that, as Viet Thanh Nguyen puts it, "anyone or any nation or any people has a unique claim to humanity, to suffering, to pain, to being the exceptional victim, a claim that almost certainly will lead us down a road to further vengeance enacted in the name of that victim. The fact of the matter is that however many millions have died in our particular tragedy, millions more have died in other tragedies no less tragic."[46] It is my hope that the archive of cultural memory this book has brought together will help us rethink in crucial ways who "we" are and the crucial role that this event played and continues to play in shaping "our" various histories as Americans, as Koreans, as Asian Americans, as people of color.

ACKNOWLEDGMENTS

Even though writing is essentially a solitary endeavor, I very much felt the presence of others as I was producing this book. I am grateful for the sustained and sustaining support I received over the many years it took to complete this project. I am certain that, in addition to those I mention here, there are others who have buoyed me along the way, and I beg their forgiveness if they have escaped my memory.

The two people who have had the most direct impact on its final shape are the readers whose insightful recommendations guided me through the very last stage of revisions, and I thank them heartily. Theirs were literally the best readers' reports I have ever received. They were the first to read this manuscript in its entirety, and their encouraging responses made clear that they understood what I was trying to do in a fundamental way; just as importantly, they also offered blunt assessments of what was not working and where I could sharpen my argument. The identity of one of these anonymous readers remains unknown to me (though I have my suspicions!), but the other, Kristin Hass, recently revealed herself to me. While I have already expressed my appreciation to her in person, I take the opportunity here to do it in writing: this book is so much better than it would have been because of her brilliant input. I would also like to thank Eric Zinner at NYU Press for his patience and judicious feedback over the many years that this project took shape as well as Dolma Ombadykow and Martin Coleman for their able assistance. The copyediting and indexing provided by Sam Martin and her team at Scribe Inc. have been meticulous and thoughtful.

I owe a debt of gratitude to Christine Hong not only for her formidable activist scholarship but also for introducing me to a group of Koreanists—including Bruce Cumings, Henry Em, Suzy Kim, Youngju Ryu, and Tammy Ko Robinson—whose work has absolutely shaped my approach to the topic of this book and whose collegiality and friendship have been a blessing.

Similarly, I want to thank Hyungji Park for first bringing me back in 2011 to the country I left as an infant to deliver a paper at the International Conference of the English Language and Literature Association of Korea (ELLAK) and enabling me to develop intellectual connections and friendships with scholars in Korea. This book has benefited immensely from the opportunities I have had to present portions of it at Yonsei University, Ewha Woman's University, and Seoul National University. For visits to those latter sites, I am grateful to Min-Jung Kim and Jee An, respectively. Thanks as well to Youngmin Kim for inviting me to present at the 2012 ELLAK International Conference.

I would like to acknowledge as well the compadres who catalyzed a fundamental shift in my thinking about the politics of diaspora as we attended several conferences of the American Studies Association of Korea and conducted extensive autoethnographic research into the *noraebang* experience: Joseph Jeon, Eun Joo Kim, James Kyung-jin Lee, Sharon Heijin Lee, Kimberly McKee, and Mary Yu Danico. I should thank Robert Ku in particular for helping me sharpen my ideas concerning the work of Chang-rae Lee.

I have had the remarkable good fortune to present material from this project at an array of universities, and I would like to thank those who organized and attended my talks at the Institute for the Humanities, University of Michigan; the James Weldon Johnson Institute for the Study of Race and Difference, Emory University; the Columbia University Seminar for American Studies; the Center for Korean Studies, University of California, Berkeley; the Institute for the Humanities, Ewha Woman's University; the American Studies Institute, Seoul National University; the Department of English, Yonsei University; the Department of English, New York University; the Center for African American Studies, Princeton University; the East Asian Studies Center, Ohio State University; the Department of English, University of California, Berkeley; the Asian American Studies Institute, University of Connecticut; the Department of American Studies, University of Connecticut at Avery Point; the Nam Center for Korean Studies, University of Michigan; the Department of English, Wesleyan University; the Department of East Asian Studies, New York University; the American Studies Program and Ethnicity, Race, and Migration Program, Yale University; the Graduate Group in Asian American Studies, University of Pennsylvania;

the Center for Korean Studies, University of Hawai'i at Manoa; and the Asian American Culture Center, Yale University.

My friends and colleagues at Brown University have been a tremendous source of support both intellectually and emotionally. In particular, I would like to give a shout-out to Susan Bernstein, Liza Cariaga-Lo, Jim Egan, Leela Gandhi, Olakunle George, Phil Gould, Matt Guterl, Françoise Hamlin, Evelyn Hu-Dehart, Tamar Katz, Nancy Khalek, Bob Lee, Kathleen McSharry, Rolland Murray, Shannon O'Neill, Rick Rambuss, Ravit Reichman, Tricia Rose, Kate Schapira, Naoko Shibusawa, Ada Smailbegovics, and Patricia Ybarra.

At Brown, I have taught several iterations of an undergraduate course titled "The Korean War in Color" that have been indispensable in working through much of the material I address here, and I am thankful to the students who have taken it over the years. Working with graduate students has been one of the most rewarding parts of my job, and I am grateful to all of them for the impact they have had on my thinking. In particular, I would like to thank Suzanne Enzerink, Nicole Fung, Claire Gullander-Drolet, Wendy Lee, Jennifer Schnepf, Jerrine Tan, and Jennifer Wang. Jennie Snow's excellent research has had the most direct overlap with this project, and I would like to acknowledge how generative for me our interactions have been.

My primary interdisciplinary home is the field of Asian American studies, and there are probably too many pioneering figures in it who have influenced and mentored me for me to properly name, but I would like specifically to acknowledge Lisa Lowe, Gary Okihiro, and Sau-ling Wong for the inspiration they have provided me and multitudes of other scholars. I would also like to voice my gratitude to the many people I have had the good fortune to get to know primarily through my membership in the Association for Asian American Studies, many of whom I now think of as kin: Tamara Bhalla, Pat Chu, Kandice Chuh, Stephanie Hsu, Eleana Kim, Jeehyun Lim, Colleen Lye, Viet Thanh Nguyen, erin Khuê Ninh, Crystal Parikh, Josephine Park, Karen Shimikawa, Cathy Schlund-Vials, Rajini Srikanth, Min Song, Jini Kim Watson, and Linda Vo.

I am grateful for several fellowships that provided crucial support for the writing of this book. Two were from Brown University: a Cogut Humanities Center Faculty Fellowship from Brown University in 2006 and a Presidential Faculty Research Fellowship at the Pembroke Center in 2018. I was also fortunate enough to receive a summer stipend from the National Endowment from the Humanities in 2013. Finally, I was able to devote my full attention to the very final revisions to this book thanks to a Norman Freehling Fellowship from the Institute for the Humanities at the University of Michigan. I am grateful to Peggy McIntosh, the institute's director, for the opportunity to enjoy the company of a brilliant and generous cohort of faculty and postdoctoral and graduate fellows as I put the final touches on this book.

I wish to express my appreciation to Jennifer Walrad and Chester P. Hound for the emotional support they provided as this project got under way.

I thank my parents, Jaejong Kim and Youngja Chun; my grandmother, Dongsun Lim; and my sister, Debbie Finch, for the love and support they have shown me over the years.

Finishing this book would not have been possible without the community with whom I trudge the road of happy destiny in Providence—I cannot convey the immensity of gratitude I feel for them.

My final words of thanks go to Annathena, Julian, and Obi for their patience and love—the idea of being able to spend more time with you guys is what helped me finally get this book done. Let it begin.

NOTES

INTRODUCTION

1 Adam Bernstein, "Al Chang, 85; Trained Lens on 3 Wars," *Washington Post*, October 5, 2007, www.washingtonpost.com.

2 Bernstein.

3 Christine Knauer, *Let Us Fight as Free Men: Black Soldiers and Civil Rights* (Philadelphia: University of Pennsylvania Press, 2014).

4 Young Ick Lew and Ki-baik Lee, "Korea," *Encyclopedia Britannica*, n.d., www.britannica.com.

5 Bruce Cumings, *The Korean War: A History* (New York: Modern Library, 2010), 35.

6 Allan R. Millett, "The Korean War," *Encyclopedia Britannica*, n.d., www.britannica.com.

7 Lew and Lee, "Korea."

8 Like every other military conflict that the United States has entered into since, the Korean War was entered into without a congressional declaration of war. It thus inaugurated what Elaine Scarry has argued is an unconstitutional state of affairs whereby Congress has illegally abdicated and the president illegally abrogated the Legislative branch's mandated power to declare war. See Elaine Scarry, "The Declaration of War: Constitutional and Unconstitutional Violence," in *Law's Violence*, ed. Austin Sarat and Thomas R Kearns (Ann Arbor: University of Michigan Press, 1992), 23–76.

9 Gregg K. Kakesako, "Photographer Brought War Home," *Star Bulletin*, October 2, 2007, http://archives.starbulletin.com.

10 Christina Klein, *Cold War Orientalism: Asia in the Middlebrow Imagination, 1945–1961* (Berkeley: University of California Press, 2003), 14.

11 Ann Laura Stoler, "Tense and Tender Ties: The Politics of Comparison in North American History and (Post) Colonial Studies," *Journal of American History* 88, no. 3 (December 1, 2001): 830–31.

12 Leerom Medovoi, "Cold War American Culture as the Age of Three Worlds," *Minnesota Review*, no. 55–57 (2002): 172.

13 Medovoi, 172, 173.

14 Medovoi, 175.

15 Mary L. Dudziak, *Cold War Civil Rights: Race and the Image of American Democracy* (Princeton, NJ: Princeton University Press, 2000); Jodi Kim, *Ends of Empire: Asian American Critique and the Cold War* (Minneapolis: University of Minnesota Press, 2010), 3; Klein, *Cold War Orientalism*; Jodi Melamed, *Represent*

and Destroy: Rationalizing Violence in the New Racial Capitalism (Minneapolis: University of Minnesota Press, 2011); Nikhil Pal Singh, "Culture/Wars: Recoding Empire in an Age of Democracy," *American Quarterly* 50, no. 3 (September 1998): 471–522; Penny M. Von Eschen, *Race against Empire: Black Americans and Anti-colonialism, 1937–1957* (Ithaca, NY: Cornell University Press, 1997).

16 Klein, *Cold War Orientalism*, 11.

17 Klein, 5.

18 Klein, 8.

19 Klein, 13.

20 Klein, 5.

21 *One Minute to Zero*, directed by Tay Garnett (1952; Burbank, CA: Warner Home Video, 2010), DVD; *Battle Hymn*, directed by Douglas Sirk (1957; Universal City, CA: Universal Studies, 2004), DVD.

22 Josephine Nock-Hee Park, *Cold War Friendships: Korea, Vietnam, and Asian American Literature* (New York: Oxford University Press, 2016), 6.

23 Park, 6.

24 *The Steel Helmet*, directed by Samuel Fuller, Eclipse Series 5: The First Films of Samuel Fuller (New York: Criterion, 2007), DVD.

25 Sara Ahmed, *Queer Phenomenology: Orientations, Objects, Others* (Durham, NC: Duke University Press, 2006).

26 Yen Le Espiritu, *Body Counts: The Vietnam War and Militarized Refuge(es)* (Oakland: University of California Press, 2014), 18.

27 Mimi Thi Nguyen, *The Gift of Freedom: War, Debt, and Other Refugee Passages*, Next Wave: New Directions in Women's Studies (Durham, NC: Duke University Press, 2012), 2.

28 Michel Foucault, *Society Must Be Defended: Lectures at the Collège de France, 1975–76* (New York: Picador, 2003); Giorgio Agamben, *Homo Sacer: Sovereign Power and Bare Life* (Stanford, CA: Stanford University Press, 1998); J.-A. Mbembé and Libby Meintjes, "Necropolitics," *Public Culture* 15, no. 1 (March 25, 2003): 11–40; Judith Butler, *Frames of War: When Is Life Grievable?* (London: Verso, 2009).

29 For a very different mobilization of this term from the vantage point of critical strategy studies, see Patrick Porter, *Military Orientalism: Eastern War through Western Eyes*, Critical War Studies (London: Hurst, 2009).

30 *Pork Chop Hill*, directed by Lewis Milestone (1959; Santa Monica, CA: MGM Home Entertainment, 2005), DVD.

31 *Nisei* is the term generally used within the Japanese American community to designate those who are in the second generation, born in the United States, while *Issei* refers to immigrants and *Sansei* to the third generation.

32 Melanie McAllister, *Epic Encounters: Culture, Media, and U.S. Interests in the Middle East since 1945* (Berkeley: University of California Press, 2005), 250.

33 *All the Young Men*, directed by Hall Bartlett (1960; New York: GoodTimes Home Video, 1990), VHS.

34 Jin-kyung Lee, *Service Economies: Militarism, Sex Work, and Migrant Labor in South Korea* (Minneapolis: University of Minnesota Press, 2010), 38.

35 *Go for Broke!*, directed by Robert Pirosh (1951; Tulsa, OK: VCI Entertainment, 2003), DVD.

36 *The Crimson Kimono*, directed by Samuel Fuller, Samuel Fuller Collection (1959; Culver City, CA: Criterion, 2009), DVD.

37 Robert J. Lentz's *Korean War Filmography: 91 English Language Features through 2000* (Jefferson, NC: McFarland, 2003) offers a literally encyclopedic account of the ninety or so English-language films that address the conflict. A more focused analysis of how movies concerning this conflict reshaped a genre that had been established during the Second World War can be found in the fourth chapter of Jeanine Basinger's *The World War II Combat Film: Anatomy of a Genre* (New York: Columbia University Press, 1986).

38 For an account of the coverage of the war in the mainstream press and how the US government attempted to manage it, see Steven Casey, *Selling the Korean War: Propaganda, Politics, and Public Opinion in the United States, 1950–1953* (Oxford: Oxford University Press, 2008).

39 Butler, *Frames of War*, 10.

40 Butler, 72.

41 Walter Benjamin, "Theses on the Philosophy of History," in *Illuminations* (New York: Schocken, 1969), 255.

42 Benjamin, 257.

43 This summary has been adapted from Daniel Y. Kim, "The Korean War," in *Asian American Society: An Encyclopedia*, ed. Mary Yu Danico, Anthony Christian Ocampo, and Association for Asian American Studies (Los Angeles: SAGE, 2014), 607–10.

44 Bruce Cumings, *The Origins of the Korean War*, vol. 1, *Liberation and the Creation of Separate Regimes, 1945–47* (Princeton, NJ: Princeton University Press, 1981); Bruce Cumings, *The Origins of the Korean War*, vol. 2, *The Roaring of the Cataract, 1947–1950* (Princeton, NJ: Princeton University Press, 1981).

45 Allan R. Millett, "The Korean War: A 50-Year Critical Historiography," *Journal of Strategic Studies* 24, no. 1 (2001): 190, 194.

46 Cumings, *Korean War*, 33.

47 While the family name precedes the given name in Korean practice—Hwang Sok-yong, for example—Korean Americans, like Chang-rae Lee, generally follow Western convention and reverse the order.

48 Alexander G. Weheliye, *Habeas Viscus: Racializing Assemblages, Biopolitics, and Black Feminist Theories of the Human* (Durham, NC: Duke University Press, 2014), 3.

49 Weheliye, 3.

50 Weheliye, 13.

51 Weheliye, 13.

52 Michael Rothberg, *Multidirectional Memory: Remembering the Holocaust in the Age of Decolonization*, Cultural Memory in the Present (Stanford, CA: Stanford University Press, 2009), 3.

53 Rothberg, 18.

54 Rothberg, 5.

55 Rothberg, 16.

56 Rothberg, 22.

57 Rothberg, 7 (emphasis mine).

58 Grace M. Cho, *Haunting the Korean Diaspora: Shame, Secrecy, and the Forgotten War*, illustrated ed. (Minneapolis: University of Minnesota Press, 2008), 12.

59 Marianne Hirsch, "Projected Memory: Holocaust Photographs in Personal and Public Fantasy," in *Acts of Memory: Cultural Recall in the Present* (Hanover, NH: University Press of New England, 1999), 3–23.

60 *Taegukgi: The Brotherhood of War*, directed by Kang Je-gyu (2004; Culver City, CA: Sony Pictures Home Entertainment, 2005), DVD.

61 Lee, *Service Economies*, 40.

62 Lee, 20.

63 Lee, 20.

64 Lee, 20.

65 Kandice Chuh, *Imagine Otherwise: On Asian Americanist Critique* (Durham, NC: Duke University Press, 2003); Hyun Yi Kang, *Compositional Subjects: Enfiguring Asian/American Women* (Durham, NC: Duke University Press, 2002).

66 Chuh, *Imagine Otherwise*, 10.

67 Lisa Lowe, *The Intimacies of Four Continents* (Durham, NC: Duke University Press, 2015), 1.

68 Lowe, 6.

69 Lisa Lowe, "The Intimacies of Four Continents," in *Haunted by Empire: Geographies of Intimacy in North American History* (Durham, NC: Duke University Press, 2006), 3.

70 Christine Hong, "The Unending Korean War," *Positions* 23, no. 4 (November 1, 2015): 598.

CHAPTER 1. "HE'S A SOUTH KOREAN WHEN HE'S RUNNING
WITH YOU, AND HE'S A NORTH KOREAN WHEN HE'S
RUNNING AFTER YOU"

1 Samuel Fuller, Christa Fuller, and Jerome Rudes, *A Third Face: My Tale of Writing, Fighting and Filmmaking* (New York: Alfred A. Knopf, 2002), 256.

2 Fuller, Fuller, and Rudes, 256.

3 Jeanine Basinger, *The World War II Combat Film: Anatomy of a Genre* (New York: Columbia University Press, 1986), 162.

4 Fuller, Fuller, and Rudes, *Third Face*, 256.

5 Basinger, *World War II Combat Film*, 56–57.

6 Basinger, 164.

7 Basinger, 26.

8 Basinger, 25–26.

9 Basinger, 26.

10 Fuller, Fuller, and Rudes, *Third Face*, 262.

11 Leslie A. Fiedler, "C'mon Back to the Raft Ag'in Huck Honey," in *The Collected Essays of Leslie Fiedler* (New York: Stein and Day, 1971), 142–51.

12 Robyn Wiegman, *American Anatomies: Theorizing Race and Gender* (Durham, NC: Duke University Press, 1995).

13 Basinger, *World War II Combat Film*, 162.

14 Basinger, 27.

15 Josephine Nock-Hee Park, *Cold War Friendships: Korea, Vietnam, and Asian American Literature* (New York: Oxford University Press, 2016), 33.

16 See Eleana J. Kim, *Adopted Territory: Transnational Korean Adoptees and the Politics of Belonging* (Durham, NC: Duke University Press, 2010); Arissa H. Oh, *To Save the Children of Korea: The Cold War Origins of International Adoption* (Stanford, CA: Stanford University Press, 2015).

17 Sahr Conway-Lanz, "Beyond No Gun Ri: Refugees and the United States Military in the Korean War," *Diplomatic History* 29, no. 1 (January 1, 2005): 50.

18 Conway-Lanz, 50.

19 Nathaniel Berman, "Privileging Combat? Contemporary Conflict and the Legal Construction of War," *Columbia Journal of Transnational Law* 43, no. 1 (2004): 4.

20 Berman, 4–5.

21 Michael Walzer, *Just and Unjust Wars: A Moral Argument with Historical Illustrations*, 2nd ed. (New York: Basic Books, 1992), 182.

22 Robert E. Park, *Race and Culture* (Glencoe, IL: Free Press, 1950), 760–61 (emphasis mine).

23 John W. Dower and American Council of Learned Societies, *War without Mercy: Race and Power in the Pacific War* (New York: Pantheon, 1993).

24 John Okada, *No-No Boy* (Seattle: University of Washington Press, 1979).

25 While I use the current popular acronym for prisoners of war (POW) throughout, some of the material I cite uses PW, which was commonly used during the 1950s.

26 Mary L. Dudziak, "The Toxic Legacy of the Korean War," *Washington Post*, March 1, 2019, accessed May 19, 2020, www.washingtonpost.com.

27 Thomas M. Franck and Faiza Patel, "UN Police Action in Lieu of War: 'The Old Order Changeth,'" *American Journal of International Law* 85, no. 1 (January 1991): 70.

28 Harry S. Truman, "172—Statement by the President on the Violation of the 38th Parallel in Korea, June 26th, 1950," American Presidency Project, October 2, 2007, www.presidency.ucsb.edu; Thomas M. Franck and Faiza Patel, "UN Police Action in Lieu of War: 'The Old Order Changeth,'" *American Journal of International Law* 85, no. 1 (January 1991): 68.

29 Harry S. Truman, "The President's News Conference," American Presidency Project, accessed May 19, 2020, www.presidency.ucsb.edu.

30 Paul Virilio, *War and Cinema: The Logistics of Perception*, trans. Patrick Camiller (London: Verso, 1989), 20.

31 Basinger, *World War II Combat Film*, 161.

CHAPTER 2. "TAN YANKS" AND BLACK KOREA

1 *The Manchurian Candidate*, directed by John Frankenheimer (1962; Santa Monica, CA: MGM Home Entertainment, 1998), DVD.

2 "The Mississippi Negro Soldier in Korea," *Atlanta Daily World*, September 2, 1950.

3 Daniel Widener, "Seoul City Sue and the Bugout Blues: Black American Narratives of the Forgotten War," in *Afro Asia: Revolutionary Political and Cultural Connections between African Americans and Asian Americans*, ed. Fred Ho and Bill V. Mullen (Durham, NC: Duke University Press, 6), 55.

4 Penny M. Von Eschen, *Race against Empire: Black Americans and Anticolonialism, 1937–1957* (Ithaca, NY: Cornell University Press, 1997), 146.

5 Von Eschen, 4–5.

6 Von Eschen, 2.

7 Von Eschen, 3.

8 Widener, "Seoul City Sue," 78.

9 McAllister, *Epic Encounters: Culture, Media, and U.S. Interests in the Middle East since 1945* (Berkeley: University of California Press, 2001).

10 Widener, "Seoul City Sue," 56.

11 Christopher Bollen and Damon Winter, "Toni Morrison," *Interview Magazine*, accessed July 12, 2016, www.interviewmagazine.com.

12 UPI, "Korean War Defector, as 'Voice' of Hanoi, Bids G.I.'s Get Out," *New York Times*, August 15, 1965.

13 Quoted in Mike Marqusee, *Redemption Song: Muhammad Ali and the Spirit of the Sixties* (New York: Verso, 1999), 214–15.

14 For a critique of how Foucault's rendering of race war actually sidelines and thus neglects the centrality of antiblack and other forms of what he terms "ethnic racism," see Alexander G. Weheliye, *Habeas Viscus: Racializing Assemblages, Biopolitics, and Black Feminist Theories of the Human* (Durham, NC: Duke University Press, 2014). My own analyses in this chapter borrow loosely from the concept of race war in ways that, according to Weheliye at least, run counter to Foucault's own emphases.

15 David Macey, "Rethinking Biopolitics, Race and Power in the Wake of Foucault," *Theory Culture Society* 26, no. 6 (November 1, 2009): 190.

16 Bill Mullen, *Afro-Orientalism* (Minneapolis: University of Minnesota Press, 2004), xv.

17 W. E. B. Du Bois, *Dark Princess: A Romance* (Jackson: University Press of Mississippi, 1995).

18 Widener, "Seoul City Sue," 55.

19 For a more comprehensive treatment of this topic, see Christine Knauer, *Let Us Fight as Free Men: Black Soldiers and Civil Rights* (Philadelphia: University of Pennsylvania Press, 2014).

20 For more comprehensive historical accounts of military integration, see William T. Bowers, William M. Hammond, and George L. MacGarrigle, *Black Soldier, White Army: The 24th Infantry Regiment in Korea* (Washington, DC: Center

of Military History, U.S. Army, 1996); Jack D. Foner, *Blacks and the Military in American History: A New Perspective* (New York: Praeger, 1974); Knauer, *Let Us Fight*; and Bernard C. Nalty, *Strength for the Fight: A History of Black Americans in the Military* (New York: Free Press, 1986).

21 Widener, "Seoul City Sue," 62.

22 Widener, 62–63.

23 Lucius C. Harper, "All Big Power Nations Have at One Time Betrayed the Koreans," *Chicago Defender*, July 8, 1950.

24 Lucius C. Harper, "How the 'Little Kingdom of Korea' Was Sold Out by the Big Powers," *Chicago Defender*, July 15, 1950.

25 Harry Paxton Howard, *America's Role in Asia* (New York: Howell, Soskin, 1943); Chris Dixon, *African Americans and the Pacific War, 1941–1945: Race, Nationality, and the Fight for Freedom* (Cambridge: Cambridge University Press, 2018), 45.

26 Walter White, "South Can't Escape Race Showdown—White," *Chicago Defender*, August 5, 1950.

27 White.

28 Lucius C. Harper, "Dustin' off the News," *Chicago Defender*, January 6, 1951.

29 For an illuminating view of the multiculturalism promoted by the Soviet Union, see Steven S. Lee, *The Ethnic Avant-Garde: Minority Cultures and World Revolution* (New York: Columbia University Press, 2015).

30 Walter White, "Remember June 25, 1950; Date May Prove Important to All Negroes," *Chicago Defender*, September 9, 1950 (emphasis mine).

31 White.

32 "It's Now or Perhaps Never," *Chicago Defender*, August 5, 1950 (emphasis mine).

33 "24th Infantry Called into Action in Korea," *Atlanta Daily World*, July 1, 1950.

34 "24th Infantry Has Long History of War Service," *Atlanta Daily World*, July 9, 1950.

35 AP, "Negro Troops Win 16-Hr. Fight for Road Center; Infiltering Cut," *Washington Post*, July 22, 1950.

36 "U.S. Hails Tan Warriors," *Chicago Defender*, July 29, 1950.

37 Thurgood Marshall, "Summary Justice—the Negro GI in Korea," *Crisis* 58, no. 5 (May 1951): 297.

38 Marshall, 351.

39 Marshall, 353.

40 Marshall, 355.

41 Harold H. Martin, "How Do Our Negro Troops Measure Up?," *Saturday Evening Post*, June 16, 1951, 31.

42 Martin, 139.

43 Martin, 139.

44 Martin, 141.

45 Martin, 141.

46 Walter White, "The Post Piece on Negro GIs Will Make You Angry, Sad, Thoughtful," *Chicago Defender*, July 7, 1951.

47 "End of Segregation in Command Closes History of 24th Regiment," *Atlanta Daily World*, July 29, 1951.

48 "24th Regiment Officially De-activated," *Atlanta Daily World*, October 4, 1951.

49 L. Alex Wilson, "Integration Is Forced to Test by War in Korea," *Chicago Defender*, February 3, 1951.

50 "Full GI Integration Reported in Korea," *Atlanta Daily World*, January 23, 1951.

51 "Integration: A Beneficial By-Product," *Chicago Defender*, August 15, 1953.

52 "Integration."

53 "Integration."

54 Robyn Wiegman, *American Anatomies: Theorizing Race and Gender* (Durham, NC: Duke University Press, 1995).

55 *The Defiant Ones*, directed by Stanley Kramer (1958; Santa Monica, CA: MGM Home Entertainment, 2001), DVD; *In the Heat of the Night*, directed by Norman Jewison (1967; Santa Monica, CA: MGM Home Entertainment, 2001), DVD.

56 Jeanine Basinger, *The World War II Combat Film: Anatomy of a Genre* (New York: Columbia University Press, 1986), 161.

57 Robert J. Lentz, *Korean War Filmography: 91 English Language Features through 2000* (Jefferson, NC: McFarland, 2003), 283.

58 *Guess Who's Coming to Dinner*, directed by Stanley Kramer (1967; Culver City, CA: Sony Pictures Home Entertainment/Columbia Tristar Home Video, 2005), DVD.

59 Edward W. Said, *Orientalism*, 25th anniversary ed. (New York: Vintage, 2003), 206.

60 Gina Marchetti, *Romance and the "Yellow Peril": Race, Sex, and Discursive Strategies in Hollywood Fiction* (Berkeley: University of California Press, 1993).

61 *Sayonara*, directed by Joshua Logan (1957; Los Angeles, CA: Hallmark Home Entertainment, 1995), VHS.

62 L. Alex Wilson, "400 to Wed Tokyo Girls," *Chicago Defender*, November 4, 1950.

63 L. Alex Wilson, "Why Tan Yanks Go for Japanese Girls," *Chicago Defender*, November 11, 1950.

64 Wilson.

65 Wilson.

66 Wilson.

67 Susan Koshy, *Sexual Naturalization: Asian Americans and Miscegenation* (Stanford, CA: Stanford University Press, 2004).

68 Colleen Lye, *America's Asia: Racial Form and American Literature, 1893–1945* (Princeton, NJ: Princeton University Press, 2005), 3.

69 Lye, 5.

CHAPTER 3. MILITARY ORIENTALISM AND THE INTIMACIES OF COLLABORATION

1 UPI, "Hollywood Film Shop," *Shamokin News-Dispatch*, August 2, 1958.

2 Bob Crompton, "Visits Father's Homeland as a Soldier; He's Just about as Confused as Anyone," *Ogden (Utah) Standard-Examiner*, June 19, 1955, sec. C.

3   Crompton.

4   Colleen Lye, *America's Asia: Racial Form and American Literature, 1893–1945* (Princeton, NJ: Princeton University Press, 2005), 5.

5   Jerry Cohen, "One in 10,000 Fighting Men Makes This Exclusive Club," *Los Angeles Times*, October 9, 1966, sec. H.

6   Cohen.

7   AP, "Shy Japanese-American POW Wins Honor Medal," *Los Angeles Times*, August 21, 1953.

8   AP.

9   See Lye, *America's Asia*.

10 Lon Kurashige, *Japanese American Celebration and Conflict: A History of Ethnic Identity and Festival, 1934–1990*, American Crossroads 8 (Berkeley: University of California Press, 2002), 120.

11 Kurashige, 120.

12 Naoko Shibusawa, *America's Geisha Ally: Reimagining the Japanese Enemy* (Cambridge, MA: Harvard University Press, 2006).

13 Robert G. Lee, *Orientals: Asian Americans in Popular Culture* (Philadelphia: Temple University Press, 1999); T. Fujitani, "Go for Broke, the Movie, Japanese American Soldiers in U.S. National, Military, and Racial Discourses," in *Perilous Memories: The Asia-Pacific War(s)*, ed. T. Fujitani, Geoffrey M. White, and Lisa Yoneyama (Durham, NC: Duke University Press, 2001).

14 Larry Tajiri, "Asians Hear the Nisei Story," *Pacific Citizen*, November 10, 1951.

15 Tajiri.

16 "Movies More Complicated Than Battle, Says 442nd Veterans," *Pacific Citizen*, November 11, 1950.

17 Larry Tajiri, "Kotonks and Boodaheads," *Pacific Citizen*, December 2, 1950.

18 Larry Tajiri, "Notes from Hollywood," *Pacific Citizen*, July 8, 1950.

19 Larry Tajiri, "Film Review: Go for Broke!," *Pacific Citizen*, March 31, 1951.

20 Tajiri.

21 Bosley Crowther, "Go for Broke!, Tribute to War Record of Nisei Regiment Opens at the Capitol," *New York Times*, May 25, 1951.

22 Fujitani, "Go for Broke," 247, 249.

23 Fujitani, 252, 244.

24 Fujitani, 250.

25 Fujitani, 248.

26 "Tommy of 442nd Film Gets Real-Life Army Training," *Pacific Citizen*, November 24, 1951.

27 "'This Time It's for Real': Tommy of 'Go for Broke!' Goes Off to War in Korea," *Pacific Citizen*, February 23, 1952.

28 "'Go for Broke' Movie Star Entering U.C.," *Pacific Citizen*, August 28, 1953.

29 Fujitani, "Go for Broke," 255.

30 "MGM Head Gets JACL Award," *Pacific Citizen*, October 28, 1950.

31 Larry Tajiri, "Dore Schary's Parlay," *Pacific Citizen*, February 16, 1952.

32 Larry Tajiri, "Behind the 442nd's Film Story," *Pacific Citizen*, April 28, 1951.

33 Tajiri.

34 Tajiri.

35 Tajiri.

36 Larry Tajiri, "MGM and Pregnant Pigs," *Pacific Citizen*, September 16, 1950; Larry Tajiri, "MGM and 'Go for Broke,'" *Pacific Citizen*, October 14, 1950.

37 Jere Takahashi, *Nisei Sansei: Shifting Japanese American Identities and Politics* (Philadelphia: Temple University Press, 1997), 87.

38 "MGM Head."

39 "Schary Presents MGM Check," *Pacific Citizen*, March 31, 1951.

40 Marita Sturken, "Absent Images of Memory: Remembering and Reenacting the Japanese Internment," *Positions: East Asia Cultures Critique* 5, no. 3 (Winter 1997): 687–707; Caroline Chung Simpson, *An Absent Presence: Japanese Americans in Postwar American Culture, 1945–1960* (Durham, NC: Duke University Press, 2002).

41 Chung Simpson, *Absent Presence*, 3.

42 Chung Simpson, 3.

CHAPTER 4. PICTURING KOREANS

1 Sontag, *On Photography* (New York: Picador, 1973), 18.

2 Bruce Cumings, *The Korean War: A History* (New York: Modern Library, 2010), 5.

3 Sontag, *On Photography*, 17.

4 Sontag, 18.

5 Steven Casey, *Selling the Korean War: Propaganda, Politics, and Public Opinion in the United States, 1950–1953* (Oxford: Oxford University Press, 2008), 45.

6 Doss, Introduction to *Looking at Life Magazine*, ed. Erika Lee Doss (Washington, DC: Smithsonian Institution Press, 2001), 2–3.

7 Doss, 2.

8 Robert Edwin Herzstein, *Henry R. Luce, Time, and the American Crusade in Asia* (Cambridge: Cambridge University Press, 2005), 1.

9 Herzstein, 2.

10 For an illuminating account of how the figure of the Asian "friendly" lies at the heart of US representations of the Korean and Vietnam Wars, see Josephine Nock-Hee Park, *Cold War Friendships: Korea, Vietnam, and Asian American Literature* (New York: Oxford University Press, 2016).

11 Carl Mydans, "Refugees Get in Way," *Life* 29, no. 8 (August 21, 1950): 22.

12 Mydans, 22 (emphasis mine).

13 Mydans, 22.

14 Osborne assumed the position of foreign news editor of *Life*'s sister magazine, *Time*, in 1945, after the death of Whittaker Chambers, whose staunch anti-Communism was increasingly reflected in that journal's coverage of the Soviet Union and China during the latter part of the Second World War. According to Herzstein, Osborne adopted the "anti-Soviet beliefs" of the man he replaced

as editor at *Time*, and its "foreign news coverage followed the same hard line"
that Chambers had established (*Henry R. Luce*, 50). In his "insider's history" of
Life, Loudon Wainwright, who served as a writer and editor at the magazine for
decades, identifies Osborne as a member of the "Editor-in-chief's Committee,"
which was headed by Luce and sought to ensure that everything that appeared
on its pages conformed to the publisher's political vision. *The Great American
Magazine: An Inside History of Life* (New York: Knopf, 1986), 175. See chapter 5
of Herzstein's *Henry R. Luce* for an account of how Luce used the advent of
McCarthyism and the Korean War as opportunities to forward his anti-
Communist agenda.

15 John Osborne, "Report from the Orient: Guns Are Not Enough," *Life* 29,
no. 8 (August 21, 1950): 77. Subsequent references to this text will be noted
parenthetically.

16 Osborne's brief description here of how the South Korean National Police and
some elements of the military negotiated the epistemological dilemma of discerning between hostile and friendly civilians with an often indiscriminate brutality
accords with the account that Bruce Cumings offers of the counterinsurgency
campaigns conducted by South Korean military forces and anti-Communist
paramilitary organizations. See chapter 5 of Cumings, *Korean War*.

17 Cumings, *Korean War*, 104.

18 Rey Chow, *The Age of the World Target: Self-Referentiality in War, Theory, and
Comparative Work* (Durham, NC: Duke University Press, 2006); Bruce Cumings,
"Boundary Displacement: The State, the Foundations, and Area Studies during
and after the Cold War," in *Learning Places: The Afterlives of Area Studies*, ed.
Masao Miyoshi and Harry D. Harootunian (Durham, NC: Duke University Press,
2002), 261–302; Harry D. Harootunian, "Postcoloniality's Unconscious/Area
Studies," in *Learning Places: The Afterlives of Area Studies*, ed. Masao Miyoshi and
Harry D. Harootunian (Durham, NC: Duke University Press, 2002), 150–74.

19 Cumings, "Boundary Displacement," 261.

20 Christina Klein, *Cold War Orientalism: Asia in the Middlebrow Imagination,
1945–1961* (Berkeley: University of California Press, 2003), 4. See also Kelly Ann
Long, "Friend or Foe: Life's Wartime Images of the Chinese," in *Looking at Life
Magazine*, ed. Erika Lee Doss (Washington, DC: Smithsonian Institution Press,
2001), 55–75.

21 "How to Tell Japs from the Chinese," *Life* 11, no. 25 (December 22, 1941): 81–82.

22 Doss, "Introduction," 8.

23 Doss, 8.

24 Carl Mydans, "Things Look Better in Korea," *Life* 29, no. 17 (October 23, 1950): 37.

25 Chang-rae Lee, *Native Speaker* (New York: Riverhead, 1995), 242.

26 Jodi Kim, *Ends of Empire: Asian American Critique and the Cold War* (Minneapolis: University of Minnesota Press, 2010), 2.

27 Chow, *Age of the World Target*, 34, 31.

28 Chow, 40–41.

29 Chow, 41.

30 See, for example, Eleana J. Kim, *Adopted Territory: Transnational Korean Adoptees and the Politics of Belonging* (Durham, NC: Duke University Press, 2010); Arissa H. Oh, *To Save the Children of Korea: The Cold War Origins of International Adoption* (Stanford, CA: Stanford University Press, 2015).

31 Klein, *Cold War Orientalism*, 113.

32 Chow, *Age of the World Target*, 39.

33 Kim, *Adopted Territory*; Oh, *To Save the Children*.

34 Hye Seung Chung, *Hollywood Asian: Philip Ahn and the Politics of Cross-ethnic Performance* (Philadelphia: Temple University Press, 2006), 141.

35 Chung, 141.

36 Harold H. Martin, "The Pious Killer of Korea," *Saturday Evening Post* 224, no. 3 (July 21, 1951): 26.

37 Martin, 26.

38 Chung suggests that Lu Wan might be partially based on Syngman Rhee, the first president of South Korea with whom Hess became close during the war. See Chung, *Hollywood Asian*, 158.

39 Maples was apparently based on Ernest Craigswell, who in Hess's memoir "similarly dispatched a group of Korean civilians (including women and children), mistaking them as enemy troops." See Chung, 148.

40 *The Postman Always Rings Twice*, directed by Tay Garnett (1946; Burbank, CA: Turner Entertainment), DVD.

41 Robert J. Lentz, *Korean War Filmography: 91 English Language Features through 2000* (Jefferson, NC: McFarland, 2003), 269.

42 Lentz, 270.

43 A rough analogue to these representations can be found in the abolitionist writings that are subjected to critique in Saidiya V. Hartman, *Scenes of Subjection: Terror, Slavery, and Self-Making in Nineteenth-Century America*, Race and American Culture (New York: Oxford University Press, 1997).

CHAPTER 5. ANGELS OF MERCY AND THE ANGEL OF HISTORY

1 Michael Rothberg, *Multidirectional Memory: Remembering the Holocaust in the Age of Decolonization*, Cultural Memory in the Present (Stanford, CA: Stanford University Press, 2009).

2 Alexander G. Weheliye, *Habeas Viscus: Racializing Assemblages, Biopolitics, and Black Feminist Theories of the Human* (Durham, NC: Duke University Press, 2014).

3 Robert J. Lentz, *Korean War Filmography: 91 English Language Features through 2000* (Jefferson, NC: McFarland, 2003), 272.

4 "Sang-Hun Choe, Charles J. Hanley and Martha Mendoza of *Associated Press*," Pulitzer Prizes, 2000, www.pulitzer.org.

5 Charles J. Hanley, "No Gun Ri," *Critical Asian Studies* 42, no. 4 (2010): 589–622.

6 Hanley, 590.

7   Cited in Hanley, 589.

8   Jayne Anne Phillips, *Lark and Termite*, Vintage Contemporaries (New York: Vintage, 2010), 258. Subsequent references to this work will be cited parenthetically.

9   Michael Dirda, "A Family Worth Knowing," *New York Review of Books*, April 30, 2009, www.nybooks.com.

10 For an excellent analysis of this novel that has affinities with my own, though it has different emphases, see the fourth chapter of Josephine Nock-Hee Park, *Cold War Friendships: Korea, Vietnam, and Asian American Literature* (New York: Oxford University Press, 2016).

11 Joseph R. Slaughter, "Humanitarian Reading," in *Humanitarianism and Suffering*, ed. Richard Ashby Wilson and Richard D. Brown (New York: Cambridge University Press, 2009), 90–91.

12 Slaughter, 104.

13 Joseph R. Slaughter, *Human Rights, Inc.: The World Novel, Narrative Form, and International Law* (New York: Fordham University Press, 2007), 105.

14 Slaughter, "Humanitarian Reading," 101.

15 Slaughter, 102.

16 Slaughter, 99.

17 Slaughter, 103.

18 Slaughter, 103.

19 Chang-rae Lee, *The Surrendered* (New York: Riverhead, 2010). Further references to this work will be cited parenthetically in the text.

20 Sahr Conway-Lanz, "Beyond No Gun Ri: Refugees and the United States Military in the Korean War," *Diplomatic History* 29, no. 1 (January 1, 2005): 50.

21 For a contrasting but compelling account of how sympathy works in this novel, see Stephanie Hsu, "The Ontology of Disability in Chang-Rae Lee's *The Surrendered*," *Journal of Literary and Cultural Disability Studies* 7, no. 1 (April 5, 2013): 19–35.

22 Slaughter, "Humanitarian Reading," 103 (emphasis mine).

23 Slaughter, *Human Rights, Inc.*, 103.

24 I owe a debt of gratitude to James Kim, who perceptively alerted me to the allusion to Walter Benjamin that is suggested by this character's name.

CHAPTER 6. "BLED IN, LETTER BY LETTER"

1   Chang-rae Lee, "Amazon Exclusive: Chang-Rae Lee on *The Surrendered*," Amazon .com, March 1, 2011, www.amazon.com.

2   Andrew S. Hughes, "Not-So-Foreign Writer Susan Choi Uses Father's Life in Korea for Story," *South Bend Tribune* (Indiana), November 15, 1998.

3   Hughes.

4   Hughes.

5   Grace M. Cho, *Haunting the Korean Diaspora: Shame, Secrecy, and the Forgotten War*, illustrated ed. (Minneapolis: University of Minnesota Press, 2008), 12.

6 H. Y. Nahm, "Susan Choi: Shadow Novelist," Goldsea, n.d., accessed July 8, 2016, http://goldsea.com.

7 Hughes, "Not-So-Foreign Writer."

8 Frederic Koeppel, "Seoul-to-South Experience Refracted in Fictional Debut," *Commercial Appeal*, October 4, 1998, sec. G.

9 Lee, "Amazon Exclusive."

10 Lee.

11 Lee.

12 Chang-rae Lee, *The Surrendered* (New York: Riverhead, 2010), 18 (emphasis mine). Subsequent references to this work will be cited parenthetically in the text.

13 For a contrasting view, see Stephanie Hsu, "The Ontology of Disability in Chang-Rae Lee's *The Surrendered*," *Journal of Literary and Cultural Disability Studies* 7, no. 1 (April 5, 2013): 19–35.

14 Susan Choi, *The Foreign Student* (New York: HarperPerennial, 1999), 51. Subsequent references to this work will be cited parenthetically in the text.

15 For analyses of how Asians are positioned racially in the South, see Susan Koshy, "Morphing Race into Ethnicity: Asian Americans and Critical Transformations of Whiteness," *Boundary 2* 28, no. 1 (2001): 153–94; and Leslie Bow, "Racial Interstitiality and the Anxieties of the 'Partly Colored': Representations of Asians under Jim Crow," *Journal of Asian American Studies* 10, no. 1 (2007): 1–30.

16 Leslie Bow notes that Asians are located in the "DMZ of indeterminate race relations." See Bow, "Racial Interstitiality," 4.

17 Lisa Lowe, *The Intimacies of Four Continents* (Durham, NC: Duke University Press, 2015), 6.

18 It would not be inappropriate to liken this gap to the one that Brent Edwards identifies in *The Practice of Diaspora: Literature, Translation, and the Rise of Black Internationalism* (Cambridge, MA: Harvard University Press, 2003) with the French word *décalage*: "This black diasporic *décalage* among African Americans and Africans . . . is not simply geographical distance, nor is it simply difference in evolution or consciousness. . . . *Décalage* is the kernel of precisely that which cannot be transferred or exchanged, the received biases that refuse to pass over when one crosses the water. It is a changing core of difference; it is the work of 'differences within unity,' an unidentifiable point that is incessantly touched and fingered and pressed" (14).

19 Elaine Scarry, *The Body in Pain: The Making and Unmaking of the World* (New York: Oxford University Press, 1987).

20 King-Kok Cheung, *Articulate Silences: Hisaye Yamamoto, Maxine Hong Kingston, Joy Kogawa* (Ithaca, NY: Cornell University Press, 1993).

21 Marianne Hirsch, "Projected Memory: Holocaust Photographs in Personal and Public Fantasy," in *Acts of Memory: Cultural Recall in the Present* (Hanover, NH: University Press of New England, 1999).

22 Hirsch.

23 Hirsch.

24 Cho, *Haunting*, 11.

25 Hirsch, "Projected Memory," 10.

26 In my view, the most powerful theoretical considerations of this conflation of injury and identity are found in Wendy Brown, *States of Injury: Power and Freedom in Late Modernity* (Princeton, NJ: Princeton University Press, 1995).

27 Alexander G. Weheliye, *Habeas Viscus: Racializing Assemblages, Biopolitics, and Black Feminist Theories of the Human* (Durham, NC: Duke University Press, 2014), 46, 47.

28 Weheliye, 49.

CHAPTER 7. THE RACIAL BORDERLANDS OF THE KOREAN WAR

1 UPI, "Korean War Defector, as 'Voice' of Hanoi, Bids G.I.'s Get Out," *New York Times*, August 15, 1965.

2 Quoted in Mike Marqusee, *Redemption Song: Muhammad Ali and the Spirit of the Sixties* (New York: Verso, 1999), 214–15.

3 Michael Rothberg, *Multidirectional Memory: Remembering the Holocaust in the Age of Decolonization*, Cultural Memory in the Present (Stanford, CA: Stanford University Press, 2009), 15–16.

4 Rothberg, 15–16.

5 Ha Jin, *War Trash* (New York: Vintage, 2005), 76.

6 Charles S. Young, *Name, Rank, and Serial Number: Exploiting Korean War POWs at Home and Abroad* (Oxford: Oxford University Press, 2014).

7 Virginia Pasley, *21 Stayed: The Story of the American GIs Who Chose Communist China—Who They Were, and the Reasons for Their Choice* (London: Farrar, Straus and Cudahy, 1955).

8 Clarence Adams, *An American Dream: The Life of an African American Soldier and POW Who Spent Twelve Years in Communist China*, illustrated ed. (Amherst: University of Massachusetts Press, 2007), 32. Subsequent references to this work will be noted parenthetically in the text.

9 It is possible to view the emphasis on American nationalism that frames Adams's memoir as a reflection of its editors' desires. For this "autobiography" was posthumously constructed by Adams's daughter, Della, and Lewis. H. Carlson, who is described on the book cover as "a retired professor of history." Adams is listed nonetheless as the author of *An American Dream*, and I will be treating him as such. It is nonetheless necessary to at least acknowledge the editorial complexities behind the composition of this work.

10 Daniel Widener, "Seoul City Sue and the Bugout Blues: Black American Narratives of the Forgotten War," in *Afro Asia: Revolutionary Political and Cultural Connections between African Americans and Asian Americans*, ed. Fred Ho and Bill V. Mullen (Durham, NC: Duke University Press, 6), 56.

11 Toni Morrison, "Toni Morrison: 'I Want to Feel What I Feel. Even If It's Not Happiness,'" *Guardian*, April 13, 2012, sec. Books, www.theguardian.com.

12 Christopher Bollen and Damon Winter, "Toni Morrison," *Interview Magazine*, May 1, 2012, www.interviewmagazine.com.

13 Hortense J. Spillers, "Mama's Baby, Papa's Maybe: An American Grammar Book," *Diacritics* 17, no. 2 (1987): 65–81.

14 Bollen and Winter, "Toni Morrison."

15 Toni Morrison, *Home* (New York: Knopf, 2012), 3. Subsequent references to this work will be noted parenthetically in the text.

16 Bollen and Winter, "Toni Morrison."

17 Rolando Hinojosa, "The Sense of Place," in *The Rolando Hinojosa Reader: Essays Historical and Critical*, ed. José David Saldívar (Houston: Arte Público Press, 1985), 19.

18 Two recent doctoral dissertations do address this topic. See Joo Ok Kim, "Untelling the Tales of Empire: Intimate Epistemologies of the Korean War" (PhD diss., University of California, San Diego, 2013); and William Arce, "Nation in Uniform: Chicano/Latino War Narratives and the Construction of Nation in the Korean War and Vietnam War, 1951–1976" (PhD diss., University of Southern California, 2009).

19 An inscription on the Korean War Veterans Memorial in Washington, DC, reads, "Freedom Is Not Free." The exhibit on Americans Wars at the Smithsonian, which includes a small section on the Korean War, is titled *The Price of Freedom: Americans at War*.

20 Rosaura Sanchéz, "From Heterogeneity to Contradiction: Hinojosa's Novel," in *Rolando Hinojosa Reader*, ed. Saldívar, 97.

21 Ramón Saldívar, "Korean Love Songs: A Border Ballad and Its Heroes," in *Rolando Hinojosa Reader*, ed. Saldívar, 155.

22 Rolando Hinjosa, *Rites and Witnesses* (Houston: Arte Público Press, 1989), 76. Subsequent references to this work will be noted parenthetically.

23 For accounts of how Mexican Americans fared during the 1950s—their uneven and limited access to upward mobility as well as the expansion of racist anti-immigrant policies—see Mario T. García, *Mexican Americans: Leadership, Ideology, and Identity, 1930–1960*, Yale Western Americana 36 (New Haven, CT: Yale University Press, 1989); Juan Gómez-Quiñones, *Chicano Politics: Reality and Promise, 1940–1990*, Calvin P. Horn Lectures in Western History and Culture (Albuquerque: University of New Mexico Press, 1990); and Manuel G. Gonzales, *Mexicanos: A History of Mexicans in the United States* (Bloomington: Indiana University Press, 1999).

24 Sanchéz, "From Heterogeneity to Contradiction," 97.

25 Limón, *Dancing with the Devil: Society and Cultural Poetics in Mexican-American South Texas*, New Directions in Anthropological Writing (Madison: University of Wisconsin Press, 1994), 15.

26 Rolando Hinojosa, *Korean Love Songs*, trans. Wolfgang Karrer, Osnabrück Bilingual Editions of Minority Authors (Osnabrück, Germany: OBEM, 1991), 98. Subsequent references to this work will be noted parenthetically.

27 Saldívar, "Korean Love Songs," 151.

28 Saldívar, 154.

29 Rolando Hinojosa, *The Useless Servants* (Houston: Arte Público Press, 1993), 184. Subsequent references to this work will be noted parenthetically.

30 Philip K. Jason, "A Conversation with Rolando Hinojosa," *Bilingual Review / La Revista Bilingüe* 25, no. 3 (September 1, 2000): 298–305 (emphasis mine).

31 Toni Morrison, *Home* (New York: Knopf, 2012), 135.

32 Allan R. Millett, "The Korean War: A 50-Year Critical Historiography," *Journal of Strategic Studies* 24, no. 1 (2001): 188–224.

33 Hinojosa, "Sense of Place," 19.

34 Bruce Cumings, *The Origins of the Korean War* (Princeton, NJ: Princeton University Press, 1981), 120.

35 Bruce Cumings, *The Korean War: A History* (New York: Modern Library, 2010).

36 Cumings, 218.

37 "Korean War—Britannica Academic," accessed September 7, 2018, https://academic.eb.com.

38 For an excellent account of how the Korean War has been memorialized in the PRC, see Keun-Sik Jung, "China's Memory and Commemoration of the Korean War in the Memorial Hall of the 'War to Resist U.S. Aggression and Aid Korea,'" *Cross-Currents: East Asian History and Culture Review* 4, no. 1 (2015): 14–39.

39 Russell Banks, "View from the Prison Camp," *New York Times*, October 10, 2004, sec. Books, www.nytimes.com; Daniel Duane, "War Trash," *Mother Jones*, November/ December 2004, accessed August 17, 2016, www.motherjones.com; John Freeman, "The Prisoner," *San Diego Union-Tribune*, October 10, 2004, accessed August 17, 2016, www.sandiegouniontribune.com.

40 Jin, *War Trash*, 5. Subsequent references to this work will be noted parenthetically in the text.

41 For a historical account of the Chinese POW experience, see Philip West and Zhihua Li, "Interior Stories of the Chinese POWs in the Korean War," in *Remembering the "Forgotten War": The Korean War through Literature and Art*, ed. Philip West and Ji-moon Suh (Armonk, NY: East Gate, 2001), 152–86.

42 Albert Wu and Michelle Kuo, "I Dare Not: The Muted Style of Writer in Exile Ha Jin," *Los Angeles Review of Books*, January 11, 2015, https://lareviewofbooks.org.

43 Banks, "View from the Prison Camp."

44 Linda Jaivin, "A Scrap Heap Made of People," *Los Angeles Times*, October 10, 2004, http://articles.latimes.com.

45 Dwight Garner, "An Interview with Ha Jin: 'Somehow I Couldn't Stop,'" *New York Times*, October 10, 2004, sec. Books / Sunday Book Review, www.nytimes.com.

46 For an illuminating account of how Jin's novel suggests the biopolitical continuities between the Korean War and contemporary US conflicts, see Joseph Darda, "The Literary Afterlife of the Korean War," *American Literature* 87, no. 1 (March 1, 2015): 79–105.

47 Mary L. Dudziak, *War Time: An Idea, Its History, Its Consequences* (Oxford: Oxford University Press, 2012), 91, 93.

CHAPTER 8. THE INTIMACIES OF COMPLICITY

1 Nak-chung Paik, *The Division System in Crisis: Essays on Contemporary Korea* (Berkeley: University of California Press, 2011), 4.

2 Paik, 5.

3 Sheila Miyoshi Jager and Jiyul Kim, "The Korean War after the Cold War: Commemorating the Armistice Agreement in South Korea," in *Ruptured Histories: War, Memory, and the Post–Cold War in Asia*, ed. Sheila Miyoshi Jager and Rana Mitter (Cambridge, MA: Harvard University Press, 2007), 242.

4 Jae-Jung Suh, "Truth and Reconciliation in South Korea," *Critical Asian Studies* 42, no. 4 (2010): 504.

5 Suh, 507, 508.

6 Jager and Kim, "Korean War," 242.

7 Jager and Kim, 242.

8 Bruce Cumings, *Korea's Place in the Sun: A Modern History* (New York: Norton, 1997), 501.

9 Cumings, 501.

10 Youngju Ryu, "Truth or Reconciliation? The Guest and the Massacre That Never Ends," *Positions* 23, no. 4 (November 1, 2015): 634.

11 Ryu, 637.

12 Ryu, 639.

13 Ryu, 639.

14 Sok-Yong Hwang, *The Guest* (New York: Seven Stories Press, 2005), 8. Subsequent references to this work will be noted parenthetically in the text.

15 According to Youngju Ryu, the group that was primarily responsible for the massacre was "an armed retaliatory unit called the 'Protestant Young Men's League' (*Gidok Cheongnyeonhoe*)" ("Truth or Reconciliation," 638).

16 Dong-Choon Kim, "The Long Road toward Truth and Reconciliation," *Critical Asian Studies* 42, no. 4 (2010): 545.

17 In her brilliant analysis of the novel, to which my own is indebted, Youngju Ryu is critical of the Hwang's recourse to the shamanistic folk tradition that is offered as a kind of cosmological explanation for the appearance and the function of the ghosts because it "succumbs to the nostalgia of precolonial, and pre–Cold War unity" ("Truth or Reconciliation," 653).

18 Cumings, *Korea's Place*, 157.

19 Chung-shin Park, *Protestantism and Politics in Korea*, Korean Studies of the Henry M. Jackson School of International Studies (Seattle: University of Washington Press, 2003), 27.

20 Park, 26.

21 Park, 28.

22 Park, 58.

23 Park, 117.

24 Park, 135.

25 Park, 152.

26 Park, 156.

27 Timothy S. Lee, *Born Again: Evangelicalism in Korea* (Honolulu: University of Hawaiʻi Press, 2010), 65.

28 Lee, 65.

29 Park, *Protestantism*, 166–67.

30 Park, 175.

31 Cumings, *Korea's Place*, 231, 230.

32 Lee, *Born Again*, 64.

33 Lee, xiii.

34 Ryu argues that while *The Guest* imagines a healing of differences taking place through the shamanistic ritual it presents itself as unfolding in purely "inter-Korean" terms, it is haunted by its recognition of "the structural impossibility of pursuing inter-Korean reconciliation as an inter-Korean affair, an impossibility sustained by the simultaneous invisibility and hyper-visibility of the United States in the historical legacy of the Korean War" ("Truth or Reconciliation," 655).

35 For a related account of this work's diasporic significance, see Jini Kim Watson, "A Not-Yet-Postcolonial Peninsula: Rewriting Spaces of Violence, Division and Diaspora," *Cambridge Journal of Postcolonial Literary Inquiry* 1, no. 1 (2014): 69–87.

36 Hoenik Kwon, *The Other Cold War* (New York: Columbia University Press, 2010), 141.

CONCLUSION

1 Jin-kyung Lee, *Service Economies: Militarism, Sex Work, and Migrant Labor in South Korea* (Minneapolis: University of Minnesota Press, 2010), 233.

2 For a comparative account of the literary traditions that emerged in the North and South, see Joanna Efving-Hwang, "Cross-border Representation in South and North Korean Literatures of the Cold War Period," in *Global Cold War Literature: Western, Eastern and Postcolonial Perspectives*, ed. Andrew Hammond, Routledge Studies in Twentieth-Century Literature 22 (New York: Routledge, 2012), 43–57.

3 Jini Kim Watson, *The New Asian City: Three-Dimensional Fictions of Space and Urban Form* (Minneapolis: University of Minnesota Press, 2011).

4 Sheila Miyoshi Jager and Jiyul Kim, "The Korean War after the Cold War: Commemorating the Armistice Agreement in South Korea," in *Ruptured Histories: War, Memory, and the Post–Cold War in Asia*, ed. Sheila Miyoshi Jager and Rana Mitter (Cambridge, MA: Harvard University Press, 2007), 242.

5 Jager and Kim, 242.

6 Jager and Kim, 244.

7 Jager and Kim, 252.

8 Daniel Y. Kim, "Nationalist Technologies of Cultural Memory and the Korean War: Militarism and Neo-Liberalism in 'The Price of Freedom' and the War Memorial of Korea," *Cross-Currents: East Asian History and Culture Review* 4, no. 1 (2015): 40–70.

9 Tessa Morris-Suzuki, "Remembering the Unfinished Conflict: Museums and the Contested Memory of the Korean War," *Asia-Pacific Journal: Japan Focus*, July 20, 2009, www.japanfocus.org.

10 Jae-Jung Suh, "Truth and Reconciliation in South Korea," *Critical Asian Studies* 42, no. 4 (2010): 507.

11 I offer more extensive analyses in Kim, "Nationalist Technologies."

12 Sheila Miyoshi Jager, *Narratives of Nation Building in Korea: A Genealogy of Patriotism* (Armonk, NY: M. E. Sharpe, 2003), 120.

13 Lee, *Service Economies*, 15.

14 Seungsook Moon, *Militarized Modernity and Gendered Citizenship in South Korea*, Politics, History, and Culture (Durham, NC: Duke University Press, 2005).

15 Lee, *Service Economies*, 28.

16 Charles K. Armstrong, "America's Korea, Korea's Vietnam," *Critical Asian Studies* 33, no. 4 (September 1, 2001): 531.

17 Armstrong, 533.

18 Armstrong, 533.

19 Cited in Viet Thanh Nguyen, *Nothing Ever Dies: Vietnam and the Memory of War* (Cambridge, MA: Harvard University Press, 2016), 138.

20 Lee, *Service Economies*, 42.

21 Lee, 43.

22 Lee, 40.

23 Lee, 45.

24 Lee, 46.

25 Lee, 46.

26 Lee, 46.

27 Lee, 48.

28 Chalmers Johnson, *The Sorrows of Empire: Militarism, Secrecy, and the End of the Republic* (New York: Metropolitan Books, 2004), 188.

29 Jinhee Choi, *The South Korean Film Renaissance: Local Hitmakers, Global Provocateurs*, Wesleyan Film (Middletown, CT: Wesleyan University Press, 2010); Mythili G. Rao, "Can a Big Government Push Bring the Nobel Prize in Literature to South Korea?," *New Yorker*, January 28, 2016, www.newyorker.com.

30 For a compelling and robust account of the emergence of this phenomenon, see Youngmin Choe, *Tourist Distractions: Traveling and Feeling in Transnational Hallyu Cinema* (Durham, NC: Duke University Press, 2016).

31 Nguyen, *Nothing Ever Dies*, 132.

32 *Shiri*, directed by Kang Je-gyu (1999; Culver City, CA: Tristar Home Entertainment, 2002), DVD; *JSA*, directed by Park Chan-wook (2000; New York: Palm Pictures, 2000), DVD; *The Host*, directed by Bong Joon-ho (2006; Los Angeles: Magnolia Home Entertainment, 2007), DVD.

33 Choi, *South Korean Film*, 39.

34 Choi, 28.

35 *Oldboy*, directed by Park Chan-woo (2003; USA: Tartan Video USA, 2005), DVD.

36 Choi, *South Korean Film*, 37 (emphasis Choi's).

37 Choi, 37, 38.

38 Choi, 39.

39 Suh, "Truth and Reconciliation," 507.

40 Jini Kim Watson, "A Not-Yet-Postcolonial Peninsula: Rewriting Spaces of Violence, Division and Diaspora," *Cambridge Journal of Postcolonial Literary Inquiry* 1, no. 1 (2014): 72.

41 Watson, 72, 77.

42 For a critique of this dimension of the novel, see Youngju Ryu, "Truth or Reconciliation? The Guest and the Massacre That Never Ends," *Positions* 23, no. 4 (November 1, 2015), 633–63.

43 For a discussion of a comparable depiction of South Korean soldiers in the writing of Hwang Sok-yong, see Lee, *Service Economies*, 66.

44 Sok-Yong Hwang, *The Guest* (New York: Seven Stories Press, 2005), 8.

45 Christine Hong, "The Unending Korean War," *Positions* 23, no. 4 (November 1, 2015): 598.

46 Nguyen, *Nothing Ever Dies*, 97.

INDEX

Page numbers in *italics* refer to figures.

Madame Butterfly (Puccini), 78–79
magazines. *See* press
magic realism, 152, 245
Malcolm X, 59
Manchuria, 18, 162, 164, 267
manhood, 211–12, 213, 214, 218
Marchetti, Gina, 79
Marshall, S. L. A., 66
Marshall, Thurgood, 3, 63–64
Martin, Harold H., 63–65, 133
Marxism, 257, 259, 260
Masaoka, Mike, 90, 92, 106, 108–9
masculinity, 211, 213–14, 215, 274
massacres, 150–52, 153, 158, 243, 244–46, 254–55
Mbembe, Achille, 12
McAllister, Melanie, 13, 35, 55
Medal of Honor, 87, 104, 112
media. *See* press
Medovoi, Leerom, 7
memory: collective, 22; cultural, 6, 20, 21–23, 112, 181, 198, 239, 288–89; false, 194–95; historical, 2, 158, 174; multidirectional, 22, 149; translation of, 196–97. *See also* postmemory
Memory of Solferino, A (Dunant), 159, 160–61, 164, 166
Mendoza, Martha, 150
Metro-Goldwyn-Mayer (MGM), 91, 102–3, 108–9
Mexican Americans, 20, 23, 218, 222–24, 310n23; as soldiers, 219, 220–21, 225
Mexico, 204, 229. *See also* US-Mexico War
MGM, Metro-Goldwyn-Mayer
militarized modernity, 272
military dictatorships, 243, 254, 277
military multiculturalism, 13, 23, 31, 35–36, 55, 67, 87, 149; African Americans and, 52; Cold War, 219; critique of, 205, 206, 210, 215
military Orientalism, 12–14, 25, 31, 36, 273–75; departures from, 276; in films, 52, 86, 113, 137; Vietnam War and, 275

Millet, Allan R., 18
miscegenation, 76, 110, 186
Miyamura, Hiroshi, 87, 88, 104, 112
model minority, 14, 85–86, 90, 177, 264; sexual, 83
Moon, Seungsook, 272
Moon Jae-in, 266
Morrison, Toni, 204; *Home*, 23, 55, 210–18
Morris-Suzuki, Tessa, 269
Moscow Radio, 60–61
Mullens, Bill, 57–58, 203, 218
multiculturalism. *See* military multiculturalism
Multidirectional Memory: Remembering the Holocaust in the Age of Decolonization (Rothberg), 22
musumes. *See* women: Japanese
Mydans, Carl, 119
My Lai massacre, 151, 152, 158

Nakamura, Henry, 103–5
Name, Rank and Serial Number (Young), 205
Narratives of Nation Building in Korea (Jager), 271
National Association for the Advancement of Colored People (NAACP), 3, 60, 63
nationalism, 90, 273, 276, 309n9; anticolonial, 209; Chinese, 204; Korean, 252, 254–55, 265; militaristic, 239, 272, 277; virtual, 270, 271
National Police (South Korea), 19, 185, 305n16
Native Americans, 62, 70, 73–75, 264
Native Speaker (Lee), 130
necropolitics, 12, 13, 137, 138, 145
neocolonialism, 25
neoliberalism, 265
newspapers. *See* press
Newton, Huey P., 69
New York Amsterdam News, 79
New York Times, 56, 92

race war, 58–59, 60–61, 74, 203, 206, 209, 300n14; in films, 77; metaphor of, 57, 70–71
racial DMZ, 12, 32, 39, 40, 47–50, 146, 187, 308n16
racial ideologies, 33, 39, 261
racialization, 21, 83, 149, 200–201
racial uniform, 38–39, 40, 43
racism, 33–34, 90, 205–6, 260; antiblack, 210–11, 257, 258, 261–62; of audience, 44; consequences of, for whites, 60; denunciation of, 94; economic dimensions of, 97; ethnic, 300n14; imperialist, 57; internalized, 111, 112; Korean War service and, 221; of white soldiers, 63, 64, 70–71, 93, 98–100, 221
Radio Free Asia, 90–91
Radio Hanoi, 56, 203, 205, 209
reconciliation, 243, 244, 246, 248, 277, 278, 280, 313n34
Red Cross, 160, 163
reframing, 15, 16
refugees, 11, 118–19, 119, 120–22, 206; Christian, 253, 254; in films, 142–43; treatment of, 37
relationality, 21, 26, 190, 200, 257, 262, 265
religion. See Christianity; Confucianism
religiosity, 49, 50, 137
remembrance, 19, 20, 22, 23, 203, 264
Republic of Korea (ROK). See South Korea
Republic of Korea Army (ROKA), 16, 185, 270, 271, 275, 281; in Vietnam War, 273, 274
"retreads," 32, 36, 88
Rhee, Syngman, 17, 18, 184–85, 269
Rites and Witnesses (Hinojosa), 23, 218, 220–24
Roh Moo-hyun, 248, 266, 269
Roh Tae-woo, 243, 266
ROK. See South Korea
ROKA. See Republic of Korea Army

romance: in films, 138, 140, 278; interracial, 141, 185–87, 193; interracial male, 35, 74–75
Roosevelt, Franklin D., 45, 102
Roosevelt, Theodore, 18, 59, 60, 62
Rorty, Richard, 160
Rothberg, Michael, 149, 203–4; Multidirectional Memory, 21–22
Russia, 59–60, 123. See also Soviet Union
Russo-Japanese War, 18, 58, 59–60
Ryu, Youngju, 244, 312n17, 313n34

sacrifice, 88–89, 91, 215, 271; civilians and, 146, 240; collective, 221; ethos of, 93, 94, 100–101
Said, Edward, 79, 123
Saldívar, Ramón, 222, 225–26
Sanchéz, Rosaura, 221
Saturday Evening Post, 63, 64–65, 133
Sayonara (Logan), 79
Scarry, Elaine, 196, 295n8
Schary, Dore, 92, 106–7, 108–9
Second Chinese Civil War, 232
Second Sino-Japanese War, 133, 158
segregation, 43, 45, 206; military, 3, 53, 64–65
sentimental attachment, 114, 117, 134
sentimentalism, 6, 132, 133, 145
Seoul, South Korea, 16, 17, 31, 86, 132
Service Economies: Militarism, Sex Work, and Migrant Labor in South Korea (Lee), 13, 274–75
shell shock. See post-traumatic stress disorder
Shibata, George, 67, 85–86, 87, 104
Shibusawa, Naoko, 89
Shiri (Kang), 277, 278, 281
Simpson, Caroline Chung, 112–13
Sinch'on massacre, 243, 244–46, 254–55
Slaughter, Joseph R., 166, 169; "Humanitarian Reading," 160–61
Smithsonian National Museum of American History, Washington, DC, 88, 310n19

ABOUT THE AUTHOR

Daniel Y. Kim is Associate Professor in the departments of English and American Studies at Brown University and author of *Writing Manhood in Black and Yellow: Ralph Ellison, Frank Chin, and the Literary Politics of Identity* (2006) as well as co-editor (with Crystal Parikh) of *The Cambridge Companion to Asian American Literature* (2015).